THE GOSPEL
ACCORDING TO
PHILIP

NAG HAMMADI
AND
MANICHAEAN STUDIES

FORMERLY

NAG HAMMADI STUDIES

EDITED BY

J.M. ROBINSON & H.J. KLIMKEIT

XXXVIII

THE GOSPEL ACCORDING TO PHILIP

THE SOURCES AND COHERENCE OF AN EARLY CHRISTIAN COLLECTION

BY

MARTHA LEE TURNER

E.J. BRILL
LEIDEN · NEW YORK · KÖLN
1996

The paper in this book meets the guidelines for permanence and durability of the Committee on Production Guidelines for Book Longevity of the Council on Library Resources.

Die Deutsche Bibliothek – CIP-Einheitsaufnahme

Turner, Martha Lee:
The gospel according to Philip : the sources and coherence of an early Christian collection / by Martha Lee Turner. - Leiden ; New York ; Köln : Brill, 1996
  (Nag Hammadi and Manichaean studies ; 38)
  ISBN 90-04-10443-7
NE: GT

ISSN 0929-2470
ISBN 90 04 10443 7

PRINTED IN THE NETHERLANDS

to

John O. Turner

TABLE OF CONTENTS

PART THREE
THE *GOSPEL ACCORDING TO PHILIP* AS A COLLECTION

PREFACE

In this volume, I have set out a view of the *Gospel according to Philip* as a collection of disparate materials. It does not follow from this assertion that the *Gospel according to Philip* is incoherent, or impossible to study, or that it has nothing interesting to say. Rather, I have argued here that its interest lies in three quite separate domains: the strands of early Christian and gnostic-Christian traditions it brings together, the organizing techniques it shares with other collections of diverse material from the same time period, and the distinctive interests of its collector. Because this document opens windows on several aspects of the early Christian world, it is of considerably more than narrowly specialized interest; I have therefore attempted to make this study as accessible to readers as possible.

I should confess at the outset that my initial view of the *Gospel according to Philip* was that it probably was a collection—although, as I have worked with it, I have been seduced by nearly every other imaginable hypothesis about its nature and organization. Readers who have found the "collection hypothesis" uncongenial might be surprised how much coherence a collection can have, and what ends it might serve.

The work presented here first took shape as my 1994 doctoral dissertation at the University of Notre Dame. I wish to thank, first of all, Harold W. Attridge, without whose very patient support of my exploration of all kinds of unpromising leads, this volume would not have become a reality. Adela Yarbro Collins and Gregory Sterling also provided valuable feedback and suggestions. I also wish to thank Hans-Martin Schenke for graciously reading and annotating an early version of this text. None of them, of course, can be blamed for the conclusions I finally reached! Nor can the people of Broadway Christian Parish, who have helped to shape my understanding of some of the things that can happen in the intersectings of multiple Christian traditions, and to whom I owe much gratitude.

This volume is lovingly dedicated to my father, John O. Turner.

CHAPTER ONE

INTRODUCTION

Composed in Greek (or mostly in Greek) during the second or third century, the *Gospel according to Philip* would be entirely lost to the world except for the discovery of a single ancient manuscript copy. Even so, that manuscript contains only a Coptic translation of the text, not the original. This "gospel" which so nearly escaped our grasp is neither a narrative (like the canonical gospels), nor a collection of Jesus' sayings (like the *Gospel according to Thomas*), nor yet an exposition of a message of salvation (like the *Gospel of Truth*). Instead, it presents a jumble of seemingly disjointed reflections on diverse topics, with spirituality and the meaning of the sacraments among the most predominant.

Because this text sprang from the intersections of gnosticisms with more or less mainstream Christianities in the first few centuries C.E., it could tell us much about those tangled milieux—more even than the much studied *Gospel according to Thomas*—if only we could ask the right questions. The great wealth of material found in the *Gospel according to Philip* has not yet been well explored, nor even adequately surveyed.

It is my contention that scholarship on the *Gospel according to Philip* has been hindered by an unresolved problem of an extremely basic nature. Where should we look for insights into the meaning of any given passage in this document? To look to any and all other passages in the *Gospel according to Philip* is tacitly to assume that the entire document expresses a single viewpoint, at least insofar as the issues at hand are concerned. Such a unity is placed in question, however, by the often-expressed judgment that the work is, at some level, a composite—and a composite of material from multiple groups within and (perhaps) beyond the Valentinian movement, at that![1]

---

[1] See, for example, Bentley Layton, *The Gnostic Scriptures* (Garden City, NY: Doubleday, 1987) 325-326, and Hans-Martin Schenke in *Neutestamentliche Apocryphon I: Evangelien* ed. W. Schneemelcher (Tubingen: J. C. B. Mohr [Paul Siebeck], 1987) 151-154.

If significant traces of diverse doctrines, perspectives, and sectarian affiliations exist within the document, then passages from different sources would have little or no relevance to each other—at least insofar as the traces of their divergent origins are concerned. I will argue in this volume that such traces do indeed occur, and that in fact there are remarkably few signs of any attempt to harmonize divergent opinions and perspectives. In such a case, only passages deriving from the same source should be used in conjunction with each other, supplemented by any other information we may be able to deduce about that source. Assertions about the interests and approaches of the collector might also be made, but with considerable caution, because he or she seems to have tampered with the materials rather little.

While tacit assumptions about these matters abound, few hypotheses have been elaborated, and not all of those have been carefully tested. Some scholars have seen in the document a cryptic coherence—but they have not been able to agree about the design, message, or origin of that coherence. Those who have seen the work as composite have seldom hazarded specific conjectures about its sources. Nevertheless, working assumptions about these matters underlie all interpretations of the document or its thought, so the clarification of these issues is urgent. The purpose of this volume is to investigate the nature of the *Gospel according to Philip* as a collection, in terms of its organizing principles, it sources, and its place within gnostic synthesis and speculation.

THE HISTORICAL AND RELIGIOUS CONTEXT

The only known ancient copy of the *Gospel according to Philip* is contained in one of a group of codices discovered inside a jar on the rocky slope beneath a cliff in upper Egypt in late 1945. These small codices were inscribed by hand on sheets of papyrus, bound together, and enclosed in tooled leather covers. The people who found them were unable to locate anyone in their villages who could read them, and early attempts to sell them were unsuccessful. Some detached leaves are rumored to have fueled cooking fires, but the bulk of the find made a slow, circuitous journey to the Cairo antiquities market. At least, that is the basic outline of the stories told by those who could be found and interviewed several years later—many of the specifics they related are open to doubt.[2]After more misadventures (which for one codex included a so-journ at the C. G. Jung Institute in Zürich), the twelve surviving codices, along with some pages which had been cut from a thirteenth, are now conserved in the Coptic Museum in Cairo.

All but one of the codices in the Nag Hammadi collection contain more than one work, and most contain several. The works span a considerable range of loosely gnostic thought, along with a few unrelated works which were (presumably) found congenial: a passage from Plato's *Republic*, a collection of maxims known as the *Sentences of Sextus*, and parts of two Hermetic dialogues, *Asclepius* and the *Discourse on the Eighth and Ninth*.

The Nag Hammadi discovery revolutionized the study of the variegated phenomena of "gnosticism." Before the find, gnostic groups and thinkers were known mostly from their opponents' descriptions of them. The accuracy and the fairness of such information was obviously questionable, but without much outside control, there was little way to assess the accuracy of the information. Since most of the Nag Hammadi find consists of writings by gnostics themselves, representing several varieties of gnosticism, they have increased our knowledge enormously, and have provided a means of evaluating the information in the anti-heretical writers. Perhaps even more importantly, the find has enriched our understanding of the varieties of Christianity in the first few centuries of the common era (including gnostic Christianities), and of their assorted ways of conceptualizing their faith.

The styles of handwriting used seem to date the manuscripts themselves to about the fourth century—although our knowledge of the early evolution of Coptic handwriting leaves something to be desired. Each volume was made by folding in half a single, thick stack of papyrus sheets; various methods were used for attaching the covers. These physical characteristics point to manufacture at a time when scrolls were still common and the codex format relatively new. This, too, suggests the third or fourth centuries. Less conjectural evidence about the date of their

---

[2] For an account of the intricacies of this journey, insofar as they can be recovered, and a critical history of earlier accounts of the discovery and transmission, see James M. Robinson, "From the Cliff to Cairo: The Story of the Discoverers and the Middlemen of the Nag Hammadi Codices," in *Colloque international sur les textes de Nag Hammadi*, ed. B. Barc (Louvain: Éditions Peeters, 1981) 21-58; for a more cautious stance toward the same data, see the long footnote by Rodolphe Kasser and Martin Krause in *The Facsimile Edition of the Nag Hammadi Codices, Introduction*, ed. J. M. Robinson (Leiden: Brill, 1984) 3-4, note 1.

manufacture is found in the papyrus scraps which were made into card-board stiffening for most of the covers. Some of this recycled wastepaper contains specific dates (on letters, bills, et cetera), and the binding of each codex must necessarily be after the last dated fragment used in its covers. This evidence establishes the binding date of at least some of the codices as just after the middle of the fourth century.[3]

---

[3] The codices are not necessarily of the same provenance. They can be divided into three groups on the basis of binding techniques. Most similarities of scribal hands and information from the cartonnage exist within these groups.

Three of the codices (4, 5 and 8) show rather primitive binding techniques. The cartonnage in these consists of accounts dealing with such large quantities that they are probably military accounts or tax records, along with official accounts (one of which, from codex 5, mentions the town of "Chenoboskion") and letters of undetermined sorts.

The codices of a second group (1, 3, 7 and 11) are bound similarly, and three of these also share two scribal hands, pointing to a shared scriptorium for codices 1, 7 and 11. Codex 3 has no cartonnage. That of 1, 7 and 11 again mentions "Chenoboskion" and includes letters, contracts and a weaver's accounts. Codex 7 is the only one with cartonnage clearly from a monastic context: there are fragments of Genesis (35.5-21 and 42.27-38) and some personal letters, some by or to monks, along with assorted contracts and an account, unrelated to monastic life. These monastic references seem to belong to a less organized and less withdrawn sort of life than that of the Pachomian communities, pointing either to an earlier time in the evolution of monasticism, or perhaps to a simpler form of monasticism which coexisted with the Pachomian. There is nothing in this material to suggest either orthodox or heterodox/heretical tendencies. The cartonnage of codex 7 includes is a deed of surety dated October 348. Other dates in the cartonnage from this group range from the 290s to the late 340s.

The group containing the *Gospel according to Philip* (2, 6, 9 and 10) is substantially better bound; some scholars have thought they could trace scribal similarities/identities through several of these, but this is debatable. Two of this group (6 and 9) also share a similar or identical hand in their cartonnage, and the personal name φαῆρις. Codex 13, buried without its cover, seems also to belong to this group, and shows scribal similarities with codex 2. Codices 2 (the *Gospel according to Philip*) and 10 are missing their cartonnage. The cartonnage in the covers of 6 and 9 yield comparatively little information: that of 6 consists of name lists and accounts plus one petition; that of codex 9 may also be tax records similar to those of 6; both are recycled from late 3rd and early 4th century materials.

Codices 6 and 8, however, may share a scribe; if this is so, the differences in binding techniques probably do not indicate different scriptoria.

The wide divergence in the cartonnage material suggests a source such as a town dump.

See the discussion (and further references) in *The Facsimile Edition of the Nag Hammadi Codices: Cartonnage*, "Preface" by James M. Robinson vi-xxiii (Leiden: Brill, 1979), and *Nag Hammadi Codices: Greek and Coptic Papyri from the Cartonnage of the Covers*, ed. J. W. B. Barns, G. M. Browne, and J. C. Shelton (Leiden: Brill, 1981).

All of the works in the Nag Hammadi find had been previously translated from Greek into the Sahidic and Subakhmimic dialects of Coptic.[4]
It was, in fact, the differences between these dialects and the later liturgical Bohairic which made these manuscripts unintelligible to a local Coptic priest to whom they were shown. The spelling of words is quite variable. This is not surprising in the case of the Subakhmimic texts, since
that dialect never underwent standardization, but the Sahidic dialect did.
The variable spelling dates the translation of the Sahidic texts (at least)

---

[4] Codices 1, 10, and parts of 11 are in the Subakhmimic dialect, while the remainder are in Sahidic, which served as the "autochthonous koine" of the Nile valley at this
time.

The language of the Sahidic codices does not conform perfectly to the usages of
later, classical Sahidic. Where the divergences are small and principally in matters of
orthography, they probably represent earlier forms of Sahidic before such matters
were standardized. In a number of codices, however, the divergences are greater and
extend to matters of syntax, morphology and lexicon. When this is coupled with a degree of internal variation unlikely in a spoken subdialect, such codices probably represent the work of a translator whose native dialect was not Sahidic attempting to translate into that more widely understood and more prestigious dialect. Bentley Layton has
argued that the usages of codex 2 represent the incompletely successful attempt of a
speaker of Subakhmimic to make a Sahidic translation, and has coined the term
"crypto-Subakhmimic" to describe the result. Birger Pearson found the language of
codex 9 to be best explained as another example of crypto-Subakhmimic. Layton
stated that codex 8 is written in a crypto-Bohairic, while Douglas Parrot has reported
that Alexander Böhlig and Pahor Labib, in 1963, suggested that the generous admix-
ture of Bohairic, Fayyumic, and Akhmimic traits (as well as Subakhmimic ones), in
the Sahidic of codex 5 could best be explained as the signs of a translator who was a
native speaker of another dialect of Coptic, most likely Fayyumic—a suggestion tanta-
mount to calling its usage "crypto-Fayyumic." See Layton, *Nag Hammadi Codex II,2-
7, vol. 1* (Leiden: Brill, 1989) 6-14; Pearson, *Nag Hammadi Codices IX and X*
(Leiden: Brill, 1981), 16-17; Layton, "Introduction" in *Nag Hammadi Codex VIII* ed.
John Sieber (Leiden: Brill, 1991), 4; and Böhlig and Labib, *Koptisch-gnostische
Apokalypsen aus Codex V von Nag Hammadi* (Halle-Wittenberg: Martin-Luther Universität, 1963) 12.

Wolf-Peter Funk's findings that the "Subakhmimic" or "Lycopolitan" of the
Manichaean texts, the Gospel of John, and of certain Nag Hammadi texts (the *Epistle
of James*, NHC I,2; the *Gospel of Truth*, NHC I,3; Rheginus' *Treatise on the Resurrection*, NHC I,4; the *Interpretation of Gnosis* NHC XI,1; the *Valentinian Exposition*,
NHC XI,2; and *Marsanes*, NHC X) together with the *Acts of Paul*, constitute three
distinct dialects does not alter the basic premise that when scribes fluctuate between a
".neutral" (or "regionally unmarked") spelling and one which is more distinctive, they
have yielded to the impact of the "neutral" spelling--which may show either an underlying regional pronunciation or an underlying regional tradition of orthography. See
W.-P. Funk, "How Closely Related are the Subakhmimic Dialects?" *Zeitschrift für
ägyptische Sprache* 112 (1985) 124-139, especially p. 126. See also Rodolphe
Kasser's catalogue of possible causes of "mixed" dialectical forms: R. Kasser, *Compléments au Dictionnaire copte de Crum* (Cairo: Institut Français d'Archéologie
Orientale, 1964) vii-xviii.

to the period before the standardization of that dialect. Unfortunately, this also occurred gradually during the third and fourth centuries, so the unstandardized Sahidic in the manuscripts confirms this general range as the time of the translations, but does not help us to narrow that range.

The composition of the writings themselves is much the hardest element to date—and for the understanding of the religious world of late antiquity, it is much the most important. Obviously, the translations must have been made somewhat before the production of the Nag Hammadi copies, and the writings themselves composed somewhat before the translations. Beyond this, however, the Nag Hammadi collection cannot be considered as a whole, for the works it contains did not originate in even approximately the same time period. Some writings in the collection date from well before the beginning of the common era, while others may have originated as late as the early fourth century, shortly before the extant copies were made.[5]

Most of the materials in the *Gospel according to Philip* come from contexts in which people clearly understood themselves as Christians. The work repeatedly returns to the theme that the Christ, by actions both cosmic and incarnate, is responsible for the salvation of humankind. Moreover, the *Gospel according to Philip* uses the term "Christian" several times, albeit with varied connotations. This is striking because, while a number of other works in the Nag Hammadi collection contain similar

---

[5] According to Bentley Layton, the "classic" gnostic works in the collection (except possibly for the *Apocalypse of Adam* and *Thunder*) could not have been written before Christian theologians began to grapple with Platonic philosophical myth, and the philosophical ideas underlying them (with the same two exceptions) seem to belong to the period after Philo Judaeus and before Plotinus. See B. Layton, *The Gnostic Scriptures*, (Garden City, NY: Doubleday, 1987) 20.

These parameters are helpful, but are based on several unstated assumptions: that gnostic thinkers did not pioneer fundamental developments in Christian theology; and, that gnostic philosophical speculation, presumably because it is "concrete" and "mythical," always derives from more academic and abstract philosophy, and never precedes it. There is nothing absolutely necessary about either of these assumptions. Marcellus of Ancyra, for example, credits Valentinus with devising the notion of three subsistent hypostases in God (*On the Holy Church* 9). With respect to Plotinian innovations, there is no reason to suppose that the philosophy reflected in every gnostic writing was up to date. Pre-Plotinian ideas undoubtedly circulated in some gnostic (and other) circles well after Plotinus' time. On the other hand, "gnostic" mythological formulations may have had more influence on Plotinus than he was willing to acknowledge. The presence of Christian elements, especially in the case of writings where these seem less than integral, only indicates the time when the writing received its final form, and does not help date the non-Christian elements.

concepts of salvation, only the *Gospel according to Philip* and one other treatise, the *Testimony of Truth*, use the term "Christian" at all.

The *Gospel according to Philip* has often been identified as deriving from some part of the Valentinian movement, because of scattered references to a doctrine of "natures," mentions of an upper and lower Sophia, and its images of salvation as nuptial union with an angelic counterpart, along with some more ambiguous shared attitudes and perceptions. Valentinian Christianity was not, however, a monolithic phenomenon, and the *Gospel according to Philip*'s "Valentinianism" may mean different things in the different materials included in the document. Moreover, as we shall see, some of the material collected in the *Gospel according to Philip* had its origin outside the Valentinian movements. The document's materials witness to a milieu in which multiple varieties of mildly gnostic Christianity coexisted, and in which at least some varieties borrowed freely from others.

Instructions and reflections on sacramental practices are frequent throughout most of the *Gospel according to Philip*. These are not descriptive, but seem to presume known rituals. So far as can be deduced from the text's oblique references to them, the practices of initiation and eucharist were roughly similar to the practices of other early Christian groups, although the interpretations were sometimes less usual. An otherwise unknown pair of sacraments known as "redemption" and "bridal chamber" may have also been known,[6] but these references, too, are in the form of allusions, from which scant inferences can be made about concrete practices. Either or both terms may, alternatively, have functioned as metaphors to describe the entire initiatory process.

The *Gospel according to Philip* was written at a time when Paul's writings had begun to circulate as a collection, for many of them are quoted or alluded to. While Matthew's and John's gospels are also frequently quoted, there is no conclusive evidence of knowledge of Mark, nor (except for a use of the story of the Good Samaritan which lacks all Lukan details) of Luke. A number of passages reflect on the opening chapters of Genesis, although the approach taken to that material varies widely. The *Gospel according to Thomas* is among the works quoted, and some of the understandings of sacramental functioning expressed in the *Gospel according to Philip* coincide with traditions surviving in the

---

[6] "Redemption" translates the Coptic word ϭⲱⲧⲉ, (probably equivalent to the Greek ἀπολύτρωσις), while "bridal chamber" translates ⲚⲨⲘⲫⲰⲚ, which is probably synonymous with ⲠⲀⲤⲦⲞⲤ and ⲔⲞⲓⲦⲰⲚ.

Acts of Thomas. Some sayings attributed to Jesus appear as well: several familiar ones from canonical or other sources, along with several otherwise unknown. Some of these sayings appear in subcollections of independent units with very loose sequential links, while others are introduced as evidence in support of a complex argument. Parallels or similarities also exist between passages in the *Gospel according to Philip* and some of the fragments of Valentinus, as also between the *Gospel according to Philip* and the cosmogony Irenaeus reports as Ptolemy's, and some of the practices he reports as Marcosian (or, more exactly, which he reports after describing the Marcosians), and also between the *Gospel according to Philip* and the *Gospel of Truth*. Our document's use of and affinities with other literature suggest a second or third century date of composition.

A number of senses of the word "gospel" (εὐαγγέλιον) were current in the *Gospel according to Philip*'s time, but the Nag Hammadi document entitled at its end (as was the practice) ΠΕΥΑΓΓΕΛΙΟΝ ΠΚΑΤΑ ΦΙΛΙΠΠΟC ("the Gospel according to Philip") corresponds to none of them. It is clearly not a gospel in the sense(s) of the synoptic gospels or John, regardless of whether these are best seen as narrative expansions of kerygma, or as a type of historiography, or as a development of biography. Nor is it a collection of Jesus' sayings, whether wise or apocalyptic or of whatever kind, as were the synoptics' Sayings Source ("Q") and the Nag Hammadi *Gospel according to Thomas*. Neither is it a collection or catena of Jesus' miracles, as seems to have lain behind canonical Mark and John. Nor yet is it a proclamation of the news of salvation—the sense in which Paul used the word, and the sense in which it is used at the beginning of the untitled document known to modern scholarship as the *Gospel of Truth*. Whatever the *Gospel according to Philip* is, it is none of these.[7]

Apart from our lone copy from Nag Hammadi, there are a few reports from antiquity of the existence of some gospel associated with the name Philip. It is not at all clear, however, that these refer to the Nag Hammadi work. Both Epiphanius and the author of *Pistis Sophia* know of some *Gospel of Philip*. Epiphanius quotes a short extract from "a fictitious Gospel in the name of the holy disciple, Philip," which he says was in

---

[7] See Helmut Koester, *Ancient Christian Gospels, Their History and Development* (Philadelphia: Trinity Press, 1990), and M. J. Suggs, "Gospel, Genre of" *The Interpreter's Dictionary of the Bible, Supplementary Volume* (Nashville: Abingdon, 1976) for discussion of these senses of εὐαγγέλιον and bibliography.

use among libertine gnostic groups in Egypt,[8] but the fragment he preserves does not appear in our *Gospel according to Philip*. While some of its themes find very remote echoes in the *Gospel according to Philip* we know, its treatment of them differs so extremely as to suggest a radically different recension at the least, or (more probably) a different document altogether. The *Pistis Sophia* narrates Jesus' choice of Thomas, Philip, and Matthew (or Matthias) as his official biographers.[9] The scene seems designed to lend support to works recording Jesus' words and deeds which circulated under these men's names, but makes no direct mention of such works. Since the *Gospel according to Philip* does not fit this description, being neither a biography nor a work recording Jesus' words and deeds, the reference in *Pistis Sophia* is probably to another document.

The titles of the works in the Nag Hammadi collection, where they exist at all, typically follow each work and are centered between the right and left margins of the page, and are set apart by extra space and by horizontal lines drawn above and below them. In codex 2, the final incomplete line of the other works is usually filled out with a decoratively penned pattern. The *Gospel according to Philip*'s title begins on the last regular text line, but is concluded in approximately the usual style for titles,[10] strongly suggesting that the copy immediately before this one was titled so irregularly that the scribe of the Nag Hammadi codex did not immediately recognize it as a title, but continued writing what he or she assumed was part of the text, only to realize the mistake after the word ⲡⲉⲩⲁⲅⲅⲉⲗⲓⲟⲛ. This irregular "title" in the immediately prior copy may have been a scribe's or librarian's conjectural attempt to identify the

---

[8] *Panarion* 26.13.2-3. "They cite a fictitious Gospel in the name of the holy disciple, Philip, as follows. 'The Lord hath shown me what my soul must say on its ascent to heaven, and how it must answer each of the powers on high. "I have recognized myself," it saith, "and gathered myself from every quarter, and have sown no children for the archon. But I have pulled up his roots, and gathered my scattered members, and I know who thou art, For I," it saith, "am of those on high."' And so, they say, it is set free. But if it turns out to have fathered a son, it is detained below until it can take its own children up and restore them to itself." *The Panarion of Epiphanius of Salamis* transl. Frank Williams (Leiden: Brill, 1987) 94.

[9] *Pistis Sophia* ed. Carl Schmidt, transl. and notes Violet MacDermot (Leiden: Brill, 1978) 44.14-47.8.

[10] See *The Facsimile Edition of the Nag Hammadi Codices. Codex II* (Leiden: Brill, 1974) 42 (title of the *Apocryphon of John*), 63 (title of the *Gospel according to Thomas*), 98 (title of the *Gospel according to Philip*), 109 (title of the *Hypostasis of the Archons*), 139 (title of the *Exegesis on the Soul*), and 145 (title of the *Book of Thomas the Contender, Writing to the Perfect*).

work, and may well have originated no earlier than that copy. Such a conjecture could have been suggested by the single mention of the apostle Philip, which occurs just a few pages from the end of the *Gospel according to Philip*, perhaps combined with a tradition (such as we find in the *Pistis Sophia*) that "Philip" made a record of Jesus' words and deeds, or figured in the title of a work which was, or might have been, in circulation.

Timotheus of Constantinople[11] and pseudo-Leontius of Byzantium,[12] both writing in the late sixth century C.E., again mention gospels associated with Thomas and Philip, which by their time were being used in Manichaean groups as well as gnostic ones. It is tempting to see in this a confirmation that the Nag Hammadi "gospels" attributed to Thomas and Philip were both in circulation in the sixth century, but this is not necessarily the case. If Timotheus and pseudo-Leontius meant either the writing known to Epiphanius, or a writing of the narrative or sayings sort implied by the *Pistis Sophia*, they bear witness to the circulation of some other document (or documents), not the *Gospel according to Philip* we know.

Apart from these dubious references, however, we have no way of knowing how widely the Nag Hammadi *Gospel according to Philip* may have circulated, if it circulated at all. It is still possible that our *Gospel according to Philip* may incorporate material from the gospel (or gospels) known to these ancient writers—or that those documents may have incorporated materials from the one preserved at Nag Hammadi.

THE INTERPRETIVE IMPASSE

Most of the *Gospel according to Philip* lacks rhetorical, logical, and thematic continuity. Without the sort of introduction, conclusion, transitions, and summaries familiar to us from original works, it sometimes seems to change both subject and type of discourse several times a page. Formal consistency is similarly lacking. The whole does not conform to the expectations of any clearly defined genre, nor are the individual parts formally consistent. Catch word associations knit some small units together. Other small units seem entirely unrelated to the material before and after them. Certain themes and their characteristic vocabulary appear

---

[11] Timotheus of Constantinople *De receptione haereticorum* PG 86.1.21.C.
[12] Pseudo-Leontius of Byzantium *De sectis* 3.2 PG 86.1.1213.C.

regularly for stretches of many pages, but are then wholly absent from other portions of the text. Often, when units of text circle around a common theme for several pages, they seem neither to build any argument nor paint any recognizable picture, however impressionistic. At other times, groups of passages can be read as coherent discussions, but their style is so abrupt and telegraphic that one is left unsure whether the text really gives one warrant to read them so.

This high degree of apparent discontinuity has lead to speculation on the document's unity and structure. Many of those who have dealt with the *Gospel according to Philip* as a whole, particularly its translators and commentators, have believed it to be a collection of materials from one or more gnostic Christian tradition. Virtually everyone who has sought to interpret some aspect of the text, such as its sacramental practice or particular points of its theology, has either silently assumed its unity or presented arguments for such a unity. Their arguments have not agreed.

If the document does indeed represent multiple traditions, interpretations which ignore this and conflate material from diverse traditions will be skewed or even valueless. Happily, many studies have focused on narrow ranges of phenomena, which sometimes may have been present in only one source, or predominantly in one source. Nevertheless, if the *Gospel according to Philip* is indeed composite, ignoring this aspect of its nature entails running the risk of expending much ingenuity in the harmonization of opinions which may never have been held by the same person or group.

A reliable source analysis should logically be foundational for the study of such a document. Unfortunately, only one person has so far attempted a source analysis of the *Gospel according to Philip*, and that source analysis was presented as a quick sketch, with little development of or argumentation for its findings.[13] It has not been used to guide any subsequent interpretation of the *Gospel according to Philip*.

By identifying some of the component traditions of the text, and by clarifying its position in the generic continuum of collections and in the practice of gnostic speculation, this study attempts to provide a new footing for the investigation of the *Gospel according to Philip*.

---

[13] That source analysis was done in 1970 by Rodolphe Kasser as part of a brief (9 page) introduction to his translation of the *Gospel according to Philip*. See "L'Évangile selon Philippe," *Revue de théologie et philosophie* ser. 3, 20 (1970), introduction: 12-20, translation: 21-35, 82-106; see also the discussion of Kasser's source analysis in chapter 2 below.

PART ONE

KINDS OF COHERENCE

INTRODUCTION TO PART ONE

The argument presented in this volume is a "circular" one, in the sense that it rests on multiple aspects both of the document and of the religious and intellectual milieu in which it was created. Part One is an inquiry into the kinds of coherence this document has been thought to have, and into the kinds of coherence other collections produced in or around its time display. The explorations here are guided, in a general way, by the findings of Part Two, which attempts to establish the composite nature of the *Gospel according to Philip* and to link certain passages within it to specific early Christian and gnostic Christian traditions.

The view that the *Gospel according to Philip* is a composite work or collection does not imply that it is nonsensical or meaningless. As a collection, its individual components (handled with appropriate care) have the power to illuminate the traditions from which they derive, of course. Its interest as a collection goes far beyond the illumination of source traditions, however, because of (not despite) the characteristics it shares with other collections of its era.

The collections of late antiquity were not mere grab bags of random materials. They were organized according to specific principles; the materials chosen for inclusion reflect the interests of their collectors; and the handling of those materials often reflects their collectors' attitudes and approaches to that material. A number of these collections share many characteristics with the *Gospel according to Philip*—including some of its most remarkable and puzzling characteristics.

The four chapters of Part One seek to illuminate the kinds of coherence we might expect to find in the *Gospel according to Philip* if it is indeed a collection. Chapter 2 reviews and evaluates previous assessments of the document's nature, with particular attention to the features of the document on which each was based; chapter 3 examines the culture of excerpting and collecting in late antiquity, and chapter 4, the organizing principles behind an assortment of loosely contemporaneous collections, and the features present in them; chapter 5 explores some "gnostic" ways of handling sacred traditions, and the role that excerpting and collecting probably played in gnostic speculative activity.

The questions here are, then, of a preliminary nature: how has the *Gospel according to Philip* been seen by previous scholarship? what do the collections produced in the late ancient world look like? how would we recognize one if we saw one? what kinds of purposes did such collections serve in their time? how might those purposes have intersected with the interests and goals of gnostic Christians?

CHAPTER TWO

ON THE TRAIL OF AN ELUSIVE COHERENCE

The *Gospel according to Philip* both intrigues and frustrates its readers. Initially it appears to be a series of non sequiturs; then, of non sequiturs circling around certain recurring and metamorphosing themes. After some exposure, it creates in the minds of many readers the suspicion of a tantalizingly elusive order: perhaps an order requiring an arcane "key" for understanding, or one partially effaced, perhaps, by severe condensation, or by physical loss, or by obscurantist literary practices. The possibilities are seductive, for the text is very rich in provocative enigma.

Such an order has, nevertheless, persisted in eluding many investigators, while those who believe they have found it do not often agree on what they have found. A discordant array of impressions and hypotheses has emerged. Few of these hypotheses can simply be dismissed as the products of over- or under-active imaginations, of fanciful projection or a pedestrian lack of insight (although occasionally scholars on both sides have tried this tactic), because concrete, observable features of the text can be cited for almost any theory about the *Gospel according to Philip*. The data itself is extremely ambiguous. This chapter will consider previous scholarly attempts to make sense of this data.[1]

CATEGORIES OF ANALYSIS

Questions of the unity and coherence of a document like the *Gospel according to Philip* do not lend themselves to binary alternatives, and

---

[1] Note that this chapter surveys only opinions relating to these issues, and does not comment on studies which have ignored them (except in the final section in which I have chronicled even tacit assumptions in scholarship of the last decade); moreover, only the stance of each investigator toward this issue will be analyzed. If mistaken for an overview of the general trends of scholarship on the *Gospel according to Philip,* or a balanced appreciation of each scholar's contributions to its understanding, it could give rise to very misleading impressions.

hence not to simple solutions. Multiple varieties, degrees, and levels of
coherence can easily coexist with multiple varieties, degrees, and levels
of disunity, as they do in many other ancient documents. Scholars have
(with varying cogency) claimed to have found, within the *Gospel according to Philip*, each of the following: a uniform and recognizable style, an
unusual set of metaphors consistently deployed, an overall plan or structure, a literary context for experimentation with genre, an identifiable
linguistic and/or sectarian provenance, clues to a purpose or function, a
coherent set of liturgical practices, and a clearly articulated doctrine. Any
of these types of coherence could plausibly exist at multiple levels: for
example, a recognizable literary or rhetorical style might distinguish editorial insertions in a collection of otherwise unredacted materials from a
single source, or characterize a revision of all (or any part) of such a
collection, or might be the stamp of a wholly original literary
composition. Similar possibilities exist for discerned consistencies of
structure, genre, milieu, liturgical practice, and theological position.

Implications about the document's compositional process and/or
redactional history lurk beneath every possible assertion about its unity,
and vary with the degree of coherence postulated as well as its kind. The
multiplicity of possibilities here is daunting, but it does not leave us to
choose between undisciplined speculation and mere description, eschew-
ing speculation about causes.

In order to assess a chaotic sea of claims and counterclaims, we
should begin by considering what data must be accounted for. A short
and reasonably non-controversial list of important, observable features
would include:

- short units which seem capable of functioning independently of
  each other (regardless of whether they ever did so function, or
  whether they do so here);
- sequences of such potentially independent units which seem to be
  random, with no discernible connections between units;
- sequences of such potentially independent units showing various
  types of connections between contiguous units, including catch
  word associations, both simple and sophisticated, and analogous
  developments;
- irregularly recurring and metamorphosing themes—i.e., seemingly
  related imagery, terms, and ideas appearing in non-contiguous
  units;

- sectarian terminology, conflicting or divergent usages, and distinctive features which are concentrated in (or wholly restricted to) certain portions of the document.

All of these features (at least) should be accounted for by any theory about the nature and/or compositional process(es) of the *Gospel according to Philip*. Beyond this, such a theory should also be capable of relating the document to its larger contexts, such as:

- the conditions of writing in late antiquity;
- the conventions of a genre or a generic context ;
- plausible motivations and commitments on the part of all agents.

These features of the document and its contextual location provide a measuring rod by which hypotheses can be evaluated. In the survey which follows, we will be asking, Which features of the text does this hypothesis try to explain? How well does it explain them? Are there other important features which have been ignored?

Beyond this, careful exploration and checking of the implications of speculative hypotheses are also possible. Any hypothesis has implications beyond the data it was originally invented to explain, and these implications should also be in harmony with other observable characteristics of the text. This provides us with some control over our own speculation. Once implications have been teased out of hypotheses, we can then check them against the text and its possible contexts. This is the only form of control we have—but it is a fairly rigorous one. The problem is not that investigators have been too speculative, but that most of their speculations have been neither carefully enough framed nor carefully enough tested.

THE EARLY "FLORILEGIUM" HYPOTHESIS: SEQUENTIAL DISCONTINUITIES AND CONTINUITIES

One of the most easily noticed features of the *Gospel according to Philip* is that much of it is composed of fairly short units which seem capable (at least) of functioning independently. This feature is very difficult to discuss without continual reference to the sequential connections that also appear to exist between such potentially independent units. While many sentences and paragraphs lack syntactic or logical connections with the preceding or following material, often a theme, image, or issue seems to continue from one unit to the next, despite the lack of more explicit sorts of connections. At times, a short, clear statement is surrounded by potentially free-standing material, which can be interpreted as making the same or an analogous point, often in either more abstract or more concrete and "mythological" terms. In other cases, only a shared word eases the abruptness of transition. There are some short units which almost everyone agrees follow each other with no discernible connection whatsoever.[2] The first serious attempts to describe the *Gospel according to Philip* focused on these features, viewing the document as some sort of collection of excerpts, often using the term "florilegium" in this loose sense.

Evaluations of the *Gospel according to Philip* as a florilegium or collection of some kind are based primarily on the appearance of potentially independent units, combined with the assessment that many of the connections between units do not represent the flow of a single continuous writing, however terse or however severely condensed. The ease with which these features can be observed, and the historical circumstance that much of the early work on the document was done in the shadow of the *Gospel according to Thomas*, have combined to give this hypothesis the feeling of something obvious and self-evident. Those who have subscribed to this view have not generally felt that the burden of proof lay with them, and few have systematically drawn out the implications of such a view for interpretation. Work on the *Gospel according to Philip* during the first half of the 1960s followed the general hypothesis that the document must be some sort of gnostic collection.

Hans-Martin Schenke inaugurated this trend when he divided the text of the *Gospel according to Philip* into units of relatively uniform length, and identified the whole as "eine Art Florilegium gnostischer Sprüche und Gedanken."[3] Schenke's was the first translation of the text into a modern language,[4] following shortly after Pahor Labib's publication of the photographic plates of codex 2.[5] Schenke's division of the text into small units was a handy form of reference and became, in slightly revised form, the most common form of reference to the text until the

---

[2] For example, much of the material on pages 64 and 65.

[3] Hans-Martin Schenke, "Das Evangelium nach Philippus" in Johannes Leipoldt and Hans-Martin Schenke, *Koptisch-gnostische Schriften aus den Papyrus-Codices von Nag Hamadi* (Hamburg: Herbert Reich, 1960) 33.

[4] Hans-Martin Schenke, "Das Evangelium nach Philippus: Ein Evangelium der Valentinianer aus dem Funde von Nag-Hamadi," *Theologische Literaturzeitung* 84 (1959) 1-26.

[5] Pahor Labib, *Coptic Gnostic Papyri in the Coptic Museum at Old Cairo. Volume 1* (Cairo: Government Press [Antiquities Department], 1956) plates 99-134.

1980s. As such, it exerted a subtle influence on perceptions of the document's continuity.[6]

Robert M. Grant introduced the often-quoted oxymoron "chaotic arrangement" in 1959 in his presidential address to the Society of Biblical Literature, referring to the text as "materials arranged chaotically, if one can speak of chaotic arrangement," although he also remarked that "both Thomas and Philip are written in order to present very special theological viewpoints."[7] It should be noted, however, that the proposition that the document contains a single coherent theological viewpoint is not necessarily the same as the proposition that the document is a coherent exposition of that viewpoint—and either proposition needs to be demonstrated. In 1960, Eric Segelberg characterized the *Gospel according to Philip* in similar terms, as "a collection of 'sayings' without any definite plan of composition"—but his interpretation of the text's "sacramental system" clearly assumed that all of these "sayings" came from a group with a single set of practices.[8]

In 1962, R. McL. Wilson expressed the *Gospel according to Philip*'s lack of sequential continuities in similar terms, but also raised more explicitly the question of the meaning of this characteristic. He wrote, "to speak of 'structure' or 'composition' in relation to such a document as the Gospel of Philip may appear at first sight to be a misuse of these terms."[9] Despite Wilson's observation that "it cannot be contended that Philip is a single coherent text, composed according to normal standards of writing," he nevertheless maintained,

> This rambling and inconsequential method of composition is not without parallel in the writings of the Fathers, or in the Bible itself. Clarity is

---

[6] The text of the *Gospel according to Philip* has been divided into sections by several different scholars. Their aims and criteria have been incommensurable, however, and as a result, the number and locations of their divisions are not immediately comparable. Schenke attempted to identify sense units on the level of paragraphs, while others have attempted to locate the seams between excerpts, or to identify multi-paragraph thematic wholes, or to enumerate the smallest possible sense divisions as an aid to analysis. Discussion about these different schemes has not usually acknowledged their different agenda, and has been strikingly unfruitful. In any case, the regularity with which any false impressions have been transcended (and deplored) suggests that their impact has been comparatively trivial.

[7] Robert M. Grant, "Two Gnostic Gospels," *Journal of Biblical Literature* 79 (1960) 2. This paper introduced the "gospels" of Thomas and Philip to an audience little acquainted with either, and pointed out some initial directions for their study.

[8] Eric Segelberg, "The Coptic-Gnostic Gospel According to Philip and its Sacramental System," *Numen* 7 (1960) 191.

[9] R. McL. Wilson, *The Gospel of Philip* (London: Mowbray & Co., 1962) 7.

sometimes introduced by modern chapter divisions, and if the texts were
written out as in Philip without these aids to comprehension we should be
faced with the same bewildering movement, as of a butterfly flitting from
one theme to the next.[10]

The point is important. Nevertheless, the propriety of any given set of
modern chapter divisions in either the Fathers or the Bible is defensible
only when they depend on markers of structure discernible in the text, or
when they make explicit a progression of themes abstracted, without vio-
lence or imposition, from the text itself. Many such divisions of biblical
and patristic texts are inappropriate to a larger or smaller degree. The
Gospel according to Philip, however, has frustrated most attempts to find
any coherent progression of themes, while even subtle structural markers
are simply not there to be found.

Wilson was well aware of the ambiguities of the situation, although he
could not foresee that they would persist stubbornly through many later
efforts at resolution. Although he called the document "an extreme case,"
he rightly insisted that this extremity "does not justify us in abandoning
the effort to discover how its author (or compiler) went to work." Wilson
made a number of observations directed toward resolving the problem.
These observations have since been repeated (or independently re-ob-
served) many, many times: (a) Schenke's "saying" or "paragraph" divisions artificially increase the impression of the document's fragmen-
tation, because a number of those units form larger sense units as well;
(b) the material on the first few pages can be blocked together under
some general headings: contrasts relating to modes of human existence,
the mission of Christ, the nature of truth; (c) certain characteristic themes
recur repeatedly; (d) the references to "bridal chamber" do not begin until
almost half-way through the document.[11] The first two of these observations point out that there are sequential connections as well as disconti-
nuities. The third and fourth address the impression of recurring and
metamorphosing themes, and the fourth also points vaguely in the direction of the uneven distribution of sectarian terminology. Wilson suggested that these observations, taken together, may "suggest a sort of
spiral movement, gradually approaching the central and deepest mystery."[12] Without further elaboration or attempted solution, however, these
remain (as Wilson offered them) only promising "leads."

---

[10] Wilson, *Gospel of Philip*, 8-9.
[11] Wilson, *Gospel of Philip*, 9-10.
[12] Wilson, *Gospel of Philip*, 10.

Jacques E. Ménard focused his attention more directly on sequential continuities, especially the catch word links between "sayings."[13] These, Ménard thought, were more than just catch words, i.e., more than just a mechanical way of linking otherwise unrelated units. Rather, they form a guide introduced by the author to help in understanding "la continuité et la progression de sa pensée."[14] Ménard's estimate of this continuity must be seen, however, against the backdrop of Schenke, Wilson, Segelberg and others, who saw the work as "chaotic" and "without definite plan or order." Ménard's claim about these exceptional catch words was that they could allow us to group together two, three, four, five or even more "sentences" for interpretation. His catalogue of such chains extends for two and one half pages in his introduction; typically, a word, concept or pair of opposed words or concepts forms a link between two consecutive "sayings," then the word/concept/pair shifts in sense or nuance to connect the second with a third "sentence," and so on.[15] After one or several such connections, another word or concept is used. The result looks a bit like free-association within a very specific universe of images; it implicitly raises the question of the nature of the links in these chains of sayings. Nonetheless, Ménard made a convincing case that the sequence of "sentences"—whatever else may be true of it—is neither completely random nor the result of a mindlessly mechanical juxtaposition of materials based on catch word association alone.

Ménard, seemingly following Wilson, went on to suggest that these form "une pareille continuité dans le texte, une semblable pensée en forme de spirale," to such an extent that it may sometimes help in reconstructing some lacunae.[16] He gave as an example "sentences" 11 and 14 (53.23-54.5 and 54.31-55.5), each spanning the damaged bottom and top of a page, both dealing with deception. Ménard did not, however, map such links onto any specific spiral structure. It is hard to know how his

---

[13] Jacques É Ménard, *L'Évangile selon Philippe. Introduction, texte, traduction, commentaire* (Paris: Letouzy & Ané, 1967), 2-6. This publication, Ménard's 1967 Strasbourg dissertation, differs little in its interpretation of the nature of the *Gospel according to Philip* from his 1964 publication, *L'Évangile selon Philippe* (Montréal: Université de Montréal, 1964; Paris: P. Lethielleux, 1964. (The 1967 work adds a Coptic text facing the translation, a commentary, and detailed indices.)
While Ménard rejected the validity of Schenke's division of the *Gospel according to Philip* into "sayings," he kept Schenke's numbering system for purely practical purposes.
[14] Ménard, *L'Évangile selon Philippe* (1967) 3.
[15] Ménard, *L'Évangile selon Philippe* (1967) 3-6.
[16] Ménard, *L'Évangile selon Philippe* (1967) 6.

view ought to be categorized. Although he wrote of an "author," he did not move beyond Wilson's observations, except to stress the linkages—sometimes causal, sometimes logical, sometimes associative—which join together small groups of statements.

None of these early "florilegium" hypotheses explored the implications of a composite *Gospel according to Philip* very carefully, nor speculated much about the processes which could have formed it. Wilson wrote now of an "author," now of a "compiler," while Ménard could write of an "author" and his concern to aid our understanding by grouping the material for us, drawing a loose comparison with the *Excerpta ex Theodoto*. Neither speculated much about the sources of the material included, nor addressed the problem of distinguishing sources from redactorial comment (since presumably this is what they had in mind when they used the word "author"). Neither asked what sorts of intelligibility are to be expected in collections.

INTEGRATIONS OF SEQUENTIAL AND RECURRENT PHENOMENA

The connections between sequential units has not been the only sort of coherence sought, and sometimes found, in the *Gospel according to Philip*. An overarching theme, or themes, or a thematic progression have been found by some investigators; these findings have been cited both as evidence of the composition of an original author and as evidence of the labors of a redactor who assembled and arranged collected materials.

In the late 1960s, Søren Giversen, Gerald Leo Borchert, William Wesley Isenberg, and Hans-Georg Gaffron each sought a way to go beyond vague references to "spiraling" structures, and attempted stronger readings of the coherence of the *Gospel according to Philip*.

Søren Giversen, in the introduction to his 1966 Danish translation of the *Gospel according to Philip*, presented an argument for a considerable unity in the document, reasoning from a sustained interest in certain key themes and concerns to an original author who was a biblical theologian.[17]

Giversen noted that the *Gospel according to Philip* does contain some small, originally independent units of traditional material—e.g., the nar-

---

[17] Søren Giversen, *Filips Evangeliet. Indledning, studier oversaettelse og noter* (Copenhagen: G. E. C. Gads Forlag, 1966) 9-38.

ratives and similes on pages 64 and 65.[18] Small, independent units appear in other ancient and patristic writers as well, he noted. On the other hand, Giversen also stressed the sequential continuities of the text, involving as much as a page or more of text. He showed that a number of Schenke's paragraphs appear together in larger thematic groups,[19] but urged a strong view of the linear continuity of the *Gospel according to Philip*, which he supported by interpreting several groups of sayings, and an attempt to trace certain themes through the entire work.

While Giversen was very much opposed to much speculative reconstruction, he made a point of demonstrating that a topic can often be shown to continue after a lacuna. He presented three specific examples: the lacuna at the bottom of 54 and the top of 55, that at the bottom of 58 and the top of 59, and the extensively damaged lower half of 69 together with the first line of 70.[20] The first and last occur in the middle of passages which Schenke also considered as single units, although Giversen gave the impression that discerning the continuity across them allowed him to extend the block of supposedly continuous text in which they occur. The passage in which the lacuna at the bottom of 58 and top of 59 occurs, on the other hand, was divided by Schenke into numerous units of a few lines each. The material from 58.17 to 59.17 was numbered 28, 29, 30, 31, 32, and 33. The material from 58.17 to 59.6, despite somewhat opaque terminology and the damage at the bottom and top of the page, does seem to form a unit concerning the production of children by "the heavenly person." The rhetorical connection from 28 to 31 is clear from repeated vocabulary and from connectors such as ⲀⲖⲖⲀ, ⲄⲀⲢ, ⲈⲦⲂⲈ ⲠⲀⲒ, et cetera, even when the thought eludes. However, the connection of the next two passages, if there is a connection, works on an analogy between two sets of three names each: Mary, Mary, and Mary Magdalene, (59.6-10) and Father, Son, and Holy Spirit (59.11-17), and is not far from being a riddle. Mary Magdalene is said to be Jesus' partner, but the link this suggests to the preceding material about spiritual parentage has nothing to do with the relation (if there is one) between that passage and the next. A chain of passages in which the relation of A to B depends on completely different aspects of B than does the relation of B to C seems like "catch word association" of a kind extrinsic to the internal logic of each part.

---

[18] Giversen, *Filips Evangeliet*, 28-29.
[19] Giversen, *Filips Evangeliet*, 23-26.
[20] Giversen, *Filips Evangeliet*, 25-27.

As examples of continuous discourse, Giversen examined 52.35-54.4 (# 9, 10, and 11 in Schenke's numbering), later adding 54.5-30 (# 12 and 13);[21] 69.1-13 (# 73, 74, and 75), later adding 69.14-70.4 9 (# 76);[22] and 73.1-18 (# 90, 91, 92).[23] He also followed what he saw to be such a con-

---

[21] Giversen, *Filips Evangeliet*, 23 and 25-26. The section 53.14-54.17 (Schenke's # 10, 11, and 12) certainly forms a coherent and sophisticated discussion of the problems of human language, as Giversen claimed. The following section, 54.18-31, deals with the same problems, in both its negative and positive aspects, from a less philosophical, more mythological perspective: the rulers tampered with language, making it deceptive, because they wanted to enslave humans, but their plan backfired in that it served to highlight the relativity of language. Most writers capable of producing the sophisticated section which precedes this would not be likely to express themselves in such mythological terms—or if they did, would put such an expression first and then exegete its "real" meaning. Some writers might move in this unexpected direction, however—see the discussion of this passage in chapter 9. In any case, Giversen has detected an intriguing connection.

When we turn to 52.35-53.14, the connections are looser. This unit of the text describes Christ's saving actions: he came to purchase some, rescue some, and ransom some. It is tempting to attach these rather ambiguous verbs to the three classes of humans in several forms of gnostic thought, but the next sentences seem to cut across these distinctions and group people differently. Possibly the same groups are under consideration here, but are here regarded as stages rather than types. The passage then turns to Christ's action of laying down his soul "from the moment the world existed." Returning to his actions in relation to humans, it states that he "ransomed those who are good in the world, and the bad." Perhaps one or more words have been omitted here. The dichotomy between good and bad forms the connection with the following material whether, by Giversen's analysis, the discussion of language is offered to explain these terms, or by a simple catchword association. The explanation, if it is one, digresses at length, into matters more sophisticated than the one being explained, and the text never comes back to the subject. On the other hand, any piece of material referring to one or more pairs of opposites, chosen at random and placed after 52.35-13, could be claimed to offer oblique explanation of the shared terms. Giversen's claim seems to have been that a substantial continuity of thought connects these two passages by means of shared terms, such as are typical of catchword association. It is undisprovable.

[22] Giversen, *Filips Evangeliet*, 24 and 26. This section seems to me to be unrelated statements about various sacraments or stages of initiation (it has been debated but remains unclear which of these is the better way of conceptualizing the *Gospel according to Philip* 's references to baptism, chrism, ransom and bridal chamber.) That is, they are unrelated statements about closely related matters, matters which are characteristically described in densely interrelated imagery, not just in the *Gospel according to Philip* but in other parts of the early Christian world as well.

[23] Giversen, *Filips Evangeliet*, 23-24. I would divide this material into two sections rather than Schenke's three. But the refutation of the doctrine that death precedes resurrection—a contention which is tied to a limited appreciation of baptism—shows thematic but not logical or rhetorical links to the following story about Joseph's woodlot, the cross, and the olive tree from which comes the oil of chrism. Moreover, the latter unit (73.8-18) is far more dense in symbolism, implication and irony than most of the *Gospel according to Philip* (or most other literature).

tinuity through 82.26-84.14 as an example.[24] His understanding of the *Gospel according to Philip* was centered in the dominance of three interlocking themes: paradise and its events, modes of creation, and the bridal chamber with its rich web of associations.[25] He did not claim that these are explored in any organized way; rather, the very fact that so much of the text concentrates on these themes in itself constitutes a plan, in Giversen's opinion. Nevertheless, these are very broad topics: the first could be paraphrased as creation and related topics, and (given what we seem to be able to deduce about the meaning of bridal chamber in Valentinian circles) the third, salvation and, perhaps, the sacramental mediation and/or depiction of salvation. The second—modes of creation—involves a distinctive way of approaching and imaging the potentialities of human beings, and the failure to attain them. It is built on a broadly gnostic base, which may also be observed in the elaborate systems of aeons and their emanations. Giversen quite correctly notes that our failure to understand much of the imagery in the *Gospel according to Philip* puts us in a poor position to evaluate its coherence. He suggested that a better understanding of special terminology, such as the association of anointing with the image of light, might help us to trace the chain of thought more accurately.[26] Giversen's bottom line was that a continuity of thought runs through the entire document and that caution about reconstructing lacunae is, in principle, the only impediment to demonstrating this.[27]

Perhaps Giversen's most lasting contribution to the study of this document is his identification of "modes of creation" as a dominant concern linking many otherwise unrelated units in the text. Nevertheless, the fact that themes come up again and again—even highly peculiar themes—does not, by itself, guarantee that the statements of them are from the same source, or are even entirely compatible with each other. (Their consistency or compatibility with each other should be checked, although, as Giversen pointed out, this is difficult when we understand them so imperfectly.) The interests Giversen pointed out could have guided a collector as easily as an author; we must look to other data to distinguish between these hypotheses.

In 1967, Gerald Leo Borchert saw more order in the sequence of materials than Giversen did, but he held that it was a collection of diverse

---

[24] Giversen, *Filips Evangeliet,* 27-28.
[25] Giversen, *Filips Evangeliet,* 35-37.
[26] Giversen, *Filips Evangeliet,* 24-25, 35-37.
[27] Giversen, *Filips Evangeliet,* 24.

materials.[28] He readily agreed that the work as a whole is a collection, "a
mixed collection of apothegmata, similitudes, parables, narratives, and
theological and etymological expositions, . . . but which do not possess
(perhaps purposely) clarifying logical connectives."[29] He contended that
its materials were assembled from both canonical and extra-canonical
sources, such as "homiletical, catechetical, apologetical and perhaps
hymnical materials," which may have included a gnostic commentary on
the opening chapters of Genesis,[30] but observed that the characterization
of the text as a "florilegium," while not incorrect, has tended to dis-
courage scholars from seeking to understand its arrangement.[31] In contrast to this impression, Borchert contended that the *Gospel according to
Philip*'s assorted materials are organized by an overall plan, not merely a
set of interconnected interests.

Borchert noted that the collector of these materials was quite a bit less
syncretistic than the person or persons who assembled the Nag Hammadi
library.[32] This collector was someone who claimed to be a Christian, and
who represented a mildly ascetic strain of gnosticism. Borchert's analysis
of the sources of the materials was relatively cursory. He was very concerned to locate the source of the seven of Jesus' sayings that correspond
to canonical material, but did not speculate on the source of the other
nine sayings.[33] He also discussed the few other direct quotations of
canonical writings contained in the *Gospel according to Philip*.[34] By lo-
cating the canonical sources of these quotations along with certain
themes and motifs to which the text alludes, Borchert was able to assemble a list of Old and New Testament books used by "Philip"
(Borchert's abbreviation for *The Gospel according to Philip*).[35] His discussion of non-canonical materials focused on their rhetorical functions
rather than their sources.[36]

---

[28] Gerald Leo Borchert, "An Analysis of the Literary Arrangement and Theological
Views in the Gnostic Gospel of Philip" (Dissertation, Princeton Theological Seminary,
1967).

[29] Borchert, "Analysis," 35.

[30] Borchert, "Analysis," 23-34 and 37-43.

[31] Borchert, "Analysis," 4-5.

[32] Borchert, "Analysis," 16-18. But no single writing in the Nag Hammadi collection embraces as wide a range of ideological positions as the collection taken as a
whole.

[33] Borchert, "Analysis," 23-25. Both figures are his.

[34] Borchert, "Analysis," 26.

[35] Borchert, "Analysis," 32.

[36] Borchert, "Analysis," 37-38.

The ambiguity of his use of the same term for both text and author/ collector/redactor coincides with the way Borchert's assumptions seem to have shifted when he turned from quotations to allusions. Instead of talking in terms of a source from which a small piece of the *Gospel according to Philip*'s text was taken, he began to speak of "the writer" making an allusion, using language such as, "The way in which Philip appears to use scriptural passages may provide some insight into his view of Scripture."[37] While he sometimes wrote in terms of "Philip" taking something from a source and deploying it in a rhetorical and doctrinal plan,[38] more often he short-circuited the distinction by attributing the gnostic meaning of a passage to the agency of the collector/redactor/ writer, without questioning how much of that meaning might (or even must) have been part of the source.[39] These moves are in harmony with Borchert's belief that the *Gospel according to Philip*'s materials were significantly redacted (as well as arranged) by their collector; in such situations it is often not possible to separate the effects of these with any certainty. Nevertheless, ignoring the distinction between appropriation and redaction or comment is not warranted, nor is the wholesale attribution of every apparently gnostic opinion to the redactor.

Borchert set out to challenge the assumption of a random or "chaotic" organization, and to explore the possibility that the *Gospel according to Philip* might be "a *grouping* of materials (some collected and some perhaps written by the editor), which are organized (and even altered) to suit his purposes but left without connectives."[40] He concluded that the text "gives the external appearance of being a disjointed collection of literary fragments but . . . contains a discernible organizing scheme."[41] He briefly contemplated two alternative scenarios under which such an organization without connectives might have come into existence: "(a) for no particular reason except that they [the materials] were collected that way, or

---

[37] Borchert, "Analysis," 33.

[38] For example, "The householder who sets different types of food before cattle, pigs, dogs, slaves and sons becomes in the hand of Philip a symbol of a disciple who understands the dispositions of men's souls (log. 119)." Borchert, "Analysis," 40. Or, "The analysis of names (in terms of etymology, translation and transliteration, and even the number of words in names) furnished Philip with a literary device by which he is enabled to support his special Gnostic formulations." Borchert, "Analysis," 41.

[39] Consider again the first example in the previous footnote: without some sort of application (which Borchert considers to be supplied by the redactor), the information that a householder gives different kinds of food to different groups of animals and people is pointless.

[40] Borchert, "Analysis," 36 (emphasis his).

[41] Borchert, "Analysis," 36-37.

(b) in order to convey by the form itself an esoteric meaning."[42] He stated
that "it is impossible to be certain which the editor had in mind" but
maintained that "it is possible that the editor may have intended to develop a treatise which would give an external appearance of confusion,
yet offer to the one who searched behind the external appearance a hidden organization."[43] For the rest of his study, Borchert simply assumed
alternative (b), claiming that

> as a clever maze-maker, the editor assembles sayings, parables, recorded
> incidents and semantic arguments to produce a work which twists and
> turns the mind of the reader as it confronts him with the fundamental dif-
> ferences in the "ways of being" and leads him by steady manipulation of
> words to consider the meaning of Gnostic salvation.[44]

Borchert believed he had found both the overarching theme and the plan
of the *Gospel according to Philip*. That theme is salvation—he even
proposed *"De salvatione"* as an alternate title. He unfolded the plan he
saw by dividing the work into seven very unequal segments, each with a
subtheme. There is, of course, no redundancy in the text of the *Gospel
according to Philip* that can support or refute such a division's appropri-
ateness: any argument of this kind can only rest on the fidelity of the
proposed themes to the materials in each section, and on the cogency of
the proposed progression of themes.

The bulk of Borchert's work deals with his thematic division of the
Gospel according to Philip into 7 sections. Here is his outline:

I. Introduction: The "Basic "Ways of Being" in the World (51.29-52.35)
   A. The Similitudes [Hebrew-proselyte, slave-son, dead-living,
      "heathen"-believer] (51.29-52.19)
   B. The World Order and the Life of the Divinely Oriented One
      (52.19-35)
II. The Conflict: the Godhead and the Archon-Dominated World
   A. The Purpose for the Coming of Christ into the World (52.35-56.15)
   B. Deceptions in the World and the Extent of God's Activity (53.14-
      55.22)
      1. The Deceptions in the World (53.14-54.31)
      2. The Activity of God in the World (54.31-55.22)
   C. Gnostic Reinterpretations Concerning Christ, the Messenger of the
      Pleroma (55.23-56.14)
III. The Message: The Illumination of Three Great Mysteries (56.15-59.6)
   A. The Mystery of the Resurrection and the Soul (56.14-57.22)
   B. The Mystery of the Hidden in the Revealed (57.22-58.17)

---

[42] Borchert, "Analysis," 36.
[43] Borchert, "Analysis," 36.
[44] Borchert, "Analysis," 46.

These sections vary from about one and one-third manuscript pages to about ten and one-half pages. Borchert's proposed structure is an attempt to get behind the apparent jumble of themes to a level of abstraction not given by the text itself, but understood to be inherent in it.

Several of the seven sections have themes so broad that nearly anything chosen at random from the text would fit as well as the material in the section. Examples of especially broad themes proposed for the main divisions are: "The Conflict: The Godhead in the Archon-Dominated World," "The Resolution of the Conflict: The Attaining of Salvation," and "The Significance of Salvation: The Great Contrast." Among the themes proposed for subdivisions, several could (and do) contain a miscellany of diverse materials: "The World Order and the Life of the Divinely Oriented One," "The Deceptions in the World and the Extent of

---

[45] This outline can be extracted from Borchert's table of contents or from the section headings in his exegesis itself. He also gave a brief survey of these seven sections and their contents; see Borchert, "Analysis," 49-58.

God's Activity;" his section, "Gnostic Reinterpretations concerning Christ," is united by little more than a reference to Christ (or Jesus or the Lord); similarly, "Life, the Resurrection and the Sacraments" might apply to many units and groups of units at different places in the text of the *Gospel according to Philip*.

Many of Borchert's categories seem superimposed on the text. They can certainly be read into it, but somewhat arbitrarily. On the other hand, one of his divisions seems quite insightful: "VII. The Life of Salvation: The Way of Knowledge." The section described, 77.15 through the end of the document, does seem quite clearly distinct, as we shall see.

Wesley William Isenberg[46] took another, quite original approach to the elusive coherence of the *Gospel according to Philip* in 1968. He based his understanding of the text on the extreme abruptness of some of the materials in it. He considered the work to be a collection of excerpts from a Christian gnostic sacramental catechesis, possibly supplemented by material excerpted from a gnostic gospel which featured dialogues in which the risen Lord expounded gnostic doctrines.[47] Like so many others, he noted that the *Gospel according to Philip* is not logically arranged, but Isenberg proposed that the apparent disorder of the text derives from someone's deliberate choice to obscure an order which was once clear (or at least, clearer).

> That certain ideas recur throughout *Philip* is evident. What seems to be partially responsible for this recurrence is an unusual literary technique employed by the author of *Philip*. This technique is the evidently intentional dissecting of paragraphs containing a continuity of thought and the distribution of the pieces to diverse parts of the document.[48]

> That the author intended to arrange some material systematically is attested by the several catenae of passages, which use either an association of ideas or catchwords as links. At the same time there is evidence

---

[46] Wesley William Isenberg, "The Coptic Gospel According to Philip" (Dissertation, University of Chicago, 1968), 24-53. Isenberg's remarks on the form, structure and content of the *Gospel according to Philip* are paralleled, in somewhat condensed form, in his introduction to the work in *Nag Hammadi Codex II,2-7* ed. Bentley Layton (Leiden: Brill, 1989) 131-9. He has also published introductions to, and translations of, our document in *The Other Bible*, edited by W. Barnstone (San Francisco: Harper & Row, 1984), and in a revised edition of *The Nag Hammadi Library in English*, edited by J. M. Robinson,*The Nag Hammadi Library in English*, ed. J. M. Robinson (San Francisco: Harper and Row, 1988).

[47] Isenberg, "Coptic Gospel," 47-51. Among the material he thought derived from a gnostic gospel is 57.28-58.10; 63.30-37; 59.23-27; 63.37-64.5; 55.37-56.3; 64.10-12; 74.24-75.2; 75.2-14; 71.3-15; 64.10-12; 60.10-15; 73.9-14.

[48] Isenberg, "Coptic Gospel," 30.

to suggest that the author purposely dissected paragraphs of thought and rather haphazardly placed the pieces in various parts of the work. One of the results of the use of this curious technique has been the impression that there is a planned recurrence of thought in the gospel. But no logically consistent plan has yet been discovered, and it is difficult to escape the thought that *Philip*'s structure is to some extent, at least, simply the result of coincidence and accident.[49]

In 1968, he was willing to conjecture at the motive for this "curious technique:"

> Presumably to heighten the effect of the mysterious, the compiler-editor chose to arrange this material strangely: sometimes logically, by means of association of ideas and catchwords, and sometimes illogically, by sprinkling ideas here and there in incoherent patches. The result is something of a literary curiosity—a "gospel" which has almost none of the obvious "gospel" characteristics.[50]

Isenberg found three types of evidence for this dissecting: 1) passages which, for grammatical reasons, must have been linked to contexts other than those in which they are now found, 2) passages similar to each other in sentence structure and thought content and hence seemingly once joined, and 3) passages with "a strikingly similar" thematic content.

The only example he gave of the "grammatical" type of evidence involves the passages 70.5-9, 76.22-77.1, 66.7-29.[51] The second and third of these begin with indefinite subjects ("they" and "he") which are difficult to relate to the actors in the immediately preceding passages, and all of them, particularly the first and third, show dubious continuity with

---

[49] Isenberg, "Coptic Gospel," 34-35.

[50] Isenberg, "Coptic Gospel," 53. His characterization of catch word and idea association links as "logical" is unhelpful: both of these occur in the *Gospel according to Philip*, but they are usually distinct from each other, and should be distinguished.

[51] Isenberg, "Coptic Gospel," 31. See also *Nag Hammadi Codex II,2-7* 133. The reconstructed passage, in Isenberg's translation, reads:

"As for those who have clothed themselves with the perfect light, the powers do not see them and are not able to seize them. But one will clothe himself with this light in the mystery, in the union.

"Not only will they not be able to seize the perfect man, but they will not be able to see him, for if they see him they will seize him. In no other way will one be able to acquire this grace for himself [unless] he clothe himself with the perfect light [and] he [himself] become perfect. Every [one who will put it] on will go [without being seen]. This is the perfect [light. Thus it is necessary] that we become [perfect men] before we come forth [from the world]. He who has received the all [without being master] over these places, will be [unable to be master over] that place, but he will [go to "the Middle" (?)] as imperfect. Only Jesus knows the end of this one.

"Either he will be in this world or in the resurrection or in the places which are in the middle. May it not be that I should be found therein. . . . "

the immediately preceding material. In Isenberg's analysis, the subject of the first sentence of the middle passage—"they"—cannot refer to anything in the preceding material, but makes sense if seen as a continuation of 70.5-9, further developing the discussion there of the powers' inability to see or seize one who has put on the perfect light: "Not only will they not be able to seize the perfect man, but they will not be able to see him."[52] Unfortunately, this "they" could equally well be understood as a pseudo-passive, and is rendered so by Layton: "The perfect human being not only cannot be restrained, but also cannot be seen."[53] The use of an undefined "they" as the subject of a sentence is the way passive constructions are routinely formed in Coptic, which lacks a true passive voice. If "the perfect human being" is understood as the real subject, there is no jarring transition from the sentence immediately preceding it in the manuscript, which contrasts those who do not know themselves with those who do. In 66.7-29, the third unit in Isenberg's proposed sequence, the subject ("he") could as easily be seen as a resumption of the discussion about "the one who comes out of the world" begun at 65.28, and interrupted by a small digression about an erroneous opinion (65.36-66.4) and an exhortation (66.4-6). While grammatical evidence sounds promising, Isenberg's lone example of it is not convincing.

His second category of evidence, passages purporting to show similarity of sentence structure and thought content, involved a theme or analogy presented in the first segment which he understood to be logically necessary to the second segment.[54] The material in Isenberg's ex-

---

[52] OY MONON ΠΡШΜΕ ΝΤΕΛΕΙΟC CΕΝΑШΕΜΑϨΤΕ ΑΝ ΜΜΟϤ ΑΛΛΑ CΕΝΑШ-ΝΑY ΕΡΟϤ ΑΝ. The translation given above is from Isenberg's 1968 translation ("Coptic Gospel," 31 and 386), but his 1989 translation does not differ much: "Not only will they be unable to detain the perfect man, but they will not be able to see him, . . ." (*Nag Hammadi Codex II,2-7*, 195)

[53] Layton, *Gnostic Scriptures* , 348.

[54] He gave three examples in 1968: 75.13-14 plus 61.36-62.5, 63.5-11 plus 70.22-29, and 59.6-11 plus 63.32-64.9. These first two of these, together with the sole example of the first category, were the only three examples given in Isenberg's 1989 introduction to the *Gospel according to Philip* in *Nag Hammadi Codex II,2-7* .

In 75.13-14 and 61.36-62.5, both passages use "receive" and "give," in the same order.

In 63.5-11 plus 70.22-29, the first passage describes how glass jars, but not earthenware ones, can be remade if broken, because they "came into being through a breath." The second passage begins, "The soul of Adam came into being by means of a breath." These clearly depend on the same or similar traditions, but this need not imply anything more than that.

Taking 63.32-64.9 as following 59.6-11 both allows Isenberg to group together material referring to Mary Magdalene but also gives him a warrant for separating 63.30-

amples, and the general type of situation envisioned by his theory, could just as easily be understood as depending on teachings which were familiar and so did not need to be stated explicitly. The same is true of the proposed sequences based on a strong similarity of theme or teaching.[55]

Isenberg argued that the *Gospel according to Philip* is the work of a compiler-editor rather than an original thinker, in part because

> . . .it is. . .irregular and unnatural for an author intentionally and frequently to dissect the very thought he has put together into a continuity and to distribute the pieces here and there in his work, especially when it is apparent that an isolated segment of thought may sometimes make little or no sense in the context in which it finds itself. It would be more likely that a compiler who was also editing his material to serve his own purposes would find use for this technique. The diversity of content in *Philip*, drawn as it appears from more than one source, also commends the conclusion that a compiler-editor is responsible for this text.[56]

Thus, Isenberg seems to have believed that some of the abrupt transitions and apparent non-sequiturs in the *Gospel according to Philip* were due to excerpting and collecting diverse materials, while others had their genesis in a deliberate dissection and dispersal of the text.[57]

In 1969, in contrast to Borchert's vision of a tightly ordered arrangement of collected materials, Hans-Georg Gaffron found the succession of ideas in the *Gospel according to Philip* loose and disjointed, and its presentation without strong thematic cohesion, despite an instructional and hortatory purpose which he discerned there. Nevertheless, he saw a strong stylistic cohesion, on the basis of which he argued that a single author's highly distinctive manner of thinking and expression shows itself throughout the entire work.[58]

In Gaffron's opinion, the document's lack of explicit connections and its athematic order show that diverse sources lie behind the text. Densely

---

32 on the barren Sophia from the discussion of Mary Magdalene. These two passages on 63 may well represent distinct traditions.
See "Coptic Gospel," 31-33 and *Nag Hammadi Codex II,2-7*, 133.

[55] His examples of this third category, based on "strikingly similar thematic content," were: 52.2-6 plus 60.1-6; 60.34-61.12 plus 78.12-25; 68.22-26 plus 70.9-22; 56.15-20 plus 73.1-8; 54.31-55.5 plus 62.35-33.4; 55.14-19 plus 59.18-27; and possibly 51.29-52.2 plus 52.21-24 plus 62.5-6. See "Coptic Gospel," 34.

[56] "Coptic Gospel," 35.

[57] As will be shown in chapter 4, other collections of diverse materials did sometimes break up and redistribute blocks of text, though in accordance with comprehensible aesthetic preferences.

[58] Hans-Georg Gaffron, "Studien zum koptischen Philippusevangelium unter besonderer Berücksichtigung der Sakramente" (Dissertation: Friedrich-Wilhelms-Universität, Bonn, 1969).

interwoven passages such as 51.29-52.18 seemed to him to embody a strong stylistic cohesion expressing a highly individual and distinctive manner of thinking. He rejected the label "florilegium," and saw the text as the work of a strong redactor who everywhere rewrote his material in an unmistakable style.[59] If such a rewriting were thorough enough, and done by someone with a reasonably sharp eye for differences in doctrine and practice, one could assume that the text in its present form presents a single viewpoint—and Gaffron went on to treat it accordingly.

Gaffron based his case for the unity of the *Gospel according to Philip* on its use of catch word and idea associations, especially complex and sophisticated catch word patterns involving multiple pairs of opposites.[60] The first four sections—from 51.29 to 52.18—are so closely bound by such pairs of opposite catchwords, Gaffron thought, that they cannot have been excerpted from a variety of gnostic sources. They form a single thought complex, he maintained, which (if not original) would have to have been taken over whole from a single source. But, he insisted, that is scarcely thinkable, since such pairs of oppositions are not restricted to the first pages of the *Gospel according to Philip* but run throughout the document.[61] Unfortunately, he derived a false conclusion from two essentially correct observations. There are few other passages in the *Gospel according to Philip* in which a series of short, independent units are as tightly interlaced by multiple catchwords as 51.29-52.18. Gaffron was neither the first nor last to attempt to found an assessment of the *Gospel according to Philip* as a whole on the peculiarities of this opening section, but the procedure is questionable. Moreover, while pairs of opposites are both frequent and important in the *Gospel according to Philip*, their use does not follow the pattern set on pages 51 and 52.

A large number of antithetical pairs in the *Gospel according to Philip* seemed highly distinctive to Gaffron, pointing to the idiosyncrasies of a specific author.[62] He wrote:

> Läßt man die allgemein gnostischen Gegensatzpaare wie Licht-Finsternis, gut-böse, rechts-links, tot-lebendig, oben-unten, hier-dort, männlich-weiblich einmal beiseite[68], so bleiben noch genügend andere übrig, die das ganze EvPh durchziehen, so z.B. grundlegend der Gegensatz verborgen-offenbar, ferner: zeugen-schaffen (bilden), Nacht-Tag;

---

[59] Gaffron, "Studien," 14-15

[60] Hans-Georg Gaffron, "Studien zum koptischen Philippusevangelium unter besonderer Berücksichtigung der Sakramente" (Dissertation: Friedrich-Wilhelms-Universität, Bonn, 1969).

[61] Gaffron, "Studien," 14-15.

[62] Gaffron, "Studien," 14-15.

Hebräer-Christen; Sklave-Freier (Sohn); Winter-Sommer[69]. Je einmal begegnen: Ernten-Pflügen (§7); sich auflösen-unauflöslich (§10); festehend-nicht festehend (§11); Kinder Adams-Kinder des vollkommenen Menschen (§28); Natur-Geist (§30); Echamoth-Echmoth (§39); Blinder-Sehender (§56); Zins-Geschenk (§59); befleckte Frauen-Jungfrauen (§73); Ackerbau Gottes-Ackerbau der Welt (§115); Hochzeit der Befleckung-unbefleckte Hochzeit (§122); geehrte Starke-verachtete Schwache (§124f.). Die Belege ließen sich leicht vermehren. Hier dürfte doch wohl eine ganz bestimmte Art zu denken vorliegen, die nicht spezifisch valentinianisch, sondern die Ausdruckweise eines bestimmten Verfassers ist.

---

[68] Licht-Finsternis: §§10.56.122.127; gut-böse: §§10.13.40.63.94; rechts-links: §§10.40.67; tot-lebend: §§3.10.14.123; oben-unten: §§33.69.113.76.125; hier-dort o.ä.: §§44.103.123; männlich-weiblich: §§61.103.

[69] Verborgen-offenbar: §§19.25.33.58.69.121.123-125.127; zeugen-schaffen (bilden): §§1.29.41.120.121; Nacht-Tag: §§122.126.127; Hebräer-Christen: §§6.49.102, vgl 1; Sklave-Sohn (Freier): §§2.13.49.73.87.110.114.123.125; Winter-Sommer: §§7.109.[63]

Unfortunately, most of these pairs of oppositions are not distinctive enough to warrant such a conclusion. Many of them are not distinctive at all, but are the commonplaces of gnostic (or Christian, or even pagan) expression. The opposition *hidden-revealed* is, as might be expected, a popular one in gnostic literature, featured (among other places) in *Gospel of Truth, Gospel according to Thomas, Treatise on the Resurrection*—not to mention the Synoptic gospels![64] Similarly, the opposition *slave-free/son* as it is employed in the *Gospel according to Philip* on page 54 (and possibly 84, after the quotation of John 8.32, in the personification of gnosis and its lack) depends on or alludes to Galatians 4; its use on page 77 is a direct quotation of John 8.34-36; its uses on pages 62 and 69 occur in longer lists of characteristics (Jew, Roman, Greek, barbarian, slave, free in the one case; in the other, animals, slaves and defiled women are contrasted with free men and virgins). Its use on page 72 of the *Gospel according to Philip* involves a reversal of expected roles strongly reminiscent of Mark 10.42-45 (and parallels). *Night-day*, again, is an opposition harder to escape than to account for; it is found, for example, in John 11.9-10 and 1 Thessalonians 5.2-8.[65] The opposition

---

[63] Gaffron, "Studien," 15 and 231 (notes).

[64] E. g., *Gos. Truth* 20.14-18 and 24.9-13; *Gos. Thom.* 1, 5, 6, 83, and 109; *Treat. Res.* 45.4-8; Mark 4.22 and parallels.

[65] See also Psalm 30.5, *Gos. Truth* 29 and 32.23-34; *Thom. Cont.* 139.12-19.

winter-summer can be found in Proverbs and the Song of Solomon along with *Gospel of Thomas* 19, but the closest usages to the *Gospel according to Philip*'s are found in the *Shepherd of Hermas* and the *Acts of Thomas*.[66]

On the other hand, *Hebrew-Christian*, (or *Jew-Christian*, as the opposition is given in one of the examples cited by Gaffron)[67] is unparalleled in the Nag Hammadi corpus. All three terms are rare in that material. Outside of the *Gospel according to Philip*, "Hebrew" appears only once unrelated to language, in the *Tripartite Tractate*, where Hebrews are paralleled with hylics. "Jew" appears twice in the Nag Hammadi materials, in *Tripartite Tractate* and *Gospel according to Thomas*; both instances are pejorative.[68] Gnostic materials which obliquely criticize the Hebrew scriptures or the Hebrew God are not uncommon, however: see, for example, the *Apocryphon of John* or Ptolemy's *Letter to Flora*. Apart from the *Gospel according to Philip*, however, the term "Christian" appears only once, in the *Testimony of Truth*, where the sense is negative. Thus the opposition *Hebrew (or Jew)-Christian* in the *Gospel according to Philip* is unusual within the Nag Hammadi corpus principally in its use of the term "Christian," and unique only in giving that term a positive valuation!

Most of the contrasts mentioned by Gaffron which appear only once in the *Gospel according to Philip*, are not much less common,[69] although

---

[66] Proverbs 10.5, Canticles 2.11, Hermas *Sim.* 4.2, and *Acts Thom.* 18.

[67] It should also be noted that one of his four examples, on page 51, not only lacks the pole "Christian," but any explicit contrast to "Hebrew."

[68] *Tri. Trac.* 112.22 and *Gos. Thom.* 43.

[69] *Sow-reap* can be found in Mark 4.3, John 4.37, 2 Cor 9.6, Gal 6.7, *Gospel according to Thomas* 63; its use at Matt 13.24-30 and *Gos. Thom.* 57, with their concern lest young plants be uprooted, is closest to *Gos. Phil.* 52. Its use as a commonplace or cliché is seen in the *Letter of Ptolemy to Flora* 33.7.1. The separation of the *destructible* from the *indestructible* is considered in such disparate places as 1 Corinthians 3.10-15, Irenaeus' account of Ptolemy's mythology (*Adv. haer.* 1.6.1), and the *Acts of Thomas* (95). The distinction between ⲚⲈⲧⲤⲘⲟⲚⲦ and ⲚⲈⲧⲤⲘⲟⲚⲦ ⲀⲚ, the latter being associated with error, is paralleled in *Gospel of Truth* 29-30, where those waking from nightmare do not consider its delusions as ⲤⲘⲟⲚⲦ.

The distinction *child of Adam-child of the perfect human* is a thread running through those gnostic traditions which trace the ancestry of gnostics back to Seth, who embodies the image of the pleromatic human being, as seen in the *Apocryphon of John,* the *Apocalypse of Adam,* and the *Hypostasis of the Archons.* The *Gospel according to Thomas* 85 and 105-105 also depend on a tradition of this general kind, though perhaps less elaborated. Related to this opposition is that of *tarnished woman-virgin,* reminiscent of the distinction between Eve and Norea in *Hypostasis of the Archons.* Also conceptually related is that of *marriage of pollution-unpolluted marriage.* The *Gospel according to Thomas,* again, knows this opposition, linking it in 75 to the term

the contrast of *Echamoth* with *Echmoth* is distinctive and creative. In the *First Apocalypse of James,* (NHC V,3) pages 34-36, Achamoth is described as the daughter of Sophia, but Sophia's name itself is said to be a translation of Achamoth. Someone has inherited a tradition of a higher and lower Sophia or Achamoth, and known enough Hebrew or Aramaic to turn it into a pun: a slight shortening of the name can be understood as *'ekh-moth,* "like death," an appropriate name for the "lower" Sophia. While Gaffron's claim that the *Gospel according to Philip* is woven together by a clearly distinctive type of thought expressed in highly individual pairs of opposites has foundered because nearly all of these antitheses are commonplaces, it remains an open question who the someone responsible for this Semitic wordplay might be.

Gaffron was, however, quite correct that the *Gospel according to Philip* opens with an extremely complex example of the interweaving of multiple "catch words." The pairs of antithetical terms appear in virtually every subject and predicate of the first several statements. The pattern is kept up for over a page, though with slightly less density, and is then abruptly dropped at the last line of page 52. The only passage offering anything like a parallel to the opening section's density of antitheses is also found early on, in a remarkably sophisticated passage about language and its complex relations to truth. That section, from 53.14 to 54.18, relates a group of four oppositions to the "worldly" pole of world-eternal realm, and then lines that opposition up with the oppositions not established-established, deceptive-creative, and multiple-unitary. Anyone who could write this passage could certainly have written, or assembled, the opening sequence as well. Nevertheless, the section on language possesses an explicit logical continuity which is not present between the components of the opening catena. While paired opposites are fairly frequent in the material contained in the rest of the Gospel *according to Philip* (and, indeed, in much of the other literature surveyed above), these two sections are the densest concatenations of them anywhere in the doc-

---

"bridal chamber;" it is present also in the *Acts of Thomas,* in chapter 14 and undergirding much of its concept of Christianity.

The opposition *nature-spirit,* which Gaffron cites as occurring on page 58 of the *Gospel according to Philip,* lacks the term "spirit" or any other term explicitly contrasted with φύσις. The image of *blindness* as opposed to *sight* is played upon in *Gospel according to Thomas* 34 and its parallels in Matthew and Luke; its form in the *Gospel according to Philip* is far less original than the related image in *Gospel of Truth* of the blinding fog produced by ignorant agitation. In *Gos. Phil.* 84, the opposition of *glorious strength-contemptible weakness* parallels the distinction of visible-hidden; the Song of Mary, various of Jesus' reversal sayings, and Paul's boasting in weakness all involve the same theme (Luke 1.46-55. Mark 10.21, 2 Cor 11-12).

The *agriculture of God-agriculture of the world* and *loan-gift,* even if unique, do not disclose a single author's shaping influence throughout the work.

ument. More typically, a passage reflects on a single antithesis, or relates one opposition to another, in a way that is not especially remarkable for gnostic works—certainly nothing like the use made of antitheses in *Thunder*! Many passages do not appeal to antithetical oppositions either logicallly or rhetorically.

Following a suggestion by Wilson, Gaffron considered that the analogy between the *Gospel according to Philip* and the *Excerpta ex Theodoto* could be fruitful.[70] Both works show "blocks" of material which stem from different sources. The problem of separating these blocks is complex in the *Excerpta*, but that text seems to fall into four major blocks. Even this sort of rough separation is not likely to be possible in the case of the *Gospel according to Philip*, in Gaffron's judgment, since he believed that a single "author" (really a strong redactor) had everywhere reworked that material, interweaving comments and additions much more tightly than are Clement's in the *Excerpta*, in keeping with his overall purpose of teaching and reminding.[71] In contrast with the *Excerpta*, Gaffron saw the traditions contained in the *Gospel according to Philip* as not so much handed on as advanced or elaborated; little or nothing appears unmediated. But Gaffron's perception of the distinctiveness of the pairs of oppositions as the core of the author/redactor's individual style is fundamental to this assessment.

Assessments of the *Gospel according to Philip* as an exposition or a well-organized collection in which the elements are subordinated to a discernible plan focus on an impression this text often creates, that something more than random juxtaposition is involved, especially the recurrence of certain themes. Such an understanding of the text justifies the attempt to discuss its theology, its ritual practice, or its perspective on any given issue. It allows one to side-step the problems raised by a theory of multiple sources, and this may have been an important part of its attractiveness to some investigators.

AN EXPERIMENT IN SOURCE ANALYSIS

In 1970, Rodolphe Kasser put forward a broad analysis of the sources and redactional history of the *Gospel according to Philip*.[72] He identified

---

[70] Gaffron, "Studien," 23. See R. McL. Wilson, *The Gospel of Philip* (London: Mowbray, 1962) 24.

[71] Gaffron, "Studien," 21-22; 220.

[72] Rodolphe Kasser, "L'Évangile selon Philippe," *Revue de théologie et de philoso-*

four original sources: "source A," "source B," a "'Philip' source," and an "'etymological' source,"[73] along with a number of additions of various types. He also sketched conjectural redactional histories for a few units. Beyond extremely brief characterizations of the sources, little or no reason was given for the assignment of material to one source or another. Kasser's article was, and remains, the most extensive previous attempt to detect the underlying sources that make up the *Gospel according to Philip*. Nevertheless, his article was offered somewhat casually; as he himself stated, "Une étude plus approfondie permettra peut-être de pénétrer dans la préhistoire du texte actuel de l'Evangile selon Philippe; nous ne pouvons que l'esquisser ici."[74] Not surprisingly, its value lies more in its provocative potential than in its concrete working out.

Kasser's source A consisted of 51.29-52.10,[75] 52.15-19,[76] 52.35-53.1 + 53.3,[77] 53.14-17,[78] 53.35-54.1 + 54.5-7,[79] 54.10-13,[80] 55.6-7? + 11-12?

---

phie ser. 3, 20 (1970), introduction: 12-20, translation: 21-35; 82-106.

[73] Kasser, "L'Évangile," 16-17.

[74] Kasser, "L'Évangile," 16.

[75] "Un homme hebreu [ne] fabrique [pas <un autre homme>] hebreu <avec un païen>; et <d'ailleurs, ce qu'il fabrique alors>, on l'apelle ainsi: 'prosélyte'; or un prosélyte <non plus> ne fabrique pas un prosélyte;--[ces hom]mes, certes, sont comme ils [sont], et ils [n']en fabriquent [pas] d'au[tres <semblables à eux>--;--ces] [h]omm[es, donc, il] leur suffit d'être--. L'[es]clave cherche seulement à être libre, mais il [ne] cherche [pas] <à acquérir> le(s) possession(s) de son maître; le fils, cependant, <ce n'est> pas seulement qu'il est fils, mais <c'est> l'héritage du père sur lequel il compte. Ceux qui héritent de (choses) qui <sont> mort(e)s, eux-<mêmes> sont morts, et <encore> ils héritent de (choses) qui <sont> mort(e)s; ceux qui héritent de ce qui vit, eux-<mêmes> sont vivants, et <encore> ils héritent de ce qui <est> vivant et de ce qui <est> mort." Kasser, "L'Évangile," 21.

[76] "Un homme païen ne meurt pas, car il n'a jamais vécu, pour qu'il meure; celui qui a cru à la vérité a vécu, et celui-(là) est en danger de mourir, car il vit depuis le jour où le Christ est venu." Kasser, "L'Évangile," 21-22.

[77] Kasser has divided the *Gospel according to Philip* into 400 verses, and has supplied Schenke's sayings numbers for convenience. Where he refers to part verses (e.g., "12a") in his introduction, it is not always clear where the division is meant to fall. This unit consists of "12a + 13a," but the exact end of Kasser's verse "12a" is not clear to me. 12 + 13a read: "(12) Le Christ est venu, les uns d'une part, pour qu'il les achète, les autres, d'autre part, pour qu'il les sauve,--<et> d'autres <encore> pour qu'il les rachète--(13) les étrangers, il les a achetés, il les a faits siens; . . . ." Kasser, "L'Évangile," 22.

[78] "La lumière et l'obscurité, la vie et la mort, les droites et les gauches, (sont) frères les uns des autres; il n'est pas possible qu'ils soient divisés <et séparés> l'un de l'autre." /Kasser, "L'Évangile," 23.

[79] ". . .les n[oms qu'on a enten]dus sont dans le mond [en tant que <signes> trompeurs." + "<Il y a> un nom unique qu'on ne profère pas dans le monde: le nom que le Père a donné au Fils;. . ." Kasser, "L'Évangile," 23-4.

[80] "Ce nom, ceux qui l'ont, ils le pensent, certes, mais ils ne le prononcent pas; cependant, ceux qui ne l'ont pas, ne le pensent pas;. . ." Kasser, "L'Évangile," 24.

-13?,[81] 57.3-5 + 7-8,[82] 57.19-22,[83] and 58.14-17.[84] He characterized these as having a very sober character and as referring to Christ simply as "Christ." He said they may have formed a small collection for "usage sacramental."

"Christ," however, is referred to in only three of these ten passages,[85] while the same form of reference is also found at 56.13, 61.30, 61.31, 68.17, 68.20, 69.7, 70.13, 71.19, and 74.16. It is hard to know what would constitute "sacramental usage;" he did not make explicit the signs by which such usage could be recognized. Perhaps he meant that the little collection was read aloud at a liturgy, or that it was used in catechesis. In any case, the first two and last two passages (51.29-52.10, 52.15-19, 57.19-22, 58.14-17) could be interpreted as referring to the effects of initiation, and two more (55.6-7? + 11-12? and 57.3-5 + 7-8) as referring to the eucharist. Of the remaining four, one deals with salvation generally (52.35-53.1 + 53.3) while three ruminate on polar opposition and the deceptive and creative aspects of language (53.14-17, 53.35-51.1 + 54.5-7, and 54.10-13). There is an abundance of material dealing with sacraments elsewhere in the document, especially in the eight or nine pages beginning with page 67, none of which was included by Kasser in "source A."

Kasser's source B consisted of "sentences isolées, et d'un caractère assez énigmatique."[86] He listed its contents: 52.19-21,[87] 52.25 + 52.30-

---

[81] Again, it is unclear where 38a ends, and also where 40a ends. Kasser's entire 38 + 40 reads: "(38) Avant que le Christ ne soit venu, il n'y avait pas de pain dans le monde." + "(40) mais lorsque le Christ est venu,--<lui> l'Homme parfait--, il a apporté le pain du ciel, afin que l'homme soit nourri avec une nourriture humaine--." Kasser, "L'Évangile," 25.

[82] "C'est pourquoi il a dit: 'celui qui ne mangera pas ma chair, et <ne> boira <pas> mon sang, n'a pas de vie en lui.' . . . Celui qui a reçu ces (choses), a <là> la nourriture, et il a <là> la boisson, et <aussi> l'habit." Kasser, "L'Évangile," 27-27.

[83] Dans ce monde, ceux qui mettent sur eux les habits <pour s'en vêtir> sont plus excellents que les habits; dans le Royaume des Cieux, les habits sont plus excellents que ceux qui les ont mis sur eux <pour s'en vêtir>." Kasser, "L'Évangile,"28.

[84] "Ne méprise(z) pas l'agneau!. . . car sans lui, il n'est pas possible de voir le roi. Personne ne pourra s'approcher du roi, (étant) nu." Kasser, "L'Évangile," 29.

[85] Kasser does indeed list ten passages, though he refers to the list as a "chaîne de douze brèves sentences." Possibly he counts 51.29-52.10 (listed by him as "v 1-3") as three separate units. Kasser, "L'Évangile," 16.

[86] Kasser, "L'Évangile,"16.

[87] "On crée le monde, on orne les villes, on emporte ce(lui) qui <est> mort." Kasser, "L'Évangile," 22. The degree of isolation of this "sentence" is debatable. Most translators have seen the phrase immediately preceeding it as a temporal cause dependant on this unit; the material from 52.15-52.25 seems to consist of three statements of structurally analogous points. Yet all are couched in flamboyant, enigmatic imagery;

32,[88] 55.19-22,[89] 67.2-5,[90] and 69.8-11,[91] but had nothing further to say about it as a whole.

The third source, the "Philip" source of fragments supposedly from an apocryphal gospel, was rather more coherent. The passages Kasser proposed were: 55.37-56.3,[92] 59.23-27,[93] 63.25-30,[94] 63.34-5,[95] 64.10-12,[96] 73.8-15.[97] He limited this source to passages including both a saying and a narrative frame (he took the latter always to be redactional), and to

---

with the possible exception of 52.17-18, nothing seems to be an explanation added later.

[88] "Ceux qui sèment en hiver moissonnent en été; . . .si (quelqu')un <veut> moissonner en hiver, il ne moissonnera pas, mais il arrachera." Kasser, "L'Évangile," 22.

[89] "La vérité, on la sème en tous lieux, elle qui e(xi)st(e) depuis les premiers <temps>; et il y en a beaucoup qui la voient semée; mais peu nombreaux <sont ceux> qui la voient moissonnée." Kasser, "L'Évangile," 25.

[90] "De l'eau et de la flamme, l'â[me] et l'esprit sont issus; de l'eau et de la flamme et de la lumière, le fils de la chambre (nuptiale)." Kasser, "L'Évangile," 86. As we shall see below, this statement is followed by an explanation of the *Gospel according to Philip* 's understanding of sacramental functioning. The material from 67.2-68.17 can be seen as a series of restatements of this principle, and it in turn introduces an eleven page section which is predominantly concerned with sacramental matters; thus, the "isolated" character of this passage, too, is in question.

[91] "Personne ne pourra se voir, ne dans (de) l'eau, ni dans (un) miroir, sans lumière; et pas plus, tu ne pourras <te> voir par la lumière, sans eau ou <sans> miroir; . . . ." Kasser, "L'Évangile," 89.

[92] "Le Seigneur a dit aux dis[ciples: '<même (?)> si] [la] sa[inteté(?)] , certes, est entrée dans la maison du Père, ne prenez <rien d'ici(?)>, ni même <de là (?)> dans la maison du Père, (et) <n'en> emportez <rien>." Kasser, "L'Évangile," 26.

[93] "C'est pourquoi un disciple a fait une demande au Seigneur, un jour, à propos d'une chose du monde; il lui a dit <en réponse>: 'demande <cela> à ta mère, et elle te donnera des (choses) étrangères'. Les apôtres ont dit aux disciples: 'que toute notre offrande soit fournie en sel!'" Kasser, "L'Évangile," 30.

[94] "Le Seigneur est entré à la teinturerie de Lévi; il a pris soixante-douze couleurs, il les a jetées au chaudron, <puis> il a fait remonter <du chaudron> les <objets à teindre>, ils étaient tous blancs! Et il a dit: 'c'(est) ainsi qu'il est venu, les fils {du fils} de l'hom[me, en] teinturier." Kasser, "L'Évangile," 82.

[95] "Le [Christ, cependant, aimait] Ma[rie] plus que [tous les dis]ciples, et il l'a saluée (par un baiser) sur sa [bouche beaucoup] de fois; le reste <des disciples lui> [faisaient des] [repro]ches à son sujet, [à par]t; ils lui ont dit: 'pourquoi l'aimes-tu plus que nous tous?' il a répondu, le Sauveur, il leur a dit il leur a dit: 'pourquoi est-ce que je ne vous aime pas comme elle?'." (Kasser notes, but does not enclose in braces, the dittography introducing the final statement.) Kasser, "L'Évangile," 82.

[96] "Le Seigneur a dit: 'Bienheureux celui qui est avant qu'il ait été!' . . . car celui qui est a été et sera." Kasser, "L'Évangile," 83.

[97] "Philippe l'apôtre a dit: 'Joseph le charpentier a planté un jardin <d'arbres>, parce qu'il avait besoin de bois pour son métier; <c'est> lui qui a fabriqué la croix, (avec) des arbres qu'il a(vait) plantés: et <ensuite>, sa "graine" était (sus)pendue à qu'il avait planté'; --sa graine (était) Jésus, et son plant (est) la croix--." Kasser, "L'Évangile," 93.

those which refer to Jesus simply as "the Lord."[98] These, along with several other passages much like them, might quite plausibly stem from an apocryphal gospel (or gospels).

Kasser's fourth source consisted of explanations of sacred names, principally by means of etymology. He said that this source may be reconstituted by placing together the following passages end to end: 62.6-17, 63.25-30, 56.3-15, 59.11-18.[99] He did not explain the logic of this order, but these passages do demonstrate a procedural consistency which might be called "etymological exegesis." This type of unit, however, can occur in a variety of generic settings: gospels, homilies, letters, treatises, catechetical material, and (probably) other contexts. The passages in question need not come from the same source nor even the same kind of source. The formal similarities alone provide only a weak ground for postulating that the etymological exegeses in the *Gospel according to Philip* came from the same source, and no warrant at all for supposing that this source consisted exclusively of this kind of material.

Every passage involved in Kasser's source separation occurs before page 74 of the *Gospel according to Philip*—that is, in the first two thirds of the document. His effort left untouched the possibility that some of the material after page 74 is, or derives from, a quite distinctive source.

In the same year as Kasser's article, William Stroud touched upon the matter of the *Gospel according to Philip*'s sources in the course of an ar-

---

[98] The latter restriction does protect his "source A." Kasser, "L'Évangile," 17.

[99] "Les apôtres qui <etaient> avant nous, <c'est> ainsi qu'ils appelaient <le Sauveur>: 'Jésus le Nazoréen' 'Messie', c'(est), <à dire> 'Jésus le Nazoréen, le Christ'; le dernier <de ces> nom(s) (est) 'le Christ'; le premier (est) 'Jésus'; celui qui <est> au milieu (est) le Nazaréen'; 'Messie' a deux significations: 'le Christ', et 'le mesuré'; 'Jesus', en hébreu, (est) 'le rachat'; 'nazara' <est> 'la vérité'; 'le Nazaréen' (est) donc 'la vérité', <soit> 'le Christ' qu'on a 'mesuré'; 'le Nazaréen' et 'Jésus' (sont) <donc> 'ceux qu'on a mesurés'."(Kasser, "L'Évangile," 33) "L'eucharistie (est) Jésus, car on l'apelle, en syrien, 'pharisatha', c'(est) <à dire> 'l'étendu'; car Jésus est venu crucifiant le monde." (Kasser, "L'Évangile," 35) "'Jésus' (est) un nom caché; le 'Christ' (est) un nom révélé; c'est pourquoi 'Jésus', certes, n'e(xi)st(e) pas <sous une autre forme>, dans aucun langage; mais son nom reste 'Jésus'--comme on l'appelle--; le 'Christ', cependant, son nom (est) en syrien 'Messie'; en grec, en revanche, (il est) le 'Christ'; assurément, tous les autres <peuples> ont (là) ce <nom>, selon le langage de chacun d'eux; le 'Nazaréen' (est) la révélation de ce qui est caché'; le 'Christ' renferme tous <les concepts> en soi: soit <celui d'>'homme', soit <celui d'>'ange', soit <celui de> 'mystère', soit <celui de> 'Père'." (Kasser, "L'Évangile," 26) "Le 'Père' et le 'Fils' (sont) des noms simples; l''Esprit saint' (est) un nom double, car ils sont en tous lieux; ils <sont> en haut, ils <sont> en bas, ils <sont> dans ce qui est caché, ils <sont> dans les <choses> qui (sont) manifestes; l'Esprit saint <est> dans la manifestation: il <est> dans le bas, ils <est> dans ce qui est caché, il <est> dans le haut." (Kasser, "L'Évangile," 30).

gument for placing the date of the *Gospel according to Philip* in the second century. Stroud attempted to separate oral from written traditions in the text, and to identify quotations from non-canonical documents.[100] His proposed criteria for separating oral and written sources were the tense used in the introductory citation formula[101] and the degree of discrepancy between the form of the saying found in the *Gospel according to Philip* and its parallels in the Greek and Sahidic New Testaments.[102] These methods did not produce results which Stroud always found entirely

---

[100] William Joseph Stroud, "The Problem of Dating the Chenoboskion Gospel of Philip" (Th.D. diss., Iliff School of Theology, 1970).

Stroud's basic premise was that the second century was marked by the use of oral traditions alongside written ones, the free adaptation of traditions, and the use of extra-canonical writings, and that the *Gospel according to Philip* was written in just such a milieu. Stroud assumed that such conditions disappeared after the end of the second century, due to the fixing of the canon and changing attitudes toward the authority of written materials. In this he depended upon the opinions of such worthies as Hans Lietzmann (*The Founding of the Church Universal*, London, Nicholson & Watson, 1938) and Adolf von Harnack (*The Origin of the New Testament*, New York: Macmillan, 1925). The assumption that these conditions did not survive into the third century would restrict the writing of the *Gospel according to Philip* to the second. Unfortunately for Stroud's thesis, the changes he used as indicators of second century origin did not take place all at once, especially among gnostic and gnostic-Christian groups, as well as other Christians who were isolated from or indifferent to the emerging "consensus" on these matters.

[101] Stroud attempted to apply to the *Gospel according to Philip* Helmut Koester's observation that in the Apostolic Fathers, citation formulas in the present tense consistently introduce written materials, while those in past tenses introduce oral traditions. See Helmut H. Koester, *Synoptische Überlieferung bei den Apostolischen Vätern* , (Berlin: Akademie-Verlag, 1957) 23; and again recently, *Ancient Christian Gospels: Their History and Development* (Philadelphia: Trinity Press, 1990) 66.

[102] While discounting minor variations in spelling, short lacunae, and the like, Stroud stated that major divergences of "grammar, syntax and especially choice of words are sufficient to show that the saying in GP is received independently of written material. Written sources are indicated when alterations are minor." Stroud, "Dating," 31-34. Unfortunately, neither G. Horner's *The Coptic Version of the New Testament in the Southern Dialect* (London: Oxford University Press, 1910) nor Nestle's 25th edition of *Novum Testamentum Graece* (ed. Erwin Nestle and Kurt Aland, Stuttgart: Württembergische Bibelanstalt, 1963) are remotely comprehensive representations of the written variations available in the second and third centuries. Quotations which do not conform to known texts might as easily point to the existence of lost text forms (variant quotations such as the *Gospel according to Philip*'s are, after all, one kind of evidence given in critical editions), or to quotation from memory, or to rhetorical adaptation to the context.

In any case, the relevance of the Sahidic version is doubtful, if (as most scholars agree) the *Gospel according to Philip* is a translation of a Greek document, and particularly if (as Stroud argues) the *Gospel according to Philip* was translated prior to the Sahidic New Testament.

clear-cut,[103] and the identifications of oral tradition about which he felt
fairly certain sometimes rested on small divergences which could easily
be due to other factors, such as copying errors or quoting with less than
complete accuracy from memory. Nevertheless, he called attention to
some factors, such as differences in citation formulas and the use of non-
canonical writings, which are worthy of further investigation.

COMMUNICATIVE STRATEGY AND GENRE

Edward Thomas Rewolinski, in a 1978 Harvard dissertation, made the
most extensive inquiry into the genre of the *Gospel according to Philip*
to date.[104] Rewolinski's judgments ultimately rested on the document's
rambling succession of small units and its apparent concern to instruct
rather than to entertain. He found that the *Gospel according to Philip* was
a document meant to be used in instruction, its form either a literary ex-
periment or dictated by an instructional situation in which the teacher
supplied the "key" necessary for full understanding.[105]

He began his analysis with a partial cataloguing of the discrete literary
structures in the *Gospel according to Philip*. He found 13 "extended
metaphors" along with "5 etymological exegeses, 1 dominical apophthegm, 1 dominical macarism, 2 dominical sayings and a small collection
of dominical sayings knit together by redactorial exegesis."[106] He also
grouped together what he called "thematic paragraphs" on various topics:
the relative rank of Christians and others, citations of biblical passages
with exegetical remarks, passages "with no shared structural features"
dealing with the soteriological role of Christ, passages showing shifts in
number or person, and passages showing Valentinian provenance.[107]
Rewolinski discerned a common thread running through this diversity of
literary structures in the *Gospel according to Philip*: the intent to instruct.
He also noted that the material "is of itself the usual stuff of gospels"—

---

[103] "While there is still some question about whether these formulas introduce written or oral material consistently, they do introduce material which GP considers
authoritative." Stroud, "Dating," 224.

[104] Edward Thomas Rewolinski, "The Use of Sacramental Language in the Gospel
of Philip (Cairensis Gnosticus II,3)" (Dissertation, Harvard, 1978).

[105] Rewolinski, however, deduced this instructional intent from its serious tone,
rather than from the presence of first- and second-person discourse, as did Gaffron.

[106] Rewolinski, "Sacramental Language," 34, 36-37.

[107] Rewolinski, "Sacramental Language," 38-42.

i.e., the categories of modern gospel form criticism could be illustrated from the *Gospel according to Philip*'s material.[108]

The *Gospel according to Philip* is similar, according to Rewolinski, to Clement of Alexandria's *Stromateis* in that both show a "loose, rambling order that is determined not so much by logical sequence but by a train of interest manifested in the subject matter itself." He cited Quasten's characterization of the tone of the *Stromateis* as light and entertaining, and contrasted the *Gospel according to Philip* as "not light and hardly entertaining" but "serious, and at times, aggressively forceful" with "no panache."[109] Citing this difference in tone, connected with the presence of extremely short, unconnected units of text in the *Gospel according to Philip*—in contrast with Clement's lengthy discussions—Rewolinski discarded the *Stromateis* as a generic parallel to the *Gospel according to Philip*.

He characterized the *Excerpta ex Theodoto* as "gleanings of a gnostic treatise, or of several treatises" gathered for later use. They are unpolished and rambling, although the work is titled ἘΠΙΤΟΜΑΙ, "epitomes," in Greek, and he pointed out that an epitome could also be a polished abridged work. A similar pair of meanings belong to the genre ὑπομνήματα. Rewolinski defined ὑπομνήματα as both "jottings or notations lacking orderliness" and more finished products, including lecture notes and learned essays, as the word is used by Sextus Empiricus for his own critical writings. He found that the *Gospel according to Philip*, with the possible exception of a few of its sections, falls short of qualifying as a ὑπόμνημα in the sense of scholarly essay. He stated,

> Likewise, that species of *hupomnemata* represented by the *Excerpta ex Theodoto* cannot be seen as the generic kin of *GPh*. The *Excerpta* are more the source material similar to that mentioned by Lucian: the raw data meant to be digested and reworked.[110]

---

[108] Rewolinski, "Sacramental Language," 42. Unfortunately, the identification of the *Gospel according to Philip*'s small formal units was far from complete, their distribution sketched rather than analyzed, and the "thematic paragraphs" neither extensive enough nor similar enough to illustrate any thesis about "the largest number of structures in the *Gospel according to Philip*."

[109] Rewolinski, "Sacramental Language," 44-45. See Johannes Quasten, *Patrology Vol. 2, The Ante-Nicene Literature after Irenaeus* (Westminster, Maryland: Newman Press, 1953) 12. A case could be made that the *Gospel according to Philip* has its playful side, however.

[110] Rewolinski, "Sacramental Language," 49.

He did not explain how the *Gospel according to Philip* differs from "raw data meant to be digested and reworked," nor what concrete indications of this intention the *Excerpta ex Theodoto* exhibit. With regard to the particular sense of "academic notes," Rewolinski commented, "*GPh* is too haphazard in layout to reflect the notes of a lecture hall, at least as examples of such notes have come down to us."[111] Thus Rewolinski concluded that the *Gospel according to Philip* did not fit any sense of the word ὑπομνήματα, but it may be that he over-restricted its meanings to either polished scholarly essays (or well-organized, if sketchy, notes from polished scholarly lectures), or a rambling set of disordered notes bearing explicit signs of their collector's intention to rework them.[112] Rewolinski found the *Gospel according to Philip* too disorganized for the former, but since it lacks explicit evidence that its material was intended to be reworked, he concluded that it must be distinct from the latter.

The third and last possible generic parallel explored by Rewolinski is Stobaeus' prose and poetry anthology, assembled as an encyclopedia of song and lore for his son, and called a florilegium. Rewolinski claimed that the florilegium "as an outgrowth of the purely poetical genre is late." He then stated, "The florilegium of Stobaeus is neither structurally, nor in terms of content, sufficiently close to *GPh* to claim kinship."[113] While this contains some truth, the florilegium or ἀνθολογία had an earlier existence than Rewolinski took into account, and was itself only one of a number of kinds of collections.[114]

For his own theory, Rewolinski took his cue from the fact that much of the material in the *Gospel according to Philip* appears to have an instructional end, but without the "tightly knit prose" of polished academic ὑπομνήματα. He suggested that the document may be a literary hybrid,

---

[111] Rewolinski, "Sacramental Language," 50.

[112] Rewolinski did not state what sort of evidence of an intent to rework the material he would expect, but one may note that the tension between Clement as compiler and the Theodotian material he was compiling does leave some traces of plans for future refutation in the *Excerpta*. Clement's disapproval of or distance from the material he records is sometimes subtle, but he occasionally makes explicit statements, for example, 3.1: "We admit that the elect seed is . . . . But the followers of Valentinus hold that . . . ."; or 30.1: "Then forgetting the glory of God, they impiously say . . . ." See Robert Pierce Casey, *The Excerpta Ex Theodoto of Clement of Alexandria* (London: Christophers, 1934) 25-33.

[113] Rewolinski, "Sacramental Language," 50. He did not discuss the structure of either.

[114] See below, chapter 4, "Organizing Principles of Some Collections" and chapter 10, "A Collection among Collections."

"perhaps notes that were never meant to be used apart from the guiding presence of the teacher-mystagogue."[115]

The principal weakness of Rewolinski's analysis is that in seeking to identify a generic parallel for the *Gospel according to Philip* he limited the field of possibilities to three, and then, in two of those cases, he focused on a single, supposedly representative example of each genre, rather than on the range of phenomena included in it. As we will see in chapters 3 and 4, the relevant genres were not sharply defined, and were prone to mutation; it is hazardous and possibly meaningless to pick any point along their "trajectories" as normative.

David Tripp was another of those who have seen an overall plan in the *Gospel according to Philip*. In a paper presented in 1979,[116] he asserted that the *Gospel according to Philip* is not "merely a collection of extracts" but displays "a continuity of argument which a *florilegium* could not provide."[117] His impression was that the bulk of the *Gospel according to Philip* is the "jottings of the author in person" and that when there are quotations, they are usually marked as such.[118] This picture of the *Gospel according to Philip* as a loosely ordered original composition contrasts sharply with Borchert's position that the *Gospel according to Philip* is a tightly ordered collection of extracts.

In Tripp's estimation, the *Gospel according to Philip*'s text could be understood as sermon-notes, and is perhaps best so understood. He wrote,

> The method of arrangement chosen is that which in our day would be called the 'retreat-address' style: concentrated exposition of major points, interspersed with substantial pauses for reflection, and moving across the

---

[115] Rewolinski, "Sacramental Language," 51-53. Ironically, he found fault with Borchert for suggesting that the *Gospel according to Philip* might be of an experimental literary hybrid without discussing the impetus for the same. André Méhat, whose introduction Rewolinski cites in support of the *Stromateis'* rambling structure, suggested in his conclusion that the *Stromateis* itself has a special place in the literary genre of ὑπομνήματα because it breaks out of "le corset étroit" under the presence of a new movement in human thought! See Méhat, *Étude sur les "Stromates" de Clément d'Alexandrie* (Paris: Éditions du Seuil, 1966), 523.

[116] David H. Tripp, "The 'Sacramental System' of the Gospel of Philip," printed in *Studia Patristica 17, part 1* ed. E. A. Livingstone (Oxford: Pergamon Press, 1982) 251-267.

[117] Tripp, "'Sacramental System,'" 251. The remark raises the important question, examined in chapter 4, of what sort(s) of continuity might be provided by a florilegium?

[118] These clarifications were expressed by Tripp to me in a conversation on October 2, 1993.

terrain to be traversed in a zig-zag fashion, rather than with the order de-manded by formal logic.[119]

"Moving across the terrain to be traversed in a zig-zag fashion," of course, describes approximately the same congeries of features charac-terized by Wilson and Ménard as "spiral progression." Themes are aban-doned or shift their meanings, but often earlier themes and perspectives are picked up again later. And the *Gospel according to Philip* is indeed liberally sprinkled with "concentrated exposition of major points"—but these are embedded in a matrix of briefer materials. While on occasion a densely stated insight is followed by more discursive explanation, or il-lustrative material (at times equally densely stated),[120] clear alternation between these two modes can account for only a fraction of the docu-ment, and, of course, any indication of pauses for reflection that might once have been in the text have been lost.[121]

Tripp saw the *Gospel according to Philip* as presenting a single domi-nant concept, "Life, and the transmission of life." He claimed that the rest of the work is ordered to the concluding sections 110-127, and that this final portion expounds on both the effect which the life of believers can have on others, and the qualities of spiritual life which are necessary for that effect.

Sections 110-115, he wrote, discuss the quality of spiritual life, chiefly in terms of generous and outreaching love; 116-127 then explore ways in which such spiritual life affects others and generates similar life in them. Tripp's observation that the final section of the *Gospel accord-ing to Philip* is more tightly structured, and that it falls into two sub-sections, the first of which deals with ethical concerns, is quite correct. It is, coincidentally, the same division that Borchert made as his final sec-tion. Tripp's second subsection of that block, however, continues to dwell on ethics and spiritual purity, and then shifts to eschatology

The claim that the rest of the work is ordered to the final section is not supported by the fragments of a "sacramental system" which Tripp traced in the earlier parts of the document. His evidence for such a system points to a pattern of practice which is by no means unique, at least in

---

[119] Tripp, "'Sacramental System,'" 252.

[120] Tripp writes that his model is the published lectures of W. Herrmann (*Systematic Theology (Dogmatik)*, English translation M. Micklem and K. G. Saunders, London: 1927). He quotes "It was his habit when lecturing to dictate a paragraph to his audi-ence and then to expatiate upon it *ex tempore.*"

[121] It may also be that Tripp's impression has been influenced by the lacunose state of the text, especially the periodically recurring lacunae at the bottoms of the pages.

most of its features. He discussed the texts that present the elements of the initiatory sequence in the order in which those texts occur in the *Gospel according to Philip*. While the elements of that ritual sequence itself probably do form a "model of spiritual progress," the arrangement of the texts which present those elements does not follow such a sequence.

The idea of life is dominant in the *Gospel according to Philip*'s thought and imagery: references to sprouting, growing, bearing fruit, ripening, harvesting, taking root, eating and being eaten, begetting, conceiving, bearing offspring, and the like are rife throughout the document, and are deployed as metaphors for spiritual realities. The theme of life, however, and this mode of expression for it, are central to many strands of Valentinianism—as, to give a single example, in the hymn preserved as Valentinus' own composition.[122] Their dominance in the pages of the *Gospel according to Philip* could suggest an author for whom such a mode of expression was congenial (as Tripp proposes), a collector working with source material naturally rich in these features, a collector and/or epitomizer who concentrated such expressions from sources originally containing them less frequently, or a redactor who added some or all of them.

"COLLECTION" HYPOTHESES REVISITED

Much more recently, in 1987, Bentley Layton and Hans-Martin Schenke have both conjectured on the components that make up the *Gospel according to Philip*, both in introductions to translations of the work.

Layton's was a cautious analysis.[123] He called the work "a Valentinian anthology containing some one hundred short excerpts taken from various other works," which he characterized as including "sermons, treatises, or philosophical epistles . . . as well as collected aphorisms or short dialogues with comments."[124] He noted that not all of the sources can be identified as Valentinian, although some material may possibly have been written by Valentinus himself. He concluded:

---

[122] See Layton, *Gnostic Scriptures* 246-249, and W. Völker, ed., *Quellen zur Geschichte der christlichen Gnosis* (Sammlung ausgewählter kirchen- und dogmengeschichtlicher Quellenschriften, n.s., 5; Tübingen: Mohr [Siebeck], 1932) 59 (= Fragment 8).

[123] Bentley Layton, *The Gnostic Scriptures. A New Translation with Annotations and Introductions* (Garden City, NY: Doubleday, 1987) 325-328

[124] Layton, *Gnostic Scriptures*, 325.

Because probably more than one Valentinian theological perspective is represented in *GPh*, it would be misleading to reconstruct a single theological system from the whole anthology. Rather, individual groups of excerpts can profitably be studied in isolation, with comparison of other works or fragments of Valentinianism or of classic gnosticism.[125]

He followed his brief introduction with an index of key words and themes in the *Gospel according to Philip*. "With due caution," he wrote, "they can be used to identify excerpts that belong together." Nevertheless, Layton did not say what procedures would constitute "due caution," nor indicate how one might assemble a group of excerpts from a single source for further study. Most of the key words and themes which he indexed are ones which could be found as important topics— albeit with different meanings or nuances—across a wide range of gnostic, gnostic-Christian and other Christian groups.[126]

The same year, Hans-Martin Schenke published a revised translation of the *Gospel according to Philip* along with a new introductory essay.[127] He had already by 1960 exchanged the designation "sayings" for an understanding of the *Gospel according to Philip*'s units as paragraphs, and had begun to readjust his estimation of their exact parameters. In 1987, he considered that there are no fewer than 175 of them. He continued to insist that the *Gospel according to Philip* is a *florilegium* or collection of excerpts, some without connecting links, some linked only by association of ideas or by catch words, and considered that this theory was on the brink of becoming the scholarly consensus.

He contended that the excerptor or compiler of the *Gospel according to Philip* did not understand the text as a "gospel" and may have intended it only for private use, but that a new understanding probably accompanied its "publication" and general diffusion. The large number of excerpts dealing with Jesus or Christ or the Lord may have contributed to an understanding of the *Gospel according to Philip* as a gospel, especially given the understanding of "gospels" shown in the *Gospel according to Thomas*. Schenke also conjectured that the *Gospel according to Philip* might have incorporated material which would have been recog-

---

[125] Layton, *Gnostic Scriptures*, 326.

[126] E.g.: "truth," "light," "paradise," "Adam," "animal," "slave," "Mary," "virgin," "garment, nakedness," "soul," "leave the world," "inherit," "mystery," "baptism, water"—to cite only the first two items from each of the seven sections of his index. See Layton, *Gnostic Scriptures*, 326-7.

[127] Hans-Martin Schenke, "Das Evangelium nach Philippus" in *Neutestamentliche Apokryphen I. Evangelien* ed Wilhelm Schneemelcher (Tübingen: J. C. B. Mohr [Paul Siebeck] 1987, 148-154 introduction, 155-173 translation.

nizable to its original readers as coming from traditions about Philip, thus suggesting the title given in the Nag Hammadi codex. This is all quite possible, although we do not know that the text was ever generally disseminated, since the ancient references to some "gospel" associated with "Philip" do not seem to match this text well. The extant copy might just as plausibly be no more than a private copy of a private translation of someone's private notebook. Nor do we know for how much of the text's career it bore either the term "gospel" or the name "Philip."

Schenke, like Layton, pointed out that the materials compiled as the *Gospel according to Philip* represent more than one school of Valentinianism (and from sources beyond Valentinianism, in Schenke's view), and that therefore one cannot meaningfully talk of the theology of this text: "Gänzlich ausgeschlossen aber ist es, etwa eine Theologie des EvPhil aus dem Text zu erheben."[128] He provided a listing of the references to Adam and paradise, creating and begetting, bridal chamber and related terms, and the sacraments, and referred the reader to Layton's index of 45 concepts and themes.[129] However, this procedure still does not address the problem inherent in interpreting a collection of excerpts: excerpts dealing with a single theme are not much more likely to present a single theology or point of view on that theme than is the document as a whole. One might as well seek to address the problems presented by the multiple authorship of the Bible by producing a thematic index. At most, it allows one quickly to locate all the passages in which a certain term appears so that their use of it may begin to be analyzed.

Jorunn Jacobsen Buckley's 1988 argument about the *Gospel according to Philip*'s unity was prefatory to her tracing of some major themes in the work.[130] In it, she stated that in contrast to some assessments of the *Gospel according to Philip* as chaotic or composite or unsystematic, Ménard argued for "unity" and "a—presumably coherent—Valentinian theology" in the *Gospel according to Philip*. This is not entirely accurate: Ménard did talk of the *Gospel according to Philip*'s author and of the text's theology, and discussed the latter at length, but he simply presumed the document's unity. The argument he presented was for a spiraling organization of materials, in which as many as five or more of Schenke's

---

[128] Schenke, "Das Evangelium," 154.

[129] Schenke, "Das Evangelium," 153-154.

[130] Jorunn Jacobsen Buckley, "Conceptual Models and Polemical Issues in the Gospel of Philip," in *Aufstieg und Niedergang der Römischen Welt* II.25.2, (Berlin: Walter de Gruyter & Co., 1988) 4167-4194.

"Spruche" could be grouped together for interpretation, and for the use of "catch words" as a literary device to point out such groupings. Jacobsen Buckley also cited with approval Giversen's introduction to his Danish translation as "the most convincing advocate of Gos. Phil.'s coherence," and his cautious approach to lacunae.[131] After a brief excursus on the impropriety of attempts to situate the document in the broader history of gnostic and Christian movements before it is clearly understood, she returned to the issue of the *Gospel according to Philip*'s unity and coherence, and rested her argument on the fact of the title and the assumption of a single author:

> It seems to me better to stay with the text, deal with it, and assume—at least for the reason of Gos. Phil.'s very title—some sort of coherence, for it must have made sense, as a putative 'gospel,' at least to the author.[132]

This, however, begs several questions at once: did the document have a single author? did the author (if any) give it its title? did the term "gospel" necessarily denote a document with "intelligible, coherent lines of thought" and "philosophical lucidity and consistency"?[133]

TACIT ASSUMPTIONS IN RECENT RESEARCH

A quick survey of the assumptions made about the nature of the *Gospel according to Philip* in the last decade will shed some light on the current state of affairs. While specific work on the document's nature has come full circle, without anyone convincing anyone else, studies of particular issues in the document continue, and continue to be based on the premise that a single position or practice can be extracted from the text—usually, without inquiry into the issue. Treatments examined above are omitted from this survey,[134]

---

[131] Buckley, "Conceptual Models," 4168. See the analysis of Giversen above.

[132] Buckley, "Conceptual Models," 4168-4169. This statement ends with a footnote, which reads, "Ménard assumes one author of Gos. Phil., L'Évangile, p. 34."

[133] Buckley, "Conceptual Models," 4169.

[134] Three translations and an interpretation published during this time period have also been omitted: Luttikhuizen, *Gnostische Geschriften I: Het Evangelie naar Maria, het Evangelie naar Filippus, de Brief van Petrus aan Filippus* (Kampen: Kok, 1986), Agourides, "To Euaggelio tou Philippou," *Deltion Biblikon Meleton* 17 (1988) 44-67, Montserrat-Torrents, "Evangelis gnòstics: Introducció, traducció i notes" in *Apòcrifs del Nou Testament*, ed. A Puig (Barcelona: Edicions Proa, 1990), and Hoeller, "Means of Transformation: The Gospel of Philip," chapter 12 in *Jung and the Lost Gospels: Insights into the Dead Sea Scrolls and the Nag Hammadi Library*,

In 1984, Catherine Trautmann presented a paper, "Le Schème de la croix dans l'Évangile selon Philippe (NH II,3),"[135] developing an interpretation of the understanding underlying the *Gospel according to Philip*'s references to the cross, based in part on symbolic values attached to the cross (such as "Limit") in other Valentinian works. In this article, she seemed to presume the internal unity of the *Gospel according to Philip* and its continuity with forms of Valentinianism.

Also in 1984, Luigi Moraldi published a volume of translations, with commentary and notes, of the Gospels of Thomas, Mary, Truth and Philip.[136] He remarked, "Non è certo una esposizione logica e articolata di un tema," but he discerned a network of sacramental references extending throughout the document; the remainder of the *Gospel according to Philip*'s material is formed of small units interwoven on two levels of meaning: a superficial, esoteric one, and a more profound—but more difficult to find—gnostic level. Echoing Wilson and Ménard, he wrote of "procedimenti a spirale."[137]

Jorunn Jacobsen Buckley's "'The Holy Spirit' Is a Double Name" was first presented as a paper in 1985 and published in 1986 and 1988.[138] She dealt with the female figures (Holy Spirit, Mary, and Sophia) in the *Gospel according to Philip* and insisted that the interaction between different levels of reality is the key to understanding these figures in the *Gospel according to Philip*. Her interpretation assumed the position, which she defended a few years later in "Conceptual Models and Polemical Issues in the Gospel of Philip,"[139] that the *Gospel according to Philip* is a unity based on a coherent underlying symbolic system, and that any part of it can be used to interpret any other part.

Kurt Rudolph's response to Jacobsen Buckley's paper (published in the conference proceedings in 1988) included only one paragraph dealing with the nature of the document.[140] In it, Rudolph agreed with Krause,

---

(Wheaton/Madras/London: Theosophical Publishing House, 1989).

[135] Catherine Trautmann, "Le Schème de la croix dans l'évangile selon Philippe (NH II,3)," *Deuxiéme journée d'etudes coptes. Strasbourg 25 mai 1984*, ed. J.-M. Rosenstiehl. (Louvain & Paris: Éditions Peeters, 1986) 123-129.

[136] Luigi Moraldi, *I vangeli Gnostici* (Milan: Adelphi, 1984).

[137] Moraldi, *I vangeli Gnostici* 158-159 and 177.

[138] This first appeared in Jorunn Jacobsen Buckley, *Female Fault and Fulfillment in Gnosticism* (Chapel Hill: University of North Carolina Press, 1986) as chapter 6, pp. 105-125, and later in a reworked and condensed version in the conference proceedings, *Images of the Feminine in Gnosticism*, ed. Karen L. King (Philadelphia: Fortress, 1988) 211-227.

[139] "Conceptual Models" in *ANRW* 25.5. For analysis, see above.

[140] Kurt Rudolph, "Response to '"The Holy Spirit is a Double Name"': Holy Spirit,

Gaffron and Tripp in considering the *Gospel according to Philip* as a
kind of homily or homiletic treatise. He found Tripp's assessment of the
document's practical purpose especially convincing with regard to the
final section (pages 77-86), and remarked, "The same is true if one reads
the entire text and its sacramental sequence along the same line as a
"model of spiritual progress." Tripp, however, claimed that the sequence
of sacramental acts (including such preparatory actions as stripping off
clothing prior to baptism) was a model of spiritual progress, not the document itself or its discussion of initiation.

Giulia Sfameni Gasparro, in her 1988 study, "Il 'Vangelo secondo
Filippo': rassegna degli studi e proposte di interpretazione,"[141] found the
document to contain a coherent message, however fragmented and
unsystematic the text. At times she used metaphors such as "un mosaico
di tessere diseguali" to describe the awkward and abrupt transitions,
seemingly implying that if an overall picture makes sense, apparent
seams and non sequiturs can be ignored.

In 1989, Jeffrey Siker[142] analyzed uses of the terms "Hebrew," "Jew,"
"proselyte," "Gentile," "Christian," along with mentions of circumcision,
the Sabbath, and sacrifice, and found "evidence of competition for adherents between Jews, non-gnostic Christians, and Valentinian gnostics in
the religious marketplace of the ancient world."[143] On the basis of this, he
speculated on the proper place of the *Gospel according to Philip* in the
trajectory of Christian-Jewish controversy in Antioch (or perhaps
Edessa). He did not seem to consider the possibility that the *Gospel according to Philip* represents more than one tradition or milieu, and did
not note that, with the exception of a brief and enigmatic reference to circumcision (*Gos. Phil.* 92.26-28), no passage or term involved in his
analysis occurs after page 75 of the *Gospel according to Philip*. Siker's
1989 article assumes the unity of the *Gospel according to Philip* without
explicitly raising the question.

Mary, and Sophia in the *Gospel of Philip*' by Jorunn Jacobsen Buckley," in *Images of
the Feminine*, ed K. L. King, 228-238.

[141] Giulia Sfameni Gasparro, ""Il 'Vangelo secondo Filippo:' rassegna degli studi e
proposte di interpretazione," in *Gnostica et hermetica. Saggi sullo gnosticismo e sull'
eremetismo* (Rome: Edizioni dell'Ateneo, 1982) 17-71. Reprinted with additions in
Aufstieg und Niedergang der römischen Welt (Berlin: De Gruyter, 1988) 4107-4166.

[142] Jeffrey S. Siker, "Gnostic Views on Jews and Christians in the Gospel of
Philip," *Novum Testamentum* 31 (1989) 275-288.

[143] Siker, "Jews and Christians," 284.

In 1991, Yvonne Janssens[144] published a new translation of the *Gospel according to Philip* with a very brief introduction, but did not remark on the unity or nature of the *Gospel according to Philip* as a whole.

Elaine Pagels' 1991 essay, "The 'Mystery of Marriage' in the *Gospel of Philip* Revisited"[145] challenged some of the assumptions underlying a long debate. Do the *Gospel according to Philip*'s references to a "mystery of marriage" refer to a practice involving—perhaps requiring—actual marriage,[146] or was it purely symbolic and probably accompanied by an encratite stance?[147] Pagels called attention to the fact that there is no unambiguous evidence with which to answer this question, and she asked why that would be, if the matter were of such central importance to Valentinians. Her solution was that the author of the *Gospel according to Philip* "expresses, precisely through his ambiguity on this topic, a deliberate refusal to take sides on this issue," a refusal linked to a more general rejection of dualistic patterns of thought. This allowed her to take at face value Irenaeus' complaints that Valentinians followed no consistent pattern with regard to marriage, celibate marriage and solitary celibacy. This may well be the case, but several things should be noted. The entire debate on this matter in the *Gospel according to Philip* has assumed that there is a single stance delineated in that document, however ambiguously. Pagels also assumed a version of this, and based her interpretation on it. But her version is a curiously dual one: it is a short step from postulating a single author whose vision embraces multiple practices to postulating a collector who assembled material on multiple practices without feeling any need to harmonize or "correct" them. She also assumed that the *Gospel according to Philip* can be identified simply with the Valentinians (or with some branch of them). The *Gospel according to Philip* turns out to contain some non-Valentinian materials, the passages in it which may be Valentinian are not necessarily from the same branch of that movement, and it is not at all obvious that all the passages relating to

---

[144] Yvonne Janssens, *Évangiles gnostiques dans le corpus de Berlin et dans la bibliothèque copte de Nag Hammadi* (Louvain-la-nueve: Centre d'histoire des religions, 1991) 97-153.

[145] Elaine H. Pagels, "The 'Mystery of Marriage' in the *Gospel of Philip* Revisited," in *The Future of Early Christianity*, ed. B. A. Pearson (Minneapolis: Fortress, 1991) 442-454.

[146] As held, with variations, by Quispel, Ménard, Grant, van Eijk and Jacobsen Buckley.

[147] As held, again with variations, by Schenke, Segelberg, Janssens, Tripp and Williams.

the "mystery of marriage" derive from a single source, or even from exclusively Valentinian sources.

In 1993, Holger Strutwolf published *Gnosis als System. Zur Rezeption der valentinianischen Gnosis bei Origenes*.[148] The first half of the book is an overview of Valentinian opinions: Strutwolf went through five topics (lines of development of the Valentinian teaching on the pleroma, the fall and the creation of the extra-pleromatic world, the creation of humans and the three-nature-teaching, the redeemer and his work, and Valentinian eschatology) and examined the position taken on each in a number of works understood to belong to the Valentinian schools. The *Gospel according to Philip* was one of the documents analyzed under each of the last four topics. The overview he provided is useful, but must be taken with a grain of salt: he did not question the unity of the *Gospel according to Philip*, nor the identification of its contents as Valentinian.

SUMMARY

As we have seen, most interpretations of the *Gospel according to Philip* have been based on the tacit assumption that a single viewpoint, theology, or set of ritual practices can be recovered from the document by considering all the passages it presents on a given theme or topic of interest. This has been true particularly for two groups: those who have defended the *Gospel according to Philip*'s coherence (whether as an original exposition or as decisively shaped by a strong redactor), and also most of those who have attempted to interpret specific issues in the *Gospel according to Philip*, regardless of whether they saw it as a disorderly collection of materials from disparate origins, or a unity, or have just ignored the question. In contrast, several of those who have focused on the nature of the document, rather than on the meaning of its contents, have insisted on its composite nature, but this assessment has had little or no impact on the actual procedures used by those who sought to interpret the document's contents.

The recurrent attempts to show the literary unity of the *Gospel according to Philip* arise partly from the fact that some themes and interests are sprinkled throughout much of the document, producing an impression of continuity or coherence which remains tantalizingly elusive. This is a

---

[148] Holger Strutwolf, *Gnosis als System. Zur Rezeption der valentinianischen Gnosis bei Origenes.* (Göttingen: Vandenhoeck & Ruprecht, 1993).

feature which must be accounted for in any assessment of the *Gospel according to Philip*. It seems to me, however, that there is also a practical motivation for arguing for the unity of the *Gospel according to Philip*. Seeing the document as a literary unity allows one to see it as a theological unity, as a document from which a coherent view on this or that subject can be extracted, from which a ritual practice can be recovered— as a document which can be interpreted. Jorunn Jacobsen Buckley came very near the heart of the matter:

> It seems to me better to stay with the text, deal with it, and assume. . . some sort of coherence. . . . To doubt the text's philosophical lucidity and consistency would mean, in some sense, to question its being worth studying at all.[149]

Yet documents widely agreed to be the product of collection and redaction have been seen as worth studying. Composite texts can have many different degrees and sorts of lucidity and consistency, at the level of sources and at a redactional level, as collections motivated by coherent interests. The real problem posed by the hypothesis that the document is composite is the lack of approaches based on this view.

If the contents of the *Gospel according to Philip* are indeed diverse in origin, a more specific understanding of its composite nature and sources is needed, an understanding which is capable of generating new approaches to its interpretation.

---

[149] Buckley, "Conceptual Models," 4168-4169.

CHAPTER THREE

THE PRACTICAL MATRIX OF COLLECTIONS
AND COLLECTION GENRES

An understanding of the collecting practices of the late ancient world, and of the organizing principles of collections formed by them, is essential if we wish to assess the possibility that the *Gospel according to Philip* might be a collection of diverse materials. Documents from late antiquity which are without doubt collections of diverse materials range from carefully edited works intended for publication to unedited notes and excerpts meant exclusively for private use, and span a wide range of subject matter.

A large body of derived or secondary literature circulated in late antiquity. It owed its existence to the conditions of reading in the ancient world, and it aimed to replace, in some degree and for some purposes, the original works on which it was based. Copies of books were expensive and sometimes difficult to acquire. They were also more laborious to read than modern books, being without word spacing or much punctuation. Until the codex supplanted the scroll, they were tedious to consult because of the unrolling (and re-rolling) necessary to consult something toward the middle or end, and they deteriorated quickly if consulted frequently. As one result, ancient people quoted texts from memory more often than modern people are inclined to, but their memories were based on reading carefully, with the knowledge that it would be difficult to return to check anything.

Yet the choice was not simply between trusting one's memory and a laborious and time-consuming consultation of the text itself. Condensations of books, summaries of opinions, school readers giving the high points of literature, handbooks for reference in medical, magical, legal, liturgical, and other matters, books of wit or wisdom, sayings of the wise, brave, rich or famous were all enormously popular. Scholars also made copious notes and excerpts as they read, to which they could later refer quickly. This would have been especially true when the book in question belonged to someone else.[1] Sometimes these collections of notes made for private use were recopied and circulated. In a cheirographic culture, there is no clear line between private use and publication. Other collections were meant for publication from the start. This heterogeneous body of derived literature was the shadow cast by original writings whenever they were exposed to the light of general or specialized interest. Such documents have figured less—far less—in the agendas of modern scholarship than the original writings from which they derived, but in their own time, the derivative works were read by more people, and consulted more often even by the scholarly, than their originals.

Since, as Part Two of this work attempts to establish, the *Gospel according to Philip* is a collection of materials from disparate sources, only collections of similarly diverse material, and their collectors, will concern us here. Works such as epitomes (condensations of single works) and doxographies (summaries of the opinions of a single philosopher, or textbook guides to a number of philosophers, both of which were often presented in the form of excerpts) are not relevant. Nor are editions of a single author's work, even when this work is in the form of brief, independent units such as maxims or epigrams. Unfortunately, the distinction is not always clear: in some types of collections, disparate materials have been more or less thoroughly organized around the conceit of authorship by a single person. The title attached to the *Gospel according to Philip* places it within this category, although a less developed or more extrinsic claim of authorship would be hard to imagine. Works loosely attributed to a single author will sometimes require some examination to determine their relevance or irrelevance to this inquiry. Nonetheless, our goal will be to discover the ways that collectors and editors of disparate material worked in the first three centuries of the common era, along with the structuring principles of some earlier collections which were widely available and may have served as models during this period.[2]

---

[1] Notes and excerpts made for private use would have met the needs served to-day not only by note taking, but also by photocopying, by the larger scale of private acquisition of books made possible by cheaper publishing technologies, and by the relatively assured possibility of renewed access to a given book created by public and institutional libraries and by interlibrary loans.

[2] This chronological restriction means that our inquiry ends before the heyday of many of the more discussed types of collection begins; the transferability of its conclusions to the Byzantine and Medieval periods will remain uncertain. Of more

The questions we may hope to answer are these: What kinds of organization and coherence are typically found in such collections? and
especially, Can any of the types of collections or collecting practices
recoverable from this period explain the arrangement of the materials in
the *Gospel according to Philip*, and the tantalizing traces of apparent
order we find there? The question about the organizational features of
different types of collections will concern us in this chapter and the
next; their specific application to the *Gospel according to Philip* will be
dealt with in chapters 10 and 11.

EXCERPTING AND COLLECTING PRACTICES IN LATE ANTIQUITY

Writing down notes and brief excerpts from one's reading was as natural
an activity in late antiquity as it is now. Just as the form of these notes
are influenced by the materials and technologies available to us—inex-
pensive paper and cards, writing instruments which do not require
frequent tending, photocopy machines, and easily portable computers all
influence the way we work—so scholarship in the first centuries of the
common era was shaped by the technologies and materials available
then.

A Scholar's Habits

The younger Pliny wrote admiringly about his uncle's dedication to
scholarship: rising hours before daylight, using every available minute
for work. The elder Pliny's single-mindedness and unremitting pace were
exceptional, but his general working procedures were typical of
scholarly practices in his time.

Post cibum saepe . . . aestate si quid otii iacebat in sole, liber leg-ebatur, adnotabat excerpebatque.	After something to eat . . . in summer when he was not too busy he would often lie in the sun, and a book was read aloud while he made notes and extracts.

immediate consequence, the relevance to our period of categories determined in
relation to that later body of works is not assured. Much of the scholarship on collections has either concerned those periods, or surveyed earlier material by means
of categories derived from them. See, for example, Henri-Marie Rochais, "Florilèges spirituels latins," and Marcel Richard, "Florilèges spirituels grecs," both in
Dictionnaire de la spritualité (Paris: Beauchesne, 1964) 5.435-460 and 5.475-512.
A survey somewhat more attentive to late antiquity may be found in Henry
Chadwick, "Florilegium," in *Reallexikon für Antike und Christentum* (Stuttgart:
Anton Hiersemann, 1969) 7.1131-1160.

Nihil enim legit quod non excerperet;	He made extracts of everything he read . . . .
Super hanc liber legebatur adnotabatur, et quidem cursim. . . .	A book was read aloud during the meal and he took rapid notes. . . .
In itinere quasi solutus ceteris curis, huic uni vacabat:	When traveling he felt free from other responsibilities to give every minute to work;
ad latus notarius cum libro et pugillaribus, cuius manus hieme manicis muniebantur, ut ne caeli quidem asperitas ullum studii tempus ciperet. . . .	he kept a secretary at his side with a book and notebook, and in winter saw that his hands were protected by long sleeves, so that even bitter weather should not rob him of a working hour. . . .
Hac intentione tot ista volumina peregit electorumque commentarios centum sexaginta mihi reliquit, opisthographos quidem et minutissimis scriptos; qua ratione multiplicatur hic numerus.	It was this application which enabled him to finish all those volumes, and to leave me 160 notebooks of selected passages, written in a minute hand on both sides of the page, so that really their number is doubled.
Referebat ipse potuisse se, cum procuraret in Hispania, vendere hos commentarios Larcio Licino quadringentis milibus nummum; et tunc aliquanto pauciores erant.	He used to say that when he was serving as procurator in Spain he could have sold these notebooks to Larcius Licinus for 400,000 sesterces, and there were far fewer of them then.[3]

The elder Pliny read nothing without making excerpts and notes from it, according to his nephew. He recorded these selected passages (presumably, along with his own notes) in scrolls which, contrary to the usual practice for book production, were written on both sides.[4] When he traveled, however, he had a secretary bring along a book and pugillares, a set of wax-coated writing tablets, the contents of which must have been copied out into a scroll upon arrival, by Pliny or the secretary. By the time of his death, Pliny had amassed 160 of his "notebooks." While these scrolls of excerpts and notes were made for

---

[3] Pliny the Younger, Letters 3.5.10-17. Text and English translation from *Pliny. Letters and Panegyricus. Volume 1, books 1-7*. transl. Betty Radice (Cambridge MA: Harvard University Press, 1969).

[4] The surface of the back of the scroll was subjected to mechanical wear, moisture, and oils every time the scroll was rolled or unrolled, and so deteriorated more quickly than the front. For personal use, when handling could be controlled and economy was important, using both sides made sense.

his own private use, he did receive at least one offer to buy them; had the sale been made, or arrangements made to copy the scrolls instead, the distinction between private use and publication would have become very thin.

The only work of Pliny's which has survived is his *Natural Histories*, a truly massive compendium of facts and reports which was undoubtedly part of the fruit of his excerpting labors. The *Natural Histories* are meticulously organized; a detailed table of contents appears at its beginning, which includes a list of authorities which Pliny consulted for each book. The presence of these "bibliographies" for each separate book affords us one small glimpse into the organization of Pliny's notebooks: extracts, or blocks of extracts, must have had the names of their authors attached.

The Materials of Ephemeral Writing

As we have seen, Pliny's notebooks were scrolls inscribed on both sides, an inherently fragile format. The codex format of folded parchment or papyrus leaves was already appearing as a format for copies of literary works, but would remain an oddity for some time to come.[5] The single-sided scroll was the only generally accepted form of the book all over the Roman empire in Pliny's day.

It was not, however, the only format for writing. Pliny or his secretary used a small sized set of wooden tablets for note taking on the road, called *pugillares*. A larger sized set was properly called either *tabulae* or *codices* in Latin; Greek terminology did not differentiate by size, but by the number of tablets involved: one could take one's notes in a δίπτυχον, τρίπτυχον, et cetera—all the way up to a δεκάπτυχον.[6] Typically, two or more thin boards were bound together along one side by a leather thong laced through a series of holes; the opposite side generally had a single hole to accommodate another thong used to keep the set closed when not in use. Inside, both faces of each board (except the outer faces of the outermost pair) would have been occupied by a large, shallow rectangular recess surrounded by a narrow margin. The

---

[5] Martial, writing around 85 C.E., seems to have made the first clear reference to literary works presented in the form of a codex (*Epigrams* 1.2), but the format remained a novelty until the third century. See Colin H. Roberts and T. C. Skeat, *The Birth of the Codex* (London: Oxford University Press, 1987), 24-29.

[6] See Roberts and Skeat, *Birth of the Codex*, 11-14, and Joseph van Haelst, "Les Origines du Codex" in *Les débuts du codex,* ed. A. Blanchard (Brepols: Turnhout, 1989) 13-35, especially 14-17.

recessed area was spread with beeswax, which could be written on by anything with a narrow point.[7] Tablets from the first few centuries of the common era have been found with their wax intact and its writing still legible;[8] judging by their example, it seems that users often placed a small lump of wax on the wooden margins of the tablets to keep the waxed surfaces spaced further apart and reduce the possibility of damage. Such "notebooks" could hold a considerable amount of text: ten tablets would yield 18 writing surfaces—half the number of pages taken up by the extant copy of the *Gospel according to Philip.*

The other principle medium for temporary notes and calculations in this period was parchment.[9] It had several major advantages: it was lighter in weight than wood, more compact, fire-retardant (rather than very highly inflammable, like cellulose products such as papyrus and wood, particularly waxed wood), and essentially waterproof. Its value for note-taking, composing, calculating, and other forms of ephemeral writing lay in the last-mentioned attribute: because carbon ink (as opposed to metallic inks and those containing dyes) did not soak deeply into parchment, it could be scrubbed clean and reused. Papyrus was sometimes also used in the same way, but was more fragile and unlikely to stand up to repeated reuse.[10] The form called *pugillares membranei*

---

[7] Occasionally unwaxed wooden tablets were also used, with chalk or with ink. See discussion in Roberts and Skeat, *Birth of the Codex*, 11, and van Haelst, "Origines," plate 2, for a photograph of inked wooden tablets.

[8] For a description (and photographs) of waxed tablets in sets of 4, 5 and 10, dating from the second to the sixth century C.E., see Patrice Cauderlier, "Quatre cahiers scolaires (Musée de Louvre): Présentation et problèmes annexes," in *Les débuts du codex*, ed. A. Blanchard (Brepols: Turnhout, 1989) 43-59; see also Rosario Pintaudi, "Tavolette lignee e cerate della biblioteca vaticana," also in *Les débuts du codex*, ed. Blanchard, 61-67.

[9] Roberts and Skeat, *Birth of the Codex*, 16-23 (and plate II for an example), and van Haelst, "Origines" in *Les débuts du codex*, 18-20.

[10] See Roberts and Skeat, *Birth of the Codex*, 17-18.

Attempts to assess the relative cost of the two materials have been inconclusive, because the recorded prices we have for each come from different periods. See Roberts and Skeat, *Birth of the Codex*, 7. Both were labor intensive to manufacture. Parchment required animal raising, which itself required considerable time and which was limited, in any given area, by the local resources and by the other demands made upon them. The papyrus plant, on the other hand, grew in quantity only along the Nile, so that its price elsewhere included shipping costs and, since Egypt held a virtual monopoly, was also subject to taxation and other manipulation. Because the availability and price of the two materials was tied to unrelated factors, there was probably considerable instability, over the course of centuries, in their relative prices. See Naphtali Lewis, *Papyrus in Classical Antiquity* (Oxford:

or simply *membranae* consisted of a sheet or several sheets of parchment folded in imitation of the more familiar waxed tablets. Quintillian made a comparison of the two media:

scribi optime ceris, in quibus facillima est ratio delendi, nisi forte visus infirmior membranarum potius usum exiget,	It is best to write on wax owing to the facility which it offers for erasure, though weak sight may make it desirable to employ parchment by preference.
quae ut iuvant aciem, ita crebra relatione, quoad intinguuntur, calami morantur manum et cogitationis impetum frangunt.	The latter, however, although of assistance to the eye, delays the hand and interrupts the stream of thought owing to the frequency with which the pen has to be supplied with ink.
Relinquendae autem in utrolibet genere contra erunt vacuae tabellae, in quibus libera adiiciendo sit excursio. Nam interim pigritiam emendandi augustiae faciunt aut certe novorum interpositione priora confundant.	But whichever we employ, we must leave blank pages that we may be free to make additions when we will. For lack of space at times gives rise to a reluctance to make corrections, or, at any rate, is liable to cause confusion when new matter is inserted.[11]

Quintillian here weighs the relative merits of these two options from the perspective of their usefulness for original composition, where unhindered speed in recording thoughts is important, and it is probable that one will want to make both minor and major changes or rearrangements. It would seem empirically that the task of arranging excerpted materials would also favor paraphernalia allowing easy erasure or very low cost, or both.

The Use of Intermediary Documents

Two unusual papyri, one from considerably before the period of our investigation and one from the first century C.E., may offer a glimpse into the use of temporary, intermediary documents by editors of collections.

One is a well-worn scroll from the third century B.C.E., containing the first line and the total number of lines of each of about 240 epigrams;

Clarendon Press, 1974) 129-134 for further discussion on the economy of papyrus.

[11] Quintillian *Institutio Oratoria* 10.3.31-32. Text and translation from *The Institutio Oratoria of Quintillian* vol. 4, ed. and transl. H. E. Butler, (Cambridge, MA: Harvard University Press, 1979) 108-109.

this list is divided into four books.[12] The roll is inscribed at its beginning τὰ ἐπιζητούμενα τῶν ἐπιγραμμάτων ἐν τῇ α΄ βύβλῳ. Alan Cameron conjectured that the roll "appears to be a librarian's (or scholar's) list of desiderata (ἐπιζητούμενα), poems that are 'missing' or 'required', presumably for the purpose of checking a corrupt or defective text."[13] This presumed purpose is possible, but it points to a very ambitious undertaking. Cameron's suggestion assumes a number of things: someone wishes to check a text which has extensive damage or corruptions, although Cameron thinks this text is not a multi-author anthology but probably only a series of rolls in which assorted small, single author collections have been recorded. His hypothetical librarian or scholar must not have expected to find another copy of the same text—if he or she did, it would be much simpler to compare the two. Cameron's understanding of the document implies a proposed search for individual epigrams preserved in other, different collections. Such a needle-in-a-haystack search would require remarkable motivation, motivation more likely to be found in the editing of a respected classic than the correction of a roll containing miscellaneous small collections.

It seems to me more plausible that a document of this kind was a collector's working document, recording choices which had been made from a source or sources known to him or her, and developing a tentative ordering of those selections. The list contains just enough information to jog the memory, enabling a provisional impression of the whole without the trouble of copying out the full text. At this stage insertions, deletions, and rearrangements could be made with a minimum of trouble, although this particular papyrus shows no traces of such activity. If and when the arrangement was deemed satisfactory, a full copy could be made, or the list could be turned over to a scribe, along with the source documents, for production. The title may indicate that this text is just such a list, from which a scribe was to work to produce a full copy.

P. Oxy. 3724, a group of fragments from the extra paper at the end of a first century C.E. papyrus roll, shows the signs of this sort of rearrangement.[14] These fragments contain six columns written on the

---

[12] See Alan Cameron, *The Greek Anthology from Meleager to Planudes* (Oxford, Clarendon, 1993) 9-10.

[13] Cameron, *Meleager to Planudes,* 10.

[14] *The Oxyrhynchus Papyri* vol. 54, ed. Peter Parsons (London: Oxford University Press, 1987) 65-84.

recto, and two on the verso. Only the first few words (not the whole first line) of 175 epigrams have been recorded. Thirty-one of these can be identified (provisionally: different epigrams were known to share the same incipit), and of these, 25 are elsewhere attributed to Philodemus, and two to Asclepiades. Evidence can be assembled to link many of the others to Philodemus, and the entire group may have come from his pen,[15] but the evidence is mostly quite circumstantial. Cameron argued against any artistic arrangement in the order of the material, but when most of the epigrams are unknown and only the first two or three words are listed in this document, any assessment of artistic merit seems ill-advised.

Most intriguingly, however, this list contains several repetitions. In some cases, the first instance of a repeated incipit is canceled. Also, two epigrams have been written out in full. The margins contain occasional check marks and sequences of numbers from one to ten. The list seems clearly to be a working list of contents for a projected anthology.

THE RELATIONSHIP OF PRIVATE NOTES TO PUBLISHED WORKS

The distinction between private notes and published works was much less clear in the days before print. Very many situations—possibly involving the majority of documents that existed in late antiquity—fell into a grey area between the two.

Inadvertent Publication

The second century C.E. physician Galen made several comments which illustrate the thin line between private notes and published works, although the material in question was principally or wholly notes on observations rather than excerpted materials. At the beginning of his ΠΕΡΙ ΑΝΑΤΟΜΙΚΩΝ ΕΓΧΕΙΡΗΣΕΩΝ, *On Anatomical Procedures*, he recalled his reason for composing that work:

> Flavius Boëthus, the Roman Consul, as keen an anatomist as ever lived, on leaving Rome for his native Ptolemais [A.D. 165] urged me to record these 'procedures.' I gave him, among other works, my *De anatomicis administrationibus libri duo*. These were of notes [only] for, while he was

---

[15] See Cameron, *Meleager to Planudes*, 379-387, and David Sider "Looking for Philodemus in P. Oxy. 54.3724," *Zeitschrift für Papyrologie und Epigraphik* 76 (1980) 229-236.

with us [162-5], he had made many observations in a short time and had asked me for some such records as memoranda. But since he is now dead and I have no copies (for those I had in Rome were destroyed by fire), at the urging of friends I decided to write others to give them.[16]

Thus we have a record of a book being written a second time by its original author because all the copies of it have perished or become unavailable.[17] The second version, at least, was intended to be shared among a circle of friends and fellow scholars.

Galen frequently referred his readers to other works of his in which topics were developed more fully; occasionally these references include some statement about the circumstances in which the other book was written, or its purpose. A little after the comment quoted above, he wrote:

De thoracis et pulmonis motu libri tres I wrote long ago, as a youth. It was for a fellow-student, returning to his own country after a long absence. He wished to display his talents in public, but lacked lecturing ability. He, too, died and thus this book became public property, so that many got hold of it, though it was not for publication.[18]

Here we have a work not intended for publication or circulation at all but "ghost-written" for a specific friend to present orally, which nevertheless became public property—i.e., "published"—after the friend died. Further along in the same work he makes another comment, that he wrote his De musculorum dissectione at the request of colleagues who needed memoranda (ὑπομνήματα) while they were traveling.[19] He recounted similar events in his book On Venesection against the Erasistrateans in Rome concerning a lecture which he re-dictated at the request of one of his hearers, and which subsequently against his explicit wishes became public; in the Nature of Man he stated that he wrote On the Elements according to Hippocrates at the request of a friend going abroad, and it too leaked out.[20]

---

[16] Galen. On Anatomical Procedures. Περι Ανατομικων Εγχειρησεων. De Anatomicis Administrationibus. Transl. and ed. Charles Singer (London: Oxford University Press, 1956), 1.1.215-216.

[17] Situations like this, in which more than one "original" version is produced are, of course, one source of complexity in later manuscript traditions.

[18] Galen, De anatomicis administrationibus 1.1.217. Translation Singer, Galen.

[19] Galen, De anatomicis administrationibus 1.3.227.

[20] For these last two, see Peter Brain, Galen On Bloodletting (Cambridge: Cambridge University Press, 1986) 41-42.

Published Miscellanies

Along with works which accidentally became public property, minimally organized miscellanies were being published, some of which were, or purported to be, unorganized notes or collections of excerpts. The elder Pliny in the first century C.E., and Aulus Gellius in the second, both reflected on the number of these, and each sought to differentiate his work from that tradition—although in Gellius' case, as we shall see, the protestations of difference were largely tongue in cheek.

The high degree of organization shown by Pliny in his *Natural Histories* was unusual. Pliny commented in his preface to that work about the titles being given to books in his day, especially by Greek writers, and complained about their contents: KHPION, KEPAΣ ΑΜΑΛΘΕΙΑΣ, ΙΑ, ΜΟΥΣΑΙ, ΠΑΝΔΕΚΤΑΙ, ΕΓΧΕΙΡΙΔΙΑ, ΛΕΙΜΩΝ, ΠΙΝΑΞ, ΣΧΕΔΙΟΝ, were popular book titles known to him: "Honeycombs," "Horn of Plenty," "Violets," "Muses," "Hold-all," "Handbook," "Meadow," "Tablet," "Impromptu"—"titles that might tempt a man to forfeit his bail," Pliny exclaimed, "but when you get inside them, good heavens, what a void you will find between the covers!"[21]

The Attic Nights *as Pseudo-Notebook*

Aulus Gellius situated his own *Attic Nights* in just such a tradition, even making the claim that the editing he had done did not extend to the organization of his materials.

Usi . . . sumus ordine rerum fortuito, quem antea in excerpendo feceramus.	. . . in the arrangement of my material I have adopted the same haphazard order that I had previously followed in collecting it.
Nam proinde ut librum quemque in manus ceperam seu Graecum seu Latinum vel quid memoratu dignum audieram, ita quae libitum erat, cuius generis cumque erant, indistincte atque promisce annotabam eaque mihi ad subsidium memoriae quasi quoddam litterarum penus recondebam,	For whenever I had taken in hand any Greek or Latin book, or had heard anything worth remembering, I used to jot down whatever took my fancy, of any and every kind, without any definite plan or order; and such notes I would lay away as an aid to my memory, like a kind of literary storehouse,

---

[21] *Pliny, Natural Histories, Preface and Books 1-2* translated H. Rackham (Cambridge, MA: Harvard University Press, 1949) 15-17.

ut quando usus venisset aut rei aut verbi, cuius me repens forte oblivio tenuisset, et libri ex quibus ea sumpseram non adessent facile inde nobis inventu atque depromptu foret.

Facta igitur est in his quoque commentariis eadem rerum disparilitas quae fuit in illis

annotationibus pristinis, quas breviter et indigeste et incondite ex eruditionibus lectionibusque variis feceramus.

Sed quoniam longinquis per hiemem noctibus in agro . . . terrae Atticae commentationes hasce ludere ac facere exorsi sumus, idcirco eas inscripsimus *Noctium* esse *Atticarum*, nihil imitati festivitates inscriptionum quas plerique alii utriusque linguae scriptores in id genus libris fecerunt.

Nam quia variam et miscellam et quasi confusaneam doctrinam conquisiverant, eo titulos quoque ad eam sententiam exquisitissimos indiderunt.

Namque alii *Musarum* inscripserunt, alii *Silvarum,* ille Πέπλον, hic Ἀμαλθείας Κέρας, alius Κηρία, partim Λειμῶνας, quidam *Lectionis Suae*, alius *Antiquarum Lectionum* atque alius Ἀνθηρῶν, et item alius Εὑρημάτων.

Sunt etiam qui Λύχνους in-scripserint, sunt item qui Στρω-ματεῖς, sunt adeo qui Πανδέκτας et Ἑλικῶνα et Προβλήματα et Ἐγχειρίδια et Παραξιφίδας. Est qui *Memoriales* titulum fecerit, est qui Πραγματικὰ et Πάρεργα et Διδασκαλικά,

---

so that when the need arose of a word or a subject which I chanced for the moment to have forgotten, and the books from which I had taken it were not at hand, I could readily find and produce it.

It therefore follows, that in these notes there is the same variety of subject that there was in those

former brief jottings which I had made without order or arrange-ment, as the fruit of instruction or reading in various lines.

Since . . . I began to amuse myself by assembling these notes during the long winter nights which I spent on a country-place in the land of Attica, I have therefore given them the name *Attic Nights*, making no attempt to imitate the witty captions which many other authors of both languages have devised for works of the kind.

For since they had laboriously gathered varied, manifold, and as it were indiscriminate learning, they therefore invented ingenious titles also, to correspond with that idea.

Thus, some called their books "The Muses," others, "Woods," one used the title "Athena's Mantle," another "The Horn of Amaltheia," still another "Honeycomb," several "Meads," one "Fruits of my Reading," another "Gleanings from Early Writers," another "The Nosegay," still another "Discoveries."

Some have used the name "Torches," others, "Tapestry," others, "Repertory," others "Helicon," "Problems," "Hand-books," and "Daggers." One man called his book "Memorabilia," one "Principia," one "Incidentals," another "Instructions."

est item qui *Historiae Naturalis*, et *Παντοδαπῆς Ἱστορίας*, est praeterea qui *Pratum*, est itidem qui *Πάγκαρπον*, est qui *Τόπων* scripserit;

Other titles are "Natural History," "Universal History," "The Field," "The Fruit-basket," or "Topics."

sunt item multi qui *Coniectanea,* neque item non sunt qui indices libris suis fecerint aut *EpistularumMoralium* aut *Epistolicarum Quaestionum* aut *Confusarum* et quaedam alia inscripta nimis lepida multasque prorsum concinnitates redolentia.

Many have termed their notes "Miscellanies," some "Moral Epistles," "Questions in Epistolary Form," or "Miscellaneous Queries," and there are some other titles that are exceedingly witty and redolent of extreme refinement.

Nos vero, ut captus noster est, incuriose et inmeditate ac prope etiam subrustice ex ipso loco ac tempore hibernarum vigiliarum *Atticas Noctes* inscripsimus, tantum ceteris omnibus in ipsius quoque inscriptionis laude cedentes, quantum cessimus in cura et elegantia scriptionis.

But I, bearing in mind my limitations, gave my work off-hand, without premeditation, and indeed almost in rustic fashion, the caption of *Attic Nights*, derived merely from the time and place of my winter's vigils; I thus fall as far short of all other writers in the dignity too even of my title, as I do in care and in elegance of style.

Sed ne consilium quidem in excerpendis notandisque rebus idem mihi, quod plerisque illis, fuit. Namque illi omnes et eorum maxime Graeci, multa et varia lectitantes, in quas res cumque inciderant, "alba," ut dicitur, "linea" sine cura discriminis solam copiam sectanti converrebant,

Neither had I in making my excerpts and notes the same purpose as many of those whom I have mentioned. For all of them, and in particular the Greeks, after wide and varied reading, with a white line, as the saying goes, that is with no effort to discriminate, swept together whatever they had found, aiming at mere quantity.

quibus in legendis ante animus senio ac taedio languebit quam unum alterumve reppererit quod sit aut voluptati legere aut cultui legisse aut usui meminisse.

The perusal of such collections will exhaust the mind through weariness or disgust, before it finds one or two notes which it is a pleasure to read, or inspiring to have read, or helpful to remember.

Ego vero, cum illud Ephesii viri summe nobilis verbum cordi haberum, quod profecto ita est πολυμαθίη νόον οὐ διδάσκει, ipse quidem volvendis transeundisque multis admodum voluminisbus

I myself, on the contrary, having at heart that well-known saying of a famous Ephesian, "Much learning does not make a scholar," did, it is true, busy and even weary myself in unrolling and running through many a scroll,

per omnia semper negotiorum intervalla in quibus furari otium potui exercitus defessusque sum,	working without cessation in all the intervals of business whenever I could steal the leisure;
sed modica ex his caque sola accepi quae aut ingenia prompta expeditaque ad honestae eruditionis cupidinem utiliumque artium contemplationem celeri facilique	but I took few items from them, confining myself to those which, by furnishing a quick and easy short-cut, might lead active and alert minds to a desire for inde
compendio ducerent aut homines aliis iam vitae negotiis occupatos a turpi certe agrestique rerum atque verborum imperitia vindicarent.	pendent learning. . . or would save those who are already fully occupied with the other duties of life from an ignorance of words and things which is assuredly shameful and boorish.[22]

Many of these titles reflect the idea of an aggregation of individual small units (as "Violets," "The Nosegay," and the less dainty titles, "Daggers" and "Torches" [or "Lamps"]); another image which many of these titles put forward as an aspect of their works is that of disorder ("Hold-all," "Meadow/Field," "Impromptu," "Fruit-basket"). Many make explicit reference to their nature as collections, or to the paraphernalia of collecting activity; "Fruits of my Reading," "Gleanings from Early Authors," "Discoveries," "Memorabilia," and "Tablet." Aulus Gellius would have known of Pliny's *Natural Histories*; this passage was a mocking play on his protests; his own title, *Attic Nights*, belongs to the subgroup of titles referring to their own collecting process. This general tradition of book titling is also the convention within which Clement christened his *Stromateis* ("Tapestries")—mention of this title by Gellius in the middle of the second century shows that Clement was not the first to use it. Many of these works probably offered miscellaneous excerpts, with or without connecting comments, in a very lightly edited form.

Gellius' belittling claims about his own work are somewhat disingenuous. The echo of Pliny's comments was entirely deliberate; Leofranc Holford-Strevens wrote:

> . . . when we find among these more elegant titles 'Natural History' (§8), far less inspired than 'Attic Nights', we cease to take Gellius' humility at

---

[22] Attic Nights, preface 2-12. Text and translation from *The Attic Nights of Aulus Gellius,* vol. 1, ed. and transl. John C. Rolfe (Cambridge MA: Harvard University Press, 1984) xxvii-xxxi.

face value. 'Pliny was a dry old stick,' he is saying, 'but I can improve on even the fancy titles, let alone his.' He was right.[23]

The *Attic Nights* appears as a sequence of notes on unrelated topics, mostly philological, biographical, historical, and legal, with some ethical philosophy and some "scientific" curiosities, arranged in a seemingly random order. René Marache observed,

> Aulu-Gelle a ainsi noté des détails de toute sorte, sans choix ni dessein prémédité. Puis il a repris ses notes en éliminant vraisemblablement pas mal, mais il le dit nettement, sans aucun souci d'y introduire un ordre, quel qu'il fût.[24]

The individual chapters range in length from a few lines to several pages, and are grouped into twenty books. It is probable that for the most part they do follow the haphazard order of his collecting efforts, but this cannot be the whole story. Four quotations from Cicero's *Orator*, from sections 158, 159, and two from 168, appear in books 15, 2, 13 and 18 respectively, while in book 10, material is cited from Hyginus' commentary on Virgil's *Aeneid* 6 dealing with verses 365-6 first, then 122-3, then 617-19.[25] More typically material from a single source is treated in a block or in close proximity. Obviously, the work had undergone some editing and rearrangement, although Marache called the composition of the individual chapters "peu rigoureuse" and Holford-Strevens characterized the final editing as "somewhat slipshod."[26] Nevertheless, Marache was correct that the excerpts are the "raison d'être" of the work. A random order of topics was both the natural result of the original collecting process and a trait which was seen as desirable, providing in variety a hedge against tedium. Despite some evidence of tampering with the original order in which the material was collected (which can partly be explained as motivated by a desire to break up an excessively long discussion of a single theme or by a single author), Gellius' claims, that he has reproduced the random order of collecting in his published work, and has striven to avoid tiresomeness, seem approximately accurate. Nevertheless, most of Gellius' text is his own

---

[23] Leofranc Holford-Strevens, *Aulus Gellius* (Chapel Hill: University of North Carolina Press, 1988) 21.

[24] René Marache, *Aulu-Gelle. Les Nuits Attiques. Livres I-IV* (Paris: Société d'édition "Les Belles Lettres," 1967) xvi.

[25] These examples, along with some others which are quite probable (but just possibly circumstantial) are given by Holford-Strevens, *Aulus Gellius*, 26.

[26] Marache, *Aulu-Gelle*, xvii and Holford-Strevens, *Aulus Gellius* 24.

prose recounting and commenting on others' ideas and opinions; excerpts there are in abundance, but his is the most frequent voice.

The following characteristics are found in the *Attic Nights*:

- an introduction by the collector;
- comments, explanations, and development by the collector;
- attribution of excerpted material;
- considerable variation in the size of units, including very short to relatively long;
- some redistribution of materials when much has been taken from a single author, in accordance with a stated aim of avoiding tedium;
- a claim that the work follows the random order of collecting;
- some thematic and motif clusters.

The Influence of Anthologies on Original Composition

We are dealing here with a curious literary phenomenon, one which it would be perilous to the investigator of ancient collections to ignore. Alongside genuine notebooks, which without a doubt existed, there were pseudo-notebooks which affected the discontinuous style of the genuine article; they seem to have been generated by subjecting real notebooks to a more or less superficial editing. Nor were these published miscellanies the limit of this trend. Excerpting and anthologizing were so popular that their disjointed style even came to influence the writings of original authors. Miriam Lichtheim commented,

> The anthologizing activity also affected the form of individual moral treatises. 1. Some treatises were so loaded with quotations as to become loose in structure. The now lost writings of the Stoic Chrysippus were said to have been thus overloaded, and the manner is apparent in some works of Plutarch, be they genuine or spurious. 2. Some moral treatises came to consist of minimally connected sequences of admonitory sayings arranged in short paragraphs. The Pseudo-Isocratean instructional speech *Ad Demonicum* is a famous early example. 3. The ultimate form—personal thoughts of a moralist formulated in aphorisms—is present in the reflections of the emperor Marcus Aurelius. 4. There was a blurring of the distinction between the work of an individual moralist and a compilation of moral sententiae attributed to a certain author. A popular collection of the latter kind was the *Sentences of Sextus*. 5. The aphoristic trend affected

moralizing poetry, such as that of Chares, and Phoinix of Colophon, the remnants of whose poetry show that they versified moral lessons in the form of short paragraphs."[27]

We will encounter the results of this trend over and over again.

THE CULTURE OF EXCERPTING AND THE CATEGORY "GENRE"

The parameters of our inquiry—works composed of relatively short units derived from multiple sources—encloses a considerable range of phenomena.

At one end of the spectrum lie private notebooks of extracts arranged only in the order in which the material was encountered, such as the elder Pliny's lost notebooks. Such private notebooks were organized by chronological circumstances and practical considerations only. Sometimes private notebooks, as we have seen, became public; moreover, some intentionally published works were (or claimed to be) generated in the same way, and expressed pride in their haphazard organization. While very few clear examples of completely unedited or minimally edited works have survived, very many of them must have existed; it would seem inherently unlikely that they would show a consistent set of formal characteristics. Analysis of the "genre" of a genuine notebook would be about as relevant as analysis of the "genre" of its nearest modern counterpart, a stack of photo-copied pages from various books and articles, made for private reference and arranged chronologically in the order in which they were copied. We must be sensitive to the possibility that some documents were shaped by excerpting practices and the limitations imposed by the materials available for those practices, by the compiler's interests, and by chance, rather than by conscious or unconscious participation in any literary form.[28]

At the other end of this spectrum, our parameters also include groups of texts which quite clearly do share conventions which are consciously literary conventions, not merely similarities derived from common needs and materials. Multiple author epigram collections constitute a genre (or several genres) wholly contained within the boundaries of our parame-

---

[27] Miriam Lichtheim, *Late Egyptian Wisdom Literature in the International Context. A Study of Demotic Instructions.* (Orbis biblicus et orientalis 52; Göttingen: Vandenhoeck & Ruprecht, 1983) 25-6
[28] Clement's *Excerpta ex Theodoto* is an example of such a notebook.

ters, in that they exhibit certain conventions which distinguish them from single-author collections of epigrams, and their units are by definition relatively short.[29] Collections of sayings and/or anecdotes can focus on a single person (in which case they fall outside the parameters of immediate relevance to the *Gospel according to Philip*),[30] or on many people—the latter sort generally find coherence in a theme (such as bravery) or a class of people (such as generals).[31] Instructions often involve the conceit of a single author, but even when this is developed, they include folk proverbs and wise sayings that circulated internationally, as well as material which may be peculiar to their author/compiler.[32]

Collections of miscellaneous wise sayings or aphorisms also circulated, with neither individual attribution nor much to develop or reinforce a link to a single author. These were generally at least titled with someone's name, but often represent collections of ideologically, as well as formally, diverse material.[33] Perhaps the oddest category of these collections are the ones which consist of brief excerpts from the work of a single dramatist. Although these were drawn from a single author, they do not represent a single point of view, since they were taken from the mouths of many different characters, with different commitments and motivations, in assorted dramatic situations.[34]

---

[29] For example, the *Garlands* of Meleager and of Philip, preserved in the *Greek Anthology*.

[30] As does, for example, Lucian's account of the wit and wisdom of the philosopher Demonax (see *Lucian I* ed. A. M. Harmon (Cambridge, MA: Harvard University Press, 1953) 141-173), or the *Gospel according to Thomas*, or the synoptic gospels' Sayings Source ("Q").

[31] For example, pseudo-Plutarch's various apophthegm collections and *Pirqe 'Abot*

[32] Such as the *Instruction* of Papyrus Insinger, or the collections included in the book of Proverbs.

[33] Such as the *Sentences of Sextus* and the collections derived from it or its sources.

[34] Two examples are the *Sentences* of Publilius Syrus (*Minor Latin Poets* ed. J. W. Duff and A. M. Duff [Cambridge, MA: Harvard University Press, 1935] 3-111), and the several collections which formed around a core of material excerpted from Menander (*Menandri Sententiae* ed. S. Jaeckel [Leipzig: Teubner, 1964]). Each of these also happens to represent not a single document but an entire tradition, in which practically every copy was a significantly different version. See Henry Chadwick, "Florilegium," *Reallexikon für Antike und Christentum*. Stuttgart: Anton Hiersemann, 1969, 7.1131-1160.
   These contrast strongly with true single author collections such as Epicurus' *Kyriai doxai,* compiled by Epicurus himself or a close disciple (quoted in full by Diogenes Laertius, *Lives* 10.138-144,) or the *Sentences of Porphyry*, which pro-

The validity with which these collections of unattributed aphorisms can be treated as a genre is open to question. By nature, they lack most of the features discussed above. Max Küchler wrote: "Die mehr oder weniger lose Aneinanderreihung kurzer, möglichst prägnanter Worte is die einzige sich durchhaltende formale Gemeinsamkeit."[35] Echoing Küchler, Miriam Lichtheim wrote, "What is shared by all collections of *logoi sophon* and makes of them a single genre despite differences in situation, intention, authorship, and level is the looseness of form."[36] If a core of demonstrable formal features is desirable for the designation of a genre—preferably accompanied by similar functions and partially analogous social settings—statements such as these are very far indeed from adequate designations of a genre.

When sample texts from this somewhat wider range of collections are analyzed for their organizing principles, a curious situation is revealed. Documents composed of material of similar subject, or of similar formal units, are not characterized by distinctive organizing principles. Conversely, collections of materials markedly different in subject or form (on the level of individual units) often share many of the same organizing principles. The literary features that have generally been used to mark out genres or subgenres of collections mostly have to do with introductory matter (proems of epigram collections, exordia of the instructions), or clues to the collection's function or social setting, or they have depended upon the nature of the materials involved, either the form of individual units (epigrams, apophthegms, monostichic sayings, et cetera), or their subject matter. As we shall see, the principles by which the bodies of collections were arranged seem to have been chosen from a smorgasbord of known possibilities, without any regard for the apparent function of the collection under construction, or the form or subject matter of the units being collected. Perhaps it is better to think in terms of the relation of the apparent purposes of the collection to its individual organizing strategies, and the degree to which the result

---

vided, in the form of excerpts gleaned from his writings (perhaps by himself) a quick guide to his thought. (See *Diogenes Laertius. Lives of Eminent Philosophers* transl. R. D. Hicks [Cambridge, MA: Harvard University Press, 1965] and Thomas Davidson, "The Sentences of Porphyry the Philosopher" *Journal of Speculative Philosophy* 3 [1869] 46-73.)

[35] Max Küchler, *Frühjüdische Weisheittraditionen* (Göttingen: Vandenhoeck & Ruprecht, 1979) 258.

[36] Lichtheim, *Late Egyptian Wisdom Literature*, 27. Lichtheim cites Küchler, among others, in support of this assessment.

is (or is not) modeled after other published collections. The former is a matter of practical considerations; the latter situates a work within a generic matrix already traversed by multiple crisscrossing trajectories.

CHAPTER FOUR

ORGANIZING PRINCIPLES OF SOME COLLECTIONS

Since the *Gospel according to Philip* was almost undoubtedly composed after the end of the first century and before the beginning of the fourth, material from the second and third centuries will be taken as constituting the document's immediate milieu. Only collections of relatively short units of material from multiple sources will be considered. Since this literature is not well preserved, we will also consider materials from the first century as evidence of trends which were already established, and probably not yet extinct, at the time the *Gospel according to Philip* was written, and editorial principles evident in earlier works which were still being edited (as opposed to merely copied) at that time.

Demotic Instructions

Demotic Egyptian instructions were still being edited and revised in the first centuries of the common era. They stand at the culmination of a very long tradition which, in the Ptolemaic period, developed in some new directions under the influence of Greek literary (and "subliterary") forms.

Pre-Demotic Egyptian instructions typically wove their component "sayings" into coherent discourses.[1] Some of these sayings were undoubtedly traditional proverbial material, and some of them may have been imported sayings of "international" circulation. Nevertheless, their existence as independent units was systematically obscured in the classical Egyptian instruction. Sections of considerable length could be organized in formulaic ways: in the *Instruction of Ptahhotep*, most sections have a three-fold organization: sketch of a possible situation, imperatives, generalizing explanation. In the *Instruction of Any* and the *Instruction of Amenope*, a command or prohibition is followed by explanation or motivation. Often the matter is immediately repeated in a second, parallel command-explanation pair. Sometimes longer tripartite forms are used, as in *Ptahhotep*. A general topic is usually considered through a number

---

[1] I am dependent on Miriam Lichtheim, *Late Egyptian Wisdom Literature*, 6-22, for the background information on pre-Demotic instructions.

of these sequences before a new reflection is introduced. The result is that classical Egyptian instructions are fairly similar in form to the integrated speeches of Proverbs 1-9, and contrast with the looser collections of predominantly bipartite statements in the collections in the later sections of Proverbs.

In Ptolemaic times, several new trends emerged. Extremely terse aphorisms came into vogue, seemingly in imitation of Greek forms. The *Instruction of Ankhsheshonqy*, according to Miriam Lichtheim, takes over material both from earlier Egyptian collections and from such internationally circulating works as the Aramaic *Wisdom of Ahiqar*. Despite the use in these sources of a varied prose style which employed sentences of different lengths and types, which were often linked in larger groupings, the *Instruction of Ankhsheshonqy* reformulates its material into simple, asyndetic statements. This stylistic move is even supplied with a fictional context: the narrative introduction describes Ankhsheshonqy in prison, allowed a writing palette but denied papyrus on which to write; he wrote instructions for his son on pottery sherds. These monostichic pronouncements are, nevertheless, arranged according to several principles in the *Instruction of Ankhsheshonqy*.[2] Lichtheim commented:

> If reliance on the monostich went hand in hand with an aphoristic manner of composition, our author yet availed himself of some elementary devices for achieving a modicum of order. His devices are three: 1. The pairing of monostichs. 2. The chain of anaphoric sentences. 3. The verbal association as a means of moving from one topic to another.[3]

Monostichic statements are often given in pairs. Lichtheim divided these pairings into several types: pairs which have the same form; pairs which state similar principles; pairs in which the second monostich gives a rationale for the first; pairs in which the second illustrates the first; pairs in which the first provides a context for the second, which would otherwise be terse to the point of obscurity.[4] For example:

> Do not be a hindrance often, lest you be reviled.
> Do not get drunk often, lest you rave. [same form]

---

[2] For further discussion, see Lichtheim, *Late Egyptian Wisdom Literature*, 28-65.

[3] Lichtheim, *Late Egyptian Wisdom Literature*, 63.

[4] Lichtheim *Late Egyptian Wisdom Literature*, 10-11 and 35-36. I have somewhat rephrased her categories.

It is better to dwell in your small house than to dwell in the large house of another.
Better is small wealth gathered than large wealth scattered. [similar principles]

Do well by your body in the days of your well-being.
There is no one who does not die. [second gives rationale for first]

Do not be impatient when you suffer so as to beg for death.
He who is alive, his herb grows. [second illustrates first]

Do not often clean yourself with water only.
Water grinds the stone. [first provides context for obscure second][5]

Lichtheim also identified three types of chains of anaphoric sentences: enumerative quatrains, quatrains building to a conclusion, and sorites.[6] Again, in her examples,

The waste of a house is not dwelling in it.
The waste of a woman is not knowing her.
The waste of a donkey is carrying bricks.
The waste of a boat is carrying straw. [enumerative quatrain]

Borrow money at interest and put it in farmland.
Borrow money at interest and take a wife.
Borrow money at interest and celebrate your birthday.
Do not borrow money at interest in order to live well on it. [quatrain
      building to conclusion]

Do not insult a common man.
When insult occurs beating occurs.
When beating occurs killing occurs.
Killing does not occur without the god knowing.
Nothing occurs except what the god ordains. [sorites][7]

This last example, in which a chain of monostichs is arranged as a series of verbally and logically interlocking statements, is an organizing principle of considerable sophistication. Known to Greek rhetoric as a *sorites*, it is a type of "repeated word" rhetorical device which extends beyond simple and mechanical "catch word association" in two ways: (1)

---

[5] Lichtheim gives these examples; they are *Ankhsheshonqy* 11.5-6, 23.8-9, 19.15-16, 8.7-8, 17.12-13.

[6] Lichtheirm, *Late Egyptian Wisdom Literature*, 63-64.

[7] *Ankhsheshonqy* 20.22-25, 16.9-12, 22.21-25.

multiple words are involved; often, one of these words is involved in the subject and predicate of each statement. (2) Logic is involved, even if the chain of reasoning is somewhat loose.

"Verbal associations" are the third type of organizing device Lichtheim found in the *Instruction of Ankhsheshonqy*. They are another sort of "repeated word" rhetorical device. Like the sorites, the linking words can involve both subject and predicate of many sentences in a series, but unlike the sorites, the result does not add up to a logical conclusion. The sequence may circle a theme tightly, or just amble along, guided by trivial verbal associations, nevertheless giving to the whole a specious sense of unity. Lichtheim cites the following passage, underlining the associating words:

(6) The friend of a fool is a fool, the friend of a wise man is a wise man.

(7) The friend of a stupid man is a stupid man.

(8) The mother gives birth, the way makes a friend.

(9) Every man acquires property; it is a wise man who knows how to protect it.

(10) Do not hand over your property to your younger brother, so as to let him become your elder brother thereby.

(11) Do not prefer one of your children to another; you do not know which of them will be kind to you.

(12) If you find your wife with her lover get yourself a worthy bride.

(13) Do not acquire a maidservant for your wife if you do not have a manservant.

(14) Do not acquire two voices.

(15) Speak truth to all men; let it cleave to your speech.

(16) Do not open your heart to your wife; what you have spoken to her goes to the street.

(17) Do not open your heart to your wife or to your servant.

(18) Open your heart to your mother; the woman is discreet.

(19) A woman—her affairs is what she knows.

(20) Instructing a woman is (having) a sack of sand whose side is split open.[8]

Lichtheim has been conservative in her underlining of the key words she has identified; their interlocking effect is, however, readily visible on the page. Her commentary makes it clear how this works, despite the unrelated nature of the individual units:

---

[8] *Ankhsheshonqy* 13.6-20, Lichtheim, *Late Egyptian Wisdom Literature*, 64.

Lines 6-7 form a pair in which the key word is "friend." Line 8 is a pun
on *mw.t,* "mother," and *my.t,* "way," in which the recurrence of the word
"friend" creates an associative link with the preceding lines without there
being a logical connection. Lines 9-10 form a pair on the new topic
"property," and the reappearance of the term "wise man" touches the
chord struck in lines 6 and 9. The new key term "brother' in line 10 leads
by mental, though not verbal, association to "children" in line 11; and
"children" in turn evokes "wife" in line 12. Thereafter, lines 12-13 are
linked through the word "wife," and the word "acquire" in line 13 carries
forward to the new topic of "not acquiring" two voices, in line 14. Lines
14-15 form a pair on the theme of speaking the truth; and the notion of
"speech" brings on the topic of "discreet speech" in lines 16-18. Then, the
word "woman" in line 18 evokes the new topic "woman," which occupies
lines 19-22.[9]

These links involve repetition of words, plays on similar-sounding
words, and associations of related ideas, but it is important to note that
this does not make of the whole a coherent discourse, much less is there
any reason to believe that these repetitions form the "key" to a second,
esoteric meaning.

The *Instruction of Papyrus Insinger* is also resolutely monostichic,
avoiding the use of grammatical connectives such as "and" or "but."[10] In
P. Insinger, each sentence is placed on a separate line, while in some
fragmentary copies, the sentences are separated by blank spaces; thus it is
evident that the monostichic form was viewed by the scribes of these
manuscripts as important. The actual ordering of its monostichs depends
on parallel or antithetical pairs, anaphoric chains, and logical (though
asyndetic) connections. The hymn in Instruction 24, together with the
monostichs which lead into it, illustrate these techniques and the remarkably high level of unity which could be achieved with them:

> The impious man does not say "there is god" in the fortune which he de-
> crees.
>
> He who says "It cannot happen" should look to what is hidden.
>
> How do the sun and moon go and come in the sky?
>
> Whence go and come water, fire, and wind?
>
> Through whom do amulet and spell become remedies?
>
> The hidden work of the god, he makes it known on the earth daily.
>
> He created light and darkness with every creature in it.
>
> He created the earth, begetting millions, swallowing (them) up and
> begetting again.

---

[9] Lichtheim, *Late Egyptian Wisdom Literature,* 64-65.
[10] Lichtheim, *Late Egyptian Wisdom Literature,* 110.

He created day, month, and year through the commands of the lord of command.

He created summer and winter through the rising and setting of Sothis.

He created food before those who are alive, the wonder of the fields.

He created the constellations of those that are in the sky, so that those on earth would learn them.

He created sweet water in it which all the lands desire.

He created the breath in the egg though there is no access to it.

He created birth in every womb from the semen which they receive.

He created sinews and bones out of the same semen.[11]

The bulk of the *Instruction* of P. Insinger is rather less unified, however, and (like that of *Ankhsheshonqy*) concentrates on moral and prudential advice and observations.

It is divided into chapters with headings indicating their contents, which are fairly consistent with the announced theme. Five chapters appear in a different order in P. Carlsberg II:

P. Carlsberg, II instruction	= P. Insinger, instruction
6	6
7	7
8	8
9	9
10	10
11	11
12	12
13	missing
14	18
15	19
16	21
17	14
18	22 [12]

Lichtheim sums up the result: "Thus, instead of P. Insinger's sequence, in chapters 14-18: Control fools—Shun greed—Enjoy life—Avoid worry—Be patient, P. Carlsberg has: Be patient—Be calm—Shun all vices—Control fools—Stay home."[13] Volten dates P. Carlsberg II to Roman Imperial times (and P. Carlsberg III to around 100 C.E. or later),[14] so it seems that the text of this instruction was still fluid around the time when

---

[11] P. Insinger 31.18-32.9. Only the first half of the hymn proper is quoted above. See Lichtheim, *Late Egyptian Wisdom Literature*, 230-231.

[12] Table simplified from Aksel Volten, *Kopenhagener Texte zum demotischen Weisheitsbuch. (Pap. Carlsberg II, III verso, IV verso und V).* (Kopenhagen: Munksgaard, 1940) 4.

[13] Lichtheim, *Late Egyptian Wisdom Literature*, 116.

[14] Volten, *Kopenhagener Texte*, 6-7.

the *Gospel according to Philip* was being compiled, not only read and copied but also rearranged and "improved."

The *Instruction* of P. Insinger ends every chapter with a somewhat formulaic sequence of paradoxical statements. Lichtheim believed that, in their original form, each consisted of two statements beginning "there is one who" (*wn pꜣ nty*), followed by a pair of negative observations (beginning with the negative particle *bn*), followed by three concluding lines which attribute the whole situation to the deity. For example, Instruction 8 concludes:

> There is one who lives on little so as to save, yet he becomes poor.
> There is one who does not know, yet the fate gives (him) wealth.
> It is not the wise man who saves who finds a reserve.
> Nor is it the one who spends who becomes poor.
> The god gives a wealth of provisions without an income.
> He also gives poverty in the purse without spending.
> The fate and the [fortune] that come, it is the god who sends them.[15]

The relativity and fatalism of these chapter endings contrast strikingly with the emphasis on self-control and accomplishment in the bulk of the instruction. The pattern, if it was followed consistently in the original, has been abbreviated in many instances; Lichtheim felt that where it was deficient in some way it was due to a deliberate attempt to soften the impact of these statements. If this is so, it points again to ongoing redactional activity.

Organizing Principles in Demotic Egyptian Instructions
Demotic instructions, at least in the form in which they are preserved from late Ptolemaic and Roman Egypt, can show the following organizing principles:

- narrative introduction presenting a real or fictional life situation of instruction;
- compiled thematic chain of monostichs to introduce instruction proper;
- reduction of source material to monostichic, asyndetic form;
- non-attribution of source materials;
- parallel, supporting, contextualizing, and antithetical pairings of monostichs;
- chains of anaphoric monostichs, topically related or unrelated;

---

[15] P. Insinger 7.13-19. Lichtheim, *Late Egyptian Wisdom Literature*, 203.

- repeating formula for sequences ending sections;
- use of multiple catch word associations in material not otherwise related;
- thematic chapters (subject to rearrangement);
- monostichs arranged into a "chain syllogism" or sorites.

The Garland *of Meleager and the* Garland *of Philip*

The *Garlands* of Meleager and of Philip are the two oldest components in a larger work now known as the *Greek Anthology* or *Palatine Anthology*. This tenth or eleventh century manuscript is an enormous collection of epigrams of every kind. A substantial revision of the work, in a manuscript signed and dated (confusingly, to both 1299 and 1301) by its editor, Maximus Planudes, also exists (the *Planudean Anthology*). Both point back to a major collecting effort on the part of one Constantine Cephalas around the beginning of the tenth century.[16] Cephalas' work, now lost but very close to the collection contained in the Palatine manuscript, was a combination of three earlier collections and supplemental materials from a number of other sources.[17] These earlier collections were the *Cycle of Agathias*, the *Garland of Philip*, and the *Garland of Meleager*. The proems introducing each of these three collections are included in the *Greek Anthology* as chapter 4, while large blocks of material from each collection are distributed throughout the whole. Agathias collected in the middle of the sixth century, and so is of little importance to an inquiry into the milieu of the *Gospel according to Philip*. Philip the collector of epigrams, however, assembled his *Garland* sometime in the first century C.E. and clearly took Meleager's work, composed in the 90s B.C.E., as a model.[18]

The ΣΤΕΦΑΝΟΣ *of Meleager*
Although Meleager spent his later life on the island of Cos, he was born in Gadara east of the Sea of Galilee and educated at Tyre; the Greek-speaking subculture that formed him was part of the complex fabric of

---

[16] The exact relation of the two extant works, and of five minor collections of the same period, is in some debate, but it need not concern us here. See Alan Cameron, *The Greek Anthology from Meleager to Planudes* (Oxford, Clarendon, 1993).

[17] Including some first century sources. The poet Strato seems to have written in the time of Hadrian or Nero, while Rufinus wrote under Nero or a little later (see Cameron, *Meleager to Planudes*, 65-69), but it is not clear that either included poetry not his own in his published work.

[18] Cameron, *Meleager to Planudes*, 49-65.

Hellenized western Syria. He assembled the first known book length
collection of epigrams from multiple authors. Before his work, we know
only of collections of the work of individual poets or the sayings of individual figures, along with small, private collections of favorite poems
and passages; Alan Cameron has speculated that librarians "might well
have had [such collections] copied seriatim into a series of consecutively
numbered rolls without ever contemplating the drastic step (and extra labor) of amalgamating and rearranging the work of different poets."[19] By
bringing together something on the order of 800 to 1000 epigrams from
many different authors, geographical areas, and time periods, on a wide
range of themes, and by interweaving them artistically, Meleager pio-
neered the literary genre of the epigram anthology.[20]

The proem of his collection likens the epigrams of each of forty-seven
poets to some flower or other plant matter.[21] The relations of the poets to
the plant matter is not always clear, but the range of botanical materials is
considerable: here are the expected lilies, roses, iris, violets, but also
greenery such as pine needles, wheat stalks, young olive shoots, "the
fine-leaved white poplar of Tymnes," and "the first grown branches from
the heaven-high palm tree;" aromatics, too, such as marjoram, mint, gin-
ger grass, spurge, and spikenard. He even includes a bunch of grapes and
some hazel-nuts. The image of this rococo and partially edible "garland"
is Hellenistic and vaguely oriental; Meleager uses it to image, at the
beginning of his work, the diversity of the authors and poems he will se-
lect. Moreover, the proem makes much use of verbs such as πλέκω,
ἐμπλέκω, συμπλέκω (all variations on "twist, braid, weave"), μίγνυμι,
ἀναμίγνυμι ("mix, mix up"), but also κείρω ("cut, cut up") and
διακρίζω ("pull to pieces"), foreshadowing one of Meleager's main
organizing principles, the alternation of authorial voices.

One of the scribes of the Palatine anthology, who also included some
notes (of dubious value),[22] claimed that Meleager's *Garland* was origi-

---

[19] Cameron, *Meleager to Planudes*, 10.

[20] He also influenced expectations as to the length of individual epigrams. Cameron
wrote of the considerable length and assorted meters of poems identified as epigrams
in early Hellenistic times, ". . . they do not look like epigrams to us, but this is because
our definitions of the Hellenistic epigram is essentially Meleager's." Cameron, *Meleager to Planudes*, 13.

[21] See *The Greek Anthology* 4.1.

[22] Cameron's opinion is that the lemmatist simply made a guess about the
arrangement of Meleager's *Garland*—a reasonable guess, based on an understanding
of the influence of Meleager on Philip and of the arrangement in Philip, but a wrong
guess nonetheless. The Palatine lemmatist makes at least one other conjecture which is

nally arranged alphabetically, but this seems unlikely, since the uninterrupted blocks of Meleagrian material which survive in the *Greek
Anthology* show no traces of alphabetical order (although some small
groups of poems begin with the same word and so necessarily with the
same letter).

Meleager did use some principles in ordering his material, however.
While Constantine Cephalas divided the material he edited into nine categories, Meleager's collection seems to have been divided into only
four.[23] Except for the fact that Cephalas attempted to divide the erotic
poems into hetero- and homosexual themes (without great success),
Meleager's categories correspond to Cephalas', so that where there are
unbroken sequences of Meleagrian authors, the order and juxtaposition of
poems within these sequences can be assigned to Meleager with a fair degree of confidence.

Within his category divisions, Meleager regularly broke up the work
of the more prolific authors with the work of others. For example, the list
of authors for one of the two Meleagrian sequences in book 9 of the
Greek Anthology, the epideictic poems, is as follows:

313 Anyte	326 Leonidas of Tarentum
314 "the same"	327 Hermocreon
315 Nicias	328 Damostratus
316 Leonidas of Tarentum	329 Leonidas of Tarentum
317 anonymous	330 Nicarchus
318 Leonidas of Tarentum	331 Meleager
319 Philoxenus	332 Nossis
320 Leonidas of Tarentum	333 Mnasalcas
321 Antimachus	334 Perses
322 Leonidas of Tarentum	335 Leonidas of Tarentum
323 Antipater of Sidon	336 Callimachus
324 Mnasalcas	337 Leonidas of Tarentum
325 Anonymous	338 Theocritus[24]

Leonidas of Tarentum, with eight epigrams out of twenty-six in this sequence (or nearly one third of the total), is clearly Meleager's most prolific writer of epideictic poems, but there are no two consecutive poems

---

highly unlikely. Cameron, *Meleager to Planudes*, 23, 49-50.

[23] Erotica (5.134-215 and 12.36-174), anathematica (6.109-157, 262-313, 351-358),
epitymbia (7.406-506, 646-665, 707-740), and epideictica (9.313-338 and 563-568)
See Cameron, *Meleager to Planudes*, 26-33. The sequences of poems given here in
parentheses are only the major sequences of Meleagrian material; numerous shorter
runs, as well as isolated epigrams, by Meleagrian authors also appear.

[24] For the poems themselves, see *The Greek Anthology III*, ed. and transl. W. R. Paton (Cambridge, MA: Harvard University Press, 1958) 168-183.

by him. His work has been divided and interwoven with the work of others in such a way that he does not seem to dominate, and we do not tire of his voice.

Meleager also grouped poems into small clusters around a particular motif[25] Among the dedicatory epigrams in book 6 of the *Greek Anthology*, in a long Meleagrian sequence, we find such groupings as 270-274, five dedications made by women after childbirth.

Meleager was sometimes willing to include an epigram in an inappropriate category, when the shared motif was striking. For example, he inserted a series of (at least) seven consecutive poems about grasshoppers into his division of sepulchral epigrams. The first of this series, the third, and the last two do have the form of tomb inscriptions, however tongue in cheek, for deceased insects. Among these, Meleager inserted three which did not conform to that convention, two of which he wrote himself:

193 ΣΙΜΙΟΥ
Τάνδε κατ᾽ εὔδενδρον στείβων
  δρίος εἴρυσα χειρὶ
πτώσσουσαν βρομίης οἰνάδος ἐν
  πετάλοις,
ὄφρα μοι εὐερκεῖ καναχὰν δόμῳ
  ἔνδοθι θείη,
τερπνὰ δι᾽ ἀγλώσσου φθεγγομένα
  στόματος.

193 Simias
This locust crouching in the leaves of a vine I caught as I was walking in this copse of fair trees, so that in a well-fenced home it may make noise for me, chirping pleasantly with its tongueless mouth.

195 ΜΕΛΕΑΓΡΟΥ
Ακρίς, ἐμῶν ἀπάπημα πόθων,
  παραμύθιον ὕπνου,
ἀκρίς, ἀρουραίη Μοῦσα,
  λιγυπτέρυγε,

195 Meleager
Locust, beguiler of my loves, persuader of sleep, locust, shrill-winged Muse of the corn fields,

---

[25] See Cameron, *Meleager to Planudes*, xvii-xviii (Table) and 19-33 for a discussion of Meleager's structure. Carl Radinger (*Meleagros von Gadara. Eine Litterargeschichtliche Skizze,* Innsbruck: 1895) and Rudolf Weisshäupl (*Die Grabegedichte der Griechischen Anthologie*, Vienna: 1889) discovered this pattern independently; see also Albert Wifstrand (*Studien zur Griechischen Anthologie*, Lund: 1926) for a summary of their findings. These three old but important works have recently been reprinted in *The Greek Anthology I* (Wifstrand and Weisshäupl) and *II* (Radinger), ed. Sonya Lida Tarán, (New York: Garland, 1987).

αὐτοφυὲς μίμημα λύρας, κρέκε
μοί τι ποθεινόν,
ἐγκρούουσα φίλοις ποσσί λάλους
πτέρυγας,ὥς με πόνων ῥύσαιο
παναγρύπνοιο μερίμνης,
ἀκρί, μιτωσαμένη φθόγγον
ἐρωτοπλάνον.
δῶρα δέ σοι γήτειον ἀειθαλὲς
ὀρθρινὰ δώσω,
καὶ δροσερὰς στόματι
σχιζομένας ψακάδας.

Nature's mimic lyre, play for me
some tune I love, beating with thy
dear feet thy talking wings, that
so, locust, thou mayest deliver mé
from the pains of sleepless care,
weaving a song that enticeth Love
away. And in the morning I will
give thee a fresh green leek, and
drops of dew sprayed from my
mouth.

196 ΤΟΥ ΑΥΤΟΥ
Ἀχήεις τέττιξ, δροσεραῖς
σταγόνεσσι μεθυσθείς,
ἀγρονόμαν μέλπεις μοῦσαν
ἐρημολάλον·
ἄκρα δ᾽ ἐφεζόμενος πετάλοις,
πριονώδεσι κώλοις
αἰθίοπι κλάζεις χρωτὶ μέλισμα
λύπας.
ἀλλά, φίλος, φθέγγου τι νέον
δενδρώδεσι Νύμφαις
παίγνιον, ἀντῳδὸν Πανὶ κρέκων
κέλαδον,
ὄφρα φυγὼν τὸν Ἔρωτα,
μεσημβρινὸν ὕπνον ἀγρεύσω
ἐνθάδ᾽ ὑπὸ σκιερᾷ κεκλιμένος
πλατάνῳ.

196 By the Same
Noisy cicada, drunk with dew
drops, thou singest thy rustic ditty
that fills the wilderness with voice,
and seated on the edge of the
leaves, striking with saw-like legs
thy sunburnt skin thou shrillest
music like the lyre's. But sing,
dear, some new tune to gladden
the woodland nymphs, strike up
some strain responsive to Pan's
pipe, that I may escape from Love
and snatch a little midday sleep,
reclining here beneath the shady
plane-tree.[26]

The second in the series of seven, 193, would perhaps make sense as a tombstone or memorial inscription, although it need not be read as such. The two by Meleager himself, however, seem to be written to living insects. Their inclusion among sepulchral epigrams violates the larger the larger thematic sequence, and seems incongruous in tone. Within the smaller cluster of epigrams about insects, however, they seem quite natural and charming.[27] They fit the motif controlling a small section, if not the general category. The inclusion of light-hearted and contrived epitymbia, along with more serious ones, is typical of Meleager's editing procedures.

[26] *Greek Anthology* 7.193, 195-196.
[27] See also Rory B. Egan, "Two Complementary Epigrams of Meleager (A. P. vii 195 and 196)" *Journal of Hellenic Studies* 108 (1988) 24-32.

Another example, also from book 7 of the *Greek Anthology,* is a series of four inscriptions on empty tombs raised for persons who have been lost at sea (7.651-654). The series is prefaced by an epigram, 650, which is not even such a memorial inscription, but which advises against going to sea:

650 [ΦΛΑΚΚΟΥ η] ΦΑΛΑΙΚΟΥ

Φεῦγε θαλάσσια ἔργα, βοῶν δ᾽
ἐπιβάλλευ ἐχέτλῃ,
εἴ τί τοι ἡδὺ μακρᾶς πείρατ᾽
ἰδεῖν βιοτῆς·
ἠπείρῳ γὰρ ἔνεστι μακρὸς βίος·
εἰν ἁλὶ δ᾽ οὔ τως
εὐμαρὲς εἰς πολιὴν ἀνδρὸς ἰδεῖν
κεφαλήν.

650 Phalaecus

Avoid busying thee with the sea, and put thy mind to the plough that the oxen draw, if it is any joy for thee to see the end of a long life. For on land there is length of days, but on the sea it is not easy to find a man with grey hair.[28]

As we have seen, Meleager not only presented a large body of work divided into rough categories, but arranged it according to an aesthetic which included regular variation of authorial voice and the clustering of variations on themes or motifs, which were sometimes allowed to violate the categories. He expressed this aesthetic in the collection's proem, which compared the collection to a garland of different flowers and fruits, artfully woven together, as pleasant as it is without practical use.

The ΣΤΕΦΑΝΟΣ *of Philip*

Philip of Cos published his *Garland* about 40 C.E., or possibly a few decades later.[29] Philip also introduced his collection with a proem which developed the image of a garland of flowers carefully arranged.[30] The proem shows quite clearly that he understood his work as a continuation of Meleager's, presenting only epigrams written since Meleager's time.

Unlike Meleager, Philip did use an "alphabetical" arrangement for his *Garland*, grouping together epigrams beginning with the same initial letter. Unfortunately, because Philip's collection has been preserved by an editor who redistributed the material thematically, these sequences of Philippan material cannot be trusted to represent consecutive runs of epigrams from Philip's arrangement. This arrangement does provide an ad

---

[28] 7.650. Text and translation *The Greek Anthology II,* ed. and transl. W. R. Paton (Cambridge, MA: Harvard University Press, 1960) 346-347.

[29] See Cameron, *Meleager to Planudes,* 56-65.

[30] *Greek Anthology* 4.1.

ditional check (beyond the list of authors in the proem) on the integrity of Philippan sequences in the *Greek Anthology* as sequences at least without insertions of foreign matter, but because his alphabetical scheme did not extend beyond the initial letter of the first word,[31] it cannot be used to reconstruct the original order of the poems.

Because of these circumstances, very much less can be learned about Philip's organizing principles than can be discovered of Meleager's. Presumably, Philip's choice of an alphabetical arrangement allowed him to present a wide variety of subject matter and approach in each section. There is some evidence that, within each initial-letter grouping, Philip (like Meleager) arranged his materials by breaking up the contributions of more prolific authors, and probably also by placing related motifs adjacent to each other. First-letter grouping would have left Philip a great deal of freedom in the actual ordering, perhaps even offering an excuse for playful incongruities.

Organizing Principles in the Garlands *of Meleager and Philip*
In the *Garlands* of Meleager and of Philip, we have seen the following practices:

- introduction by a proem listing the authors included and describing the arrangement of their work by an elaborate metaphor;
- attribution of each item to its author;
- interrupting the work of more prolific authors with other authors' work to avoid large blocks ;
- collection of material of a certain form only, which by definition imposes a variable but relatively short unit;
- organization of materials by broad category;
- organization of materials by initial letter;
- the appearance of a mostly chance order within categories or letter groupings;
- arranging of some small clusters of material by theme or motif;
- adjacent placement of interestingly or amusingly antithetical material.

---

[31] More thorough alphabetization was rare in antiquity. See Lloyd W. Daly, *Contributions to a History of Alphabetization* (Brussels: Latomus, 1967).

Anecdote and Sayings Collections

This section will examine the apophthegm collections attributed to Plutarch, along with his ΓΥΝΑΙΚΩΝ ΑΡΕΤΑΙ (*Virtues of Women*), and the collection *Pirqe ꞋAbot.*

Plutarch (and pseudo-Plutarch)

Plutarch of Chaeronea assembled his collection of anecdotes about virtuous women toward the end of his life, perhaps in the decade 115-125 C.E.[32] Others had made collections of similar subject matter. The Byzantine patriarch Photius[33] recorded that he had read a twelve volume collection of extracts, entitled ΕΚΛΟΓΑΙ ΔΙΑΦΟΡΟΙ, *Various Extracts*, by one Sopater, which contained among many other things extracts from three such collections: an *Accounts of Deeds Done Courageously by Women* by one Artemon of Magnesia, a *Women Who Were Philosophers or Otherwise Accomplished Something Noteworthy, or through Whom Houses Were Joined in Good Will*, by Apollonius the Stoic, and an anonymous *Women Lifted to Great Fame and Brilliant Reputation.*[34] The *Suda* also

---

[32] Philip Stadter defends this date on the basis of correspondences with other of Plutarch's works and the datable activities of the dedicant of the work, Flavia Clea. The authenticity of this collection has seldom been doubted, and stylistic studies have supported it. See Stadter, *Plutarch's Historical Methods. An Analysis of the Mulierum Virtutes*, (Cambridge, MS: Harvard University Press, 1965) 1-3.

[33] Photius probably assembled his ΒΙΒΛΙΟΘΗΚΗ between the years 843 and 858, after the banning of iconoclast authors and before the first of his two patriarchates. See Warren T. Treadgold, *The Nature of the Bibliotheca of Photius* (Washington, DC: Dumbarton Oaks/Harvard University, 1980) 26-28.

Treadgold remarked of the work itself: "To say that it is a collection of descriptions by Photius of ancient and medieval books which he had read is true as far as it goes. But the *Bibliotheca* belongs to no recognized category of writing. In certain places and in certain respects it resembles a history of literature, a literary autobiography, a work of literary criticism, an anthology, an annotated bibliography, a library catalogue, or a research notebook; but it is none of these consistently." We see here, much later, a work shaped by the needs of the situation rather than by the conventions of a literary genre. Treadgold, *Nature*, vii.

[34] Sopater's latest author was Diogenes Laertius (fl. in the first half of the third century); Sopater himself may have been Sopater of Apamea, who died under Constantine, or possibly Sopater of Athens, who taught around 500 C.E. We know nothing more of Artemon, but if Apollonius the Stoic was Apollonius of Tyre, he wrote in the first century B.C.E. The materials Sopater collected included material from the last centuries before the common era as well as Plutarch and materials up to the early third century, so inclusion in Sopater's twelve volumes gives us little clue as to the date (relative to Plutarch) of authors otherwise unknown.

Sopater's *Various Excerpts* itself is fascinating in its unkempt diversity. It seems to represent the notebooks of a scholar with habits not unlike those of the elder Pliny, which somehow became public, and could possibly date from the third century, and so be roughly contemporaneous with the *Gospel according to Philip*. Its contents were

reported concerning one Charon of Carthage, who wrote four books of biographies of men and four books of biographies of women, possibly somewhat before 146 B.C.E.[35] It, too, is lost. An anonymous collection entitled *Women Intelligent and Courageous in Warfare* has survived and consists of fourteen short histories, most of them attributed to their sources. It is impossible to determine how many similarities of presentation might accompany this similarity of subject matter.

Plutarch's ΓΥΝΑΙΚΩΝ ΑΡΕΤΑΙ (*Virtues of Women*) addressed the specific situation of the death of a woman named Leontis, and Plutarch's conversation with one Clea, for whom he also wrote his exposition on

---

reported by Photius as:

Book 1 was mostly about Greek mythology, with a treatise on the subject by Apollodorus the Athenian, and also contained parts of the second book of a *Treatise on Painting* by Juba, and from the *Banquet of the Sophists* by Athenaeus of Naucratis.

Book 2 contained excerpts from our *Accounts of Deeds Done Courageously By Women* as well as from the *Summaries* of Pamphilia daughter of Soteridas, the *Apophthegms* of Diogenes the Cynic, material from Sappho, and other material.

Book 3 consisted of sections taken from the *Varied Materials* of Favorinus, on the attribution of certain names and similar matters.

Book 4 was composed half from an anonymous *Collection of Wonders* and half from the *Melanges* of Aristoxenus, along with some astonishing and incredible bits from Rufus' *History of the Theatre*.

Book 5 consisted of extracts taken from the first three books of Rufus' *History of Music*.

Book 6 consisted of extracts taken from books 5 and 4 of the same *History of Music*, along with material from the second book of the *Halieutiques* of Damostratus and from books 1, 5, 9 and 10 of Diogenes Laertius' *Lives of the Philosophers*, and from a *History of Alexandria* by Elius Dios and from a *History of Egypt* by Hellanicus of Mitylene.

Book 7 contained material gathered from the history of Herodotus.

Book 8 contained an old anonymous collection, or perhaps a collection of collections, including our list of *Women Lifted up to Great Fame and Brilliant Reputation*, along with other subject matter, some from Plutarch.

Book 9 was a series of extracts from works attributed to Plutarch, including a *Sayings of Famous Men* and the *Sayings of Kings and Commanders*.

Book 10 contained extracts taken from Cephalion's work on the history of Alexandria, our *Women Who Were Philosophers or Otherwise Accomplished Something Noteworthy*, and material from a number of Plutarch's lives.

Book 11 was also a collection of excerpts from Plutarch's lives.

Book 12 was a collection of material from diverse sources: from a work by Callixenus on painters and sculptors, from one by Aristonicus on the Museum at Alexandria, and from Aristotle's *Constitutions*.

See *Photius. Bibliothèque*. Ed. René Henry (Paris: Société d'Édition "Les Belles Lettres," 1960) vol. 2, 123-8; and René Henry, "Remarques a propos des 'codices' 161 et 239 de Photius," *L'Antiquité Classique* 7 (1938) 291-93.

[35] Χάρων, Καρχηδόνιος, ἱστορικός. ἔγραψε . . . Βίους ἐνδόξων ἀνδρῶν ἐν βιβλίοις δ', Βίους γυναικῶν ὁμοίως ἐν τέσσαρσιν. *Suidae Lexicon*, ed. Ada Adler (Stuttgart: Teubner, 1971) Part 4 (P-Y) 791.

Isis and Osiris. The collection is an extension of their conversation. Plutarch meant to refute Thucydides' opinion that the best woman is the one least talked about, and the idea that women's virtues are not the same as men's. His method was to put "lives beside lives and actions beside actions" and consider whether women's virtues have the same character and pattern as men's. He did not quite literally carry out this plan, however: the work lacks acccounts of the lives or actions of men—perhaps they were presumed to be familiar enough to the reader.

After his introduction, Plutarch recounted fifteen stories of women acting together, and twelve of individual women's deeds. The structure consists of the introduction (it lacks any conclusion), the division into stories about groups and about individuals, the parallel nature of the material itself, plus Plutarch's easy mastery of the technique of using multiple historical examples to demonstrate a moral argument. Indeed, these anecdotes were meant to function like miniature parallel lives demonstrating "manly" virtue in women as in men.

Plutarch did not mention his sources for these anecdotes, although he sometimes alluded to his own biographical writings for a fuller account of the circumstances. The substance of nineteen of these twenty-seven stories appeared not quite forty years after Plutarch's death in the *Stratagems* of Polyaenus.[36] It has been debated whether Polyaenus used Plutarch's *Virtues of Women* as his source, or both writers depended on a common source. Each has his own ordering scheme: Plutarch simply divides the stories into those of groups of women and those of individual women, while Polyaenus also divides them geographically; where these schemes are not in conflict, however, the same order is followed. This observation, together with the facts that most of Polyaenus' text also appears in Plutarch, that Polyaenus' accounts are briefer than Plutarch's, and that Polyaenus only occasionally includes details not included by Plutarch (and etiologies for these details can easily be proposed) suggest that Polyaenus used Plutarch's *Virtues of Women* and not a common source, but they do not make a conclusive case for either hypothesis.[37]

Many of Plutarch's stories are connected in various ways to other works of his; some stories are retold, in part or in whole, in some of his

---

[36] Plutarch's stories 5, 10, 8, 6, 1, 14, 4, 16, 17, 18, 19, 20, 24, 25, 27, 11, 7, 2, and 3 appear, in the order given, from book 7.45 through 8.66 of Polyaenus' *Stratagems*.

[37] See Stadter, *Plutarch's Historical Methods*, 13-29 for an overview of the debate (which mostly raged in the late 1800s) and Stadter's own defense of Polyaenus' dependence on Plutarch.

Lives. Some of those other Plutarchan texts make reference to a source for the stories; the nature of these references makes it more unlikely that Plutarch found most of his stories in a single source. For example, the story of the Trojan (soon to be Roman) women (*Virtues of Women* 1) was also narrated by Plutarch in *Romulus* 1 and *Quaestiones Romanae* 6; in the latter text Plutarch mentioned that he knew of multiple versions of the story, set in various locales, but that he followed the version given by Aristotle.[38] The material has been so thoroughly reworked and subordinated to a clearly stated overall purpose that the only structural element left of a collection is that (after the introduction and with the transition from fifteen to sixteen excepted) it consists of a string of short stories. While Plutarch undoubtedly used sources, for isolated facts and for whole stories, this is really a collection of his own work (using those sources) rather than a collection of excerpts or extracts or free-standing pieces of others' work.

Several sayings collections have been attributed to Plutarch. The ΑΠΟΦΘΕΓΜΑΤΑ ΒΑΣΙΛΕΩΝ ΚΑΙ ΣΤΡΑΤΗΓΩΝ (*Sayings of Kings and Commanders*), ΡΩΜΑΙΩΝ ΑΠΟΦΘΕΓΜΑΤΑ (*Sayings of Romans*), ΑΠΟΦΘΕΓΜΑΤΑ ΛΑΚΩΝΙΚΑ (*Sayings of Spartans*), and ΛΑΚΑΙΝΩΝ ΑΠΟΦΘΕΓΜΑΤΑ (*Sayings of Spartan Women*) make use of more of the conventions for ordering collections of material. The *Sayings of Kings and Commanders* is organized both by person, geography and chronology: they are ordered chronologically, except that when attention shifts from one part of the world to another, the chronology must start again; and since all the sayings of each person treated appear together, there is inevitably some overlap in time. The *Sayings of the Romans* follows a similar order, except (of course) that only person and chronology are involved. The first collection has an introduction dedicating it to Trajan; the second lacks any introduction or conclusion. The *Sayings of Spartans* most surprisingly arranges the Spartans whom it treats in true alphabetical order (not just first-letter groupings), a rare practice in antiquity. The much shorter *Sayings of Spartan Women* starts out in alphabetical order also, but after the first three names, one appears out of place, and the rest of the book deals with anonymous women. Neither has introduction or conclusion.

---

[38] Recorded by Dionysius of Halicarnassus, *Roman Antiquities* 1.72.3-4.

Organizing Principles in Plutarch and pseudo-Plutarch
In the collections attributed to Plutarch, the following organizing principles can be seen:

- organization of material by chronology, modified by geography;
- absolute alphabetization;
- collections of material of a single (loosely construed) form: apophthegms;
- collections of materials on a single subject;
- use of repetition of similar or analogous material to make a point.

Pirqe ʾAbot
The Mishnah tractate ʾAbot, composed around 250 C.E., also presents short units of text ascribed to multiple authors, and manages to be one of the most tightly organized of the multi-author collections.[39]

The four of the tractate's five chapters are structured differently from the fifth, and in the first chapter extra care has been taken to make the significance of the structure of the first four apparent.

Chapter one carefully describes the links between each of the people whose sayings are given. It begins with a very brief statement that Moses received the Torah and handed it on to Joshua, Joshua to the elders, the elders to the prophets, the prophets to the men of the great assembly. Three brief maxims are attributed to "them" collectively, and then the actual collection begins with Simeon the Righteous, "one of the last survivors of the great assembly." Typically each speaker's link in this chain is described, then one or a few maxims are given. Some context is given for some sayings.

Explicit references to this chain of authority become scarce after the first chapter, but notations of who was the disciple of whom continue. As Neusner wrote, "The structural program of The Fathers is transparent: (1) a list of names, together with (2) wise sayings."[40] Sometimes a theme continues through a few speakers, but the collection is organized by speaker until chapter five.

There, we encounter a number of lists of things, seemingly unrelated

---

[39] For a convenient text and some analysis of structure, see Jacob Neusner, *Form-Analytical Comparison in Rabbinic Judaism. Structure and Form in The Fathers and The Fathers According to Rabbi Nathan.* (Atlanta: Scholar's Press, 1992). The bulk of this work concerns the directions taken by *ʾAbot de Rabbi Nathan* from *m. ʾAbot* as its base text.

[40] Neusner, *Form-Analytical Comparison*, 4.

to each other except by the number of items in each list. Lists of ten things begin the chapter—ten acts of speech by which the world was made, ten generations from Adam to Noah, ten trials inflicted upon Abraham, ten wonders done in Egypt, and ten at the Red Sea, and ten in the Temple, ten things created on the eve of the Sabbath—then come lists of seven items, then of four. Then follows some unattributed material, developments of a few things at paragraph length. A single list of three items, with a development, follows, and then a few more unattributed sayings.

Organizing Principles in Pirqe ʾAbot
The materials included in *Pirqe ʾAbot* are arranged by the following principles:

- attribution + wise saying;
- carefully drawn links between speakers;
- chronological organization of speakers;
- some weak thematic groupings;
- disparate material involving numbered lists grouped together by number of items.

Clement of Alexandria and Stromateis 8

Clement of Alexandria's *Excerpta ex Theodoto* has frequently been suggested as an analog to the *Gospel according to Philip*: it includes both the opinions and the actual words of more than one person, and is probably an unedited notebook of excerpts, the collector's reflections on the excerpts, and experimental formulations of ideas. It appears in a block of materials titled as the eighth book of Clement's *Stromateis*, sandwiched in between some unconnected explanations of logical matters and a work which develops its themes by alternately quoting and expounding scriptural verses.

Stromateis 8
Book eight of the *Stromateis* of Clement of Alexandria has been preserved in only two manuscripts, the eleventh century Laurentianus V 3 and the sixteenth century Parisinus Suppl. Graec. 250; the latter is a copy of the former.[41] In both manuscripts, the seven books of the *Stromateis*

---

[41] For a fuller description, see Otto Stählin, *Clemens Alexandrinus. Protrepticus und Paidagogus* (Berlin: Akademie-Verlag, 1972) xxix-xlii.

are followed by material titled as an eighth book. The material falls into three main parts: a section on logic, the *Excerpta ex Theodoto*, and the *Eclogae propheticae*. The first section is neither a coherent whole nor a collection: a discussion of logical demonstration (ἀπόδειξις; 1-15.1) is followed by an argument against the skeptics (15.2-24.9), which in turn is followed by a part of a treatise on different kinds of causes (25.1-33.9). Then follows a section entitled *Epitomes from Theodotus and from what is Called the Eastern Teaching from the Time of Valentinus* (ΕΚ ΤΩΝ ΘΕΟΔΟΤΟΥ ΚΑΙ ΤΗΣ ΑΝΑΤΟΛΙΚΗΣ ΚΑΛΟΥΜΕΝΗΣ ΔΙΔΑΣΚΑΛΙΑΣ ΚΑΤΑ ΤΟΥΣ ΟΥΑΛΕΝΤΙΝΟΥ ΧΡΟΝΟΥΣ ΕΠΙΤΟΜΑΙ); then, a section titled *Prophetic Extracts* (ΕΚ ΤΩΝ ΠΡΟΦΗΤΙΚΩΝ ΕΚΛΟΓΑΙ). While the *Stromateis* make a virtue of loose connections and seemingly random juxtaposition, these materials do not form anything so coherent as an eighth book of that work—although all three do display, at times, some of Clement's characteristic terminology and ideas.

One approach to this puzzle, the one most commonly pursued, is to postulate that these sections represent excerpts and epitomes compiled by Clement, with some annotation by him. Later, probably after Clement's death, someone (perhaps his "literary executor") recognized that these notes were made by Clement and were of considerable interest, and saw in the loosely knit *Stromateis* a reasonable (or at least a forgiving) place for them. This hypothesis corresponds well with what we have seen of the literary culture of antiquity and its interest in making and transmitting collections of excerpts.[42] Another hypothesis is that these sections represent lecture notes from Clement's days as a student of Pantaenus.

Pierre Nautin has postulated a third scenario, in which a scribe, copying Clement's *Stromateis* and feeling pressure either for time or materials, abandoned direct transcription after book seven and began excerpting the material.[43] Nautin cites Clement's occasional statements of his plans

---

[42] Pierre Nautin's protest that antiquity did not have the same taste for personal papers, letters, and the like which we have may be true in general, but leaves out of account the culture of excerpting and collecting, and the practical necessities which motivated it. His objection was that in antiquity friends, on the occasion of someone's death, would be more likely to destroy unfinished works than to publish them, especially if they contained anything that might damage the late author's reputation. Again, this presumes that the unfinished works were considered by the friends both useless and easily replaceable, neither of which is likely. He also presumes an atmosphere of doctrinal suspicion perhaps typical of the Christian world a few centuries later but anachronistic in Clement's Alexandria. See Nautin, "La fin des Stromates et les Hypotyposes de Clément d'Alexandrie" *Vigiliae Christianae* 30 (1976) 270-273.

[43] Nautin, "La fin des Stromates," 268-302.

for developing the *Stromateis*, and is able to locate the fulfillment of many of them. In *Stromateis* 4.1.1-3.3, Clement makes such an announcement, claiming that he will deal with martyrdom and human perfection, then with the physical doctrines of the Greeks and their elementary principles, then a refutation from prophecy of the heterodox, and then the science of nature and sacred things, which will include cosmology and theology. At the end of the seventh book, he remarks that ethics has been treated; he proposes to "proceed to what we promised." The book closes with a comparison of its plan to an irregularly planted hill on which fruitless and fruit-bearing trees are mixed; he advises the reader that they "study neither arrangement nor diction," and then proposes to "give the account of what follows from another commencement." Clement clearly promises more writing, and perhaps more of the *Stromateis* (although the "new beginning" is puzzling). Nautin claims that the rest of the plan announced in book four is carried out in the book eight we possess, but that it has been severely condensed. The "elementary principles" of the Greeks mean the discussion of kinds of causes; heterodox doctrine is certainly addressed in the *Excerpta ex Theodoto*; and a consideration of cosmology and theology is found in the *Eclogae propheticae*. Citing Photius' description of Clement's (now lost) *Hypotyposes*, Nautin solves the puzzle by claiming that the original *Stromateis* ran from 1.1.1 to 8.24.6 (thus containing originally eight books), and the *Hypotyposes* ran from 8.25.1 to 33.9, plus the original material behind the *Excerpta* and *Eclogae*. The fact that various ancient authors cite material from the *Eclogae propheticae* as from the eighth book of the *Stromateis* only shows that an abridged version similar to the eleventh century codex Laurentianus was already in circulation as early as Acacius of Caesarea's time (bishop from 340-366), and it, rather than the original *Stromateis*, was what his predecessor Eusebius knew.[44]

Nautin's scenario seems tempting, although his refutations of alternate theories are much less cogent. A structure of the *Stromateis* with seven books on ethics and one on apologetics against the Greeks and the Jews (especially when this latter seems to deal with concepts of demonstration and arguments against skepticism) seems so unbalanced as to be unlikely. The possibility that the material in *Stromateis* 8 (or part of it) has been subjected to some condensation after it left Clement's hands remains open.

---

[44] Eusebius, *H. E.* 6.13.1.

The Philosophical Material and the Eclogae propheticae

The *Eclogae propheticae*, in contrast to the *Excerpta ex Theodoto*, shows considerable unity of thought. Carlo Nardi, who has done most work on them, has argued persuasively that they move from baptism (1-26) to an exposition of "gnosis" which is positive and thoroughly Clementine (27-50), to a consideration of the spiritual world and the progressive divinization of the soul (51-65).[45] Unlike the "progression of themes" found by some in the *Gospel according to Philip*, these so-called ἔκλογαι, though usually rhetorically unconnected, develop their topics without digressions or excurses. Certain terms and concepts current among the "heterodox" exponents of gnosis are used, but these terms are made to express biblical understandings of morality and doctrine—a typically Clementine move. Nardi states, "Moltissime idee che Clemente esprime nelle *EP* trovano riscontro quasi verbale nelle opere la cui paternità clementina è fuori de ogni dubbio."[46]

The text is full of scriptural quotations, which, along with interwoven commentary, are used to develop a larger picture; the citations only occasionally and briefly follow a sequential path through scripture. It is the argument that controls the choice of scripture to be expounded. EK TΩN ΠΡΟΦΗΤΙΚΩΝ ΕΚΛΟΓΑΙ would seem to be another artistic but disingenuous title: these are not randomly assembled snippets of scripture with incidental comments, but are deployed as part of an overall plan.[47] The sense in which "sources" may be considered is not "which books have been excerpted," but "what are the cultural and intellectual influences which are here apparent." The possibility remains that the

---

[45] *Clemente Alessandrino. Estratti Profetici.* Ed. Carlo Nardi (Firenze: Nardini, 1985) 7-35, especially 28-33.

[46] Nardi, *Estratti*, 10.

[47] The nearest analogy to the *Eclogae propheticae*, without turning to a later time, is the so-called 4QFlorilegium. This group of fragments has been misleadingly titled by modern scholars; the two columns which survive with some completeness present citation followed by interpretation of verses from 2 Samuel 7 and Psalms 1 and 2. In both cases, the biblical text is interpreted with reference to the community. Further quite small fragments show materials dealing with Deuteronomy 33 and perhaps Genesis 49, Daniel 11 and Numbers 24. The size of the sample makes it impossible to say much about the organization of the whole (study of the methods of exegesis employed has been more fruitful). Possibly these biblical texts (like those of the *Eclogae propheticae*) were chosen to develop a coherent argument, or perhaps they had already been juxtaposed in a liturgical setting, and the 4QFlorilegium merely commented on them (a possibility which should not be ruled out with respect to portions of *Eclogae propheticae*). See George J. Brooke, *Exegesis at Qumran. 4QFlorilegium in its Jewish Context.* (JSOT Supplement Series 29, Sheffield, England: JSOT Press, 1985) especially 161-174.

Eclogae propheticae may be slightly condensed by the omission of some transitional material. It is not a close analog to the *Gospel according to Philip*, nor (except for its continual use of scripture) an anthology or collection of excerpts in any sense.

The first part of book eight is made up of three substantial passages on technical philosophy which are grouped together; presumably each is a long excerpt or epitome, and their juxtaposition is a purely practical one, as in someone's private notebooks. Something comprised of so few separate units, which are so large, tells us very little about the way people took notes, except that they sometimes copied out whole passages (or condensed them).

The Excerpta ex Theodoto

The *Excerpta ex Theodoto* has been the most studied portion of *Stromateis* 8. Sagnard, building on and adjusting earlier conjectures, attempted to separate the sources contained in it;[48] the validity of his separation of the opinions expressed in it does not depend on the resolution of the chicken-and-egg question introduced by Nautin.

One group of sections—4-5, 8-9, 18-20, and 27—seems clearly to express Clement's own views. Sagnard added to these a second group, 10-15, which seems to develop Clement's position in most respects, but experiments with a Stoic materialism which is uncharacteristic of Clement. Presumably, Clement was experimenting with the use of this terminology in the privacy of his own notebook. (Alternatively, the section 10-15 may come from another source.)

Excerpta 43-65, on the other hand, seems to parallel closely the doctrine of Ptolemy, as reported by Irenaeus.[49] This section contains no attributions to Theodotus, nor even any attributions to "him" or "them." It must be either a copy or a condensation of a single source.

This leaves the non-Clementine, non-Ptolemaic material, which is sprinkled with five attributions to Theodotus, six to "him" and four to "them," as probably Theodotan or mostly Theodotan. Here, Clement's method resembles Pliny's in that some record was kept of the origin of these excerpts. A high proportion of these attributions occur after passages which seem to be Clementine—that is, he notes when he returns to his source material after a digression. This, too, follows the pattern of a

---

[48] F. Sagnard, *Clément d'Alexandrie. Extraits de Théodote.* Ed. F. Sagnard (Paris: Éditions du Cerf, 1948) 5-50.

[49] Irenaeus *Adv. haer.* 1.1-7.

private notebook: the excerpts seem to have been taken in the order in which they were found; the notes that accompany them indicate that Clement approached his material with an open mind, willing to learn from it while at the same time intending to refute its most unacceptable positions.

The following characteristics are found in the *Excerpta ex Theodoto*:

- alternation of excerpts and commentary on/rebuttal of excerpted material;
- frequent but casual attribution of excerpts when they are interspersed with the collector's comments;
- development of the collector's opinions in contrast to excerpted material;
- experimentation in expressing the collector's opinions using terminology borrowed from material excerpted;
- excerpting some material in an unbroken block, without attribution or interruption by commentary.

The Sentences of Sextus *and Related Collections*

The *Sentences of Sextus* is a collection of brief statements of moral and spiritual advice. Typically each is phrased as a simple, declarative sentence, or sometimes as a rhetorical question; self-control, wisdom, and purity are among the predominant virtues.[50] The first surviving news of the work appears in Origen's writing in the late 240s. Origen mentions the work explicitly on two occasions (*Contra Celsum* 8.30 and the *Commentary on Matthew* 15.3), and quotes or paraphrases its words several other times. By the time of Rufinus' translation of *The Sentences of Sextus* into Latin (around 400), the work had become attributed to the popular figure of Xystus II (martyred in 258). Although Jerome saw its underlying pagan character, doubted its Xystine authorship, and roundly disapproved of it,[51] the collection remained popular through the middle ages. Only a few medieval manuscripts preserve Jerome's doubts or note that the attribution to Pope Sixtus (= Xystus) might rather be to a philosopher of the same name.

---

[50] For an overview of "Sextus'" teachings, see Robert L. Wilken, "Wisdom and Philosophy in Early Christianity, *Aspects of Wisdom in Judaism and Early Christianity* (Notre Dame, IN: University of Notre Dame Press, 1975), 143-168, and Henry Chadwick, "The Moral Teaching of Sextus" in his book, *The Sentences of Sextus. A Contribution to the History of Early Christian Ethics.* (Cambridge: Cambridge University Press, 1959), 97-106.

[51] *Comm. in Ierem.* 4.41, *Comm. in Ezech.* 6, *Ep.* 133.3.

The many Latin manuscripts of Rufinus' version, together with the single Greek manuscript that corresponds closely to them, give us our earliest snapshot of the text: a Greek collection of (probably) 451 units, called ΣΕΞΤΟΥ ΓΝΩΜΑΙ, *The Gnomai (or Maxims) of Sextus*.[52] While it was a work that ungrudgingly accepted minor interpolations, omissions, and rearrangements, something very close to this sequence of these Greek maxims must have circulated freely, for it was the form of the text used to make both a Coptic[53] and a Syriac translation.[54]

Some Christian elements appear in this collection. Henry Chadwick listed 17 maxims "which could have no other origin than a Christian au-

---

[52] Rufinus' Latin text is attested by 15 extant manuscripts, from the 7th to the 15th century, edited by J. Gildemeister (*Sextii Sententiarum Recensiones*, Bonn, 1873) and by A. Elter (*Gnomica I*, Leipzig, 1892). The work is attested in Greek by only two manuscripts, one corresponding closely to Rufinus' translation, the 14th century Vaticanus Graecus 742, and another with closely similar material in a quite different order, the 10th century Patmiensis 263.

Henry Chadwick has provided an edition of the Greek and Latin texts, with critical apparatus, and several interpretive studies: *The Sentences of Sextus. A Contribution to the History of Early Christian Ethics* (Cambridge: Cambridge University Press, 1959). Richard A. Edwards and Robert A. Wild have published a slightly different edition of the Greek together with an English translation and short introduction, *The Sentences of Sextus* (Chico, CA: Scholars Press, 1981).

Curiously, both Greek manuscripts run on beyond sentence 451 without a break. The generally accepted opinion is that Rufinus translated from a Greek manuscript that ended at 451. Apart from the ample Latin manuscript tradition, however, there is little specifically textual evidence to support this. The argument rests mostly on the fact that little Christian influence can be seen after 451. Most of the other versions either support the two Greek manuscripts in extending beyond sentence 451 (a full Syriac translation, an independent Syriac epitome, and two of the three smaller collections selected from the material, preserved in Armenian), or are physically missing the pages which could decide the matter (the Coptic). Only the first and largest of the three small collections in Armenian seems to support a manuscript tradition ending with 451: there we find exactly 100 sentences, drawn entirely from 1-451, with only 3 items out of the sequence given in the Latin manuscripts of Rufinus' version.

[53] From the ruined remains of Nag Hammadi Codex 12, disassembled probably at the time of the discovery of the codices, all that remains of the *Sentences of Sextus* is an isolated leaf, presumed to be pages 15/16, and four leaves together, pages 27-34. The first block contains sentences 157-180 (but lacks 162a), while the second contains sentences 307-397. There are two passages in the latter block where the order is slightly different: 332, 334, 333, transition, 335; and again, 354, 356, 357, and a sentence only partially corresponding to 355. These small divergences from the Latin and Greek witnesses correspond to the order found in a Syriac version, suggesting that the Syriac and Coptic both go back to a Greek text earlier than the ones extant. See Paul-Hubert Poirier, *Les Sentences de Sextus. (NH XII, 1)* (Quebec: Presses de l'Université Laval, 1983) 7-28.

[54] Edited by Paul de Lagarde, *Analecta syriaca* (Leipzig, 1858) 10.22-25.11. See also V. Ryssel, "Die syrische Übersetzung der Sextussentenzen," *Zeitschrift für wissenschaftliche Theologie* 38 (1895) 617-630; 39 (1896) 568-624; 40 (1897) 131-148.

thor," including nine maxims dependent on Matthew, two dependent on Romans, and one on Proverbs. Beyond these, a much larger number of others make use of more or less distinctively Christian terminology.[55] As Chadwick notes, the Christian or Christianized units are particularly dense at the start of the work, and perhaps were placed there to secure its acceptance in Christian circles. On the other hand, the majority of the maxims are innocent of any Christian reference, but they could be seen as compatible with a mildly ascetic Christianity. Their non-Christian origin is confirmed by the fact that many of these maxims reappear in Byzantine collections (such as that compiled by John Stobaeus in the fifth century C.E.), where they are attributed to Pythagoras. The concatenation of the Christian and Pythagorean strands reflects the enterprise, seen also in Clement and Origen, of presenting the Christian faith in the trappings of the best of the ancient philosophical tradition.

The Sources of the Sentences of Sextus

Parts of an alphabetically arranged sequence[56] of many Sextine maxims, along with some others, appear in four separate witnesses: a fifteenth century Greek manuscript of 119 maxims, a sisteenth century Greek manuscript of 45 maxims, a sixth or seventh century Syriac manuscript of 98 maxims, and a sequence of 15 maxims appearing in Stobaeus. All four collections are ascribed to Pythagoras or the Pythagoreans. The same alphabetic order runs through all these and is followed even in the Syriac version, although there of course translation obliterates the effect. Of the three smaller collections, only the Syriac collection contains material not in the largest one, and even there this extraneous material amounts to only four sayings out of 98. It would seem that the three smaller collections were either taken from the collection of 119 sentences, or that all four came from a collection only slightly more ample. In any case, the source behind them was already associated with Pythagoras and was already arranged alphabetically. We can only guess

---

[55] See Chadwick, *Sentences*, 138-140 and 154-155.

[56] That is, they were grouped together according to the first letter of the maxim, and the groups were arranged in the order of the alphabet. This sort of alphabetization begins to be used fairly often by librarians, tax office workers, and others needing to keep track of large amounts of information, by the 1st century B.C.E. Second letter and absolute alphabetization remained quite rare throughout the middle ages; probably the use of papyrus for the slips or lists required to fully alphabetize a large project was felt to be extravagant, and the gain in convenience not commensurate to the effort involved. See Lloyd W. Daly, *Contributions to a History of Alphabetization in Antiquity and the Middle Ages* (Brussels: Latomus, 1967).

how much this alphabetical collection of Pythagoreana might antedate the sixth or seventh century Syriac text.

Very many of the same sayings also appear quoted or paraphrased in Porphyry's letter to Marcella (around 300 C.E.). While Porphyry and the Pythagorean collection share material which is absent from the *Sentences of Sextus*, Porphyry and *Sextus* share material absent from the Pythagorean collection, and the Pythagorean collection and *Sextus* share material absent from Porphyry. Thus they cannot depend on each other, but each represents a different usage of a common original. Since Porphyry's wording is usually closer to that of the Pythagorean collection than to Sextus', and those two often agree on a sequencing of sentences not found in *Sextus,* they are probably better witnesses to the source of the three than is the work of the Christian redactor.

There is, moreover, another group of collections related to Sextus'. A Greek manuscript (Parisinus gr. 1630) contains the largest collection of the group, 93 maxims, 59 of which are found in *Sextus* in the same order. A fifteenth century manuscript (Vaticanus gr. 1144) contains 59 maxims, 22 of which are contained in the largest collection. The fifteenth century manuscript (Bodleianus Auct. F. 6. 26) contains a collection of 38 maxims, all of which are found in the largest collection. Each maxim in this collection has a periphrastic exegesis attached. Finally, the thirteenth century manuscript (Parisinus gr. 1168) preserves a group of 23 maxims, including some shared with the largest collection of the group, and others shared with the collection in the Vatican manuscript; the maxims in this collection are in an order quite different from the first three manuscripts. It would seem that the largest and second largest collections, sharing only 22 maxims in common, drew independently on a more ample common source, as did the smallest collection, which also reorganized its materials significantly. The collection in the Bodleian manuscript drew on an epitome of that common source, one essentially identical to the largest collection of the group. Two of the four collections attribute their material to one Clitarchus; speculating from the title given to one of them,[57] the original collection may have been titled, ΑΙ ΚΛΕΙΤΑΡΧΟΥ ΠΡΑΓΜΑΤΙΚΑΙ ΧΡΕΙΑΙ, *Clitarchus' Useful Sayings.*

---

[57] The collection in Vaticanus gr. 1144 is titled ΕΚ ΤΩΝ ΚΛΕΙΤΑΡΧΟΥ ΠΡΑΓΜΑΤΙΚΩΝ ΧΡΕΙΩΝ ΣΥΝΑΓΩΓΗ Parisinus gr. 1168 places its 23 maxims under the heading ΚΛΕΙΤΑΡΧΟΥ; the other two are without titles. See Chadwick, *Sentences,* 73-74.

The material in the Clitarchan collections has not been Christianized, and a number of the maxims shared with *Sextus* are ones which show, in their Sextine versions, the light but insistent touch of the Christian redactor. The possibility that Clitarchus' material could be a re-paganized redaction of *Sextus* is undercut by the fact that the wording of Clitarchus is sometimes close to Porphyry and the alphabetical Pythagorean collections and distinct from the wording of *Sextus*. Moreover, Clitarchus and Porphyry join some maxims which appear separately in *Sextus*, but —at least, in Henry Chadwick's opinion—not so often that it is likely that Clitarchus depends directly on Porphyry. More likely, Clitarchus, Sextus, Porphyry and the Pythagorean collector all drew on a single common source. Chadwick in the end threw up his hands: "It is not profitable to inquire too closely into the exact source-relationship here for the reason that there is no category of literature with a less rigid and consistent existence than an anthology of aphorisms."[58] An overview of the probable relationships among this material is presented schematically on the next page.

Chadwick, like most investigators, analyzed smaller collections and epitomes for what they could contribute to the clarification of the "original" text, and tried to determine how that might relate to an even earlier source. Here, however, we must look at the collections in their own right, if they are to illuminate the ways collections of excerpts were organized and reorganized in late antiquity. The only one which certainly represents major redactional activity—the decisive shaping of a new, albeit derived, collection—during the period in which the *Gospel according to Philip* was shaped is the Christian revision responsible for the *Sentences of Sextus* as Rufinus knew it. Porphyry's letter to Marcella was composed late enough to be of dubious relevance, a couple of years beyond the end of the third century, but is the more interesting because it also contains a section drawn not from *Sextus* but from Epicurus. No date can be attached to any of the rest of the material, but it may well be that the Pythagorean tradition received an alphabetical form during this period, that the epitome of *Sextus* which survives as the shorter Syriac text was made then, and perhaps that some of the three independent epitomes of Clitarchan material received their form as well. It is somewhat less likely, though not impossible, that the epitome of 100 sentences ascribed to Evagrius in the Armenian tradition was also made this early.

---

[58] Chadwick, *Sentences*, 159.

A Rough Stemma of the *Sentences of Sextus* and Related Collections

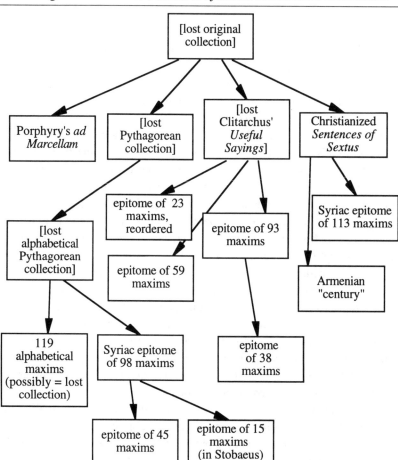

The Christian Redactor of the Sentences of Sextus

The organizing principles in the ΣΕΞΤΟΥ ΓΝΩΜΑΙ have mostly been ignored. Robert Wilken's description of it has a familiar ring to investigators of the *Gospel according to Philip:*

> The organization is apparently haphazard, reflecting a tradition which had been a long time in the making and which grew simply by the addition of new maxims. At times the maxims seem grouped together around a common theme (sometimes three to five maxims are related), but in most

cases they are loosely strung together with no transitions from one to another. They touch on one subject, go on to another, and sometimes return to the same or a similar topic a hundred or two hundred sentences later.[59]

While this is a generally valid description, it requires several qualifications. First of all, an "organization which is haphazard" and which seems to have grown "simply by the addition of new maxims" is not necessarily "one which had been a long time in the making." Such a scenario is certainly possible: many scribes over many years may have each added many or few maxims to the collection. It is, moreover, certain that the Christian who gave the collection its final touches was a redactor reworking an already existent (and fairly well known) non-Christian text, neither the original author nor the collector of the whole. But we have very slender evidence on which to speculate whether the earlier work used by the Christian redactor was the project of a single collector or of centuries of aggregation, or something in between. Secondly, Wilken is much too pessimistic in his quantification of the size of groups of maxims sharing a common theme: for example, 149-165f all deal with speaking, 230a-240 deal with marriage (with the exception of 234, which may not be meant to stand alone but as a motivation for the behaviors recommended), 350-368, except for 363-364, deal with the specific hazards of speaking about God, and 415b-427 deal with the sage. Thirdly, there are signs that the arrangement may not be entirely haphazard, at least as far as the contribution of the Christian redactor is concerned. Beyond common themes, certain units stand in logical or rhetorical relation to others, and recurrent organizing principles are not hard to locate.

The first page or so, which has (as Chadwick noted) an unusually high concentration of Christian sayings, is considerably more than a politically astute placement for a redactor's pious but unorganized additions. In the following text, the maxims Chadwick considered as "specifically and unambiguously Christian" are marked with "+" while those derived from the Pythagorean tradition are marked with "π." (Note that these categories are not mutually exclusive.)

+1 Πιστὸς ἄνθρωπος ἐκλεκτός   +1 A faithful man is an elect man.
   ἐστιν ἄνθρωπος.

+2. ἐκλεκτὸς ἄνθρωπος   +2 An elect man is a man of God.
   ἄνθρωπός ἐστι θεοῦ.

---

[59] Wilken, "Wisdom and Philosophy," 145.

π3. θεοῦ ἄνθρωπος ὁ ἄξιος θεοῦ.	π3 A man of God is worthy of God.
π4. θεοῦ ἄξιος ὁ μηδὲν ἀνάξιον θεοῦ πράττων.	π4 One worthy of God does nothing unworthy of God.
π+5. ἐπιτηδεύων οὖν πιστὸς εἶναι μηδὲν ἀνάξιον θεοῦ πράξῃς.	π+5 Therefore if you wish to be faithful, do nothing unworthy of God.[60]

The first five sentences are very tightly interwoven: A is B, B is C, C is D, D does not do E. Therefore, if you wish to be A, then do not do E. The work opens with a classic sorites. After it, 6, 7a and 7b each deals with the idea of faithfulness (concept A again). At least for this opening section, the atomization of the text into separate sentences, although derived from the ancient manuscript tradition, has taken a quite coherent argument and artificially created the impression of unrelated sentences. The argument in question was, however, a new creation: it is woven together from both Pythagorean and Christian statements. This neo-Pythagorean-Christian cento was crafted as an introduction to the collection, and displays accurately the distinctive approach of the entire collection, in its Christianized form.

Sentences are frequently grouped into parallel or antithetical pairs:

310 ὅσα θεοῦ κτήματα, καὶ σοφοῦ.	310 Whatever God possesses belongs also to the sage.
311 κοινωνεῖ βασιλείας θεοῦ σοφὸς ἀνήρ.	311 A wise man shares in the kingdom of God.
—	—
388 ὃ δεῖ ποιεῖν, ἑκὼν ποίει.	388 Do willingly what you must do.
389 ὃ μὴ δεῖ ποιεῖν, μηδενὶ τρόπῳ ποίει.	389a Do not ever do what you must not do.
—	—
404 ὅσα δίδωσιν ὁ θεὸς οὐδεὶς ἀφαιρεῖται.	404 Whatever God gives, no one takes away.
405 ὃ παρέχει κόσμος βεβαίως οὐ τηρεῖ.	405 Whatever the world offers, it does not keep secure.

A variation on this principle involves two parallel sentences in which the first is somewhat metaphorical or complex, and the second restates the idea in a more literal or blunt manner.

---

[60] Text and English translation from Edwards and Wild, *Sentences of Sextus*, 16-19.

295 ὅπερ μεταδιδοὺς ἄλλοις αὐτὸς οὐχ ἕξεις, μὴ κρίνῃς ἀγαθὸν εἶναι.	295 Do not consider anything good which you cannot share with others and still have yourself.
296 οὐδὲν ἀκοινώνητον ἀγαθόν.	296 Nothing is good which is not shared.

A surprisingly coherent argument is sometimes woven out of these tiny components:

115 μὴ πλέον κτῶ ὧν τὸ σῶμα ἐπιζητεῖ.	115 Do not acquire more than the body needs.
116 ψυχὴν χρυσὸς οὐ ῥύεται κακῶν.	116 Gold does not rescue the soul from evil.
117 οὐ γέγονας ἐντρυφήσων τῇ τοῦ θεοῦ παρασκευῇ.	117 You were not born to luxuriate in what God provides.
118 κτῶ ἃ μηδείς σου ἀφαιρεῖται.	118 Acquire those things which no one can take from you.
119 φέρε τὰ ἀναγκαῖα ὡς ἀναγκαῖα.	119 Bear with what must be as something that must be.
120 μεγαλοψυχίαν ἄσκει.	120 Practice magnanimity.
121a ὧν καταφρονῶν ἐπαινῇ εὐλόγως, τούτων μὴ περιέχου.	121a Do not surround yourself with those things which, if you despised them, would rightfully bring you praise.

This section continues on the topic of possessions with about the same degree of thematic coherence through 137, although it is clearly made up of separate items. A similar degree of cohesion is usually seen in other long runs of sentences on the same topic, and in many sequences of three to five sentences.[61]

Porphyry and the Pythagorean collections both contain sentences which are considerably longer than anything in *Sextus,* composed of as many as six members. In a number of cases in which those two agree on the form of such a sentence, *Sextus* has only one of the members, or places the members widely apart.[62] In a few cases, a plausible motive can be found: the omitted member was sometimes one which would have been offensive to Christian sensibilities; but that still leaves the majority of instances unaccounted for. Chadwick remarks that "the first impres-

---

[61] *Sentences of Sextus* 41-44, 207-208b, 265-267, 278-282, 320-324, 369-372, for example.

[62] See Chadwick, *Sentences,* 149-153, for examples and discussion.

sion made by this evidence might be that Sextus has consistently and deliberately split up sentences which were originally united," a remark eerily reminiscent of Isenberg's theory that the compiler-editor of the *Gospel according to Philip* "purposely disjoined paragraphs that had a continuity of thought and deposited the pieces in diverse places in the work."[63]

The documents form a sort of synoptic problem. Porphyry and the Pythagorean collections sometimes agree in the wording of a saying against Sextus, and Sextus and the Pythagorean collections sometimes agree against Porphyry, but Sextus and Porphyry seldom agree against the Pythagorean collections. Hence, a Pythagorean collection must have been the source of the other two. Certain sentences, however, are found in Porphyry and Sextus but omitted from the extant Pythagorean collections, so the version used by them must have differed significantly from the extant ones. Herein lies the problem. The lost collection may have contained more connected blocks of discourse, which were sundered by Sextus; or, Sextus may have used a more primitive collection in which they were not yet joined, while Porphyry and the extant Pythagorean collections both represent a later stage in the evolution of the collection which had joined the materials. Here the simplistic nature of the stemma above becomes evident.

The Christian editor, in handling the non-Pythagorean materials, has demonstrated a preference for simple sentences and an ability to string them together into longer logical units which, however, remain asyndetic. The dispersal of the component parts seems unmotivated, but since the Christian editing of the *Sentences of Sextus* was comparatively intensive, it seems plausible. The other alternative, that the editor of *Sextus* used a more primitive version of the Pythagorean collection than the version behind the extant Pythagorean collection and Porphyry, involves the postulation of another rather energetic editor who joined brief sentences together into longer compound sentences. But Porphyry did major editing too, by either of these hypotheses, as did the person responsible for the alphabetical order of the extant Pythagorean collection: the postulation of yet another energetic editor does not make a significantly more complex, or less plausible, theory. The current state of scholarship on this problem does not offer reasonable grounds for a decision between these two alternatives.

---

[63] See Chadwick, *Sentences,* 152, and Isenberg's introduction to the *Gospel according to Philip* in Layton, *Nag Hammadi Codex II,2-7* vol. 1, 133.

With respect to the possible analogy between an editor of the *Sentences of Sextus* who disjoined more coherent discourse and Isenberg's view of the editor of the *Gospel according to Philip,* it is clear that the sentences in *Sextus,* if they ever were disjoined, are whole ones. There is nothing particularly remarkable about them. Brief, quintessentially "gnomic," there is no incompleteness that calls for explanation, as Isenberg claimed for passages in the *Gospel according to Philip.* Were it not for the other collections, we would not give their state a second thought. Thus, if it could be demonstrated that the Christian redactor who produced *Sextus* did deliberately dismember once complete sentences, we should have to say (1) that it was done in such a way that whole sentences resulted, which retained no sign of the violence done them; (2) that it was done in the name of consistency of style: the stark simplicity, with a touch of mystery, of wisdom won by hard experience. Both these observations greatly weaken the analogy to Isenberg's understanding of the *Gospel according to Philip.* If the *Gospel according to Philip*'s editor engaged in the same practices that, by this hypothesis, the *Sentences of Sextus'* editor may have, the result should be undetectable, the disjoined members seemingly whole in themselves, and the style of the document more uniform as a result. In other words, the results are not analogous, even if it could be demonstrated that roughly similar practices underlay them.

Organizing Principles in the Sentences of Sextus *and Related Documents*
The *Sentences of Sextus* and related materials have brought to light a number of practices used in editing collections. The Christianizing revision that resulted in the *Sentences of Sextus* itself is a collection of material from both Christian and secular sources, on ethical and spiritual topics; it shows the following characteristics:

- juxtaposition of many individual maxims unrelated to each other;
- loose groupings of maxims by subject and/or motif and/or key word;
- analogous and antithetical pairs of maxims;
- logically and rhetorically coherent passages fabricated from individual maxims;
- a chain-syllogism or sorites fabricated from individual maxims of disparate origin;
- the omission/revision of ideologically offensive material present in sources;

- omission of the name of author/source even when available, perhaps to make the result more palatable to a Christian audience;
- the grouping of monostichic units into larger logical wholes which remain asyndetic;
- the production of an introductory sequence by combining material from disparate sources;
- possibly, the division of larger sentences with syntactic connectors into smaller independent maxims, to enhance gnomic style.

In the related material, which is less certainly datable to the first three centuries of the common era, we encounter a number of other practices:

- epitomizing in a way that leaves the original order intact;
- the addition of explanations, motivations, and applications;
- the production of epitomes of exactly 100 items;
- first letter "alphabetization" (the extant Pythagorean collections);
- major reworking and rearrangement of material into an overall argument (Porphyry);
- possibly, the combination of separate items into larger compound sentences.

SUMMARY

As we have seen, there was a continuum between notes made for private use, private notes shared with limited others, private (or limited circulation) notes which inadvertently became public, minimally edited notes published as miscellanies, carefully polished miscellanies and collections of various kinds, and individually authored works which affected some of the characteristics of notebooks or multi-author collections.

Notebooks, miscellanies, and multi-author collections employed organizing principles chosen from a common group of possibilities, with little reference to the subject matter of their contents. Within this continuum, the identification of works as belonging to literary genres or subgenres rests on the choice of subject matter, the form of individual units, and on the presence and characteristics of a literary "frame," not on the set of organizing principles involved. Notebooks governed by the contingencies of the collecting process itself, and some of the miscellanies which imitated them, lacked such a frame, and were not restricted in the form or content of their subject matter. Thus there existed a precedent (albeit a non-literary one) for compositions outside the definitions of the recognized genres of collections. Such a matrix allowed for the rapid evolution of genres.

We have seen a number of organizing techniques which do not appear in the *Gospel according to Philip*. These include:

- use of a narrative introduction or frame;
- attribution of excerpted material (except for Jesus' words and the saying of Philip);
- organization of material by author;
- chronological or geographical organization of material;
- organization of material into a repeating formula;
- organization of material into a chain-syllogism or sorites .

We have also seen a number of organizing principles which are found in the *Gospel according to Philip*. They are:

- use of an introductory sequence woven out of disparate material;
- removal of attributions of most material;
- division of blocks of source material and interleaving of material from different sources;
- inclusion of units of varying size, but mostly prefering short units;
- clustering of material by motif or image;
- juxtaposition of material using analogous arguments or making analogous points;
- arrangement of material into parallel or antithetical pairs;
- sequencing of material by broad themes.

These principles can explain many of the features of the *Gospel according to Philip*, including some of its most perplexing ones. Their impact on that document will be explored in chapter 10. Nevertheless, they provide a relatively minimal organization. Much of the tantalizingly elusive coherence of the *Gospel according to Philip* resides in its collector's interests and choices of materials. Chapter 5 examines the nature of collecting in the context of gnostic speculation, and chapter 11 offers a few insights into our collector's distinctive approaches.

CHAPTER FIVE

RECOMBINANT MYTHOGRAPHY

If we take seriously the possibility that the *Gospel according to Philip* may have been assembled from diverse excerpts, we must inquire about the motivation behind its assembly, copying, and translation. Presumably any collection was valued because it served some purpose or purposes. The determination of the function of any piece of literature, or of a non-literary document, is always a more speculative endeavor than the description of its structural features—especially given the scarcity of information on the social context of many works from antiquity. This does not excuse us from the task, however. If we could not find plausible motives for the work as a collection, this understanding of it would be drawn into question.

This chapter will argue that the jostling and jarring of contradictory and divergent opinions within the *Gospel according to Philip* is an aspect of the potential which its collector saw in its diverse materials, and that an interest in such provocative juxtapositions as we find there is intelligible within the religious and intellectual context of gnostic speculation.

THE GNOSTIC PROLIFERATION OF SYSTEMS

Gnostics were notorious for their tendency to generate multiple systems. The trait was a stock complaint of heresiologists, who mostly sought to deal with it by producing intricate taxonomies of gnostic groups. Despite the fact that many of the specific opinions recorded by the heresiologists find parallels in the material recovered from Nag Hammadi, the heresiologists' groupings do not correspond well to the documentary evidence. It is plain that there was a very remarkable proliferation of speculations, but apparently the heresiologists were wrong in assuming that there were as many sects as there were systems. I would propose that they made this mistake because speculative expositions that looked to the heresiologists like systems demanding rigorous adherence were actually something quite different.

My claims are twofold: (1) Adherents of the gnostic systems adhered to them much less closely than the heresiologists assumed they did, or wanted members of their own groups to adhere to the faith as they understood it. (2) The manufacture of systems by the recombination of myths and traditions served a heuristic function: it was seen to be provocative of insights, and was undertaken in pursuit of them, not as a means for uncovering or conveying a literal, univocal truth.

The Phenomenon of Recombinant Mythography

The sets of elements that make up the famous gnostic systems overlap to a marked degree. The same images and motifs show up over and over again, with adjustments primarily in their relation to one another. The traditions involved were treated very freely, with little regard for their origin, original meaning, or literal truth value; their manipulation seems to have been based, rather, on the premise that insight could be both sought and found by means of new juxtapositions and recombinations.

Irenaeus, in the course of complaining bitterly about the handling Christian traditions received at the hands of gnostic writers and teachers, gives a remarkably clear description of the way his opponents handled sacred traditions.

Τοιαύτης δὲ τῆς ὑποθέσεως αὐτῶν οὔσης, ἣν οὔτε προφῆται ἐκήρυξαν οὔτε ὁ κύριος ἐδίδαξεν οὔτε ἀπόστολοι παρέδωκαν,	Such is their system which neither the prophets preached, nor the Lord taught, nor the apostles handed down.
ἣν περισσοτέρως αὐχοῦσιν πλεῖον τῶν ἄλλων ἐγνωκέναι, ἐξ ἀγράφων ἀναγινώσκοντες καὶ τὸ δὴ λεγόμενον ἐξ ἄμμου σχοινία πλέκειν ἐπιτηδεύοντες,	They boast rather loudly of knowing more about it than others do, citing it from non-scriptural works; and, as people would say, they attempt to braid ropes of sand.
ἀξιοπίστως προσαρμόζειν πειρῶνται τοῖς εἰρημένοις ἤτοι παραβολὰς κυριακὰς ἢ ῥήσεις προφητικὰς ἢ λόγους ἀποστολικούς, ἵνα τὸ πλάσμα αὐτῶν μὴ ἀμάρτυρον εἶναι δοκῇ,	They try to adapt to their own sayings in a manner worthy of credence, either the Lord's parables, or the prophets' sayings, or the apostles' words, so that their fabrication might not appear to be without witness.

τὴν μὲν τάξιν καὶ εἱρμὸν τῶν γραφῶν ὑπερβαίνοντες καὶ ὅσον ἐφ᾿ ἑαυτοῖς λύοντες τὰ μέλη τῆς ἀληθείας. Μεταφέρουσι δὲ καὶ μεταπλάττουσι καὶ ἄλλο ἐξ ἄλλου ποιοῦντες ἐξαπατῶσι πολλοὺς τῇ τῶν ἐφαρμοζομένων κυριακῶν λογίων κακοσυνθέτῳ φαντασίᾳ.

They disregard the order and the connection of the Scriptures and, as much as in them lies, they disjoint the members of the Truth. They transfer passages and rearrange them; and, making one thing out of another, they deceive many by the badly composed phantasy of the Lord's words which they adapt.

῝Ονπερ τρόπον εἴ τις, βασιλέως εἰκόνος καλῆς κατεσκευασμένης ἐπιμελῶς ἐκ ψηφίδων ἐπισήμων ὑπὸ σοφοῦ τεχνίτου, λύσας τὴν ὑποκειμένην τοῦ ἀνθρώπου ἰδέαν, μετενέγκοι τὰς ψηφίδας ἐκείνας καὶ μεθαρμόσοι καὶ ποιήσοι μορφὴν κυνὸς ἢ ἀλώπεκος καὶ ταύτην φαύλως κατεσκευασμένην,

By way of illustration, suppose someone would take the beautiful image of a king, carefully made out of precious stones by a skillful artist, and would destroy the features of the man on it and change around and rearrange the jewels, and make the form of a dog, or of a fox, out of them, and that a rather bad piece of work.

ἔπειτα διορίζοιτο καὶ λέγοι ταύτην εἶναι τὴν τοῦ βασιλέως ἐκείνην εἰκόνα τὴν καλήν, ἣν ὁ σοφὸς τεχνίτης κατεσκεύασεν, δεικνὺς τὰς ψηφίδας τὰς καλῶς ὑπὸ τοῦ τεχνίτου τοῦ πρώτου εἰς τὴν τοῦ βασιλέως εἰκόνα συντεθείσας, κακῶς δὲ ὑπὸ τοῦ ὑστέρου εἰς κυνὸς μορφὴν μετενεχθείσας,

Suppose he would then say with determination that this is the beautiful image of the king that the skillful artist had made, at the same time pointing to the jewels which had been beautifully fitted together by the first artist into the image of the king, but which had been badly changed by the second into the form of a dog.

καὶ διὰ τῆς τῶν ψηφίδων φαντασίας μεθοδεύοι τοὺς ἀπειροτέρους τοὺς κατάληψιν βασιλικῆς μορφῆς οὐκ ἔχοντας καὶ πείθοι ὅτι αὕτη ἡ σαπρὰ τῆς ἀλώπεκος ἰδέα ἐκείνη ἐστὶν ἡ καλὴ τοῦ βασιλέως εἰκών·

And suppose he would through this fanciful arrangement of the jewels deceive the inexperienced who had no idea of what the king's picture looked like, and would persuade them that this base picture of a fox is that beautiful image of the king.

τὸν αὐτὸν δὴ τρόπον καὶ οὗτοι   In the same way these people
γραῶν μύθους   patch together old women's fables,
συγκαττύσαντες, ἔπειτα   and then pluck words and sayings
ῥήματα καὶ λέξεις καὶ   and parables from here and there
παραβολὰς ὅθεν καὶ ποθὲν   and wish to adapt these words of
ἀποσπῶντες,ἐφαρμόζειν   God to their fables.[1]
βούλονται τοῖς μύθοις αὐτῶν
τὰ λόγια τοῦ Θεοῦ.

Irenaeus is, of course, hostile to the practices he is describing, but his enumeration of them deserves careful examination. In this passage, he described several specific practices: (1) the development of new systems or syntheses; (2) citation of non-"scriptural" works; (3) use of Christian and Hebrew scripture (and perhaps of unwritten Christian tradition) to reinforce speculations; (4) a very free handling of scripture which interprets without reference to context, rearranging and recombining its elements into a new and unintended design; (5) the inclusion of sources which are no longer taken seriously—the sort of things that may once have had sacred status but which have been relegated to the nursery or the gossip of old women. Despite Irenaeus' hostility, this turns out to be a relatively accurate and enlightening list of some key characteristics of gnostic handling of sacred traditions, and thus helps describe the intellectual and spiritual context in which the *Gospel according to Philip* was assembled.

Irenaeus' second and third complaints (as listed above) have to do with gnostics' choice of sacred writings—specifically, with their choice to use other people's sacred writings. Irenaeus was bitter that gnostics were "stealing" material that he viewed as belonging to his own group. He also complained that they were using writings that he did not view as belonging to his own group, but to groups from which his tradition dissociated itself. Part of the problem was that many different groups were reading partially overlapping bodies of literature, and the sense of competition for "ownership" was keen. Some of these groups were making overlapping (i.e., "rival") claims about their corporate identity as well. For example, Valentinus, to judge by the few preserved fragments of his writing, wrote about Jesus, quoted his words, tried to forge a philosophical framework for the terms "Father," "Son," and "Holy Spirit," and re-

---

[1] *Adv. haer.* 1.8.1 *Irénée de Lyon Contre les hérésies. Livre I,* ed. Adelin Rousseau and Louis Doutreleau (Paris: Éditions du Cerf, 1979) 2.112-116. English translation *St. Irenaeus of Lyons Against the Heresies,* transl. Dominic J. Unger (New York: Paulist Press, 1992).

ferred warmly to "the church."[2] "Jesus" and "the Christ" are prominent in the economies of salvation of the systems Irenaeus recounts as Valentinus' and Ptolemy's.[3] On the other hand, the terms "gnosis" and "gnostic" were used in positive senses by people like Clement of Alexandria as well as by the "gnostics,"[4] and Irenaeus entitled his own polemic ΕΛΕΝΧΟΣ ΚΑΙ ΑΝΑΤΡΟΠΗ ΤΗΣ ΨΕΥΔΩΝΥΜΟΥ ΓΝΩΣΕΩΣ, *The Refutation and Overthrow of the So-Called Knowledge*,[5] implying that γνῶσις had an application which he considered proper and which was distinct from the gnostics' "misuse" of the term. Given the extent of the disputed territories in jargon, imagery, history, and texts, complaints such as Irenaeus' about gnostics' choice of texts are not especially surprising.

Irenaeus' other three complaints concern the proliferation of systems, an associated manner of handling texts, and the inclusion of motifs which have been demoted from religion to folklore. These observations illustrate the structure of a basic mode of thought common to many "gnostic" phenomena and which, I would argue, is foundational to the *Gospel according to Philip*'s collector's way of proceeding.

A little later in the first book of his ΕΛΕΝΧΟΣ ΚΑΙ ΑΝΑΤΡΟΠΗ, Irenaeus returns to his criticism of gnostic handling of traditional materials, this time drawing an analogy between such reworking and the poetic form of the cento.[6] His argument does not add to our list of textual practices, but the analogy is illuminating. Here again is the complaint that bits of scripture were being handled too freely, without regard for their proper context, made in this case by a comparison with a form of poetry in which all the lines were taken from another poem (most often Homer, in the Greek speaking world) but were rearranged to tell a completely different story. The procedures are indeed analogous, and the image of the cento parallels that of the rearranged mosaic. Nevertheless, the cento does not appear normally to have been intended as a fraud or forgery, but frankly as an ingenious piece of literary recycling, not a deception but a

---

[2] Fragment 3 (in Völker's enumeration; = Clement *Stromateis* 3.59.3) is concerned with Jesus' physical nature; fragment 4 (= Clement *Stromateis* 2.114.3-6) quotes Jesus' words from Matt 19:17 and 5:8; fragment 9 (Marcellus of Ancyra *On the Holy Church* 9) credits Valentinus with the notion of three subsistent entities or hypostases; fragment 6 (Clement *Stromateis* 6.52.3-4) speaks warmly of God's church as "the people of the beloved, which is beloved and which loves him."

[3] Irenaeus, *Adv. haer.* 1.11.1 and 1.1-1.8.

[4] See Clement's *Stromateis*, book 7.

[5] This long version of the title is preserved in Eusebius *H.E.* 5.7.1.

[6] *Adv. haer.* 1.9.4.

somewhat lighthearted collage in imitation of and tribute to a master poet's work.[7] Irenaeus misunderstands the purposes of the only literary practice he cites as parallel to the gnostics'.

Irenaeus complains that bits of scripture not only were chosen promiscuously but also handled too freely, without regard for their proper context, as freely as those who ransacked the pagan classics to concoct recycled poems on completely new subjects. The complaint that gnostics "disregard the order and the connection of the Scriptures" and "transfer passages and rearrange them" is all too easy to interpret anachronistically, at least for modern exegetes who might think of a heedless and insensitive prooftexting in contrast to a careful search for the meaning of texts in relation to their original historical context. For Irenaeus or interpreters like him, however, the proper context for a passage of scripture would have been the context of the traditions of his or her own group. The "beautiful image of a king" was the way that the whole of scriptures could be read to yield the "one faith" which Irenaeus claimed was held by the church "throughout the whole world."[8] In other words, the "order and connection" that counted was a particular web of symbolic relationships between the texts. Irenaeus objected to disrupting this web in any way, whether by severing connections between texts or by proposing different connections. Juxtapositions of texts, along with allegorical interpretations of them, were legitimate as long as they corroborated the faith of the church, and illegitimate when they did not. His opponents, however, were playing quite another game: they shuffled their texts and dealt them out, again and again, hoping for combinations full of meaning, productive of insight. They seem not to have judged the results strictly by their correspondence to an existing system, nor by internal consistency, but by their capacity to provoke insight. And, of course,

---

[7] A couple of centuries later, Christian centos were being produced, certainly without any intent to disparage either their subject matter or their sources. See, for example, *Grégoire de Nazianze. La Passion du Christ. Tragédie,* ed. André Tuilier (Paris: Éditions du Cerf, 1969), a Euripidean cento attributed to Gregory of Nazianzus, and *The Golden Bough, The Oaken Cross,* ed. Elizabeth A. Clark and Diane F. Hatch (Chico, CA: Scholars Press, 1981) a Virgilian cento about salvation history from the creation to Christ's ascension, by Faltonia Betitia Proba. Proba, at least, makes her mode of expression explicit: "praesens, deus, erige mentem; Virgilium cecinisse loquar pia munera Christi."

[8] Irenaeus, *Adv. haer.* 1.10.

what counted as insight could vary noticeably from one person to the next.[9]

The fifth complaint in Irenaeus' characterization of gnostic exegesis was the incorporation of discredited or "lowbrow" motifs into mythological syntheses which expect to be taken seriously. Irenaeus referred to a phenomenon which deserves much fuller treatment than it can be given in this context. The term he used, γραῶν μύθοι, "old women's fables," is an allusion to 1 Timothy 4.7, but both passages point to folkloric ele-

---

[9] This understanding of speculation is quite distinct from "allegorical interpretation." It is important to make the distinction explicit, since the latter is sometimes over-attributed to gnostics, as, for example, by David Dawson in his *Allegorical Readers and Cultural Revision in Ancient Alexandria* (Berkeley: University of California Press, 1992). Dawson makes a number of insightful remarks about the meaning of Valentinus' fragments and the *Gospel of Truth*, especially in relation to their social and cultural context, and I have no quarrel with his position *vis a vis* "symbolism" and "typology," nor with his definition of "allegory."

Nevertheless, many of the things he observes (usually with accuracy) in Valentinian texts are quite unlike the allegorical treatments he traces in Philo and Clement, and unlike most things denoted by the word "allegory." When recognizable elements from several distinct traditions are woven together into an new story which is nuanced by values and associations from all of them, it seems misleading to call the result a "commentary" on any one of them (however carefully camouflaged) or an "interpretation" of any one of them. It is something else. This is not, of course, to say that Valentinus or other gnostics did not engage in explicit allegory of several different kinds. They did, of course—but much of what they did was not so obviously allegory, and is likely to be misinterpreted if forced to fit that mold.

Dawson's basic premise was moored in the paradigm of the deceptive revaluation of a single text—the paradigm used by Irenaeus. Dawson wrote of "layers of interpretation, each layer seeking to *hide its interpretive character*" (128, emphasis mine), of a "new story, into which he [the "allegorist"] surreptitiously weaves *the* old story" (129, emphasis mine). Despite his exploration of the contribution from sources like the *Apocryphon of John* or the *Hypostasis of the Archons* to Valentinus' thought, he continued to view Valentinus' synthesis predominantly from the perspective of one of its elements, namely the works that would become canonical.

Dawson's presuppositions blinded him to a major aspect of Valentinus' thought: its emphasis is often neither on the elements (from wherever borrowed) nor on new (and allegedly "allegorical") interpretations of their meanings, but on the analogies that can be drawn within the big picture of a speculative system. To say that A is to B as C is to D (A:B::C:D) is not to say that A means C, or is even like C. One is invited to ponder the similarities between the relationships. Dawson correctly drew out much of the analogical structure of Valentinus' fragments on the creation of Adam, but at the end of his discussion returned to talk of "identifications" and using the verb "equate." (136-142)

This chapter seeks to propose a more appropriate paradigm for some of those elements that are not well served by the paradigm of allegorical exegesis.

ments in the culture, some perhaps never taken seriously by intellectuals or religious authorities, others possibly the survivals of older and out-moded mythologies. The inclusion of such material was a major point of friction between gnostic and non-gnostic Christians. It is one thing to tell a somewhat anthropomorphic story about God when such a story is a venerable part of tradition, especially if it had a long tradition of allegori-cal interpretation. It is quite another to include such a thing, without warrant of tradition, within the framework of a lofty and philosophically oriented account of good and evil. In late antiquity, many groups (including gnostic, Christian, and Jewish) felt the attraction of a high-brow philosophizing about mythology. Traditions already venerable with age were equated with the clear, colorless abstractions of philosophy in such a way that the prestige of each was enhanced. But it was shocking to combine philosophy with "common," low-brow, discredited folklore, perhaps even women's lore: to hear of divine or semi-divine beings resorting subterfuge or to makeshift measures to compensate for lack of proper tools and materials, or achieving unsatisfactory results, or requiring unsuccessful attempts before achieving success. Without the garments of antiquity and their accompanying prestige, an anthropomorphic demiurge becomes comic in the new context of philosophical sophistication, acquiring the character of a trickster. The degree to which this happens in gnostic literature varies, but it is one of the elements considered most unacceptable by other groups laying claim to some of the same mythological framework and philosophical presuppositions. The gnostic willingness to incorporate such material points to a certain detachment; it is part of the same approach seen in the heuristic shuffling and reshuffling of texts and mythical images.

Myth, Belief, and the Claim to Truth

While ancient heresiologists sought to use the proliferation of systems to discredit their authors, modern scholars of gnostic phenomena have stud-ied these systems in detail and sometimes with respect. Nevertheless, we have not often asked the question of the function of this proliferation. Scholars of mythology and anthropology have frequently asked similar questions, but their context has been almost entirely the origins of mythology, and its function in preliterate tribal settings, not the rear-rangement of mythological elements in a literate and cosmopolitan soci-ety such as the Roman empire. Nevertheless, some of their insights seem transferable to this other setting. I will not here attempt to survey the range of theories about the function of mythology, or their history, but only to glean certain concepts that will help elucidate the phenomenon of gnostic speculation.

In some modern Western typologies of narratives, "myth" is characterized as, among other things, stories which are absolutely and unquestioningly believed to be true—though always by "primitive" others, not by the investigator. Raffaele Pettazzoni's analysis provides an explicit example. Pettazzoni traced an extremely widespread dichotomy between religious myths (especially myths of origin) and fictions.[10] He compiled many indications of what "true" can mean in these dichotomies, drawing primarily on North American, African, and Australian indigenous cultures. "True" can mean stories recited at prescribed times (e.g., cult ceremonials, in certain seasons of the year or at certain times of the day); those restricted to being told only at certain times; those which, while known to all, may only be told by certain authorized persons; those which carry a danger to their hearers, which can be averted by certain actions (especially washing); those which certain classes of people are forbidden to hear; et cetera. "False," in Pettazzoni's composite dichotomy, means under no such restrictions.

It is unclear why Pettazzoni chose to attach the concepts "true" and "false" to the poles of this dichotomy. It is evident from his data that a story which possesses several of these characteristics is special and different from one which does not, but there is little indication in these attributes that the stories possessing these characteristics were regarded as "true" in the sense of "corresponding to objective reality" or something of that kind, nor that the absence of such restrictions on a story means that it was regarded as "fictitious" and therefore "false," as Pettazzoni assumed.[11] As a corollary, changing such a story might (or might not) involve serious hazards, but the result of falsehood (as failure to correspond to reality) is not necessarily one of them. Assumptions like Pettazzoni's seem to underlie a common "naive" understanding of mythology in our culture (possibly due to its permeation by Greek philosophical ideas

---

[10]"Raffaele Pettazzoni, "The Truth of Myth," in *Sacred Narrative. Readings in the Theory of Myth* ed. Alan Dundes (Berkeley: University of California Press, 1984) 98-109.

[11] It should be noted that some kinds of legends—especially those of a "tall tale" nature, told largely for entertainment—are sometimes restricted in their time of telling and/or "owned" by certain storytellers who have the right to authorize others to tell the story. See William Bascom, "The Forms of Folklore: Prose Narratives" in *Sacred Narrative*, ed. Dundes, 5-29.

of truth, as mediated by Christianity), and persists in some of the scholarly theories about the meaning and origin of mythologies.

Such assumptions, however, are not universally accepted. Anthropology's treatment of the myths of primitive peoples as inherently fixed and unchanging has, as Raymond Firth pointed out, been conditioned by a general lack of evidence by which to trace a tradition's changes through time. Where such evidence exists, sacred traditions often prove themselves to be quite adaptable. Firth cited a story in which divine brothers build the heavenly prototype of a temple. Its earthly exemplar, and presumably some form of the story, date from around 1700 C.E.—but the myth of its origin has come to include, as a major theme, a series of actions explaining a situation which did not come about until a century later. In another case, political pressure and Christian harassment induced pagan Tikopias to abandon a ritual involving a stone image—but the harassment soon gave rise to widespread accounts of how the stone repeatedly rescued itself from would-be kidnappers and returned to its spot, much to the kidnappers' discredit and the stone's—and its devotees'—prestige.[12] Such traditions seem almost infinitely adaptable.

Th. P. van Baaren has also cited multiple examples of deliberate adjustments of myths to accommodate changing dynasties, changing laws (such as a shift in stories from human sacrifice to animal sacrifice at the time when the former was banned), and new awareness of other groups of people and their attributes (by expanding myths of origins to include newly encountered peoples). In the case of Tahitian genealogies, which validate rule by tracing the parentage of the current ruler back to the gods, the policy of deliberate change was able to coexist with a prescribed penalty of death for any priest making an error in the recital.[13] The change in the genealogy brought it into greater correspondence with "objective" reality—albeit reality on the social and political level.

---

[12] Raymond Firth, "The Plasticity of Myth: Cases from Tikopia" in *Sacred Narrative*, ed. Dundes, 207-216.

[13] Th. P. Van Baaren, "The Flexibility of Myth" in *Sacred Narrative*, ed. Dundes, 217-224. While van Baaren's examples are all from the literature of contemporary ethnology and deal with Tahiti, Borneo, the Nilotic Anuak and Papua New Guinea, his assessment of the interplay of stability and change in these bodies of myths is reminiscent of John A. Wilson's famous thesis that ancient Egyptian culture was enormously successful (and long-lived) by making continual adjustments which, over time, amounted to major changes in essence, all the while denying change and blithely asserting that their system was eternal. See *The Culture of Ancient Egypt* (Chicago: University of Chicago Press, 1951) 91-21 and *passim*.

Claude Lévi-Strauss has made several observations which are particularly relevant to the study of late and literate reshufflings of mythology, although this was not his context. Underlying his structuralism but broader than it, he contended that it is the relation of the elements in a myth to each other which gives it its meaning, not the elements themselves. Many might wish to revise this to "not exclusively the elements themselves," but the importance of the relationship remains.[14] And if the meaning of a sacred tradition lies, even in part, in the relation of its elements, so does its importance—or even its "truth," if that is the right word.

Like many primitive and non-Western peoples, gnostic speculators in the first few centuries of the common era seem to have held their beliefs lightly.[15]

The Function of Recombinant Mythography

Claude Lévi-Strauss' famous characterization of mythological thought as a *bricoleur* is based on the insight that the meaning of myth lies in the relation of its elements; it is strikingly similar to Irenaeus' analogies of the rearranged mosaic portrait and the cento. The French term *bricoleur* designates a sort of tinker, a person who makes and/or fixes things, not by tooling up and manufacturing the parts needed from raw materials but by re-using and adapting existing objects. *Bricolage* is a duct tape and hairpin approach to life, and Lévi-Strauss claims that "mythological thought is . . . a kind of intellectual 'bricolage.'"[16] That is, mythological thought "builds up structures by fitting together events, or rather the remains of events," using "remains and debris of events," "the fossilized evidence of the history of an individual or a society."[17]

---

[14] After discussion of Lévi-Strauss' view that the underlying structure alone constitutes the meaning of a myth and that its surface elements are irrelevant, G. S. Kirk comments, "It would be preferable to say that the message conveyed by a myth is a product of its overt contents and the relation between them." G. S. Kirk, *Myth, Its Meaning and Functions in Ancient and Other Cultures* (Cambridge: Cambridge University Press, 1970) 43.

[15] See Jean Pouillon's "Remarks on the Verb, 'To Believe,'" in *Between Belief and Transgression. Structuralist Essays in Religion, History, and Myth* (Chicago: University of Chicago Press, 1982) 1-9.

[16] Claude Lévi-Strauss, *The Savage Mind* (Chicago: University of Chicago Press, 1966) 17.

[17] Lévi-Strauss, *Savage Mind*, 22.

He saw the function of myth as allowing adjustment to changing and future institutions. Mythology provided the means for readjustments to the conditions of life, both present and changing. Lévi-Strauss claimed that these readjustments could not be the work of individuals, however. The "thinking" that is done in mythology is, according to him, normally done collectively and below the level of consciousness.

> Although the possibility cannot be excluded that the speakers who create and transmit myths may become aware of their structure and mode of operation, this cannot occur as a normal thing, but only partially and intermittently. It is the same with myths as with language: the individual who conscientiously applied phonological and grammatical laws in his speech, supposing he possessed the necessary knowledge and virtuosity to do so, would nevertheless lose the thread of his ideas almost immediately. In the same way the practice and the use of mythological thought demand that its properties remain hidden: otherwise the subject would find himself in the position of the mythologist, who cannot believe in myths because it is his task to take them to pieces. Mythological analysis has not, and cannot have, as its aim to show how men think. . . .I therefore claim to show not how men think in their myths, but how myths operate in men's minds without their being aware of the fact.[18]

The analogy with grammar is a misleading one, however. Re-telling a sacred story is never a matter of putting events or ideas into words for the first time, much less of making up a story as one goes along. True, the words may vary, and changes both small and large are made on occasion. But the story has been heard before, year after year, generation after generation. It is likely known by heart both by the teller and the listeners. It is a part of life—to tell, to hear told, to remember, to reflect upon at crucial and trivial moments, and idly over chores. It can be a matter of discussion or allusion, of patterns of words and images, borrowed solemnly or lightheartedly or as a shorthand critique of the matter to which they are applied. The roots of a mythology are deep and broad. There is room enough for every imaginable kind of consciousness to co-exist—though not perhaps simultaneously—without conflict. In fact, this is what one would expect if the analogy to language were applied carefully!

The world of late antiquity was a literate one in which many different traditions, sacred and otherwise, had been reworked time and again, to such an extent that the entire period is useless to those trying to recover

---

[18] Claude Lévi-Strauss, *The Raw and the Cooked, Introduction to a Science of Mythology* (New York and Evanston: Harper Torchbooks, 1969) 11-12.

the origins or pristine state of mythologies. Nevertheless, Lévi-Strauss' analysis of mythology as *bricoleur* turns out to be applicable to late, literate, and conscious efforts to rethink traditional mythological themes and to use them as a means for speculation on a variety of issues.

A key aspect of the intellectual *bricolage* that is mythological thought is that it uses a limited and heterogeneous repertoire of material which is the sum of what has accumulated, "the contingent result of all the occasions there have been to renew or enrich the stock or to maintain it with the remains of previous constructions or deconstructions."[19]

> . . .the possibilities always remain limited by the particular history of each piece and by those of its features which are already determined by the use for which it was originally intended or the modifications it has undergone for other purposes. The elements which the 'bricoleur' collects and uses are 'pre-constrained' like the constitutive units of myth, the possible combinations of which are restricted by the fact that they are drawn from the language where they already possess a sense which sets a limit on their freedom of maneuver.[20]

The relation of mythological *bricolage* to its component elements is ambivalent: on the one hand, the process is limited to a finite set of imagery which is both familiar and meaningful; on the other hand, such *bricolage* need not owe great allegiance to the traditions on which it builds. Indeed, it cannot work in those few cases where reverence for the tradition takes the form of rendering it inalterable.

The "pre-constrained" quality of the elements of mythological thought results in a constant web of apparent allusion and cross-reference in its products. There are always more possible chains of connection, more than anyone could intend at any one time, more than are needed to carry forward the speculation at hand. (This additional richness allows and encourages the imagery's use as raw material for future endeavors of *bricolage*.) It is, however, often possible to detect which strands of the web are being emphasized in any given telling.

Both of Irenaeus' images of Valentinian exegesis share, and share with Lévi-Strauss' image of *bricolage*, the feature that something new has been made out of the cultural remains of a previous work. Such remains are not free from signs of their previous uses, however. The "pre-constrained" aspect of the elements is what could fool simple folk into believing that they are looking at the previous (for Irenaeus, the original)

---

[19] Lévi-Strauss, *Savage Mind*, 17.
[20] Lévi-Strauss, *Savage Mind*, 19.

construction, i.e., the original mosaic portrait or a genuine passage from Homer.

It is unlikely that this kind of mistake was either the intention of gnostic Christian exegesis or the mode in which it was normally received. Irenaeus was hostile to the re-use of the elements of the Christian story as the means of new speculation on the meaning of life, and hence unable or unwilling to recognize it for what it was. Still, his witness is valuable confirmation that gnostics were re-using Christian mythology in the manner of a *bricoleur*. Not surprisingly, this instance of *bricolage* in late antiquity shows a key mark of a limited and heterogeneous "stock" of materials: an "intertextuality" which is built in rather than always intended, which becomes both a source of richness and of confusion.

COLLECTING ACTIVITY WITHIN THE CONTEXT OF SPECULATION

It might be easy to assume that while a few brilliant gnostics devised and recorded great systems of speculative myth, the less gifted studied the systems of a Ptolemy or a Theodotus, and preached and taught those systems with scrupulous care (unless and until overcome by a desire to outdo their teachers and create their own system). This would be a misreading of the *Gestalt* of the gnosticizing movements of the first several centuries, however. If the quest for individual insight was a hallmark of these movements, and the systems that their greatest thinkers produced were valued for their ability to provoke intuitive insight rather than for their literal truth, the tendency to tinker with images and constellations of images was probably more common than the studious acceptance of authority. True, it was a path to enlightenment which could only be followed by literate people who had some leisure for reflection, but such people were not in short supply in and around the Roman empire in those times, and they were the sort of folk attracted to gnosticisms anyway. It was not a path which required either rigorous logic or specialized training for success.

If the sort of textual and mythological *bricolage* described above was an important *modus operandi* in gnostic speculation, it would normally have been preceded by the compilation of promising materials, and followed by the excerpting labors of those who found in the resulting systems something of value. If this tendency to mythological speculation and the "centonisation" of sacred imagery and texts extended far into the rank and file of gnostics, then such excerpting and collecting of provocative (and sometimes discordant) materials would have been widespread. In such an atmosphere, even people who had no intention of developing a whole system or writing up their findings for publication would be likely to collect excerpts that particularly interested them, that shed some light on their own situation, or that had the power to put other teachings or texts into a new perspective.

The Gospel according to Philip *as a Sourcebook for Speculation*

The *Gospel according to Philip* is not a speculative system, nor does it contain materials which have been reworked and coordinated into such a system, but it does contain some rather good elements from which such a system could be built. *Bricolage* with sacred traditions was an accepted path to enlightenment within that milieu. The intersection of the excerpting and collecting activity typical of ancient writers and readers with this more specifically gnostic quest of speculative recombination of materials recommends itself as a context in which to understand this remarkable document. Our document's elusive coherence may result from the adaptability of the texts chosen, the "accidental" but provocative intertextuality that accompanies materials reappropriated from previous uses, and their deliberate juxtaposition by its collector. Such a collection makes an implicit invitation to the reader to speculate on the meanings and interrelationships of the patterns there. To read as historians, we must bracket that invitation, for the time being, and ask what sources went to make up this collection, and seek to discover how and why these materials were brought together.

PART TWO

THE COMPONENTS OF THE *GOSPEL ACCORDING TO PHILIP*

INTRODUCTION TO PART TWO

The material included in the *Gospel according to Philip* is demonstrably diverse; the demonstration of this is the matter of Part Two.

No single piece of evidence, taken by itself, proves beyond all doubt the composite nature of this document, but there are many pieces of evidence which come rather close. Nevertheless, it is the cumulative force of many pieces of evidence, and their fit with the collecting process, the attributes of known collections, and the nature of gnostic speculation, which together make it clear that we are dealing with a collection of materials of diverse origins, assembled and edited according to the conventions of such works.

Chapter 6 presents methods by which source material may be identified within such a collection. The peculiarities of collections, as seen in chapters 3 and 4, call for some special precautions in this task.

Chapter 7 begins to survey the document by means of those methods, tracing the primary differences between large blocks of text and noting signs of divergent materials within them. A major rift divides the *Gospel according to Philip* at 77.15. Themes, interests, and approaches which characterize the first three-quarters of the document vanish when we cross that divide. Although certain interests remain constant, the jostling of divergent opinions abruptly ceases, and something like a single voice emerges, employing different exegetical and rhetorical strategies, making distinctive points.

The final quarter of the text, from 77.15 to the end, is distinguished by considerable stylistic uniformity, by longer units presenting carefully developed argumentation, by a tendency to allude to (rather than quote) scripture frequently, by a distinctive understanding of the basic problematic of human life and its solution, and by an utter lack of interest in a dozen or so highly visible sectarian issues belonging to the first three quarters of the text. This final section shows strong affiliations with the *Gospel of Truth*, and breathes the air of an early or a conservative Valentinianism. Chapter 8 explores the nature of this block of text.

The section before 77.15 is not only distinct from the material before that point, but is itself clearly heterogeneous. The surface traces of most of the smaller fault lines have been obscured by editorial practices common to collections from late antiquity. Potentially independent excerpts have sometimes been strung together in an artfully "random" order, sometimes arranged in thematic or analogous clusters, sometimes linked by "catch word" rhetorical devices which range from the mechanical and purfunctory to the extremely sophisticated. Chapter 9 attempts to trace identifiable strands of tradition through the first three quarters of the *Gospel according to Philip*.

CHAPTER SIX

METHODS AND CRITERIA

Since the hypothesis under investigation is that the *Gospel according to Philip* belongs to an organizational and stylistic continuum which made a virtue of several of the kinds of aporiae used by traditional source analysis, we must proceed cautiously in attempting to identify material from different sources within it. Incongruous juxtapositions, the impression of random or fortuitous sequencing, an enigmatic brevity of expression, the omission of such textual markers as introductory or connective statements, and the ambiguous richness of potential inter-reference produced by the clustering of "pre-constrained" elements—these were all symptomatic of the excerpting and collecting process, but they were also given a positive value by collectors and editors of collections. The dominance of these features in the *Gospel according to Philip* situates it within the rather large and flabby continuum of collections and pseudo-collections, but within that continuum, such features cannot be taken to mark redactional seams or preexisting units in any reliable way.

As a consequence, we cannot frame an argument about the unity or diversity of this text by appeal to the traditional data of source analysis without careful re-evaluation. Breaks in continuity and changes of topic, however jolting, might represent carefully achieved effects (either within a single block of material or between blocks from disparate sources) rather than badly stitched redactional seams. And, of course, we can hardly expect an editor to supply linking statements or summaries if he or she was working in a tradition that sometimes deliberately deleted them!

A number of indicators of diverse origins remain, however, which do not seem likely to have been affected either by the excerpting process or by editorial preferences for variety, gnomic reserve, and fortuitous polysemy. Shifts in word choices (especially terms involved in the sensitive matters of sectarian self-designation and differentiation), divergent interests and approaches, differing assessments of the basic human problem, and distinctive ways of framing and supporting positions allow us to begin to differentiate excerpts from disparate sources, and to trace the use of these sources through the document. Though largely obscured by translation, where shifts in style can be discerned, they can reveal similar phenomena. Evidence of affiliations with specific milieux in the early Christian and gnostic world allow us to link some passages with known groups and developments.

The analysis in Part Two depends on several basic kinds of argument. The situation is one of accumulated probabilities, some stronger than others, not of absolute certainties—but this is generally the case in the investigation of anything in the past. Four basic types of arguments have been used here to differentiate and disentangle sources within the *Gospel according to Philip*: (1) When two passages use a term in incompatible ways, or in sharply differentiated ways, or otherwise show radically divergent tendencies, those passages did not derive from the same source. (2) When a group of terms, ideas, approaches, and the like appear frequently in some parts of the document and not at all (or only in radically transformed senses) in other parts, which contain their own set of characteristic terms, ideas, et cetera, a discontinuity must be postulated: a different selection criteria (possibly indicating a different collector or redactor), or different sources, or both.[1] (3) When multiple distinguishing characteristics (special vocabulary, approaches, et cetera) appear together in several passages, especially when they appear only (or primarily) as a group—that is, in conjunction with each other—those passages probably came from the same or closely related sources. (4) When passages share unusual characteristics with another document, or with the documents of a particular and distinctive tradition, those passages probably came from a source or sources associated with that document or tradition.

The first two of these methods differentiate passages or blocks of text as derived from different sources, and are, together, the primary focus of chapter 7. The third and fourth criteria above allow the grouping of passages derived from the same or related sources, and (together with the findings of chapter 7) guide the investigation in chapters 8 and 9.

---

[1] Analysis of what has changed and what has remained constant may be hoped to shed some light on which of these possibilities is more likely: chapter 11 below argues that a single collector's interests are manifest in choices of material derived from some fairly divergent sources.

DIVERGENCES, DIFFERENTIATIONS, AND INCOMPATIBILITIES

Divergent, inconsistent, or incompatible terms, usages, concepts, and approaches allow us to form relatively strong hypotheses that passages with these divergent markers did not come from the same source. For example, if passages A and B use a term positively, and passages X, Y, and Z use it negatively, we may hypothesize that neither A nor B came from the same source(s) as X or Y or Z. The underlying assumption is that neither individual writers nor communities usually affirm both a thing and its negation—at least, not if it matters much to them, and provided they are not indulging in deliberate paradox. Incompatible and mutually exclusive statements obviously fit this class of evidence, but so do developments and understandings which clearly diverge from each other.

Hypotheses based on this criterion are relatively strong—how strong depends upon the divergence or inconsistency in question—but they are also extremely particular. In the above situation, we actually have many small (but strong) hypotheses:

- A did not come from the same source as X.
- A did not come from the same source as Y.
- A did not come from the same source as Z.
- B did not come from the same source as X.
- B did not come from the same source as Y.
- B did not come from the same source as Z.

We may have two sources here, or five, or any number in between.

A second kind of hypothesis may also be made from the same data, but it is a weak one: since there can only be a finite number of sources involved, there is some probability that passages with a similar usage, et cetera, came from the same source. In our hypothetical situation, it is somewhat probable that A and B came from a single source (or closely related sources), and that X, Y and Z came from a single source (or closely related sources). The existence of multiple points of similarity between two passages, or other factors (see below), may increase this probability so that, taking the evidence together, we may come to have quite good reason to see A and B as derived from the same source, or X, Y, and Z.

The exception to this rule is the paradox constructed to point beyond the categories involved. The paradoxical statements in *Thunder, Perfect Mind* are a good source of examples of paradox: "It is I who am the wife: and the virgin. . . . . It is I who am the barren: and who has many children."[2] Such a paradox says, "I am above both this category and its negation: there is a level of reality at which these categories are not valid."

Deliberately paradoxical statements include the conflicting affirmations in close conjunction with each other. They can be distinguished by this feature; without it, they fail to communicate their point. For example, a person who made the assertions we find in *Thunder* as separate statements, not in conjunction as paired opposites, would not be pointing to a truth beyond these dichotomies, but lying or insane—or at best attempting paradoxical communication in such an ineffective way as to be dismissed as lying or insane. The test here is: Are the opposed statements in a conjunction which would lead their hearers or readers to seek to understand them paradoxically?

Qualification of the sense in which a term is employed may also make the application of this criterion unclear. A category may be claimed in one sense, while it is rejected in another. For example, both Irenaeus and Clement of Alexandria handled the term gnosis in this way, claiming that the so-called gnostics did not have the true claim to the term. Such qualifications take the form, "I affirm x, but in a different sense than others affirm it." The point is lost without the statement of the comparative status of the different senses. Explicitness is of the essence for hairsplitting.

The uses of religious jargon, especially as it is involved in sectarian self-understanding and differentiation, is a particularly good place to look for such incompatible or divergent usages, because the terms used in sectarian conflict are particularly touchy matters. Passages which use a term in self-reference are unlikely to come from the same individual or group as passages which reserve that term for their opponents or who make a point to distinguish themselves from those who use the term. For example, while one may certainly consider the leaders of one's group to be personally immoral, obtuse with respect to the defining teachings of the group, or even dangerous to the group's present or future morals or doctrine, one does not define one's group as authorized by the fact of possessing a certain sort of leadership, and at the same time condemn one's opponents as hopelessly misguided simply because they possess

---

[2] *Thunder* 18, 22.

the same sort of leadership. As separate, serious statements, these positions can hardly come from the same source.

Different or divergent positions or understandings with respect to any matter can warrant the hypothesis that those passages which differ markedly did not come from the same source. Different views of salvation, the human dilemma, the workings of sacraments, exegetical strategies, and different interests are all employed in Part Two to differentiate material derived from different sources. Style is also a type of evidence on which this sort of hypothesis can be based, despite the obscuring and leveling effect of the Coptic translation.

PATTERNS OF SOURCE UTILIZATION

A second category of evidence consists of patterns of usage, conceptuality, approach, et cetera, as they appear throughout the document as a whole, and particularly the congruence of many such patterns. Certain characteristics appear in certain portions of the text, and not in other portions: for example, the term ΝΥΜϤⲰΝ (and its near synonyms) does not appear at all until page 65. The distribution of terms, ideas, and the like can be traced across the document; it yields a rough map of differences in interest and focus, pointing to the utilization of different sources. Multiple instances of a characteristic certainly need not have come from the same source (as argued above). But for any composite work, large portions of text in which many features recur frequently must depend (in part or wholly) on one or more sources in which those features were present. If all these characteristics then disappear for a sizable block of text, it would seem that the block from which they are absent depended on another source or sources, some of them perhaps shared with the first, but not the sources from which these absent characteristics derived.[3]

Caution must be used here: a number of modifiers in the above paragraph point to matters of judgment: how big is a "sizable" block of text?

---

[3] A different selection criterion might, instead, have been involved, but the possibility is dubious. The new criterion of selection would have to involve the avoidance of many, previously favored, ideas, images, et cetera. One would have to ask why a collector with such different interests would choose to continue a collection so seemingly uncongenial to him or her. When (as we shall see in Part Three) strong evidence points to a uniting set of interests throughout the work, the assumption of different sources seems much the more economical.

how many appearances of a feature constitutes "frequently"? how similar must statements, positions, images, et cetera, be, to count as "recurrence"? Such matters cannot be entirely quantified; they remain a matter
of judgment—though they should, nevertheless, be subjected to as careful and self-doubting a judgment as possible.

A rough kind of quantification, however, is possible, and it can serve
as an aid to judgment. Terms and interests which occur rarely in the
work show us little or nothing. For example, the restriction of the Greek
loan word ἀθάνατος to the first three quarters of the text is insignificant:
the word appears only once, on page 75. If it appeared ten times in the
same short passage on page 75, its absence from the final quarter would
still be insignificant. When, however, a number of separate passages
spread over a number of pages[4] habitually use a certain term to express
their ideas, while another section is entirely devoid of that term, then we
must wonder.

We may gain some control over our wondering by considering the
frequency with which a characteristic occurs in a portion of the text as
the number of recurrences divided by the number of pages in that
portion of text. For example, a term might appear twelve times, in seven
different passages, in the first twenty-seven pages, and not at all in the
final nine pages. Its occurrence in the first twenty-seven pages (i.e., in a
little more than one passage every four pages) would lead us to expect
two or three occurrences in the final nine pages. The absence of any
appearance may well be significant: may, not must. (If the characteristic
appeared on every page in the first three-quarters of the text, then disappeared, it would be virtually impossible to discount!) Moreover, such a
"statistic" again rests on a judgment: the number of passages or excerpts
in which a term, image, et cetera, occurs is much more important than the
total number of occurrences, but the detection of the seams between
separate excerpts is controverted. Nevertheless, when many
characteristics follow the same pattern or recurrence and absence, even
if each seems, by itself, only marginally significant, the utilization of
different sources becomes a reasonable—or even a necessary—
hypothesis.

---

[4] Since the paragraph or excerpt divisions are so disputed, patterns of distribution have been analyzed herein with reference to the pages of the Coptic
manuscript. The pagination of the manuscript itself supplies ready-made divisions
of convenient size which do not pre-judge the findings.

Such patterns of distribution show differences between large blocks of text, not the precise boundaries between them (unless, by good fortune, several characteristics of each block of text happen to occur immediately on either side of such a seam). Moreover, this criterion does not insure against small inclusions of foreign traditions within such blocks. Its results need to be refined by examination of other characteristics.

Stylistic differences might be supposed to parallel differences in author and/or tradition. While translation into Coptic has obscured very many features which could be analyzed if we possessed the original Greek text, we do indeed find differences in rhetorical strategies. The patterns of their appearance, where they can be detected, should be analyzed in the same way as other characteristics of blocks of text.

In fact, very many indicators, including some which have been considered typical of the *Gospel according to Philip* as a whole, occur only in the first three quarters of the work, and are nowhere to be seen in the final quarter, which (as we shall see) has a number of distinctive peculiarities of its own.[5]

PECULIARITIES SHARED BY GROUPS OF PASSAGES

A third kind criterion considers similarities between passages—in approach, doctrine, presupposition, manner of expression, et cetera—and works toward the identification of groups of passages similar in these respects. Still, the hypothesis that two passages came from the same source because they show a single common characteristic is a weak one. Unless the characteristic in question is extremely peculiar, it could easily have been present in any number of potential or actual source documents. The fact that any collection can have only a finite number of sources does a little, but very little, to strengthen it.

On the other hand, when multiple points of similarity are shared by a group of passages, even if each passage contains only a few characteristics of the group, the probability rises sharply that these passages derive from the same source or from closely related sources.

Even so, this criterion is generally more ambiguous than the first two. One key is the characteristics involved: if they are truly unusual, the

---

[5] These are listed at the end of chapter 7.

case is quite strong; if they are more common, it is rather weak.[6] Another
key is the number of characteristics in each passage and the degree to
which they interlock. Suppose one passage has characteristics A and B,
another B and C, two more, A and C, and another B and D. These
passages seem closely related, more likely than not dependent upon the
same source. But even so, characteristics A and C (each of which occurs
three times in this hypothetical group of passages) are somewhat more
secure markers than B, which occurs only twice. Another passage
involving either A or C would be a strong candidate for membership in
this group. Characteristic D, on the other hand, is a less clear indicator: it
appears only once in the group, in conjunction with the rather less
strong B. The hypothesis that another passage involving only
characteristic D derived from the same source as the others in this group
is still plausible, but weaker.

Short excerpts, however, can hardly be expected to each contain every interest of their sources, every favored bit of jargon, every distinctive
doctrine or practice. This category of evidence, more than the other
three employed here, is directly affected by the relative brevity of the
excerpts in question. Nevertheless, these are the restrictions imposed by
the document being studied; there is enough evidence to allow some
tentative groupings, some of which can also be supported by arguments
of other types.

PECULIARITIES SHARED WITH SPECIFIC TRADITIONS OR MILIEUX

Correspondences between the *Gospel according to Philip* and other
texts allows the hypothesis that there is some connection between this
text and those others. Again, some limits apply.

One subgroup of this type of evidence is the citation of other literature. Most of the references to non-biblical works which have been
identified by translators and others, however, are cases of similar uses of
imagery, or parallel ideas. Some (or many) of these may well have been
intended as allusions to specific passages, but most do not include
enough verbal similarity, or imagery sufficiently distinctive, to make it
clear that the allusion is to a specific text. The problem is compounded

---

[6] "Commonness," however, is a relative thing: judged against the background of
the other Nag Hammadi writings, the use of the word "Christian" is quite uncommon!

by the fact that much gnostic and gnostic Christian literature has simply been lost. What was once crisply and unmistakably an allusion to a text now lost may seem to us to echo, indistinctly, other allusions to that text or statements of related ideas.

The use of widely-known literature, nevertheless, shows that this literature was (at least) not considered unacceptable by the source, and was—perhaps, depending on the use made—even considered authoritative. The citation of Matthew's gospel, for example, is so common in second- and third-century writings associated with Christianity that such citations show relatively little beyond some association with Christianity in some form. The citation of less ubiquitously utilized literature, on the other hand, may be an important clue linking together material associated with relatively specific traditions. When passages depend on a relatively little-quoted source, they probably represent the same tradition or are extracts from the same source. Again, this will yield small groups of passages.

The occurrence of a very distinctive idea can also be used to link passages, but the idea must be quite distinctive. This criterion, like the last, is capable both of linking together passages within the *Gospel according to Philip,* and of linking those groups of passages with other streams of traditions in the early Christian and gnostic worlds.

Some of the positions articulated in this rather fragmented collection bear strong resemblances to specific gnostic and gnostic Christian traditions. On this basis, sections can be marked out and identified as originating in those traditions. Small groups of passages linked to the same external tradition, even if they contain no characteristics in common with each other, can be joined together into a larger group of materials all derived from that tradition.

CHAPTER SEVEN

INDICATIONS OF A COMPOSITE CHARACTER

The argument for the composite nature of the *Gospel according to Philip* rests, of course, on both evidence for the disunity of the whole and evidence for smaller identifiable unities. This chapter will survey the distribution of terms used in sectarian self-definition and differentiation, the sometimes opposed or sharply divergent senses in which such terms are used, and the distribution of other indicators of interests, approaches, and tendencies. The next two chapters will build on this evidence, and on other indicators, to group together some specific passages.

THE DISTRIBUTION OF SECTARIAN TERMINOLOGY

The terms "Christian," "apostle," "apostolic," "perfect," "Hebrew," "Jew," and "gentile" are all restricted to the first three quarters of the *Gospel according to Philip*. The issues of group identity to which they point are of interest in at least some of the sources of that material; these are absent from the final quarter of the document. Within the material before 77.15, however, many of these terms are used in distinct, conflicting, and at times mutually contradictory senses, showing the passages in which they appear to be of diverse provenance.

"Christian"

The fact that the term "Christian" is used at all in the *Gospel according to Philip* is striking. Apart from its occurrences here, "Christian" appears only one other time in the entire Nag Hammadi corpus, in the *Testimony of Truth*. The term does not seem to have been used by most of those responsible for the other Nag Hammadi works, either as a self-designation or as a label for others. The fact that it is used at all in the *Gospel according to Philip* points to a provenance for (at least) some of its materials which is distinct from those of the other Nag Hammadi documents.

The use of the term "Christian" in the *Gospel according to Philip* is not consistent, however. It appears seven times.[1] Four times it is used in a positive sense, as a term of self-designation, although these uses do not necessarily point to a single group. They include one use which draws a

---

[1] The spelling in the *Gospel according to Philip* is also not consistent; ΧΡΗСΤΙΑΝΟС is used four times and ΧΡΙСΤΙΑΝΟС twice (in the remaining instance, the first part of the word falls in a lacuna). Iotas and etas seem to have been pronounced much the same around the Graeco-Roman world at this time. Substitution of ι for η was common, although the reverse was less common. Χριστός (which was a comprehensible adjective in Greek, but not a personal name) could therefore easily be confused with the popular name Χρηστός. This undoubtedly explains Suetonius' note that Claudius expelled from Rome Jews who were stirred up *impulsore Chresto* (*Lives* 25), but the understandable confusion of outsiders does not seem to me to account for the spelling Χρηστιανός in codex Sinaiticus at Acts 11:26, 26:28, and 1 Peter 4:16. In the face of the opinions recorded in Blass-Debrunner-Funk and Moulton and Howard (which explain those readings in Acts as the result of confusion with the name Χρηστός), it seems to me that this usage by a skilled scribe who cannot have been ignorant of Christianity must point to an orthography accepted or acceptable in some part(s) of the early Christian world. The fact that the third century Greek writer Alexander of Lycopolis used the spelling Χρηστός (*C. Manich.* 24) tends to support this interpretation.

Given the fluidity of orthography in the Coptic dialects in this period and the position taken above with regard to Greek orthography, several possibilities seem about equally likely: the Greek original might have contained both spellings (which were simply reproduced), the translator or a later Coptic scribe might have known of an accepted (if minority) Greek usage not contained in the underlying document and followed it sometimes, the translator or scribe might have freely transcribed the sounds, or there may have been an accepted (if, again, perhaps local or regional) Coptic spelling. (Χριστός is always abbreviated [ΧС, ΧΡС] in the *Gospel according to Philip*, and so its form sheds no light on the matter.)

The loan word χρῖσμα is ususally spelled ΧΡΙСΜΑ in the *Gospel according to Philip,* but twice it appears as ΧΡΕΙСΜΑ; the passage 74.12-19 uses ΧΡΕΙСΜΑ at its beginning, but switches to ΧΡΙСΜΑ (and uses ΧΡΙСΤΙΑΝΟС) for the statement ΕΒΟΛ ΓΑΡ 2Μ ΠΧΡΙСΜΑ ΑΥΜΟΥΤΕ ΕΡΟΝ ΧΕ ΧΡΙСΤΙΑΝΟС, "because of chrism we were called Christians." It is tempting to imagine a scribe unencumbered by notions of standard orthography but sensitive to etymology coming to this passage and realizing the connection between the two words; such a scenario could have happened in either the Greek or the Coptic stage of the document's history.

See F. Blass and A. Debrunner, *A Greek Grammar of the New Testament*, transl. and revised R. W. Funk (Chicago: University of Chicago Press, 1961) § 24; J. H. Moulton and N. F. Howard, *A Grammar of New Testament Greek* (Edinburgh: T & T Clark, 1919) 72; W. Bauer, W. F. Arndt, F. W. Gingrich, and F. W. Danker, *A Greek-English Lexicon of the New Testament* (Chicago: University of Chicago Press, 1958) 886-887; *Bibliorum Codex Sinaiticus Petropolitanus IV Novum Testamentum cum Barnaba et Pastore* ed. C. Tischendorf (Hildesheim: Georg Olms, 1969) 107, 116*, 121*. See also G. H. R. Horsley, *New Documents Illustrating Early Christianity* (North Ryde, Australia: Macquarie University, 1983) 128-130.

sharp distinction between Christians and "Hebrews,"[2] another strongly
concerned with the importance of anointing,[3] and two in which
"Christian" is a name of power, designating "the true people" which is
"renowned in the world."[4]

In contrast to these unambiguously positive (though varied) uses, we
find two passages which question other people's claim to the term; the
second of these denies any proper use of the term. Both passages deal
with those for whom baptism was somehow not fully efficacious.

On page 64, we read:

ЄРЩА ОУА ВШК ЄПЄСНТ	Anyone who goes down into the
ЄΠΜΟΟΥ Ñ΄ЄΙ Є2ΡΑÏ ЄΜΠЄ΄ΧΙ	water and comes up without having
ΛΑΑΥ Ñ΄ΧΟΟΟ ΧЄ ΑΝΟΚ	received anything and says, "I am a
ΟΥΧΡΗСΤΙΑΝΟΟ ÑΤΑ΄ΧΙ	Christian," has borrowed the
ΜΠΡΑΝ ЄΤΜΗСЄ	name.
Є΄ЩΑΧΙ ΔЄ ΜΠΠΝΑ ЄΤΟΥΑΑΒ	But one who receives the Holy
ΟΥÑΤΑ΄ ΜΜΑΥ ÑΤΑШΡЄΑ	Spirit has the gift of the name.
ΜΠΡΑΝ	
ΠЄΝΤΑ2ΧΙ ÑΟΥΔШΡЄΑ	Anyone who has received a gift
ΜΑΥ΄ΙΤ͞Ç ÑΤΟΟΤ΄	will not have it taken away.
ΠЄΝΤΑ2ΧΙ ΔЄ ЄΧШ΄ ЄΤΜΗСЄ	But one who has borrowed some-
ЩΑΥЩΑΤ΄	thing will have it taken back.[5]

Here, the name "Christian" has been misappropriated by persons or by a
group who are asserted not to have a right to it. The name is said to be
"borrowed," and hence subject to repayment, even collection. Their state
is contrasted with the state of one "who receives the Holy Spirit" and

---

[2] *Gos. Phil.* 52.21-24: "When we were Hebrews we were orphans with (only)
our mother, but when we became Christians we got father and mother."

The English translations for the *Gospel according to Philip* are those of Bentley
Layton, *The Gnostic Scriptures* (Doubleday, Garden City, NY, 1987) 329-353,
except where noted. Capitalization has been modified without comment in some
cases.

[3] *Gos. Phil.* 74.13-14: "because of chrism we were called Christians" (translation
modified).

[4] *Gos. Phil.* 62.26-34: [after statements that if you say "I am a Jew/Roman/
Greek--or a barbarian, a slave, free" no one will be disturbed] "If you [say], 'I am a
Christian,' the [. . .] will shake;" and probably 75.25-76.2, a lacunose discussion of
spiritual progeny, involving the idea that levels of being produce after their own
kind; the list culminates in Christians, after which there is some discussion of "the
chosen people," "the true human being" and the "true people," "renowned in the
world."

[5] *Gos. Phil.* 64.22-29, translation modified.

"has the gift of the name." The passage implies that these other people are those who have a true claim to the term "Christian," if anyone does.

The second passage, from page 67, presents a somewhat more complicated situation:

ϢϢⲈ ⲀⲚⲈⲦⲬⲠⲞ ⲀⲚ ⲘⲘⲀⲦⲈ ⲘⲠⲢⲀⲚ ⲘⲠⲈⲒⲰⲦ ⲘⲚ ⲠϢⲎⲢⲈ ⲘⲚ ⲠⲦⲠⲚⲀ ⲈⲦⲞⲨⲀⲀⲂ ⲀⲖⲖⲀ Ⲁ<ⲚⲈⲚⲦⲀ>ⲨⲬⲠⲞⲞⲨ ⲚⲀⲔ ⲈⲰⲞⲨ	Not only must those who produce the names of Father, Son, and Holy Spirit do so, but also <those who> have acquired these.
ⲈⲦⲘ ⲞⲨⲀ ⲬⲠⲞⲞⲨ ⲚⲀϤ ⲠⲔⲈⲢⲀⲚ ⲤⲈⲚⲀϤⲒⲦϤ ⲚⲦⲞⲞⲦϤ	If someone does not acquire them, the name too will be taken from that person.
ⲞⲨⲀ ⲆⲈ ⲬⲒ ⲘⲘⲞⲞⲨ ⲈⲘ ⲠⲬⲢⲒⲤⲘⲀ ⲘⲠⲦⲤⲞ[.] ⲚⲦⲀⲨⲚⲀⲘⲒⲤ ⲘⲠⲤϮ[Ⲟ]Ⲥ ⲦⲀ[Ⲉ]Ⲓ ⲚⲈ ⲚⲀⲠⲞⲤⲦⲞⲖⲞⲤ ⲘⲞⲨⲦⲈ ⲈⲢⲞⲤ ⲬⲈ [ⲦⲞ]ⲨⲚⲀⲘ ⲘⲚ ⲦⲈⲈⲂⲞⲨⲢ	But if one gets them in the chrism of [. . .] of the force of the cross, which the apostles called right and left.
ⲠⲀⲈⲒ ⲄⲀⲢ ⲞⲨⲔⲈⲦⲒ ⲞⲨ[ⲬⲢⲎ]Ⲥ̅Ⲧ[Ⲓ]ⲀⲚⲞⲤ ⲠⲈ ⲀⲖⲖⲀ ⲞⲨⲬⲢⲤ ⲠⲈ	For this person is no longer a Christian but rather is a Christ [i.e., "an anointed one"].[6]

Here we find the acquisition of a "name" in initiation coupled with the idea that if the "names" of Father, Son and Holy Spirit are not acquired, "the name too" ("Christian"?) will be taken away. In contrast to that unhappy situation, however, one who does receive the appropriate gifts is no longer a "Christian," but a "Christ." This passage, like the one on page 64, protests an inappropriate usage of the term "Christian," but it presents a picture in which there is no correct referent for the term. Those who use it inappropriately can do so only temporarily; those for whom the name might be imagined appropriate have, in fact, left it behind: such a one is now a "Christ" and no longer a "Christian." The passage suggests a close dialogue with people who do call themselves "Christian," and makes use of some common Christian terminology and ritual. Nevertheless, a need to distinguish themselves from other individual "Christians" and groups has pushed the person or community behind this passage to give up on a much-conflicted term, building their rationale upon a distinctive understanding of initiation.

---

[6] *Gos. Phil.* 67.19-27, translation modified.

Finally, one passage in which "Christian" appears is simply too lacunose to determine the sense of the term.[7]

The passage on page 67 and probably that on page 64 come from a different source (or sources) than the source(s) behind the uses of "Christian" on pages 52, 62, 74, and 75. All of the uses of ХРICTIANOC /ХРHCTIANOC in the *Gospel according to Philip* appear in the first three quarters of the document.

"Hebrews," "Jews," "Gentiles"

The term "Hebrew" appears once (in the compound M̄NT2EBPAIOC) to designate a language, but in the other four passages where 2EBPAIOC occurs, it is used of a group of people, and it is used negatively. These passages dissociate the group(s) of their author(s) from others called "Hebrews." On page 51, the term refers to a deficiency involving an inability to pass on the fullness of one's religious identity to converts.[8] On the next page, it is stated that "when we were Hebrews we were orphans with (only) our mother, but when we became Christians we got father and mother."[9] This passage depicts a group associated with a "mother" in a way that is problematic: possibly these folk are understood to be associated with an entity rather like the lower Sophia, perhaps unknowingly. Nevertheless, the group understands itself as having been "Hebrews," at one time. A passage concerning a dispute about Mary, on page 55, identifies "Hebrews" with "apostles and apostolic persons;" here, the term is used to mean some other sort of Christians, not Jews, or speakers of "Hebrew" or Aramaic.[10] At the top of page 62, "Hebrew" is again associated with deficiency: "Anyone who has received something other than the Lord is still a Hebrew."[11] Thus "Hebrew," in the passages on pages 51, 52, 55, and 62 of the *Gospel according to Philip*, describes a group which is contrasted with the favored group: the group of the author(s) of these units was conceived, among other ways, as being what these "Hebrews" were *not*. In one passage, "Hebrews" means

---

[7] The passage (74.24-75.1) deals with sacraments, despising something, laughter, and entering the kingdom of heaven. It is unclear how these elements are related, and also unclear how "a Christian" who is mentioned (between two of the several substantial lacunae at the bottom of page 74) might relate to any of these.

[8] *Gos. Phil.* 51.29-52.2.

[9] *Gos. Phil.* 52.21-24.

[10] References to "Hebrew" as a language sometimes designate Aramaic; see Acts 21.40, 22.2, and 26.16.

[11] *Gos. Phil.* 52.5-6.

another kind of Christian, and this meaning could lie behind all four passages, though this is not clear.

"Gentile" is given a negative sense in its only secure occurrence, at
52.15: "A gentile does not die, for he has never become alive so as to
die."[12] The opposite with which "gentile" is contrasted here is "one who
has believed in the truth."

"Jews" are mentioned in two places. Neither passage is positive. On
page 62, "Jews" are included in a recital of all known people—along
with Romans, Greeks, barbarians, slaves, free people: i.e., just about ev-
erybody. All these are contrasted to "Christians," at whose name some
entity, lost to lacunae, will tremble.[13] A passage at the bottom of page 75
is extremely lacunose, but seems to include "Jews" [IOYΔAI] and
"Christians" in an argument based on the principle of "like produces
like." One lacuna in this passage, preceded by the letters Ñ2Є, might be
conjecturally restored as a Ñ2Є[ΛΛHN] (Greeks), or Ñ2Є[BPΔIOC]
(Hebrews), or Ñ2Є[ΘNIKOC] (gentiles).[14]

All of these terms are confined entirely to the first three quarters of
the document; most of them (i.e., all except the occurrence of "Jews"
with one other group designator on page 75) appear in the first third.
Since all of these terms have been given the basic meaning of "not part
of the favored group" (though with different nuances), the passages in
which they appear may (but need not) come from the same source.[15]

"Apostolic" and "Apostle(s)"

The terms "apostle" and "apostolic" are used only in the first three quarters of the text, but appear there both as pejorative labels and to refer to
sources of authority for favored teachings and practices.[16]

On page 55, lines 28-30, it is said of Mary (the virgin "whom the
powers did not defile"), ЄCЏOOTT ÑNOYNOб ÑNANOЏ ÑÑ2ЄBPΔIOC
ЄTЄ NATTOCTOΛOC NЄ ΔYШ [Ñ]ATTOCTOΛIKOC—"Her existence is

---

[12] *Gos. Phil.* 52.15-18, translation modified.

[13] *Gos. Phil.* 62.26-35.

[14] See the critical apparatus in Layton, *Nag Hammadi Codex II,2-7*, 174.

[15] The hypothesis that their source (or sources) was (were) mostly drawn upon
in the first third of the *Gospel according to Philip* will find some corroboration
when we examine evidences of a Syrian or bilingual milieux later in this chapter.

[16] On the unusual nature of a negative appeal to apostolicity, i.e., to discredit an
opinion by association with apostles, see Farkasfalvy in William R. Farmer and
Denis M. Farkasfalvy, *The Formation of the New Testament Canon. An Ecumenical
Approach.* (New York: Paulist, 1983) 132-34.

anathema to the Hebrews, meaning the apostles and apostolic persons." Since the term "Hebrew" in the *Gospel according to Philip* invariably designates those outside the community, the equation of "apostles and apostolic persons" with "Hebrews" assigns a strongly negative understanding to these terms. Moreover, these apostles and their followers do not subscribe to the understanding of Mary endorsed by the text. They may be the same people who hold the opinion with which the passage opens (that Mary "conceived by the Holy Spirit"), which is immediately stated to be in error.

A passage spanning pages 59 and 60 also uses the term "apostles" in a negative sense, although the passage is somewhat lacunose.

ⲡⲉϫⲉ ⲛⲁⲡⲟⲥⲧⲟⲗⲟⲥ ⲛ̄ⲛⲙⲙⲁⲑⲏⲧⲏⲥ ϫⲉ ⲧⲙ̄ⲡⲣⲟⲥⲫⲟⲣⲁ ⲧⲏⲣⲥ̄ ⲙⲁⲣⲉⲥϫⲡⲟ [ⲛ]ⲁⲥ ⲛ̄ⲟⲩ2ⲙⲟⲩ	The apostles said to the disciples, "May all of our offering get salt!"
ⲛⲉⲩⲙⲟⲩⲧⲉ [ⲉⲧⲥⲟⲫ[ⲓ]ⲁ ϫⲉ 2ⲙⲟⲩ ⲁϫⲛ̄ⲧ̄ⲥ̄ ⲙⲁⲣⲉ ⲡⲣⲟⲥⲫ[ⲟⲣⲁ ϣ]ⲱ]ⲡⲧⲉ ⲉ4ϣⲏⲡ	They were referring [to wisdom] as "salt." Without it, no offering is acceptable.
ⲧⲥⲟⲫⲓⲁ ⲇⲉ ⲟⲩⲥⲧⲉⲓⲣ[ⲁ ⲧⲉ ⲁϫⲛ̄] ϣⲏⲣⲉ ⲇⲓⲁ ⲧⲟⲩⲧⲟ ⲉⲩⲙⲟⲩⲧⲉ ⲉⲣⲟ[ⲥ ϫⲉ ⲡⲕⲉ]ⲥⲉⲡⲉⲓ ⲛ̄2ⲙⲟⲩ	Now wisdom [is] barren, [without] offspring. For this reason, [she] is called "[. . .]. . .of the salt."
ⲡⲙⲁ ⲉⲧⲟⲩⲛⲁϣ[. . . .] ⲛ̄ϣ ⲛ̄ⲧⲟⲩ2ⲉ ⲡ̄ⲡⲛ̄ⲁ̄ ⲉⲧⲟⲩⲁⲁⲃ[. . . . . ⲁⲩ]ⲱ ⲛⲁϣ[ⲉ] ⲛⲉⲥϣⲏⲣⲉ	Wherever [. . .] can [. . .] like them, the Holy Spirit [. . .], [and] many are her offspring.[17]

The structure of the passage seems to be: (a) a reminiscence of an apostolic remark involving special terminology: the apostles express a pious hope which, through Mark 9.49, depends on Lev 2.13: "May all our offering get salt!", (b) an explanation of what the apostles meant by the remark—they were making an allegorical interpretation of Lev 2.13, identifying the "salt" prescribed there as "wisdom," (c) a gnostic reinterpretation of that allegory, identifying the wisdom referred to as Sophia, the problem child of the Pleroma, and (d) a comment on this reinterpretation, contrasting this barren, lesser Sophia with the Holy Spirit. Much of the final part of the passage is at the bottom of page 59 and is severely damaged, but the attempt to associate the apostles with the fallen nature of Sophia is clear enough. The passage is a piece of one-

---

[17] *Gos. Phil.* 59.27-60.1.

up-manship based on the myth of the fall of Sophia, which reveals the apostles' lack of understanding.

66.29-67.1 is unfortunately too damaged to determine the tone of its reference to "an apostolic person." ογαπτοcτολικο̣c [2]ν̄ ο̣[γ]οπτacιa aчnaγ a2oeine eγoττ [e2oγ]n eγhei ν̄κω2τ aγω e[γ]mhp 2ν̄ [. . .] ν̄κω2τ: "In a vision, an apostolic person saw certain people imprisoned in a house of fire and bound with [. . .] of fire." The text becomes even more lacunose after this point. There are several fragmentary phrases in the next six lines—bits of description and bits of a conversation about the meaning of the situation—but not enough survives to make it clear whether this "apostolic" visionary is being represented as an authority or as a deluded fool.

On the other hand, passages on pages 62 and 67 pass on terms used by the apostles, without any hint of the superiority present on pages 55 and 59. The phrase "Jesus the Nasoraean Messias" is stated on page 62 to have been used by "the apostles before us," and the etymology of each component is carefully explained. On page 67, almost as an aside, it is stated that what the writer of the passage calls the "force of the cross,"[18] was called "the right and the left" by "the apostles." This passage recognizes a reality shared with "the apostles" but prefers to use a different terminology for it. These statements occur in the passage discussed earlier in this chapter, where the term "Christian" has been discarded, leaving only pretenders to the name and those who have gone beyond it.

On page 73, lines 8-19, there is a puzzlingly and painfully ironic saying about Joseph the carpenter, attributed to Philip the apostle, in which Joseph planted the tree from which his son's cross was fashioned; this tree is then associated first with the tree of life in paradise and then with the olive tree from which comes chrism, the source of resurrection. Despite the irony created by the interweaving of different senses of wood lot/paradise, the ambiguity of the word "seed," and the overlapping semantic fields of planting, begetting, and making, and despite the pain inherent in the story line itself, the saying seems to be presented as an insight into the underlying truths of salvation. At least, no disparagement of Philip "the apostle" seems implied by putting this carefully wrought anecdote in his mouth.

---

[18] Or "the chrism of the force of the cross."

On page 74, however, the use of the term is very strongly positive. This group's spiritual authority is traced through the apostles:

. . . ⲚⲦⲀⲨⲘⲞⲨⲦⲈ ⲈⲡⲈⲭ̄ⲥ̄ ⲈⲦⲂⲈ ⲡⲭⲣⲓⲥⲙⲁ	. . . it was because of chrism (anointing) that the Christ (the anointed) was named,
ⲀⲡⲈⲓⲱⲦ ⲅⲀⲣ Ⲧⲱ2ⲥ Ⲙⲡⲧⲩ̄ⲏⲣⲉ Ⲁⲡⲧⲩ̄ⲏⲣⲉ ⲁⲉ Ⲧⲱ2ⲥ Ⲛ̄ⲀⲡⲟⲥⲦⲟⲗⲟⲥ ⲀⲚⲀⲡⲟⲥⲦⲟⲗⲟⲥ ⲁⲉ ⲦⲀ2ⲥⲚ̄	for the Father anointed the Son; and the Son anointed the apostles, and the apostles anointed us.
ⲡⲈⲚⲦⲀⲨⲦⲟ2ⲥ̄ⳡ ⲞⲨⲚ̄ⲦⲈⳡ ⲡⲦⲏⲣ̄ⳡ Ⲙ̄ⲘⲀⲨ	Whoever has been anointed has everything; . . . .[19]

The statement "the Father anointed the Son, and the Son anointed the apostles, and the apostles anointed us," taken together with "because of chrism we are called Christians" (for this is one of the passages in which "Christian" is used in a positive sense) makes it unambiguously clear that this group understood themselves in terms of a succession of anointing going back through the apostles and through Christ to the Father. There is no attempt in this passage to distinguish between different groups or different senses of the term. "The apostles," without any further specification, are an essential link in the chain of actions that constitutes the group.

Thus, two passages in the *Gospel according to Philip* stem from traditions frankly hostile to the "apostolic" churches and their history: apostles and their followers misunderstand Mary, the incarnation, and the powers; the apostles were foolishly impressed by the barren Sophia. These seem to represent a source or sources different from that/those behind one passage which bases its spiritual authority on the apostles, and several others which cite apostles as sources of lore of enduring importance. The two passages employing "apostles" in negative senses fall on pages 55 and 59-60, before the positive senses (on pages 62, 73 and 74). None of these passages occurs in the final quarter of the document, where there is no sign of interest in any of these disputes.

---

[19] *Gos. Phil.* 74.15-18, translation. modified to show emphasis created by the use of the second perfect. Layton's translation reads, ". . .the anointed (Christ) was named for chrism. . . ."

The "Perfect"

Another term sometimes used as a self-designation in the *Gospel according to Philip* is "the perfect human being" (Ⲡ̄ⲦⲈⲖⲈⲒⲞⲤ Ⲣ̄ⲢⲰⲘⲈ) or "the perfect ones" (Ⲛ̄ⲦⲈⲖⲈⲒⲞⲤ Ⲣ̄ⲢⲰⲘⲈ or Ⲛ̄ⲦⲈⲖⲈⲒⲞⲤ).[20] This term is used in both an initiatory and a moral sense, the former confined to the first three quarters of the text, the latter appearing only after the divide at 77.14.

The borrowed Greek adjective τέλειος is more often used in other ways: the *Gospel according to Philip*'s text refers to "the perfect light,"[21] "perfect (things)," i.e., the entire level of being which is perfect,[22] the "perfect day" (paired with "holy light"),[23] and, once, to a full or complete meal.[24] "The perfect human being" (Ⲡ̄ⲦⲈⲖⲈⲒⲞⲤ Ⲣ̄ⲢⲰⲘⲈ) appears in apposition to "the Christ" (ⲠⲈⲬⲤ̄) once,[25] and seems to have the same sense in another passage, where it is asserted that "the cup of prayer" belongs to "the perfect human being" and when we drink it we receive "the perfect human being."[26] Both these uses are associated with the eucharist: in the former, "the Christ, the perfect human being" brings bread from heaven to those who have had only animal food to eat. On page

---

[20] The Coptic word ⲢⲰⲘⲈ has two principal meanings: (1) a human being irrespective of sex, and (2) a male human being. The term derives from the Egyptian *rmṯ*, with the same two meanings; in the plural, it could be written with the determinatives for both man and woman.

In Coptic, ⲢⲰⲘⲈ was regularly used to translate both ἄνθρωπος and ἀνήρ. Crum cites a usage from Shenute showing that the former meaning persisted and was at least sometimes used without contamination from the latter: ⲢⲰⲘⲈ . . . ⲈⲒⲦⲈ ϨⲞⲞⲨⲦ ⲈⲒⲦⲈ ⲤϨⲒⲘⲈ. The semantic range of ⲢⲰⲘⲈ thus corresponds closely to that of the word "man" in Middle and early Modern English (as in usages such as "And yet thaie [a husband and wife] riht riche men ware," or "The Lord had but one paire of men in Paradise." [from a metrical homily, c. 1325, and J. King *On Jonas*, 1597, both cited in the *Oxford English Dictionary*).

See: W. E. Crum, *A Coptic Dictionary* (Oxford: Clarendon Press, 1939) 294b; J. Cerny, *Coptic Etymological Dictionary* (Cambridge: Cambridge University Press, 1979) 136; W. Westendorf, *Koptisches Handwörterbuch* (Heidelberg: Carl Winter, 1977) 163-164; Werner Vycichl, *Dictionnaire étymologique de la langue copte* (Leuven: Peeters, 1983) 172; A. Erman and H. Grapow, *Wörterbuch der aegypytischen Sprache* (Berlin: Akademie-Verlag, 1982) 2.421-424; *The Oxford English Dictionary* 2nd edition, ed. J. A. Simpson and E. S. C. Weiner (Oxford: Clarendon Press, 1989) 9.284.

[21] *Gos. Phil.* 58.12, 70.5, 76.27, 76.28 (and possible in the lacuna at 76.30, although this is conjectural since no letter traces remain), and 85.26.

[22] *Gos. Phil.* 85.18.

[23] *Gos. Phil.* 86.17.

[24] *Gos. Phil.* 81.14.

[25] *Gos. Phil.* 55.12.

[26] *Gos. Phil.* 75.14-21.

60 there is a lengthy passage (by the standards of the first three quarters of the *Gospel according to Philip*) which makes a double analogy: just as human beings plow the fields using domesticated animals, and thereby increase the food supply for themselves, for domesticated animals, and for wild animals, so the "perfect human being" plows with domesticated forces, and in the same way the Holy Spirit pastures and rules all the forces. The meaning of the perfect human being is unclear here: it could mean the fully realized sectarian, or Jesus Christ, or possibly the pleromatic Human Being which is part of the primary octet in Valentinus' and Ptolemy's systems.[27]

In three passages, however, the term is used to designate humans other than Jesus: twice quite unambiguously to designate the fully realized sectarian, once to refer to the ethically perfect as exemplified by Jesus Christ.

The passage 58.17-59.5 opens by asserting the greater generative power of the heavenly person (ΠΡⲘⲘ̄ΠⲈ) or perfect person (ΠⲦⲈⲖⲈⲒⲞⲤ ⲢⲢⲰⲘⲈ) in comparison to the earthly person (ΠⲢⲘ̄ⲚⲔⲀ2) or Adam. So far, these phrases might refer to Christ in a familiar pattern of Christ-Adam opposition. This discussion of generativity is, however, brought to bear on the situation of the humans with whom the author of this passage identifies in two ways: they seem to understand themselves as the offspring of the heavenly or perfect person, taking their nourishment from "the promise of the heavenly place," but initially like young children in that they produce no offspring of their own. In contrast to this condition of immaturity, "the perfect ones" (Ⲛ̄ⲦⲈⲖⲈⲒⲞⲤ) conceive and give birth by means of a kiss. This possibility is held out to members of the group in the sentence immediately following: "For this reason we too kiss one another: it is by the grace residing in one another that we conceive."[28]

A second mention of "the perfect human" also attributes unusual powers to the sectarian: "The perfect human being not only cannot be restrained, but also cannot be seen."[29] This is linked with two of the mentions of "perfect light" examined above: "no one can obtain this grace without putting on the perfect light [and] becoming, as well, per-

---

[27] Cf. Irenaeus *Adv. haer.* 1.11.1 and 1.1.1.

[28] Or, "Because of this we too kiss one another, conceiving by the grace which is in each other;" ⲆⲒⲀ ⲦⲞⲨⲦⲞ ⲀⲚⲞⲚ 2ⲰⲰⲚ ⲦⲚ̄ϯ ΠⲒ ⲈⲢⲚ̄ Ⲛ̄ⲚⲈⲠⲎⲨ ⲈⲚⲬⲒ Ⲙ̄ΠⲰ̈ ⲈⲂⲞⲖ 2Ⲛ̄ ⲦⲬⲀⲢⲒⲤ ⲈⲦ2Ⲛ̄ Ⲛ̄ⲚⲈⲠⲎⲨ.

[29] *Gos. Phil.* 76.22-77.1.

fect light." The fully initiated member of the group has gained not only immunity but invisibility with respect to some kind of hostile powers (which are not, however, described in this passage).

The third passage using "the perfect" to designate humans other than Jesus, on pages 79-80, also links "the perfect human" with Christ in such a way that others are encouraged to strive to attain this status. Unlike the two passages examined above, however, the focus is not on some unusual power available to the fully initiated and mature member of the group, but on an interpersonal virtue. The passage opens with a macarism in which the virtue is described; unfortunately, the operative verb has been lost to the damage at the bottom of page 79: "[Blessed] is that one who has not [. . .] a soul." The last part of "blessed" can be made out ([ΟΥΜΑΚΑ]ΡΙΟC), making the saying's character as a macarism certain, but only the beginning of the verb is present: ЄΜΠЄЧΑΛ[. . . .], followed by a lacuna four to four and a half average letter spaces in length. The first letter of the verb, given the context, suggests "caused grief" (ῬΛΥΠЄΙ);[30] in any case, the context demands a verb which can parallel "burden," since the blessed one who has not done this thing is immediately identified as Jesus Christ, who "has encountered the whole place and has not burdened anyone." That is not the end of the matter, however. The next sentence states, "For this reason, blessed is such a person: this person is a perfect human being." The passage goes on sympathetically to acknowledge that this is indeed difficult, to ask how it can be achieved, and to give first practical advice and then a parable (with an interpretation) in answer to the question. In other words, the hearers of 79.33-81.13 were encouraged to strive for this variety of perfection, and the possibility that they might attain it is not ruled out. Thus the "perfect human being" is a goal for the group member, perhaps understood as an attainable one, but it differs sharply from the uses on pages 58-59 and 76 in that it is not used to describe the fully initiated member of the group, and the issue centers around human relationships rather than unusual or uncanny abilities.

Thus the "perfect" of the earlier part of the text (on pages 58-59 and 76-77) are perfectly initiated and possess different powers than others; the "perfect" of the final quarter (on pages 79-81) are the morally perfect—or, to be more exact, an invitation is made to people to attempt to

---

[30] Layton reconstructs: ЄΜΠЄЧΑΛ[ΥΠЄΙ ῬШ Ν] ΝΟΥΨΥΧΗ. See *Nag Hammadi Codex II,2-7*, 202.

be morally perfect.[31] These divergent senses, and the values and goals to which they point, indicate the use of a different source (or sources) after 77.14.

DISTRIBUTION OF INTERESTS AND APPROACHES INDICATIVE OF AFFILIATION OR MILIEU

The presence (and absence) of interests and approaches involved in the religious self-understanding of groups also provide evidence about the milieu in which a writing originated. The inclusion of etymologies involving Semitic (and other) roots, accounts of the words and actions of Jesus (or the Christ or the Lord), interest in other biblical persons or places, the evocation of the creation story from Genesis, and ways of framing the basic human problematic point to aspects of group identity. Again, we find a major divide at 77.14, and some indicators of a source or sources behind part of the material in the first third.

Etymological Exegesis and "Syrian" Provenance

Several passages in the *Gospel according to Philip* involve the etymologies of words or names. In four of these, the etymology is the point, and three of them follow a very direct form: introduce word/name, explain etymology. To these, we may apply the term "etymological exegesis" as a formal category. A fourth depends wholly on the etymologies involved, and a fifth passage reinforces one of its points by reference to an etymology.

Each of the three etymological exegeses, and the passage which depends wholly on two etymologies, depend on Semitic languages. These four passages are built on some accurate knowledge, although one also includes a seemingly fantastic etymology[32] (along with three sound ones). These passages have also been put forward in support of the premise that the *Gospel according to Philip* was originally written in Syriac, or was written in a bilingual milieu.[33] This claim, as we shall see,

---

[31] This latter emphasis lines up with other concerns typical of the final quarter of the text, as we will see in chapter 8.

[32] That "*Nazara*" means "truth," is asserted at 62.14.

[33] See: Eric Segelberg, "The Antiochene Background of the Gospel of Philip," *Bulletin de la Société d'Archéologie Copte* 18 (1965-66) 205-223, and "The Antiochene Origin of the 'Gospel of Philip' II," *Bulletin de la Société d'Archéologie Copte* 19 (1967-68) 207-210.

goes beyond the evidence, though it is not impossible. Provocatively, however, all the passages which take the form of etymological exegesis or which show clear evidence of some acquaintance with a Semitic language (like most of the appearances of the terms "Hebrew," "Jew," and "gentile") are restricted to the first third of the document; in fact, they are all concentrated in a single eight page stretch, from 56 to 63.

The invocation of a (probably) Greek etymology appears later, in a passage on page 74, examined above for its positive treatment of apostles. The focus of the passage is not the etymology but a discussion of the value of chrism.[34]

The first reference to "Syriac," and the first etymological exegesis in the *Gospel according to Philip*, occur on page 56 in an explanation of the names of Jesus.[35] The passage explains that "Jesus" is a personal name, not a word in any language (ϥϣⲟⲟⲡ ⲁⲛ ϩⲛ ⲗⲁⲁⲩ ⲛ̄ⲛⲁⲥⲡⲉ) and hence not subject to translation,[36] while "the Christ" (or "the Anointed")

Jacques-É Ménard, "La sentence 53 de l'Évangile selon Philippe," *Studia Montis Regii*, (1963), 149-52, "Le milieu syriaque de l'Évangile selon Thomas et de l'Évangile selon Philippe," *Revue des sciences religieuses* 42 (1968), 261-66, "Syrische Einflüsse auf die Evangelien nach Thomas and Philippus," in *XVII Deutscher Orientalistentag vom 21 bis 27 July 1968 in Würzburg, Vortrage, Teil 2*, ed. W. Voight (Wiesbaden: Franz Steiner, 1969) 385-91 [this article is very similar, but not identical, to the 1968 "Milieu syriaque" above], and "Beziehungen des Philippus- und des Thomas-Evangeliums zur syrischen Welt," in *Altes Testament-Frühjudentum-Gnosis Neue Studien zu "Gnosis und Bibel"* ed. Karl-Wolfgang Tröger (Berlin: Evangelische Verlagsanstalt, 1980), 317-325.

Otto Betz, "Der Name als Offenbarung des Heils (Jüdische Traditionen im koptisch-gnostischen Philippusevangelium," in *Das Institutum Judaicum der Universität Tübingen in den Jahren 1971-1972*, reprinted in *Jesus, Der Herr der Kirche: Aufsätze zur biblischen Theologie II* (Tübingen: J. C. B. Mohr [Paul Siebeck], 1990) 396-404.

[34] It is impossible to tell whether this discussion originally rested on the relation between the Greek words χρῖσμα and Χριστός or the Syriac words *mš*[c] and Messiah—the pun works in either language, and in Coptic as well, where the Greek terms have become usual as loan words. Thus the passage gives little clue of its original provinance, or of the provenance of the *Gospel according to Philip* as a whole.

[35] *Gos. Phil.* 56.3-13.

[36] Note the contrast to 62.11-17 (discussed below), where the Hebrew meaning of "Jesus" is given, and a fantastic meaning attached to *Nazara*.

and "the Nazarene" are epithets.[37] Comparative information is given on
the former term:

ΠΕΧΡC ΔЄ ΠЄЧΡΔΝ {ΠЄ} ⲘⲘⲚ̄ΤⲤⲨⲢⲞⲤ ΠЄ ⲘⲈⲤⲤΙⲀⲤ	But the word for Christ in Syriac is *messias,*
ⲘⲘⲚ̄ΤⲞⲨⲀⲈΙⲀΝΙΝ ΔЄ ΠЄ ΠⲬⲤ̄	and in Greek is *khristos,*
ΠⲀ(Ν)ΤⲰⲤ Ν̄ⲔⲞⲞⲨЄ ΤⲎⲢⲞⲨ ⲞⲨⲚ̄ΤⲀⲨЧ ⲘⲘⲀⲨ ⲔⲀΤⲀ ΤⲀⲤΠЄ Ⲙ̄ΠⲞⲨⲀ ΠⲞⲨⲀ Ν̄ⳢⲎΤⲞⲨ	and probably all the others have it according to the particular language of each.[38]

The author of this passage obviously knew that *christos* and *messias*
were equivalent terms, and that they were ultimately words rather than
names, hence translatable. Beyond that, not much can be inferred from
the passage with respect to language. It might indicate that the author
of the passage had some knowledge of a Semitic language, at least at a
rudimentary level,[39] or this information might have circulated as a piece
of basic Christian instruction, as it sometimes does now. The act of explaining the terms shows an expectation of readers to whom this lore
might be news. Perhaps the passage had a bilingual author, but he or she
did not expect readers to be bilingual.

On page 59, a writer familiar with the name "Achamoth" as an alternate name for Sophia, and familiar with the tradition of using the same
name on the higher and lower levels, and also familiar with some Semitic
language, has combined these materials to make a revealing play on
words. A slight shortening of Ekhamoth (derived from "wisdom") yields
a fitting name for the lower Sophia: Ekh-moth, "like death."

ⲔЄⲞⲨⲀ ΠЄ ЄⲬⲀⲘⲰⳐ ⲀⲨⲰ ⲔЄⲞⲨⲀ ΠЄ ЄⲬⲘⲰⳐ	Ekhamoth is one thing: and ekh- moth, another.

---

[37] I have here followed Layton's understanding in the face of considerable
(mostly earlier) opinion. The text runs: ⲒⲤ̄ ⲞⲨⲢⲀ(Ν) ΠЄ ЄЧⳢⲎΠ ΠЄⲬⲢⲤ̄ ⲞⲨⲢⲀΝ ΠЄ
ЄЧⲞⲨⲞΝⳢ ЄⲂⲞⲖ and ΠΝⲀⳌⲀⲢⲎΝⲞⲤ ΠЄΤⲞⲨⲞΝⳢ ЄⲂⲞⲖ ΠЄ Ⲙ̄ΠΠЄⲐⲎΠ. The first
part of this has been understood along the lines of "'Jesus' is a hidden/secret name,
'Christ' is a revealed/publicly known name:" it is (approximately) so translated by
Schenke 1960 (41), de Catanzaro 1962 (40), Wilson 1962 (83), Till 1963 (15-17),
Ménard 1967 (57), Borchert 1967 (85), Kasser 1970 (26), Moraldi 1984 (52),
Luttikhuizen 1986 (84), Schenke 1987 (157), Isenberg 1989 (153) and Janssens
1991 (103-104). Translations of the explanation of "the Nazarene" show a wider
range of senses, but none of them seeks to understand the hidden/revealed
dichotomy along idiomatic, rather than mysteriosophic, lines.

[38] *Gos. Phil.* 56.7-11.

[39] The fact that the form used, *messias*, is a Hellenized one, is not encouraging
for the construction of theories of strong Semitic contacts.

ЄХАМШѲ ТЄ ТСОФІА ҆ЂАПЛШС	Ekhamoth refers to wisdom proper;
ЄХМШѲ ΔЄ ТЄ ТСОФІА ҆ЂПТМОУ	but ekh-moth to the wisdom of death—
ЄТЄ ТАЄІ ТЄ ЄТСООУΝ ҆ЂПТМОУ	that is, the widsom who is ac-
ТАЄІ ЄТОУМОУТЄ ЄРОС ХЄ	quainted with death, and who is
ТКОУЄІ ҆ЂСОФІА	called the little wisdom.[40]

This passage is not quite an etymological exegesis, but it is closely related to them: its whole point rests on the underlying etymology, but it
does not make that etymology explicit. Since most of its point would be
lost without such information, the passage either (1) presumes readers
who have a basic familiarity with the languages involved, or (2) presumes readers who have been exposed to information about the meanings of these particular names, or (3) is an excerpt from a more discursive
source which has just explained the meanings of these names. The passage seems rhetorically whole, and specific knowledge of these terms (as
in scenario 2) might be unlikely unless insured by attached explanation
(as in scenario 3), so perhaps a bilingual audience is most likely.

Another etymological exegesis again mentions "the Syriac language,"
on page 63:

ТЄУХАРІСТЄІА ПЄ Ⲓ̄С̄	The eucharist is Jesus.
ЄУМОУТЄ ГАР ЄРОϤ	Now, in Syriac it is called *phar-*
҆ЂМΝТСУРОС ХЄ ФАРІСАѲА	*isatha,* that is, "that which is spread
ЄТЄ ПАЄІ ПЄ ПЄТПОРШ ЄВОЛ	out."
аⲓ̄С̄ ГАР ЄІ ЄϤСТАУРОУ	For Jesus came to crucify the
҆ЂПКОСМОС	world.[41]

The author of this passage had some specific and correct knowledge of
Christian sacramental terminology in "Syriac," and presumes that the
reader will also be interested in such terms, at least to the extent that
they can be used to make some interesting or enlightening point. The
text, however, explains everything from the perspective of Greek. It
does not say, "Pharisatha is Jesus. Now, in Greek it is called *eucharist*,
that is, 'thanksgiving'. . ."! That is to say, this text too presumes Greek-
speaking readers who do not necessarily know "Syriac."

Terminology used for Semitic languages during this period can be
quite ambiguous. The time around the end of the second century and
the beginning of the third century C.E. was marked by considerable lin-

---

[40] *Gos. Phil.* 60.10-15.
[41] *Gos. Phil.* 63.21-24.

guistic chaos east of the Mediterranean basin. Greek was the official language of the Roman empire in the east, and had been an important language of learning, commerce, and government there since Hellenistic times. The dialects of Aramaic that followed the breakdown of the widely used Imperial or Official Aramaic of the neo-Babylonian empire were in a state of flux. The phase of the language known as "Middle Aramaic" stretches from Alexander's time to about 200 C.E., and includes literary survivals of Imperial Aramaic (such as the Aramaic parts of Daniel and some of the Aramaic Qumran fragments) alongside numerous local and regional dialects, of which Nabatean, Palmyrene, Edessan, and Hatran are best attested.

The period from 200 C.E. until around 700 ("Late Aramaic") is marked by further divergence along geopolitical and ethnic lines, resulting in Western and Eastern groups of dialects. Palestinian Jewish Aramaic, Palestinian Christian Aramaic, and Samaritan evolved in the west, while Babylonian Jewish Aramaic (the Aramaic of the Babylonian Talmud), Mesopotamian Christian Aramaic (the "classical Syriac" derived from the dialect of Edessa) and Mandean evolved in the east.[42] If the *Gospel according to Philip* is a late second-century or third-century work, its context is the beginning of the trend from local or regional dialects toward eastern and western groups of dialects specific to certain religious groups.

The semantic ranges of the term "Syriac language" (ТṀ̄NTCΥPOC) and "Hebrew language" (ТṀ̄NT2ЄBPΑIOC) demand attention. The Greek συριστί was used by Xenophon to denote the language understood in the city of Babylon at the time of its capture by Cyrus, i.e., Imperial Aramaic;[43] the term was used in the second century C.E. by Plutarch[44] and Lucian[45] in the same sense. "Syriac" could probably refer to any of the forms of Aramaic spoken in the areas called "Syria," and the term "Syria" was used in both stricter and looser senses: to denote regions at one or another time included in the various Roman provinces bearing that term as part of their name, i.e., Syria, Syria Palaestina, Syria

---

[42] See Wolfhart Heinrichs, "Introduction" in *Studies in Neo-Aramaic*, ed. W. Heinrichs (Atlanta, GA: Scholars Press, 1990), x; and Sebastian Brock, "An Introduction to Syriac Studies" in *Horizons in Semitic Studies*, ed. J. H. Eaton (n.p.: 1980) 11-12.

[43] *Cyropaedia* 7.5.31.

[44] *Antonius* 46.

[45] *Alexander* 51.

Phoenice, and Coele Syria,[46] or to include Mesopotamia ("Assyria") as well.

'Εβραϊστί refers to the Aramaic dialect of first century Judea in John 20:16 (and probably 19:20). ἑβραΐς διάλεκτος is used in the same sense in Acts 21:40, 22:2, and 26:16. Irenaeus uses ἑβραϊκός in relation to a gnostic initiatory formula of uncertain affiliations; the text he gives is garbled beyond reasonable hope of reconstruction.[47] The exotic and "magical" appeal to some gnostics of claiming something to be "Hebrew" seems as likely to underlie the remark as any real use of a Hebrew (or Aramaic) formula. Since "Hebrew" was also used as a synonym for "Jew," it seems unlikely that the term would be used for an Aramaic dialect not somehow associated in the users' mind with Judaism. But since Jews were spread throughout the Aramaic-speaking (and the rest of the known) world, this does not restrict things much.

One etymological exegesis names "the Hebrew language," as the source of its etymologies. The passage appears on page 62. Like the discussion about Jesus' names on page 56, this passage seems to be more comfortable with the term "Christ" than with "Messias," and like it, uses a Hellenized form of the latter name. It attributes that term, however, not to a foreign usage, but to a more primitive usage within its own tradition. The two terms must now must be explained to readers ignorant of the "Christ-Messias" equivalence! It begins,

ⲚⲀⲠⲞⲤⲦⲞⲖⲞⲤ ⲈⲦ2Ⲓ ⲦⲚⲚⲈ2Ⲏ ⲦⲈⲈⲒ2Ⲉ ⲚⲈⲨⲘⲞⲨⲦⲈ ⲬⲈ Ⲓ̅Ⲏ̅Ⲥ̅ ⲦⲠⲚⲀⲌⲰⲢⲀⲒⲞⲤ ⲘⲈⲤⲤⲒⲀⲤ	The apostles before us used to employ the terms "Jesus the Nasorean Messias,"
ⲈⲦⲈ ⲠⲀⲈⲒ ⲠⲈ Ⲓ̅Ⲏ̅Ⲥ̅ ⲦⲠⲚⲀⲌⲰⲢⲀⲒⲞⲤ ⲠⲈⲬ̅Ⲥ̅	which means "Jesus the Nasorean the Christ (anointed)."
Ⲡ2ⲀⲈ p̄ⲢⲀⲚ ⲠⲈ ⲠⲈⲬ̅Ⲥ̅ ⲠⲦϢⲞⲢⲠⲦ ⲠⲈ Ⲓ̅Ⲥ̅ ⲠⲈⲦ2Ⲛ ⲦⲘⲎⲦⲈ ⲠⲈ ⲦⲠⲚⲀⳅⲀⲢⲎⲚⲞⲤ	The last name is "Christ" (anointed), the first name is "Jesus," the middle name is "the Nazarene."[48]

The text goes on, however, to bring out three etymologies, one of which it attributes to "Hebrew."

---

[46] These regions included, in some cases for a brief period only, Commagene, eastern Cilicia, Ituraea, Judea, and Nabataea.

[47] *Adv. haer.* 1.21.3

[48] *Gos. Phil.* 62.6-11.

ⲘⲈⲤⲤⲒⲀⲤ ⲞⲨⲚ̄ⲦⲀϤ ⲤⲎⲘⲀⲤⲒⲀ ⲤⲚ̄ⲦⲈ ⲀⲨⲰ ⲠⲈⲬⲢ̄Ⲥ̄ ⲀⲨⲰ ⲠⲈⲦⲰⲎⲨ	*Messias* has two meanings, "Christ (anointed)" and "the measured."
Ⲓ̄Ⲥ̄ ⲘⲘⲚ̄Ⲧ2ⲈⲂⲢⲀⲒⲞⲤ ⲠⲈ ⲠⲤⲰⲦⲈ	"Jesus" in Hebrew means "ransom."
ⲚⲀ2ⲀⲢⲀ ⲦⲈ ⲦⲀⲖⲎⲐⲈⲒⲀ ⲠⲚⲀ2ⲀⲢⲎⲚⲞⲤ ⟦ⲚⲈ⟧ ϬⲈ ⲦⲈ ⲦⲀⲖⲎⲐⲈⲒⲀ	*Nazara* means "truth," thus "the Nazarene" means "truth."
ⲠⲈ ⲠⲬ̄Ⲥ̄ Ⲛ̄ⲦⲀⲨⲰⲒⲦϤ ⲠⲚⲀ2ⲀⲢⲎⲚⲞⲤ ⲘⲚ̄ Ⲓ̄Ⲥ̄ ⲚⲈⲚⲦⲀⲨⲰⲒⲦⲞⲨ	It is the anointed (Christ) whom they have measured out; it is the Nazarene and Jesus who have been measured out.[49]

While the first meaning given for *messias* is common to all the Semitic languages in question, the second meaning ("measured") cannot be derived from Hebrew, but it seems to have been common across much of the range of Aramaic dialects in the first few centuries.[50] "Jesus," on the other hand, could be equated with "ransom" in Hebrew only, it seems: the Aramaic targums render words related to $yš^c$ with words related to prq.[51] References to "Hebrew" sometimes only meant the Aramaic of Aramaic-speaking Jews, as we have seen, but here the information is correct only if Hebrew itself is meant. It is possible that nothing more than Matt 1:21 lies behind the etymology given for "Jesus," but it is striking that this passage both correctly identifies the one language in which "Jesus" can mean something like "ransom," and gives a second meaning ("measured") for "Messias." These two together make it clear that the section was written by someone who knew both Hebrew and some form of Aramaic, or at least had detailed and correct information about certain usages in these languages and their differences.[52] This passage, in

---

[49] *Gos. Phil.* 62.11-17.

[50] Both meanings are present in Syriac. See *A Compendious Syriac Dictionary*, R. Payne Smith (Mrs. Margoliouth) (Oxford: Clarendon Press, 1903, 1967) 305.
They are also present in Palestinian Christian Aramaic, and are used in the Samaritan Targum of the Pentateuch, Targum Neophyti, and the Palestinian Talmud. See Michael Sokoloff, *A Dictionary of Jewish Palestinian Aramaic of the Byzantine Period* (Ramat-Gan, Israel: Bar Ilan University Press, 1990) 333.

[51] See *The Theological Dictionary of the Old Testament*, ed. G. J. Botterweck & H. Ringgren, vol 6 (Grand Rapids, MI: Eerdmans, 1990) 441-463.

[52] Walter Bauer described a situation in early Syrian Christianity in which the more numerous Marcionites used the term "Christian" to describe themselves, while the "orthodox" group had to be content to be known as followers of their bishop Palût. He then recounted an anecdote in which the sixth-century oriental patriarch Mar Aba, prior to his conversion, was dumbfounded by an ascetic who claimed to

contrast to the first two, would make sense for a Greek-speaking audience, or a bilingual audience, or even (if we can account for the Hellenized form "Messias" as an effect of translation) an Aramaic/Syriac speaking one.

Jacques Ménard has claimed that the use of the term CMONT in the *Gospel according to Philip* to denote "truth" indicates a *Rückübersetzung* dependent Syriac, since the Syriac *šrārā* "truth' is derived from the verb *šar*, "establish" (feststehen) = "be true."[53] This is a bit misleading. CMONT (the qualitative of CMINE) appears in the *Gospel according to Philip* nine times. One instance conveys the physical meaning "to be placed."[54] Of the other eight instances, seven are in a single passage (53.23-54.5) which describes the deceptive action of "names," i.e., language. The words "God," "Father," "Son," "Holy Spirit," 'life," "light," "resurrection," and "church" are cited as examples; their effect is to turn one's thoughts from NETCMONT to NETCMONT ⲁN; unfortunately, this argument is not paraphrased in any other terms which might help us refine our understanding of CMONT; rather, the terms are repeatedly contrasted. Things that are unstable, not established, are contrasted with things that are stable and established— but the usage here does not necessarily go beyond this sense to involve a more specific meaning of "untrue/true."

Thus, most of the evidence which has been proposed for a Syriac or Semitic milieu for the *Gospel according to Philip* is rather weak. Two passages (56.7-11 and 63.21-24) indicate only an author/authors who had some specific knowledge of Semitic usages (with or without a general knowledge of the language), writing for audiences whom they assumed to be ignorant of them. The passage on page 62, involving both Hebrew and Aramaic, shows wider knowledge on the part of its author, but reveals little about the language(s) of its readers. The paronomasia

---

be at once a Jew, a Christian, and a worshipper of the Messiah, since these usually meant different things: "Christians," i.e., Marcionites, rejected everything to do with Judaism, while the equivalence of "Christ" and "Messiah" was apparently unknown. It is possible that the original point of the texts in the *Gospel according to Philip* exegeting multiple names of the Lord was to preempt other groups' claims to these names and, by extension, to the group designations which derive from them. See Walter Bauer, *Orthodoxy and Heresy in Earliest Christianity* (Philadelphia: Fortress, 1971) 22-24.

[53] Ménard, "Le milieu syriaque," 262, "Syrische Einflüsse," 386.

[54] *Gos. Phil.* 83.12-13: HⲆH TⲀⲌⲈINH CⲘMONT ⲀTNOYNⲈ ⲚⲚⲰHN translating Matt 3.10: ἤδη δὲ ἡ ἀξίνη πρὸς τὴν ῥίζαν τῶν δένδρων κεῖται.

on page 60, on the other hand, expects an audience which could appreciate underlying etymologies without an explanation.

Nevertheless, these passages point to the use of a source (or sources) with distinctive interests and information, the use of which seems to have been restricted to the first third of the *Gospel according to Philip*.

Interest in Words and Actions of "Jesus," "the Christ," or "the Lord"

The tendency to make christological references of any kind whatever says something about the religious commitments of an author or group, and the terminology used, and the information conveyed, say more.

The *Gospel according to Philip* contains approximately sixteen dominical sayings, some with and some without context or accompanying action, and two actions attributed to Jesus.[55] Of these, four certainly come from Matthew's gospel; one could come from Matthew or Mark; one could come from Matthew or Luke; two come from John's gospel; two are from the *Gospel according to Thomas*; and six are from otherwise unknown sources.

Nearly all of this interest appears in the first three quarters of the document. Only once in the final quarter are words of Jesus from other known sources attributed to him—and then, they are ambiguously ascribed to "the Logos," which is also used to introduce a saying of John the Baptist's, and a comment about an unidentified macarism.[56] The final quarter also contains a quotation of Matt 15:13, but without any hint that the words are Jesus', or indeed a quotation at all. The final quarter of the document, while rooted in traditions about Jesus, is not particularly concerned to report his words.

---

[55] "Approximately" because there are several ambiguous cases: one statement is not attributed to anyone, but in Matt 15.13 it is spoken by Jesus; at another place a phrase is attributed to Jesus: "he called corruption 'outer darkness'"; two statements are attributed to the Logos--but one of them, in its canonical context, was spoken by John the Baptist. In either or both of these two cases, "the Logos," may not refer to Jesus at all, but to scripture--the word. Another reference to the Logos has to do with an elaboration of the meaning of an unattributed macarism. If all of the above are counted, the total comes to 17.

Beyond these, there are a number of cosmic actions, usually though not always attributed to "the Christ:" purchasing, rescuing and ransoming (53.35-54.13), bringing appropriate food into the world (55.6-13), rectifying the separation of the sexes (70.9-21), weeding "the whole place" (83.16-17) et cetera.

[56] *Gos. Phil.* 84.7-8 (= Jesus in John 8.32); 83.11-12 (= John the Baptist in Matt 3:10 and Luke 3:9); 80.4-6 (comment on macarism).

In contrast, interest in sayings and stories about Jesus is high before the divide at 77.14. Some of these dominical sayings seem to be independent units, or at least to have no rhetorical or syntactic connections to the preceding or following material in the *Gospel according to Philip*. These sayings include 55.37-56.4, 58.10-14, 63.28-30, 64.9-12, and 68.26-28.

Twice as many of Jesus' sayings are introduced to support an argument already in progress, such as 55.33-36, 57.3-5, 59.25-27, 63.32-64.9, 68.6-8[57], 68.9-12, 72.33-73.1, 74.25-27, 79.33-34 and 80.4-6,[58] 83.11-13, 84.7-9 and 85.28-29. Elaborations of the introductory formula, such as "The Lord [would] not say,"[59] "because of this he said,"[60] "well did the Lord say,"[61] sometimes make explicit this subordination to a larger discussion.

With respect to the form of these sayings, most consist of a bare statement with an attribution. In a significant minority, a context is given. At 58.10-14, a prayer is quoted: "He said that day in the prayer of thanksgiving." At 59.23-26, he replies to a request from a disciple. At 63.32-64.9, his action (kissing Mary Magdalene) prompts a question from the disciples, which Jesus answers. At 63.25-30, the Lord enters the dye works of Levi, casts seventy-two hues into the caldron, and brings them all out white before announcing, "For this did the child of the human being come—to be a dyer." The cry of dereliction (68.26-28) is accompanied by reference to an action, though a somewhat ambiguously earthly one: "for he [had] withdrawn from that place." Two actions of the earthly Jesus are mentioned without any verbal comment from him attached, but they do not take the form of an anecdote of which his action forms the high point.[62] The sayings which involve a context, answer a question, or describe an earthly action of Jesus appear in the first three quarters of the text only, and all but one of them (the cry of dereliction) appears in the first third.

---

[57] A phrase only, but specifically attributed.
[58] The unattributed macarism with its discussion attributed to the Logos.
[59] *Gos. Phil.* 55.33-36: N[ЄϥNAϪ]OOC AN Ñϭɪ ⲠϪOЄIC ϪЄ.
[60] *Gos. Phil.* 57.3-5: ⲀIⲀ ⲦOⲨⲦO ⲠⲈϪⲀϥ ϪЄ.
[61] *Gos. Phil.* 74.25-27: ⲔⲀⲖⲰⲤ ⲀⲠϪOЄIC ϪOOC ϪЄ.
[62] The two wordless actions of the earthly Jesus are found in 57.28-58.9: "Jesus tricked everyone, for he did not appear as he was, but appeared in such a way that he could be seen," and in 70.34-771.2, which (though lacunose) seems to refer to his baptism, and begins, "Jesus appeared [. . .] Jordan, the fullness [of the] kingdom of heavens."

The compound "Jesus Christ" (I͞C Π͞X͞C) occurs only once, on page 80. The name "Jesus" occurs eighteen times in the first three quarters of the document, and twice in the final quarter; the title "the Christ" occurs twenty-one times in the first three quarters of the document and once in the final quarter.[63] A few of the occurrences of XOЄIC, XЄC- are used with other meanings: the master of a slave (52.4 and 79.16), the owner of a pearl (62.22) or of an estate (80.23); at 68.27 it is inserted into the cry that "he" spoke from the cross: "[My] God, my God, why *O Lord* have you forsaken me?" The remaining uses of Π͞XOЄIC refer to "the Lord" as (approximately) equivalent to Jesus/the Christ. Unlike the terms explored in the first part of this chapter, these titles are not restricted to any one part of the document, but the nature of the interest they reveal is not uniform.

In the first three quarters of the text, the term "the Lord" always appears in the context of sayings of Jesus, or anecdotes about him, or explanations of his names. After 77.14, the interest shifts. On page 78 the term occurs twice in the same sentence: "You then, who live with the son of God, do not love the world: rather, love the Lord, so that those whom you produce might come to resemble not the world but the Lord."[64] On page 81, the term again occurs in the context of a teaching in which reproduction points metaphorically to some other capacity. The passage begins, "The child of the human being exists, and the child of the child of the human being exists. The child of the human being refers to the Lord, and the child of the child of the human being refers to the one who creates by the child of the human being." In the final quarter of the *Gospel according to Philip*, Π͞XOЄIC has mystical connotations and is linked to teachings about human spiritual potentialities. These uses are significantly different from the more "historical" and matter-of-fact interest shown in the citation formulae, reminiscences, and etymological exegeses of the earlier pages.

The different understandings of Jesus/the Christ, are just as striking. On page 80, "Jesus Christ" is presented as the ideal of moral perfection, the one fulfilling a difficult macarism. On page 83, "Jesus" appears again as an example to follow in digging the root of evil from one's heart—again, a difficult task involved in ethical and spiritual purity. The text

---

[63] If the number of occurrences were proportionate to the first three quarters, "Jesus" would appear six times in the last quarter, or three times as often as it does, and "the Christ" seven times, seven times as often as it does.

[64] *Gos. Phil.* 78.20-24.

adds: "Jesus has weeded the whole place, while others did so one part at a time," a reference to cosmic rather than a human action. Up to the middle of page 77, in contrast, these terms mostly refer to the sayings of Jesus or to his cosmic saving actions.

References to Other Biblical Persons and Places

The first three quarters of the document contains nearly all of the specific references to persons and places. Adam, Eve, Joseph, Mary, Mary Magdalene, and Philip are mentioned in the first three quarters of the *Gospel according to Philip*, as are Jerusalem, the Jordan river, and Nazareth. This does not represent an overwhelming interest in either history or geography, but it does betray some interest in these matters and the biblical narratives in which they are contained. The final quarter is almost completely lacking in any such references: there, the only person mentioned by name is Abraham, in an exegesis of John 8:56. [65]

Retellings of the Creation Story from Genesis

Seven passages in the *Gospel according to Philip* interpret or retell some part of the creation story in Genesis. A few more passages make oblique references to it. Two passages are "revisionistic" only to the extent that they read the tale through a Christian lens.[66] Another is rather mildly revisionistic in a way reminiscent of *Thomas the Contender*— there is talk of a tree that produces animals.[67] Two more read into the story a report of a primordial unity of the sexes,[68] while three passages show a tendency to invert the values of some of the actors and symbols (e.g., bad creator, bad creation, good tree of gnosis).[69] Such inversions have been considered a hallmark of gnostic interpretations of Genesis, but this idea should be approached with caution.

"Powers" and "Rulers"

Six passages using the word ⲆⲨⲚⲀⲘⲓⲤ denote personified, hostile powers. Two more passages referring to "unclean spirits" (ⲡⲚⲀ ⲚⲀⲔⲀⲐⲀⲡⲧⲟⲚ), two refer to "rulers" (ⲁⲣⲬⲰⲚ), and one reference each

---

[65] Excluding "Philip" in the title, which is likely a scribe's or librarian's annotation, and in any case is not part of the text.

[66] *Gos. Phil.* 71,16-21 and 73.8-18.

[67] *Gos. Phil.* 71.22-72.3.

[68] *Gos. Phil.* 68.22-25 and 70.9-21.

[69] *Gos. Phil.* 60.34-61.11, 70.22-33, and 73.27-74.11.

to "demons" (ΔⲀIMONION) and "robbers" (ΛHCTHC) round out the roster of malevolent spiritual beings in the *Gospel according to Philip*.[70] They are distributed similarly—rulers appear on pages 54 and 55, unclean spirits appear on page 65 as seducers, and are associated with demons on page 66; robbers or brigands take the soul captive on page 53. The word ⲀⲢⲬⲰN is used in the plural on both occasions when it is used; there is no reference in the *Gospel according to Philip* to a single evil Archon. On page 54, seeing the kinship of human beings with the good they wish to enslave them, and cause confusion in language in order to achieve that end. On page 55, while they think they act by their own power (ϬOM) and will, the Holy Spirit secretly acts through them, much as the powers were on page 59. This entire cast of infamy appears only in the first three quarters of the document.

The assimilated Greek word ΔⲨNⲀMIC, "power," turns up in the *Gospel according to Philip* in eleven passages. Three of these passages, on pages 64, 67 and 72, use the term in an unpersonified and positive sense of "strength" or "ability," and are irrelevant to the present inquiry.[71] Two more passages use ΔⲨNⲀMIC to refer to personified beings without any hint that their nature might be hostile. A passage on page 60 argues that just as humans work the fields with domesticated animals and increase the food supply for themselves, for the domesticated animals, and for wild animals, so the perfect human being plows with domesticated forces, and so also the Holy Spirit pastures and rules all forces, both domesticated and wild. These uses of ΔⲨNⲀMIC seem to in-

---

[70] The native word ϬOM, which also means "power" or "force," is used eight times, once for benevolent spiritual beings (in 65.1-26) and the other times in non-personified, non-"mythological" ways.

[71] On page 72, ΔⲨNⲀMIC is used in a positive and quite remarkable context: one's deeds (ϨBHⲨⲈ) are asserted to come from one's power or abilities (ΔⲨNⲀMIC). The passage considers also a specific kind of "deed," children, who result from a moment of repose. The whole complex of works and offspring are then compared to the works and offspring of the imaged person, ⲠⲢⲰMⲈ N̄ϨIKONIKOC. Thus, ΔⲨNⲀMIC here has a positive meaning, the "force" seen in human artifice and procreation, on both mundane and spiritual levels.

On page 67, in the context of a discussion of the way truth comes into the world by means of types and images, there is a passing mention of "the force of the cross," N̄TΔⲨNⲀMIC M̄ⲠC⳨[O]C, "which the apostles called right and left." It is associated with chrism; some of the surrounding text is damaged. ΔⲨNⲀMIC, here, is positive again.

Another lacunose passage, at the end of page 64, occurs in the context of the mystery of marriage. The passage seems to assert that this mystery possesses power or powers, but there are about seven letters immediately preceding the word which are missing.

clude friendly entities, or at least ones who are securely under control and who benefit from the arrangement, without causing harm. At 63.11-20, a donkey turning a millstone makes no progress, just as some people travel and see nothing, "neither cities nor villages nor constructions nor the natural order nor forces nor angels." These forces seem important only as spectacle.

The remainder of the occurrences of ΔΥΝΑΜΙΟ refer to hostile entities: two related passages on page 54, two unrelated passages on 55, one on 59, two passages on 65-66, and two passages on 70.

Several different attitudes can be discerned, however. One attitude, concentrated on pages 65 and 66, is that such beings are extremely dangerous and must be eluded at the cost of considerable exertion and ingenuity. The first of these passages involves the famous and enigmatic matter of the "bridal chamber." Its interest for us at present, however, is in the ways hostile forces are characterized, the kind of threat they pose, and the means necessary for avoiding them.

[Ñ]ϹΧ[ΗΜ]Ⲁ ΜΠ̄Ñ[Ⲁ] Ñ̄ⲀΚⲀⲐⲀⲢΤΟΝ ΟΥÑ ϩΟΟΥΤ Ñ̄ϩΗΤΟΥ ΟΥÑ ϩÑ̄Ϲϩ ⲒΟΜⲈ	Among the shapes of unclean spirits there are male ones and female ones.
Ñ̄ϩΟΟΥΤ ΜⲈΝ ΝⲈ ⲈΤⲢ̄ΚΟΙΝⲰΝⲈⲒ ⲀΜⲮΥΧΗ ⲈΤⲢ̄ΠΟΛΙΤⲈΥⲈⲤⲐⲈ ϩÑ̄ΝΟΥϹΧΗΜⲀ Ñ̄Ϲϩ ⲒΜⲈ Ñ̄Ϲϩ ⲒΟΜⲈ ⲆⲈ ΝⲈ ΝⲈΤϩ̄ϩ ΜÑ̄ ΝⲈΤ2Ñ̄ ΟΥϹΧΗΜⲀ Ñ̄ϩΟΟΥΤ ⲈΒΟΛ ϩΙΤÑ̄ ΟΥⲀΤΤⲰΤ	It is male spirits that have sexual intercourse with souls who conduct their lives within a female shape, and female ones that mingle promiscuously with those within a male shape.
ⲀΥⲰ ΜÑ̄ ΛⲀⲀΥ ΝⲀϢⲢ̄ ΒΟΛ ⲈΝⲀⲈⲒ ⲈΥⲈΜⲀϩΤⲈ Μ̄ΜΟϤ ⲈϤΤΜ̄ΧΙ Ñ̄ΟΥϬΟΜ Ñ̄ϩΟΟΥΤ ΜÑ̄ ΝΟΥϹϩ ⲒΜⲈ ⲈΤⲈ ΠΝΥΜⲪΙΟϹ ΠⲈ ΜÑ̄ ΤΝΥΜⲪΗ	And no one can escape if seized by them, unless by taking on a male or female power, namely (one's) bridegroom or bride.
ϩΟΤⲀΝ ⲈⲢϢ ⲀϤ Ñ̄Ϲϩ ⲒΜⲈ Ñ̄ⲀΤϹΒⲰ ΝⲀΥ ⲀΥϩΟΟΥΤ ⲈϤϩΜΟΟϹ ΟΥⲀⲀϤ ϢⲀΥϤⲰ ϬⲈ Ⲉϩ ⲢⲀⲒ ⲈΧⲰϤ Ñ̄ϹⲈϢⲰΒⲈ ΝΜ̄ΜⲀϤ Ñ̄ϹⲈΧⲟϩ ΜⲈϤ	Whenever the foolish female ones see a male sitting by himself they leap upon him and fondle him and pollute him.
ΤⲈⲈⲒϩ Ⲉ ΟΝ ϩⲢ̄ΡⲰΜⲈ Ñ̄ⲀΤϹΒⲰ ⲈΥϢ ⲀΝΝⲀΥ ⲈΥϹϩ ΙΜⲈ ⲈϹϩΜΟΟϹ ΟΥⲀⲀΤⲤ̄ ⲈΝⲈϹⲰϹ Ϣ ⲀΥΠΙⲐⲈ Μ̄ΜΟϹ Ñ̄ϹⲈⲢ̄ΒΙⲀⲌⲈ Μ̄ΜΟϹ ⲈΥΟΥⲰϢ ⲈΧΟϩ ΜⲈϹ	So also when the foolish male ones see a beautiful woman sitting alone they seduce her and do violence to her in order to pollute her.[72]

---

[72] *Gos. Phil.* 65.1-19 (translation modified).

A discussion of the qualities of the person who leaves the world begins near the bottom of page 65. Like the bottoms of most pages of codex 2, especially near the center, it is lacunose. One who leaves the world is above desire and perhaps fear, and superior to envy. Such a one "will no longer be restrained as though in the world"—ⲚⲤⲈⲦⲘ̅ϢⲈⲘⲀϨⲦⲈ Ⲙ̅Ⲙⲟⲩ ⲈⲦⲒ ⲬⲈ ⲚⲈⲩϨⲘ̅ ⲠⲔⲞⲤⲘⲞⲤ. The discussion then seems to shift to consideration of a person in the opposite situation, and remarks,

ⲈϢⲬⲈ [. . .]Ⲩ ⲈⲒ ⲤⲈⲀⲘ[Ⲁ]ϨⲦⲈ Ⲙ̅Ⲙⲟⲩ ⲤⲈⲰϬ[Ⲧ Ⲙ̅Ⲙⲟⲩ]	If [. . .] then that person is seized and strangled.
ⲀⲨⲰ ⲠⲰ[Ⲥ Ⲉⳡ]ⲚⲀϢⲠ̅ ⲂⲞⲖ ⲀⲚⲚ[ⲞϬ Ⲛ̅Ⲁ ⲨⲚ]ⲀⲘⲒ[Ⲥ. . .] ⲦⲈ	And how can that person escape the [great] forces [. . .]?
ⲠⲰⲤ ⳡⲚⲀϢϨ[. . .]ⲔⲒⲤ	How can that person [. . .]?
ⲞⲨⲚ̅ ϨⲞⲈⲒⲚⲈ ⲈⲨ[ⲬⲰ Ⲙ̅ⲘⲞⲤ ⲬⲈ] ⲀⲚⲞⲚ ϨⲘ̅ⲠⲒⲤⲦⲞⲤ ϨⲞⲠⲰ[Ⲥ.. . . [Ⲡ]Ⲛ̅Ⲁ̅ Ⲛ̅Ⲁ[ⲔⲀⲐⲀⲢⲦⲞ]Ⲛ ϨⲒ ⲆⲀⲒⲘⲞⲚⲒⲞⲚ	There are some people who [say], "We are faithful," in order that [. . .] [unclean] spirit(s) and demons.
ⲚⲈⲨⲚ̅ⲦⲀⲨ ⲄⲀⲢ Ⲙ̅ⲘⲀ[Ⲩ] Ⲙ̅ⲠⲚ̅Ⲁ̅ ⲈⲦⲞⲨⲀⲀⲂ ⲚⲈ ⲘⲚ̅ ⲠⲚ̅Ⲁ̅ Ⲛ̅ⲀⲔⲀⲐⲀⲢⲦⲞⲚ ⲚⲀⲢ̅ⲔⲞⲖⲖⲀ ⲈⲢⲞⲞⲨ	For if they possessed the Holy Spirit, no unclean spirit could attach itself to them.[73]

These beings are dangerous, deadly opponents; the most extraordinary measures must be taken against them, and the battle is taken very seriously.

Another, contrasting conception of hostile powers is found in two groups of passages, on pages 54 and 55 and on pages 59 and 60. Here, while the evil powers are depicted as personified and malevolent, actively seeking to harm human beings, their plans either backfire or are rendered innocuous by the activity of the Holy Spirit. A faintly slapstick quality is conveyed: the forces of evil are not in control, do not have what it takes to be in control, and can be mocked. Two classic statements of this understanding appear on pages 55 and 59. Each passage is found in a cluster of material with the same perspective.

A discussion of language extends from 53.13 to 54.30. The discussion establishes that language and the dualities with which it often deals are deceptive. The conclusion of the discussion, with which we are here concerned, affirms the value of a philosophically sophisticated understanding of language in mythological terms. The rulers, seeking to de-

---

73 *Gos. Phil.* 65.32-66.4 (translation modified).

ceive by tampering with language, only succeed in making this relativity
of language apparent to their intended victims.

ⲀⲚⲀⲢⲬⲰⲚ ⲞⲨⲰϢ ⲀⲢⲀⲠⲀⲦⲀ	The rulers wanted to deceive
ⲘⲠⲢⲰⲘⲈ ⲈⲠⲈⲒⲀⲎ ⲀⲨⲚⲀⲨ ⲈⲢⲞϤ	humanity, inasmuch as they saw
ⲈⲨⲚ̄ⲦⲀϤ Ⲙ̄ⲘⲀⲨ	that it has kinship with truly good
Ⲛ̄ⲚⲞⲨⲤⲨⲄⲄⲈⲚⲈⲒⲀ ϢⲀ	things;
ⲚⲈⲦⲚⲀⲚⲞⲨⲞⲨ ⲚⲀⲘⲈ	
ⲀⲨϤⲒ ⲠⲢⲀⲚ Ⲛ̄ⲚⲈⲦⲚⲀⲚⲞⲨⲞⲨ	they took the names of the good
ⲀⲨⲦⲀⲀϤ ⲀⲚⲈⲦⲚⲀⲚⲞⲨⲞⲨ ⲀⲚ	(plur.) and gave them to the non-
	good
ⲬⲈⲔⲀⲀⲤ ϨⲒⲦⲚ̄ Ⲣ̄ⲢⲀⲚ ⲈⲨⲚⲀⲢ̄	to deceive humanity by the names
ⲀⲠⲀⲦⲀ Ⲙ̄ⲘⲞϤ ⲀⲨⲰ Ⲛ̄ⲤⲈⲘⲞⲢⲞⲨ	and bind them to the non-good
ⲈϨⲞⲨⲚ ⲀⲚⲈⲦⲚⲀⲚⲞⲨⲞⲨ ⲀⲚ	
ⲀⲨⲰ Ⲙ̄ⲘⲚ̄Ⲛ̄ⲤⲰⲤ ⲈϢϪⲈ ⲈⲨⲈⲒⲢⲈ	and—then what a favor they do for
ⲚⲀⲨ Ⲛ̄ⲞⲨϨⲘⲞⲦ	them!—
Ⲛ̄ⲤⲈⲦⲢⲞⲨⲤⲈϨⲰⲞⲨ ⲈⲂⲞⲖ	to remove them (the names) from
Ⲛ̄ⲚⲈⲦⲚⲀⲚⲞⲨⲞⲨ ⲀⲚ ⲀⲨⲰ	the non-good and assign them to
Ⲛ̄ⲤⲈⲔⲀⲀⲨ ϨⲚ̄ ⲚⲈⲦⲚⲀⲚⲞⲨⲞⲨ	the good!
ⲚⲀⲈⲒ ⲚⲈⲨⲤⲞⲞⲨⲚ Ⲙ̄ⲘⲞⲞⲨ	These they were acquainted with:
ⲚⲈⲨⲞⲨⲰϢ ⲄⲀⲢ ⲈⲦⲢⲞⲨϤⲒ	for they wanted the free to be taken
ⲦⲈⲖⲈⲨⲐⲈⲢ[Ⲟ]Ⲥ Ⲛ̄ⲤⲈⲔⲀⲀϤ ⲚⲀⲨ	and enslaved to them in
Ⲛ̄ϨⲘ̄ϨⲀⲖ ϢⲀ ⲈⲚⲈϨ	perpetuity.[74]

The passage immediately following is unrelated to the discussion of language, but reveals a similar understanding of evil forces and the success
of their plans. In this passage, the powers are identified with the pagan
deities, particularly the theriomorphic ones. Animals were slaughtered as
sacrifices to them: that is, they were offered live and became dead as a
result of the offering. In place of this, however, human beings in their
usual unsaved "dead" state are now being offered to God, and as a result
they become alive. Here, the plan of the powers has not so much backfired as it has been made obsolescent.

ⲞⲨⲚ ϨⲚ̄ⲆⲨⲚⲀⲘⲒⲤ ϢⲞⲞⲠ	There exist forces that [. . .] human
ⲈⲨϮϨ[. . .] ⲠⲢⲰⲘⲈ ⲈⲤⲈⲞⲨⲰϢ ⲀⲚ	beings, not wanting them to [attain
ⲀⲦⲢⲈϤⲞⲨ[ϪⲀⲈⲒ] ⲬⲈⲔⲀⲀⲤ	salvation], so that they might
ⲈⲨⲚⲀϢⲰⲠⲈ ⲈⲨⲘ[. . .]Ⲁ	become [. . .].
ⲈⲢϢⲀ ⲠⲢⲰⲘⲈ ⲄⲀⲢ ⲞⲨⲬ[ⲀⲈⲒ	For if human beings attain salva-
Ⲛ̄ⲚⲞⲨ]ϢⲰⲠⲈ Ⲛ̄ϬⲒ ϨⲚ̄ⲐⲨⲤⲒⲀ	tion, sacrifices [will not] be made
[. . .] ⲀⲨⲰ ⲚⲈⲨⲦⲀⲖⲈ ⲐⲎⲢⲒⲞⲚ	[. . .], and animals will not be of-
ⲈϨⲢⲀⲓ̈ Ⲛ̄Ⲛ̄ⲆⲨⲚⲀⲘⲒⲤ	fered up unto the forces.

---

[74] *Gos. Phil.* 54.18-31.

ΝΕ [2]Ν̄[Θ]ΗΡΙΟΝ ΓΑΡ ΝΕ ΝΕΤΟΥΤΕΛΟ Ε2ΡΑῚ ΝΑ[Υ]	Indeed, the ones to whom offer- ings used to be made were animals.
ΝΕΥΤΕΛΟ ΜΕΝ Μ̄ΜΟΟΥ Ε2ΡΑῚ ΕΥΟΝ2 Ν̄ΤΑΡΟΥΤΕΛΟΟΥ ΔΕ Ε2ΡΑῚ ΑΥΜΟΥ	Now, they were offered up alive: but when they had been offered up, they died.
ΠΡΩΜΕ ΑΥΤΕΛΟϤ Ε2ΡΑῚ Μ̄ΠΝΟΥΤΕ ΕϤΜΟΟΥΤ ΑΥΩ ΑϤΩΝ2	Human beings were offered up dead unto God; and they became alive.[75]

On page 54, the "rulers" wish to deceive humanity and enslave them, so
they confuse language; immediately following that passage is this partial
parallel, in which the "powers" wish to thwart human salvation, lest animals cease being sacrificed to them. The passage identifies the gods of
paganism with these hostile powers.

On page 55 we read about the Holy Spirit's part in all this:

ΝΕΡΕ Ν̄ΑΡΧΩΝ ΜΕΕΥΕ ΧΕ 2Ν̄ ΤΟΥϬΟΜ ΜΝ̄ ΠΟΥΩϢ ΕΥΕΙΡΕ Ν̄ΝΕΤΟΥΕΙΡΕ Μ̄ΜΟΟΥ	The rulers thought that it was by their own power and will that they did what they did:
ΝΕΡΕ ΠΠ̄Ν̄Α ΔΕ ΕΤΟΥΑΑΒ 2Ν̄ ΟΥΠΕΘΗΠ ΝΕϤΕΝΕΡΓΕΙ Μ̄ΠΤΗΡϤ ΕΒΟΛ 2ΙΤΟΟΤΟΥ Ν̄ΘΕ ΕΤϤΟΥΩϢ	but the Holy Spirit was secretly ac- tivating the entirety through them, as it willed.[76]

On page 59, again the evil forces are blinded by the Holy Spirit, and
tricked into acting against their own interests by ministering to the
saints.[77]

ϹΕϢΜ̄ϢΕ Ν̄ΝΕΤΟΥΑΑΒ 2ΙΤΝ̄ Ν̄ΔΥΝΑΜΙϹ Μ̄ΠΟΝΗΡΟΝ	The holy are ministered to by evil forces:
ϹΕΟ ΓΑΡ Ν̄ΒΛ̄ΛΕ 2ΙΤΜ̄ ΠΝ̄Α ΕΤΟΥΑΑΒ	for the latter have been blinded by the Holy Spirit
ΧΕΚΑΑϹ ΕΥΝΑΜΕΕΥΕ ΧΕ ΕΥР̄2ΥΠΗΡΕΤΕΙ Ν̄ΝΟΥΡΩΜΕ 2ΟΠΟΤΕ ΕΥΕΙΡΕ Ν̄ΝΕΤΟΥΑΑΒ	so that while they will think that they are helping [their] human be- ings whenever they help the holy.[78]

The assertion that providence works itself out even through the acts of
those opposed to it is not especially unusual, but the description of the
Holy Spirit as a trickster is less common.

---

[75] *Gos. Phil.* 54.31-55.5.
[76] *Gos. Phil.* 55.14-19
[77] *Gos. Phil.* 59.18-26.
[78] *Gos. Phil.* 59.18-23, translation modified.

It is not incompatiblê with the underlying conceptuality of the two passages on page 70, although its connection with the first is less clear than with the second. At the top of page 70, the forces are said to be unable to see or seize those who have put on the perfect light.[79] This is reminiscent of an understanding mentioned in Irenaeus' catalog of rites of "redemption" (ἀπολύτρωσις): one group anoints its members at the point of death, in order that they "might become incomprehensible and invisible to the Principalities and the Powers, and that their inner man might ascend above the invisible things."[80] This seems to confer the ability to trick the powers, but it is not stated that this is the gift of the Holy Spirit. Later on the same page of the *Gospel according to Philip*, however, the forces envy the newly created Adam because he speaks words superior to them.[81] The idea that the rulers or powers fashioned Adam but were surprised when they learned that a spirit had been secretly given him is present in a number of texts from various streams of gnostic thought, such as the *Hypostasis of the Archons*,[82] the *Apocryphon of John*,[83] as well as the Ptolemaic version of Valentinianism.[84] Sometimes, as here, the gift involves an action by his "mother" and/or "blowing" (the breath/spirit). The story in the *Gospel according to Philip*, however, adds that the rulers' surprise comes when the superior element in Adam is revealed by his speech, a detail absent in the above accounts but shared with a fragment of one of Valentinus' own writings quoted by Clement of Alexandria.[85]

One passage about hostile powers remains, which may belong with the group of texts that regard these powers as capable of being outsmarted or outmaneuvered: the passage on page 55 that identifies Mary the mother of Jesus as "the virgin whom the forces did not defile," a striking phrase found identically as a description of Norea in *Hypostasis of the Archons*.[86]

---

[79] *Gos. Phil.* 70.5-8.

[80] Irenaeus, *Adv. haer.* 1.21.5.

[81] *Gos. Phil.* 70.22-33.

[82] *Hyp. Arch.* 87.33-88.16.

[83] *Ap. John* 15.1-20.8, especially 19.10-20.8.

[84] Irenaeus *Adv. haer.* 1.5.5-6.

[85] Clement *Strom.* 2.36.2-4 = Völker's Fragment 1. The phrasing is similar but not identical in the two texts: [ⲁϥϫ]ⲱ Ⲛ̄2Ⲛ̄ϣⲁⲭⲉ ⲉⲩⲭⲟⲥⲉ ⲁⲛⲁⲩⲛⲁ[ⲙⲓⲥ] ⲁⲩⲢ̄ⲃⲁⲥⲕⲁⲛⲉ ⲉⲡⲟϥ. Valentinus, however, offers a sophisticated reflection on the partial analogy offered by human artistic creation, which is absent here in the *Gospel according to Philip*.

[86] *Gos. Phil.* 55.23-32 and *Hyp. Arch.* 91.34-93.1.

The Human Problematic

It is difficult to escape the conclusion that the *Gospel according to Philip* does not have any coherent theory of the underlying problematic of the human condition. The assessments of the mess and the solutions offered differ widely both in concept and sophistication.

Several passages point to a lost primordial unity of the sexes;[87] others blame a faulty creation that was never right;[88] others blame the activity of hostile beings, as seen above, or even the Spirit;[89] still others see the basic human problem stemming from human choices.[90] For other passages, the underlying problem results from failure to gain some spiritual good, perhaps linked to a sacrament, in some passages;[91] or to a lack of knowledge;[92] others subsume an unstated lack under the image of a poor diet: humans have had only food fit for animals to eat, or food that makes them animals, or corpses.[93] In some passages the problem is denied as only apparent;[94] or as applying only to certain groups of people.[95]

The assessments in the *Gospel according to Philip* of the underlying nature of the human condition are legion. Nearly all of them are jumbled together throughout the first three quarters of the document. A large number of the passages that trace the basic human problem to sin or freely chosen harmful actions occur in the last quarter of the document: 66.21-29, 74.24-36; 77.15-34, 78.12-24, 79.13-17, 82.30-84.13.

Ethical Exhortation

From time to time, the *Gospel according to Philip* gives advice about how to behave. This advice is usually more than a little oblique; it often needs a key to render it intelligible; and does not generally address the issue of behavior toward other human beings. For example, "Let us sow in the world so that we might reap in the summer;" or, "Do not despise

---

[87] *Gos. Phil.* 65.1-26, 68.17-21, 68.22-25, and 70.9-12 are the clearest examples.

[88] *Gos. Phil.* 60.34-61.11, 61.11-20, and 75.2-12—again, only the clearest examples.

[89] *Gos. Phil.* 60.6-9.

[90] *Gos. Phil.* 66.21-29, 74.24-36, 77.15-34, 78.12-24, 79.13-17, 82.30-84.13.

[91] *Gos. Phil.* 65.1-26, 66.1-6, 66.16-20, 73.1-7.

[92] *Gos. Phil.* 53.14-23, 61.20-35, 82.30-84.13.

[93] *Gos. Phil.* 54.6-13, 71,22-72.3, 73.19-27, respectively.

[94] *Gos. Phil.* 62.17-25.

[95] *Gos. Phil.* 64.1-8, 69.1-3, 75.25-76.5, 81.14-33.

the lamb, for without it one cannot see the door" (or, "king").[96] The *Gospel according to Philip* talks occasionally about "going astray:" "It is the ones who have gone astray that the spirit gave birth to;" it even mentions "sin:" "It is good to leave the world before a person commits sin."[97] But it is unclear what constitutes "going astray" or "sinning." Nor is the spiritual advice given in the first three quarters of the *Gospel according to Philip* based on a paradigm of loving relationship with God and the transference of interpersonal virtues to that relationship. The examples above are typical of the little advice found in the first three quarters of the document. The nearest to a specifically ethical passage before the final quarter is found on page 72, where there is a description, unaccompanied by exhortation or even application, of how the free will render service to the servants in the kingdom of heavens.

In contrast, most of the document's passages dealing with human relationships or spiritual purity occur in the final quarter of the *Gospel according to Philip*, and they occur there with such a density that they constitute a major focus of most of that final section. Viewed from this perspective, a major change can be located precisely, between 77.14 and 77.15. The nature of spiritual love, the relation of love and gnosis, fidelity of devotion to God imaged as sexual fidelity, the preconditions for spiritual growth, avoidance of needlessly distressing others, the importance of discerning the spiritual condition of others in dealing with them, the nature of spiritual parenthood, fidelity of devotion to God again, the mortification of the flesh, and the need to "burrow for the root of evil that is within" hold sway after 77.15.

THE DISTRIBUTION OF SACRAMENTAL REFERENCES

Sacraments are mentioned frequently throughout the *Gospel according to Philip*: as rituals, as metaphors of transformation, and in the course of discussion of other matters. The density of such references, however, is considerably greater between page 67 and page 74 than in the earlier pages of the document, and after the middle of page 77, virtually all interest disappears, except for a few oblique and metaphorical usages in the last few pages.

---

[96] *Gos. Phil.* 52.27-28 and 58.14-15.
[97] *Gos. Phil.* 60.6-7 and 66.21-22.

The exact nature of the sacraments in the *Gospel according to Philip* is notoriously controverted. A passage on page 67 is traditionally the starting place:

ⲁⲡⲭⲟⲉⲓ[ⲥ ⲡ]ⲣ̣ϩⲱⲃ ⲛⲓⲙ ϩⲛ̄ⲛⲟⲩ ⲙⲩⲥⲧⲉⲣ̇ⲓⲟⲛ	The Lord [did] all things by means of a mystery:
ⲟⲩⲃⲁ[ⲡ]ⲧⲓⲥⲙⲁ ⲙⲛ̄ ⲟⲩⲭⲣⲓⲥⲙⲁ ⲙⲛ̄ⲛⲟⲩⲉⲩⲭⲁⲣ[ⲓⲥⲧ]ⲓ̣ⲁ ⲙⲛ̄ⲛⲟⲩⲥⲱⲧⲉ ⲙⲛ̄ⲛⲟⲩⲛⲩⲙⲫⲱⲛ	baptism, chrism, eucharist, ransom, and bridal chamber.[98]

The table on page 179, "The Distribution of Sacramental References in the *Gospel according to Philip*," gives a quick impression of the uses of these, and some related, terms. Terminology typically involved in sacramental matters, when used in what appears to be its ritual sense, are marked "X", while clearly non-ritual usages are marked "ø", and doubtful ones, "?" (See Notes below for more details.) A glance at this table should put to rest any claims that the majority of the material in the *Gospel according to Philip* is sacramental in nature, or that the work as a whole—as distinct from some of its sources—is some kind of sacramental catechesis.

Notes to Table "The Distribution of Sacramental References"

Each occurrence of the names (and related verbal forms) of the five supposed sacraments—as listed at 67.27-30—is tabulated here. Despite the ambiguity related to these, the employment of these terms provides a rough index to sacramental matters.

The "additional" references represent terms which are often found in conjunction with fairly clear references to each sacrament (or sacramental action, or aspect of initiation). Because the relevance of each term to ritual or non-ritual matters is inevitably a judgment call, every occurrence of each term selected is represented. When a ritual seems to be in mind, the reference is indicated by an "X" (when it refers to the sacrament in question), by an "ø" (when it is used in other ways), or occasionally by a "?" when the nature of the reference is unclear.

The terms tabulated as "possible references" are as follows: for baptism, ⲙⲟⲟⲩ; for chrism, ⲧⲱϩⲥ, ⲛⲉϩ(ⲛⲏϩ), ⲥⲟϭⲛ, ⲥⲧⲟⲉⲓ; for eucharist, ⲟⲉⲓⲕ, ⲁⲣⲧⲟⲥ, ⲏⲡⲧ, ⲡⲟⲧⲏⲣⲓⲟⲛ, ⲥⲁⲣⲝ, ⲥⲛⲟϥ, ⲧⲣⲟⲫⲏ, and ⲥⲱ; for "ransom" (ⲥⲱⲧⲉ), and for "bridal chamber" (ⲛⲩⲙⲫⲱⲛ), only the occurrences of the terms themselves are shown, plus (with ⲛⲩⲙⲫⲱⲛ) ⲡⲁⲥⲧⲟⲥ and ⲕⲟⲓⲧⲱⲛ. It is impossible securely to recognize an allusion or oblique reference to these matters from our current state of knowledge.

---

[98] *Gos. Phil.* 67.27-30.

The Distribution of Sacramental References
in the *Gospel according to Philip*

	ΒΑΠΤΙCΜΑ ṖΒΑΠΤΙΖΕ	other refs. to baptism	ΧΡΙCΜΑ	other refs. to chrism	ΕΥΧΑΡΙCΤΕΙΑ ṖΕΥΧΑΡΙCΤΕΙ	other refs. to eucharist	CΩΤΕ	ΝΥΜϢΩΝ
51								
52								
53							??	
54								
55						?????		
56						XXXX		
57		XXX	X			14X		
58					X			
59								
60								
61	XX	X						
62				ø			ø	
63					X			
64		X				øøø		
65								X
66				øøø		øø		
67	X	XX	XXX		X		X	XXX
68						øø		
69	XXX	XXX	X	X			XXX	XXXXX
70								XXXX
71				XX		øø	XX	??
72		X						??
73	XX		X			øøøø		
74	XX	X	XXX	XXXX		øøøø		X
75		XX ø		ø	X	XXXXX		
76								?
77	X	XX		ø		XX ø		
78						ø		
79		ø						
80						ø		
81						ø		
82						øø		????
83								
84								ø
85			?				?	øø
86								ø

Most investigators have seen the items listed on page 67 of the *Gospel according to Philip* as the names of sacraments or sacramental actions; opinions differ as to what they are or how they relate to each other. It is by no means agreed upon whether these terms refer to separate sacraments, or to individual ritual elements in an initiatory sequence, or whether some of the terms are metaphorical or elliptical ways of referring to initiation or its effects,[99] or even sometimes used to refer metaphorically to salvation, received with or without such rites.

One of the problems the data presents is that the same results (the reception of "light," resurrection, the Holy Spirit, et cetera) are in different passages associated with different ones of these names. The impossibility of making clear functional distinctions between these allegedly separate rites does not necessarily mean that they were not separate—functional distinctions that do not overlap are not available in proto-orthodox references to baptism and chrism either, which were nevertheless clearly distinguishable actions. This issue may not be capable of being resolved definitively, at least without new information. In any case, some occurrences of the terms seem to refer literally to ritual actions, while in other places they are used metaphorically.

Note that neither baptism nor eucharist is mentioned by name after the middle of page 77. The single use each of the words "chrism" and "redemption" (ϹⲰⲦⲈ) after the same point both occur in an eschatological passage, which may draw metaphorically on their sacramental or ritual symbolism.

"Water" often appears in baptismal contexts, but after the middle of page 77, the two passages in which it appears are unrelated to baptism. On 79, water is listed along with earth, air, and light as a necessity for agriculture; each term is interpreted allegorically: water is hope, and the others faith, love and gnosis respectively. This passage has no relevance to ritual matters. On pages 84-85, water again appears in a dense and

---

[99] Specifically, the text can be interpreted as witnessing to six sacraments (taking ⲘⲨϹⲦⲈⲢ︤ⲒⲞⲚ as an item on the list rather than a characterization of items which follow), five (as is assumed here, solely for heuristic purposes—see Segelberg, "The Coptic-Gnostic Gospel according to Philip and its Sacramental System," *Numen* 7 (1960) 189-200, and Ménard, *L'Évangile* (1967) 25-29), four (taking ⲚⲨⲘⲪⲰⲚ as referring generally to the whole sequence—see Isenberg, *Nag Hammadi Codex II,2-7*, 136-137), three (taking ϹⲰⲦⲈ as referring to baptism and anointing together, and ⲚⲨⲘⲪⲰⲚ as referring to the eucharist, or both these terms as referring generally to the sequence of the first three—see Rewolinski, "Sacramental Language," 123-140, and Tripp, "'Sacramental System,'" 256-257); other solutions may also be possible.

enigmatic account of salvation or enlightenment, told in the imagery of eschatological cataclysm. The (inferior?) deity, unable to mix with un-mixed light, will take refuge under the wings of the cross, and the ark (from the Temple, it seems, from earlier references to the rending of the veil) will be "the people's" salvation from surging floodwaters. Ritual im-agery is among the many sorts invoked in this richly tangled metaphoric skein, so the floodwaters here may well be meant to carry some bap-tismal reverberations. Nevertheless, (1) this is no direct reference to bap-tism; (2) "the people" who find refuge in this way are soon contrasted to others belonging to the tribe of the priesthood, who are able to enter in-side the veil—so to the extent this "water" evokes baptismal connota-tions, it does so to criticize the action and those who take part in it; (3) as with the uses here of the imagery of the Temple and its priesthood, evocation of the imagery of baptism in this sort of context need not im-ply literal use of the ritual.

Terms sometimes associated with the eucharist appearing in the final quarter of the *Gospel according to Philip* also turn out to be unrelated to a ritual context. "Loaf" (ⲀⲢⲦⲞⲤ) appears on page 80 in a parable about a landowner who gave his several kinds of animals, servants and children each their proper kind of food. The passage could conceivably be given a eucharistic interpretation, but only by considerable vio-lence.[100] A reference to different kinds of instruction as appropriate to more than three different groups is more likely, given the larger context of 79.33-81.13.[101] "Bread" (ⲞⲈⲒⲔ) appears on page 81 in the same pas-sage, in the idiom ⲘⲀⲘⲞⲨ Ⲛ̄ⲞⲈⲒⲔ, "urine of bread," i.e., excrement (but possibly also spoiled food?). It is combined with acorns to feed hogs.

---

[100] One might assume a three-fold division of humanity is meant (despite the care to distinguish three different kinds of "animals" [pigs, cattle, and dogs] in addition to two kinds of humans [slaves and sons], each requiring quite different kinds of food); the result would be that "slaves" get "a loaf," understood as the eucharist, while "children" get something more—but this does not seem likely.

[101] Note that it is not specified, however: at this point Isenberg's translation, "To slaves he will give only the elementary lessons, to the children he will give the complete instruction," is based on the statement that the disciples of God "will consider the condition of the soul of each one, and will speak to him." The concluding reiteration of the terms of the parable (it is not exactly an interpretation) only says that he will give the slaves "a first" (ϥⲚⲀϯ Ⲛ̄ϢⲞⲢⲡ— Layton interprets this as "a first course" or one-dish meal), while he will give the children "a complete" (ϥⲚⲀϯ ⲚⲀⲨ Ⲛ̄ⲦⲈⲖⲈⲒⲞⲚ) i.e., a full meal. Isenberg's interpretation that the phrase Ⲛ̄ϥϢⲀⲬⲈ Ⲙ̄ⲘⲞϥ, "and speak to him" determines the thrust of the whole is gratuitous. Without clearer specification, it would be safer to interpret the whole as referring to an unspecified range of "nurturing" activities.

"Flesh" (ⲤⲀⲢⲜ) appears twice on page 82, but in the non-eucharistic statement, "When Abraham [. . .] to behold what he was going to behold, [he] circumcised the flesh of the foreskin, telling us that it is fitting to mortify the flesh."

These references are not metaphorical evocations of sacramental matters but belong to their own quite separate and distinct frames of reference.

Neither ⲚⲨⲘⲪⲰⲚ (bridal chamber) nor its approximate synonyms ⲠⲀⲤⲦⲞⲤ (bridal chamber or bridal bed) and ⲔⲞⲒⲦⲰⲚ (bed chamber) appear at all in the *Gospel according to Philip* before page 65; after page 77, these terms reappear on pages 82, and 84-86. In the last several pages of the document, the terms seem to be used more metaphorically or eschatologically, but this is difficult to judge, especially since it is unclear whether they ever referred to a distinct ritual.[102] It can be noted, however, that (except for the famous list on page 67) these terms never occur in a passage that refers explicitly to the eucharist, while they are found with some frequency in conjunction with baptism and chrism.

SUMMARY

The first three quarters of the *Gospel according to Philip* contains:

- all uses of the term "Christian;"
- all references to "Hebrews," "Jews," and "Gentiles;"
- all uses of the terms "apostle" and "apostolic;"
- all uses of "perfect" in an initiatory sense;
- all interest in Semitic language etymologies;
- all citations of or references to words or earthly actions attributed to "Jesus," "Christ," "Jesus Christ," or "the Lord;"
- all references to persons (other than Jesus) mentioned in the New Testament (and 95% of all references to biblical persons);[103]

---

[102] A few people have noted aspects of this, without developing the insight. Catherine Trautmann considered that the *Gospel according to Philip* presents "celestial marriage" in two ways—as part of the mythology of the original marriage between the father and the virgin, and as part of the final act inaugurating the new time (84-85). Her subsequent development of parentage in both terrestrial and celestial marriage does not return again to those final pages. See Trautmann, "La Parenté dans l'Évangile selon Philippe," in *Colloque International sur les textes de Nag Hammadi* ed. B. Barc (Québec: Presses de l'Université Laval, 1981) 267-278.

[103] Both excluding "Philip" in the title, positioned at the end of the work.

- all references to biblical place names;
- all allusions to the creation story in Genesis ("revisionist" or not);
- all concern with hostile powers, however understood;
- all references to "Sophia;"
- all uses of "baptism" and all plausibly ritual uses of "water;"
- all uses of "eucharist," "*pharisatha*," "cup," "blood" "eat," and "drink," along with all plausibly ritual uses of "bread," and "wine;"
- all plausibly ritual uses of "chrism," "anoint," "oil" "ointment," and "perfume;"
- all plausibly ritual uses of "redeem/redemption."

The final quarter, in contrast, contains:

- none of the above;
- all references to "gnosis" as a spiritual quality or abstraction, and to its opposite as "ignorance;"
- all use of "perfect" in a moral sense;
- all citation formulae employing "logos."

The distribution of these features, along with other trends and tendencies, which will be analyzed in the next two chapters, amounts to strong evidence that there is a major disjunction at 77.14-15.

Nevertheless, the material in the first three quarters is not homogeneous. That portion of the *Gospel according to Philip* derives from people who called themselves "Christians" and from others who opposed the use of the term, from ones tracing their spiritual ancestry back to apostles and from ones who considered the apostles and their heirs to be fundamentally deluded, from those who considered demonic forces real and still dangerous, and from those who believed them to have been rendered laughable and obsolescent.

CHAPTER EIGHT

THE "PRIMITIVE" VALENTINIAN BLOCK

The final section is set apart from the rest of the *Gospel according to Philip* by the absence of a number of characteristics, all of them present in abundance in the first three quarters of the document:

- the absence of terms of sectarian self-reference and polemic such as "Christian," "apostle/apostolic," "Hebrew," "perfect" (in an initiatory sense);
- a very limited use of sacramental vocabulary; that which is used has acquired a metaphoric sense;
- the almost complete absence of interest in hostile powers; the few references are metaphorical;
- absence of any reference to the creation story from Genesis, whether revisionist or not;
- a lack of interest in the historical context (or even the speaker) of dominical sayings quoted.[1]

The final section of the *Gospel according to Philip* is also united by the presence of a number of characteristics not typical of the rest of the work:

- longer rhetorical units;
- the use of the term "gnosis" to refer to a psychological or spiritual quality;
- provocative parallels to the *Gospel of Truth*;
- several distinctive ways of handling scripture:
  - distinctive citation formulae used when scripture is quoted;
  - some quite literally gnosticizing interpretations;
  - a preference for allusions over quotations, and the combination of multiple allusions into a single image;
  - a sort of reverse allegorization;

---

[1] These characteristics were surveyed and evaluated in chapter 7 as evidence for a major disjunction between the first three quarters of the document and its final quarter; their presence in the first three quarters will be explored more fully in chapter 9.

- an interest in moral exhortation, understood as a matter of (a) interactions between people, and (b) inner purity;
- a distinctive transformation of sacramental imagery.

I have (somewhat playfully) labeled the material in this final section "primitive" Valentinian, because it most probably originated in either an early or a conservative part of the Valentinian movement. The character of this section, as defined primarily by its positive characteristics, is the subject of this chapter. There are also two passages in the first three quarters of the *Gospel according to Philip* which seem to belong to the same source; they will be discussed in chapter 9.[2]

LENGTH AND STRUCTURE OF TEXTUAL UNITS

There are several long blocks of continuous argumentation in this section: 77.15-78.11 form a single unit, as do 79.33-81.13 and 82.30-84.13. They offer a blend of exegesis, application, exhortation, and invitation that is distinctively homiletical.

This final section of the *Gospel according to Philip* opens on the middle of page 77 with a consideration of gnosis and love which extends almost to the middle of the next page.[3] It may be outlined as follows:

- Gnosis confers freedom, especially freedom from sin.
- Gnosis "puffs up," love "builds up"—here, both are construed as positive effects.
- One freed by gnosis is nevertheless a servant through love to those who have not yet found gnosis.
- Spiritual love is not possessive, but shares freely.
- Spiritual love is like perfume: both those anointed with it and those nearby have the use/pleasure of it.
- Spiritual love is like wine and ointment: the Samaritan gave only wine and oil to the man who was beaten.
- Wine and ointment healed his wounds: love covers a multitude of sins.

The sharing of possessions and use or enjoyment unite 77.31-34 with 77.35-78.6, while the story of the Samaritan returns to the image of 77.35 (spiritual love is wine and perfume), to love's characteristic unposses

---

[2] These are *Gos. Phil.* 53.14-54.31 and 56.26-57.21.
[3] *Gos. Phil.* 77.16-78.13.

siveness, and to the servanthood which those who have been made free
by gnosis adopt for the sake of love.

Another unit of considerable length (by the *Gospel according to
Philip*'s standards) extends from the bottom of page 79 to almost the
middle of page 81.[4] Its argument goes as follows:

- A macarism, its attribution and sense both lost to a lacuna;
- Jesus Christ was able to fulfill conditions of the macarism by encountering the whole place and not burdening anyone.
- The logos (Jesus? scripture? reason? divine inspiration?) tells us it is difficult to do so.
- A rhetorical question: "How can we be successful at this great virtue? How can it give help to everyone?"
- Recommendations: their exact meaning is unclear, but they involve considering how one should treat people in relation to their social and spiritual condition.
- A parable: the owner of an estate treats animals and personnel according to their natures; just so, the disciples of God perceive the condition of each person's soul and deal with them accordingly.

The parable is an integral part of the argument: it answers the questions
asked at 80.6-8, and the answer it gives parallels the advice given in
80.8-22.

Another longer unit is found at 82.30-84.13. Its argument runs:

- In the world, what is hidden is strong and gives life while it stays hidden: examples: intestines, tree roots.
- Evil is strong while it is hidden, but withers when it is revealed.
- The logos (Jesus? scripture?) says the ax is at the root of the trees, to extract the root so it cannot resprout.
- We should root out evil from our hearts, for it dominates us while it is hidden.
- Lack of gnosis is the mother of evils, but it becomes powerless when gnosis comes.
- The logos (Jesus? scripture?) said, If you know the truth, the truth will make you free.

The passage postulates opposite dynamics for evil/lack of gnosis and for
gnosis: evil, like worldly things, is strong when hidden and ineffectual
when exposed; gnosis is ineffective when hidden, but triumphant when

---

[4] *Gos. Phil.* 79.33-81.13.

revealed, sweeping away all that is contrary to it. The passage is a power-ful one, presenting an elegantly simple conception of salvation through gnosis, presenting it by means of vivid and earthy imagery combined with a web of scriptural allusions and quotations, without digression or excursus. Within it, as its climax, is an expansion of the formula known both from the *Gospel of Truth* and from Irenaeus' reports, which has been used to suggest that Valentinus may have been responsible for *Gospel of Truth*.[5]

The following passage, from 84.14 to 85.20 deploys the dichotomy hidden-revealed in a different way. This passage contrasts conventional wisdom about the visible and the hidden with the true situation. It is con-ventionally held that visible things are strong and glorious, while things not seen are powerless and contemptible, but in reality this is backward: it is the hidden which is truly strong and glorious.

- Conventional wisdom is wrong: the hidden, not the visible, is strong.
- The "mysteries of truth" stand as visible types, the bedroom (equated with holy of holies) is hidden.
- Once, the veil concealed how God controlled the creation.
- Cataclysm ensues when the veil is torn and what is inside revealed:
  - "this house" will be left desolate;
  - the (inferior?) deity will flee, seeks refuge under wings of cross, be-cause it cannot mix with unmixed light;
  - "this" (cross? refuge of lower deity there?) serves as ark for salva-tion of the people from raging flood waters.
- Those who belong to priesthood can enter inside veil with high priest (i.e., into holy of holies).
- The veil was torn completely so that both of these can happen, and to reveal upper realm (= hidden realm of truth) to lower realm.
- We enter upper/hidden realm through (comparatively) contemptible things;
- their reality, which exceeds the image, is made visible, invites us in.

The concluding section, from 85.21 to 86.18, again makes use of the hid-den-revealed dichotomy as its starting point. Though its images are of es-chatological consummation phrased mostly in the future, it bristles with a sense of urgency and with the perception that the eschatological fulfill-ment can be present now.

---

[5] *Gos. Phil.* 83.39 to 84.6.

- Evil is inactive but present while seed of Holy Spirit is hidden.

- When seed is revealed, perfect light will stream forth, and all who belong to it will be anointed, slaves will be freed, captives will be ransomed, weeds will be rooted up, those separated will be joined.

- Everyone who will enter bedroom will kindle fire (lacunose material follows for last lines on page 85).

- Mysteries of that marriage are performed in day and light, that day's light does not set.

- Someone who becomes a ϢΗΡⲈ ⲘⲠⲚⲨⲘϤⲰⲚ will receive the light: if not receive it "here" cannot receive it elsewhere.

- Those who receive that light will be invisible and unrestrainable, exempt from harassment while living in this world;

- on leaving this world, such a person has already received the truth in the form of images, and the world has already become the eternal realm;

- to this person (now?), eternal realm is manifest.

The three and a half pages from 82.30 to the end—which includes 82.30-84.13, outlined above—circle incessantly around the dichotomy hidden-revealed. The different deployments of the dichotomy could come from the same thinker without contradiction, but their combination in the same passage (of a sermon or epistle or essay) would be rhetorically very confusing. They are a clear indicator of the rhetorically independent nature of these last three passages.

PARALLELS WITH THE *GOSPEL OF TRUTH*, AND THE MEANING OF "GNOSIS"

Nine of the twelve occurrences of the term "gnosis" fall in the last quarter of the document, from the middle of page 77 to the end. The three occurrences that come before that division all appear in a single unit on page 74, and use this word in a different sense. It appears there as part of the phrase "tree of gnosis," imported from Genesis 2.

The nine occurrences of the word in the final quarter are not anchored in the Genesis story. The appear in three passages, and refer to a intellectual or spiritual grace or good. "Gnosis" is given an explicit object twice: "gnosis of the truth" (ⲅⲚⲰⲤⲓⲤ ⲚⲦⲘⲈ, ⲅⲚⲰⲤⲓⲤ ⲚⲦⲀⲖⲎⲐⲈⲓⲀ) brings freedom (in a paraphrase of John 8:34) and "puffs up" (in a partial rehabilitation of Paul's comparison of love and gnosis),[6] Gnosis takes its place

---

[6] *Gos. Phil.* 77.15-34. Cf. 1 Cor 8:1.

alongside faith, hope and love in the "agriculture of God."[7] In a meditation strongly resonant with certain passages in the *Gospel of Truth*, the
lack of knowledge[8] is the source of evil and a slave, while gnosis is freedom.[9]

Within the larger unit 82.30-84.13, the section from 83.30 to 84.6
parallels, at greater length, a formulaic statement which is found in the
Gospel of Truth twice, at 18.7-11 ("Since oblivion came into existence
because the Father was not known, then if the Father comes to be known,
oblivion will not exist from that moment on."), and at 24.28-32 ("Since
the deficiency came into being because the Father was not known, therefore, when the Father is known, from that moment on the deficiency will
no longer exist."), and in Irenaeus' *Adversus haereses*, at 1.21.4 ("Since
both degeneracy and passion came from ignorance, the entire substance
which came from ignorance is destroyed by knowledge."). The version in
the *Gospel according to Philip* reads:

ТМ̄НТΑΤС[ООΥΝ] ЄСШООТ М̄МΑΑΥ Ν̄Ν̄ΠЄ[ΘΟΟΥ ТНРОΥ] ТМ̄НТΑΤСООΥΝ [ЄС]ΝΑШЄ ΑΠ[МОΥ. . . .	Lack of [knowledge] is the mother of [all evils]. Lack of knowledge will lead to [death]. . .
[. . . . . . .] СЄΝΑΧШΚ ЄΒΟΛ 2ОТΑΝ ЄРШΑ ТΑΛΗΘЄΙΑ ТНРС ОΥШΝ2 ЄΒΟΛ . . .	[. . .]will become perfect when the whole truth appears. . . .
ЄСШΑОΥШΝ2 ΔЄ ЄΒΟΛ Ν̄СЄСОΥШΝС̄ ШΑΥТΝΑС ЄООΥ 2ОСОΝ С6Ν̄ 6ОМ ЄТМ̄НТΑΤСООΥΝ ΑΥШ ΑΠΛΑΝΗ	When it (i.e., truth) appears and is recognized, it is glorified insofar as it overpowers lack of knowl- edge and error.[10]

The correspondence between this passage of the *Gospel according to
Philip* and the other statements of this "formula" or "slogan" strongly indicates shared traditions at the level of verbal expression, probably a
common sectarian origin, and possibly a single author.[11]

---

[7] *Gos. Phil.* 79.18-33. Cf. 1 Cor 13:13.

[8] ТМ̄НТΑΤСООΥΝ: the Coptic translator employed native roots for both verbal and
privative forms in this passage, but the Greek loan word, ΠΓΝШСΙС, for the substan-
tive.

[9] *Gos. Phil.* 83.30-84.13: cf. *Gos. Truth* 18.7-11 and 24.28-32.

[10] *Gos. Phil.* 83.30-32, 83.35-84.2, 84.4-6., translation modified.

[11] See Hans Jonas, *The Gnostic Religion* (Boston: Beacon, 1963) 309-319, and
"Evangelium Veritatis and the Valentinian Speculation," in *Studia Patristica* 6 (Berlin:
Akademie-Verlag, 1962) 96-111.

In Irenaeus' *Adversus haereses*, the passage does not occur in the discussion of Valentinus or of any specific one of his followers, but in a chapter devoted to interpretations of the sacrament of redemption, ἀπολύτρωσις, of which the heresiologist complains that "there are as many redemptions as there are mystery-teachers of this doctrine."[12] He describes some who "prepare a bridal chamber and complete the mystic teaching with invocations on those who are being initiated," asserting that this is a spiritual marriage, like the conjugal unions in the pleroma; others mix oil and water together and place it on the heads of initiates, saying that leading them to the water, i.e., for baptism, is useless. Several of these practices might very well underlie remarks in the earlier parts of the *Gospel according to Philip*, which are intensely concerned with ritual, but not this final section. The formula expanded in the final section of the *Gospel according to Philip* appears in *Adversus haereses* at the end of this recital of ritual variants of ἀπολύτρωσις, in a description of an explicitly anti-ritual interpretation of the meaning of this concept:

ἄλλοι δὲ ταῦτα πάντα παραιτησάμενοι	Others, however, reject all these things.
φάσκουσι μὴ δεῖν τὸ τῆς ἀρρήτου καὶ ἀοράτου δυνάμεως μυστήριον δι᾽ ὁρατῶν καὶ φθαρτῶν ἐπιτελεῖσθαι κτισμάτων,	They assert that the mystery of the unspeakable and invisible Power ought not to be consecrated by visible and corruptible creatures;
καὶ τῶν ἀνεννοήτων καὶ ἀσωμάτων δι᾽ αἰσθητῶν καὶ σωματικῶν.	nor the mystery of the unthinkable and incorporeal, by the sentient and corporeal.
εἶναι δὲ τὴν τελείαν ἀπολύτρωσιν αὐτὴν τὴν ἐπίγνωσιν τοῦ ἀρρήτου μεγέθους·	[They maintain] that the very knowledge of the unspeakable Greatness is perfect redemption;
ἀπ᾽ ἀγνοίας γὰρ ὑστερήματος καὶ πάθους γεγονότων, διὰ γνώσεως καταλύεσθαι πᾶσαν τὴν ἐκ τῆς ἀγνοίας σύστασιν,	for, since both degeneracy and passion came from ignorance, the entire substance which came from ignorance is destroyed by knowledge;
ὥστ᾽ εἶναι τὴν γνῶσιν ἀπολύτρωσιν τοῦ ἔνδον ἀνθρώπου.	and so knowledge is the redemption of the inner man.

---

[12] *Adv. haer.* 1.21.1.

καὶ μήτε σωματικὴν ὑπάρχειν αὐτήν, φθαρτὸν γὰρ τὸ σῶμα,	And this redemption is not corporeal, since the body is corruptible;
μήτε ψυχικήν, ἐπεὶ καὶ ἡ ψυχὴ ἐξ ὑστερήματός ἐστι καὶ τοῦ πνεύματος ὥσπερ οἰκητήριον·	nor is it ensouled, since the soul also is from Degeneracy and is, as it were, the dwelling of the spirit.
πνευματικὴν οὖν δεῖν καὶ τὴν λύτρωσιν ὑπάρχειν. λυτροῦσθαι γὰρ διὰ γνώσεως τὸν ἔσω ἄνθρωπον τὸν πνευματικὸν	Therefore, the redemption too must be spiritual; for the inner spiritual man is redeemed by knowledge.
καὶ ἀρκεῖσθαι αὐτοὺς τῇ τῶν ὅλων ἐπιγνώσει·	And this deeper knowledge of all things is sufficient for them. [13]

Irenaeus points to a group somehow related to the Valentinian movement which used this formulation to support their rejection of ritual observances.[14] If *Gospel of Truth* and this passage in the *Gospel according to Philip* come from the milieu Irenaeus discusses, they also represent proponents of this anti-sacramental approach.[15] There is nothing in *Gospel of Truth* to discredit this possibility, nor in this distinctive and unsacramental final section of the *Gospel according to Philip*.

There are two other passages within this subsection which have close parallels in the *Gospel of Truth*. The two sections in question, from the top and bottom of page 83 respectively, read:

ΤΕΕΙϨΕ ΟΝ ΜΠΤϢΗΝ ϨⲰⲤ ΕΤΕϥΝΟΥΝΕ ϨΗΠ ϢⲀϥϯ ΟΥⲰ ⲚϥⲀⲈϨΗΤ	. . trees sprout and grow (?) while their root is hidden.
ΕΡϢⲀ ΤΕϥΝΟΥΝΕ ϬⲰⲀΠ ΕΒΟⲖ ϢⲀΡΕ ΠΤϢΗΝ ϢΟΟΥΕ	If their root is uncovered, the trees wither.[16]

---

[13] *Adv. haer.* 1.21.4. *St. Irenaeus of Lyons. Against the Heresies. Vol.. 1.* translation by Dominic J. Unger, with further revisions by John J. Dillon. (New York: Paulist Press, 1992).

[14] He may, of course, have misunderstood this position or exaggerated it slightly in caricature, or both.

[15] For an appropriately cautious assessment of groups holding such a stance, see David E. Aune, "The Phenomenon of Early Christian 'Anti-Sacramentalism,'" in *Studies in New Testament and Early Christian Literature. Essays in Honor of Allen P. Wikgren,* ed. D. E. Aune (Leiden: Brill, 1972) 194-214.

[16] *Gos. Phil.* 83.3-5.

NETϢOOTT ЄBOΛ 2Ñ   . . . those who existed as a result of
TMNT[ΑTCOOYN] OYTE   the [lack of acquaintance] neither
NEYϢOOTT ΑN OYTE [CEϢOOTT   (truly) existed nor [do exist] nor
Α(N)] OYTE CENΑϢϢTTE ΑN   will exist.[17]

The corresponding material in *Gospel of Truth* appears in a continuous
passage:

TTETEMÑTEϤ NOYNE MMEY   . . . he who has no root has no fruit
MÑTEϤ OY[Α . . .]TΑ2 MMEY ΑN   either, but though he thinks to
ΑΛΛΑ EϤMEYE NEϤ ХE   himself, "I have come into being,"
Α2IϢϢTTE EITE ΑN ϤNΑBϢΛ   yet he will perish by himself.
ΑBΑΛ 2ITOOTϤ

ЄTBE TTEEI TTETENEϤϢOOTT   For this reason, he who did not
TTTHPϤ ЄN EϤNΑϢϢTTE   exist at all will never come into
                                    existence.[18]

There are enough similarities here to make literary dependence probable,
although this is somewhat weakened by the fact that it involves material
that is separated by almost a page in the *Gospel according to Philip*.
Perhaps this passage of the *Gospel according to Philip* paraphrases the
Gospel of Truth (or vice versa!), but possibly there is no more here than
several very strongly similar patterns of imagery. Even that would be
hard to account for unless the texts originated within the same tradition;
it is plausible that they may have had a common author. If, as Bentley
Layton has suggested, some parts of the *Gospel according to Philip* may
have been written by Valentinus himself,[19] this passage would probably
be the best candidate for such authorship, since both the style and content

---

[17] *Gos. Phil.* 83.32-35.
[18] *Gos. Truth* 28.16-23, in *Nag Hammadi Codex I (The Jung Codex).* ed. and transl.
Harold W. Attridge and George W. MacRae)Leiden: E. J. Brill, 1985).
[19] Layton, *Gnostic Scriptures*, 325. For an analysis of the style of Valentinus and
Gospel of Truth, see Benoit Standaert, "'L'Évangile de Vérité': Critique et Lecture,"
New Testament Studies 22 (1976) 243-275. It is not, however, clear that Valentinus did
write *Gospel of Truth.* Fundamental differences include the absence in the latter of a
clear statement of the fall within the Godhead and of the doctrine of three types of
human beings—unless these things are very obliquely expressed, in which case one
must ask why this would be so. On the differences of *Gospel of Truth* and Valentinus
or Valentinian theologies, see: Christoph Markschies, *Valentinus Gnosticus?*
(Tübingen: Mohr/Siebeck, 1992) 339-356, and Holger Strutwolf, *Gnosis als System*
(Göttingen: Vandenhoeck & Ruprecht, 1993); for a development of the idea that much
that may seem like theological differences may instead show differences in emphasis
chosen to meet the needs of different audiences, see Harold W. Attridge, "The Gospel
of Truth as an Exoteric Text," in *Nag Hammadi, Gnosticism, and Early Christianity*,
ed. C. W. Hedrick and R. Hodgson (Peabody, MA: Hendrickson, 1986) 239-255.

of this passage of the *Gospel according to Philip* are reminiscent of some of the fragments of Valentinus' own writings, as well as of the *Gospel of Truth* and Irenaeus' reports. Nevertheless, in Irenaeus the passage is not identified as Valentinus' own, but as belonging to an unidentified group[20] who abstained from ritual behavior and offered the formula as their motivation for this.

DISTINCTIVE TREATMENT OF SCRIPTURE

Several distinctive methods of treating scripture appear in this section: a group of citation formulae using "logos," some very literally "gnosticizing" interpretations, and some sophisticated handling of texts akin to, but not identical with, allegorical interpretation. Along with these methods of handling scripture, we find over and over again a preference for allusion rather than quotation, and a tendency to combine multiple allusions into a single image.

The "Logos" Citation Formulae

The *Gospel according to Philip* contains approximately sixteen sayings which it attributes to Jesus, some with and some without context or accompanying action, and two reports of wordless actions attributed to him. Four of these sayings—one quarter of them—appear in the final quarter of the document, but the way they are handled there raises doubts about whether they were intended to represent words of Jesus at all.

The last of these, on page 85, is taken verbatim from Matt 15:13 but has no quotation formula or attribution of any kind, or anything else that would call attention to its derived nature. The statement has been so successfully naturalized into the surrounding prose that, were it not from a known text, we would have no clue that it was not original composition.

The other three are introduced by closely related, ambiguous citation

---

[20] Probably the miscellany of practices about "redemption" in *Adv. haer.* 1.21 all deal with various sorts of Valentinian groups, although this is inferred from its position in book 1 rather than explicitly claimed by Irenaeus. Possibly they were all Marcosian groups, although the last mention of Marcosians or Marcus is several chapters before (modern translations tend to insert these terms into chapter headings where their relevance is doubtful). On the order of book 1 of *Adversus haereses,* and its relevance to the grouping of Valentinian sects, see David H. Tripp, "The Original Sequence of Irenaeus 'Adversus Haereses' I: A Suggestion" in *The Second Century* 8 (1991), 157-162—although Tripp's reordering is certainly not necessary to the recognition that Marcus has probably been left behind by 1.21.

formulae: (80.4-5) ⲠⲖⲟⲅⲟⲥ ⲬⲚⲟⲨⲚ ⲘⲘⲟⲛ, "the word tells us,"[21] (83.11-12) ⲠⲖⲟⲅⲟⲥ Ⲭⲱ Ⲙⲙⲟⲥ Ⲭⲉ, "the word says,"[22] and (84.7-8) ⲠⲉⲬⲁϤ ⲚϬⲓ ⲠⲖⲟⲅⲟⲥ Ⲭⲉ, "the word said." None of the citation formulae in the rest of the document use "logos."

Moreover, this block of text also employs citation formulae involving "the word" to introduce scriptural quotations and periphrases other than Jesus' sayings.

The first appearance of a citation formula using Ⲗⲟⲅⲟⲥ, at 80.4-5, introduces not a statement but a periphrastic summary: "The word tells us how difficult it is to accomplish this," but "this" refers back to an unattributed macarism a few lines earlier, at the bottom of page 79: [ⲟⲨⲘⲁⲕⲁ]Ⲣⲓⲟⲥ Ⲡⲉ Ⲡⲁⲉⲓ ⲉⲘⲠⲉϤⲀⲗ [. . . . Ⲛ]ⲚⲟⲨⲯⲨⲬⲏ, "[Blessed] is he who has not [. . .] anyone." The paraphrase introduced at 80.4-6 seems to refer back to this unidentified macarism, but it remains unclear who was understood to be the speaker.[23]

At 83.11-12, John the Baptist's words are attributed to "the Logos:" ⲠⲖⲟⲅⲟⲥ Ⲭⲱ Ⲙⲙⲟⲥ Ⲭⲉ ⲎⲀⲎ ⲦⲀⲌⲉⲓⲚⲎ ⲤⲘⲘⲟⲚⲦ ⲀⲦⲚⲟⲨⲚⲉ ⲚⲚϢⲎⲚ —"The Logos says that 'even now the ax is laid to the root of the trees.'" It is unclear what is being claimed by the formula. Possibly the text is simply declared to derive from scripture—"the Word." On the other hand, despite the attribution of these words to John the Baptist at Matt 3:10 and Luke 3:9, the second part of John's statement (every tree that does not bear good fruit is cut down and thrown in the fire) is repeated by Jesus at Matt 7:19, so perhaps the first part of the statement had also become associated with Jesus in some part of the tradition. We must assume something like this if "the Logos" is here taken to mean Jesus. A third possibility is that the term refers to the divine power active in Jesus, or John, or scripture generally.

A similar formula is used at 84.7-8 to introduce Jesus' words from John 8:32: ⲠⲉⲬⲁϤ ⲚϬⲓ ⲠⲖⲟⲅⲟⲥ Ⲭⲉ. Although the statement quoted is attributed by John to Jesus (in a gospel that uses "the Word" to refer to him), the two earlier introductory formulae raise the question of whether the point here is that the statement derives from scripture, or that it is

---

[21] Layton translates, "the rational faculty tells us."

[22] Layton translates, "scripture says."

[23] Conjecturally, since the surrounding discussion deals with not causing grief or distress, this might represent a development of the teaching at Matt 18:5-9 that σκάνδαλα or temptations to sin are bound to occur, with the "woe" pronounced on those who cause them transformed into a beatitude for whoever does not.

specifically Jesus' statement, or that it is somehow inspired, or perhaps even just reasonable.

The presence of these quotations (along with other quotations and allusions without citation formulae) shows an interest in some of the writings we know as the canonical New Testament. The confused attribution, ambiguous introductions, and in one case, the complete lack of attribution show very little interest in the status of these statements as those of Jesus. In this final section, there is only one statement attributed to Jesus in a known source which is here attributed to him at all—and that, only if ΠΛΟΓΟC is understood personally. There are no sayings introduced as his from unknown sources. The author (or authors) responsible for this material simply was not interested in buttressing arguments with the authority of Jesus' words.

Gnosticizing Interpretations

The final quarter of the *Gospel according to Philip* contains a number of passages which are "gnosticizing" in an extremely forthright manner: scriptural passages which did not originally refer to a saving gnosis are re-presented so that they do so, and passages that did are strengthened.

The confluence of knowledge of the truth and freedom from sin, derived from John 8:32-34, appears twice in the section. The first of these appears at the beginning of the final quarter, 77.14-19. The possibilities inherent in the Johannine text are simply drawn a little more explicitly, and followed with the statement "Truth is the mother, gnosis the father." Note that, although this statement attaches further concepts to "truth" and "knowing/knowledge", it is an independent statement, not an allegorical "key" by which to extract a gnostic meaning from John 8:32. In the section extending from 82.30 to 84.14, a paraphrase of John 8:32 is produced as a summary near the end a meditation on the formula of salvation which appears (in variant forms) in the *Gospel of Truth* (18.7-11 and 24.28-32) and in Irenaeus (*Adv. haer.* 1.21.4). Neither is asserted to be derived from the other. They are presumed to mean approximately the same thing, and are juxtaposed here, as familiar and trusted patterns of words, to resonate against each other.

Later in the passage on page 77, 1 Corinthians 8:1 is quoted: "Knowledge puffs up, but love builds up." The statement is taken as an unproblematic endorsement of both gnosis and agape, with the "puffing up" (or "lifting up": ϪICE ṄT2HT) seen as a metaphor for the freedom brought by gnosis of the truth. Nevertheless, gnosis is still subordinated to agape, at least for the time being: "whoever has become free through gnosis is a slave on account of love toward those who have not yet taken up [the] freedom of gnosis."[24]

On page 79, gnosis is added without comment to the famous triad of faith, hope, and love from the end of 1 Corinthians 13. The resulting list of four is produced as an allegorical interpretation of the four elements, considered as the requirements for farming "in the world" (ТⲘⲚⲦⲞⲨⲈⲒⲈ ⲘⲠⲔⲞⲤⲘⲞⲤ): so, faith, hope, love, and gnosis are the elements of God's farming (ТⲘⲚⲦⲞⲨⲈⲒⲈ ⲘⲠⲚⲞⲨⲦⲈ).

Another passage, on page 83, takes up the imagery of slavery from Romans 7:14, and adds to it a paraphrase of Paul's complaint from the next verse:

ⲈϢⲰⲠⲈ ⲆⲈ ⲦⲚⲚⲞ ⲚⲀⲦⲤⲞⲞⲨⲚ ⲈⲢⲞⲤ ⲤⲬⲈ ⲚⲞⲨⲚⲈ ⲈϨⲢ[Ⲁ]Ï Ⲛ2ⲎⲦⲚ ⲀⲨⲰ ⲤⲦⲈⲨⲞ ⲈⲂⲞⲖ ⲚⲚⲈⲤⲔⲀⲢⲠⲞⲤ ϨⲢⲀÏ 2Ⲙ ⲠⲚ2ⲎⲦ	If we are ignorant of it [i.e., the root of evil], it sinks its root within us, and yields crops within our hearts;
ⲤⲞ ⲚⳜⲞⲈⲒⲤ ⲈⲢⲞ(Ⲛ) ⲦⲚⲚⲞ Ⲛ2Ⲙ2ⲀⲖ ⲚⲀⲤ ⲤⲢ̄ⲀⲒⳜⲘⲀⲖⲰ[Ⲧ]Ⲓ̈ⲌⲈ ⲘⲘⲞⲚ	dominates us; we are its slaves; it takes us captive
ⲈⲦⲢ̄ⲚⲈⲒⲢⲈ ⲚⲚⲈⲦⲚ̄ⲞⲨⲞϢ[ⲞⲨ ⲀⲚ] ⲚⲈⲦⲚ̄ⲞⲨⲞϢⲞⲨ ⲦⲚⲈⲒⲢⲈ̄ ⲘⲘⲞⲞⲨ [ⲀⲚ]	so that we do the things we do [not] want, and we do [not] do the things we want[25]

This root of evil, however, has nothing to do with a conflict between the flesh and the spiritual law; here, the root of evil is ignorance, lack of gnosis, error—and Paul's complaint leads into a meditation on the Valentinian formula of salvation familiar from Irenaeus and the *Gospel of Truth*.

All of these passages are "gnosticizing" in the simplest, most transparent sense. None of them are overtly polemical: none claims or hints that other interpretations are false, or even that other interpretations exist. Each reads its text as referring to gnosis as if that were simplest and most obvious thing to do.

"Reverse" Allegorization

Several passages in this section are built on a passage of scripture, and draw correspondences between it and another level of reality, but are not

---

[24] *Gos. Phil.* 77.26-28, translation modified.
[25] *Gos. Phil.* 83.22-27.

quite instances of allegorical interpretation, for the simple reason that they do not make interpretation their objective. Neither are they attempts to produce a proof text for a position already held. They are better seen as a subtype of the interweaving of multiple allusions and references into a new, but richly nuanced, whole.

A very graceful piece of writing which employs something akin to allegorical interpretation appears on pages 77 and 78:

ТАГАПН ΜΠΝΕΥΜ[ΑΤΙΚΗ] ΟΥΗΡΠ ΤΕ 2Ι СΤΟΕΙ	Spiritual love is wine and perfume.
СЕРАПО[ΛΑΥΕ Μ]ΜΟС ΤΗΡΟΥ Ν6Ι ΝΕΤΝΑΤΟ2СΟΥ ΜΜΟС СЕРАПОΛΑΥΕ 2ΩΟΥ Ν6Ι ΝΕΤΑ2ΕΡΑΤΟΥ ΜΠΟΥΒΟΛ 2ΩС ΕΥΑ2ΕΡΑΤΟΥ Ν6Ι ΝΕΤΤΟ2С	Those who anoint themselves with it all have the use of it, as do also those who are outside their company so long as the anointed ones stand there.
ΝΕΤΤΑ2С ΝСΟ6Ν ΕΥΩΑΛΟ ΕΤΟΥΩΟΥ ΝСΕΒΩΚ ΩΑΡΕ ΝΗ ΕСΕΤΟ2С ΑΝ ΜΟΝΟΝ ΕΥΑ2Ε ΕΡΑΤΟΥ ΜΠΟΥΒΑΛ ΩΑΥ6Ω ΟΝ 2Μ ΠΟΥСΤΒΩΩΝ	When those anointed with ointment leave them and depart, the ones who are not anointed but are only outside their company still remain within their fragrance.
ΠСΑΜΑΡΙΤΗС ΝΤΑΥΤ ΛΑΑΥ ΑΝ ΑΠΕΤΩΟΟ6Ε ΕΙ ΜΗ ΗΡΠ 2Ι ΝΕ2 ΚΕΛΑΑΥ ΑΝ ΠΕ ΕΙ ΜΗΤΙ ΑΠСΟ6Ν	The Samaritan gave nothing to the man who had been beaten except wine and oil, which means none other than ointment.
ΑΥΩ ΑΥΘΕΡΑΠΕΥΕ ΝΜΠΛΗΓΗ ΤΑΓΑΠΗ ΓΑΡ 2ΩΒС ΝΟΥΜΗΝΩΕ ΝΝΟΒΕ	And it healed his wounds, "since love covers a multitude of sins."[26]

This passage begins by moving from an abstraction (spiritual love) to concrete images (wine and perfume/ointment), and then provides two narrative contexts for those images. The first merely sketches a recurrent situation among people (and involves only perfume); the second invokes the story of the good Samaritan (and involves both wine and ointment).

The rhetorical structure of this passage is far more sophisticated than, for example, the instances of Ptolemaean allegory given by Irenaeus. There, a scriptural passage is first cited, then equivalences drawn up between its actors or images and another level of reality. In Ptolemy's allegories of scripture, that other level is usually that of the aeons. The allegory of the "offering places in Jerusalem" on pages 69 and 70 of the *Gospel according to Philip* follows the same pattern, although it is not

---

[26] *Gos. Phil.* 77.35-78.12.

concerned with the aeons: the Temple is first described, then the equivalences are laid out and commented upon.[27] The pattern of presentation is the same in Philo: the literal images of the text, followed by exegesis by reference to another level of reality. The domain of the allegorical meaning varies, but the paradigm of "allegorical interpretation" remains the same: it is a form of commentary on a text.

In *Gos. Phil.* 77.35-78.12, the scriptural reference is not introduced first but last. The author of the passage does not make a claim—even a fanciful claim—to have used a valid method to extract a deeper meaning from the story, nor is it claimed that the story had this meaning all along. But the reference to the Samaritan's story is not mere ornamentation, either. The story has clearly contributed to the formation of the thought here, but does not wholly determine it.

On page 79, the triad of faith, hope, and charity from 1 Corinthians 13.13 receives a remarkable treatment. "Gnosis" is joined to the three, and these four concepts are supplied with concrete corollaries: earth, water, air, and light, the four requisites of a successful harvest in the "agriculture of the world." Just so, the text asserts, faith, hope, love, and gnosis operate within the "agriculture of God." This concretizing "back-formation" of physical correlatives for the abstractions under discussion is a sort of inverted allegorization, and bears witness to a milieu well acquainted with allegory.

MORALITY AND GNOSIS

The final quarter of the *Gospel according to Philip* refers repeatedly to questions of proper dealings with other humans, the motivations for such dealings, and the underlying spiritual purity that supports such motivation. Right relationships and right behavior, largely ignored in the first three quarters of the *Gospel according to Philip*, are of real concern here. Nevertheless, these are seen as the reflection or fruit of gnosis. The obstacle to ethical purity is not conceived of as temptation but as wrong apprehension, wrong decision, wrong preoccupation, misguided contemplation: that error which is the antithesis of gnosis.

Gnosis and sin do not coexist, because gnosis necessarily produces the love, which results in right actions.

---

[27] *Gos. Phil.* 69.14-70.4.

ΠΕΤΕΥΝΤΑϤ ΜΜΑΥ ΝΤΓΝШСІС
ΝΤΜΕ ΟΥΕΛΕΥΘΕΡΟС ΠΕ
ΠΕΛΕΥΘΕΡΟС ΔΕ ΜΑϤⲢ ΝΟΒΕ
ΠΕϮΡΕ ΓΑΡ ΜΠΝΟΒΕ ΠⲀ2Μ2ΑⲀ
ΜΠΝΟΒΕ ΠΕ . . . .

One who possesses acquaintance
[gnosis] of the truth is free, and
the free person does not sin: for,
"one who commits sin is the slave
of sin." . . . .

ΠΕΤΑ2Ⲣ ΕΛΕΥΘΕΡΟС ΔΕ 2ΙΤΝ
ΤΓΝШСІС ϤΟ Ν2Μ2ΑⲀ ΕΤΒΕ
ΤΑΓΑΠΗ ΝΝΑΕΙ ΕΜΠΑΤΟΥШϤΙ
Ε2ΡΑΪ [ΝΤΕ]ΛΕΥΘΕΡΙΑ
ΝΤΓΝШСІС

Now, whoever has become free
through acquaintance [gnosis] is a
slave on account of love toward
those who have not yet taken up
[the] freedom of acquaintance.

ΤΓΝШ[СІС ΔΕ] СΕΙΡΕ ΜΜΟΟΥ
ΝШΙΚΑΝΟС ΕС[ΤΡΟΥ]ШШΠΕ
ΝΕΛΕΥ[Θ]ΕⲢ[ОС]

[And] acquaintance makes them
capable of becoming free.[28]

Similarly, the passage beginning at the bottom of page 79 with an unknown (and partially destroyed) macarism, and continuing to 81.13, re-
volves around treating people appropriately. Not burdening or causing
grief to others, and helping everyone regardless of their social or eco-
nomic status, or religious affiliation, is held out as the ideal. The parable
of the owner of the estate who gave proper food to children, slaves, cattle, dogs and hogs, and its interpretation, show that the key to treating
people properly is discerning their true natures:

ΤΑΕΙΤΕ ΘΕ ΜΠΜΑΘΗΤΗС
ΜΠΝΟΥΤΕ ΕШШΠΕ ΟΥСΑΒΕ ΠΕ
ΕϤΑΙСΘΑΝΕ ΝΤΜΝΤΜΑΘΗΤΗС

Just so are the disciples of God: if
they are wise they are perceptive
about discipleship.

ΜΜΟΡϤΗ ΝСШΜΑΤΙΚΗ
СΕΝΑⲢΑΠΑΤΑ ΑΝ ΜΜΟϤ ΑⲀⲀΑ
ΕϤΝΑ6ШШΤ ΝСΑ ΤΔΙΑΘΕСІС
ΝΤΕϤϤΥΧΗ ΜΠΟΥΑ ΠΟΥΑ
ΝϤШΑΧΕ ΝΜΜΑϤ

Bodily forms will not deceive
them: rather, what they consider is
the condition of each person's
soul, and they speak with that person accordingly.

ΟΥΝ 2Α2 ΝΘΗΡΙΟΝ 2Μ
ΠΚΟСΜΟС ΕΥΟ ΜΜΟΡϤΗ
ⲢΡШΜΕ ΝΑΕΙ ΕϤШΑСΟΥШΝΟΥ
ⲢΡΙΡ ΜΕΝ ϤΝΑΝΕΧ ΒΑⲀΑΝΟС
ΕΡΟΟΥ ΝΤΒΝΟΟΥ ΔΕ ϤΝΑΝΕΧ
ΕΙШΤ ΕΡΟΟΥ 2Ι ΤШ2 2Ι ΧΟΡΤΟС
ΝΝΟΥ2ΟΟΡ ϤΝΑΝΕΧ ΚΑΑС
ΕΡΟΟΥ

In the world, there are many
animals that have a human form. If
the disciples of God recognize that
they are hogs, they feed them
acorns; if cattle, barley, chaff, and
fodder; if dogs, bones;

Ν2Μ2ΑⲀ ϤΝΑϮ ΝΑΥ ΝШΟΡΠ
ΝШΗΡΕ ϤΝΑϮ ΝΑΥ ΝΤΕΛΕΙΟΝ

if slaves, a first course (that is, a
single dish); if children, a
complete meal.[29]

---

[28] *Gos. Phil.* 77.15-19, 26-31.
[29] *Gos. Phil.* 81.1-13.

While the gnosis that prevents sin and produces agape is left vague in the passage on page 77, here its content is specified: knowledge of people's natures gives the key to appropriate treatment.

Related to this interest in interpersonal morality is a tendency to understand relationship to God in the imagery of sexual fidelity. In *Gos. Phil.* 78.12-24, a piece of folklore is presented: a child might resemble its mother's lover if her heart was set on him, and not her husband, during intercourse with the latter. The power of thought or contemplation is seen to have a creative power, and the moral drawn is: "You, then, who live with the son of God, do not love the world; rather, love the Lord, so that those whom you produce might come to resemble not the world but rather the Lord."[30] The consequences of wrong priorities or wrong attachments—ultimately, of wrong contemplation—are parallel to those of adultery: the generation of some sort of "offspring" whose nature or appearances betray its origin.

The text continues on (for 78.12-79.13 circles around the themes of sexual intercourse and identity) to point out that only connatural beings can have intercourse with each other, and the same is true of spirit, mind, light, et cetera. The passage is partially parallel to both 61.20-35 (in which people cannot see anything in the realm of truth unless they become it) and 75.25-76.5 (in which horses, human beings, and the divine all beget offspring of their own nature); it may possibly be the collector/redactor's own synthesis of these two passages. In any case, this passage transposes taboos against bestiality into a broader call to purity, to be like and associate with the "upper" or "inner" sorts of reality (spirit, reason, light), and to be unlike, and avoid association with, the "animals." Again, the precise actions involved are not specified, but the call is to a purity reaching to the level of one's identity and involving an intensity of attention comparable to intercourse.

In 77.35-78.12 (the meditation on wine and perfume, ending with the allusive reference to the Good Samaritan), the unifying topic is announced clearly: "spiritual love" (ⲦⲀⲄⲀⲠⲎ ⲘⲠⲚⲈⲨⲘⲀⲦⲒⲔⲎ). This quality is symbolized both in the pleasurable charm of perfume and wine and in the concrete giving of help (which is, perhaps, somewhat tough-minded in its limitation).

---

[30] *Gos. Phil.* 78.20-24.

THE TRANSFORMATION OF SACRAMENTAL IMAGERY

Sacramental terms are relatively plentiful in the first three quarters of the *Gospel according to Philip*, and especially dense in the section between pages 67 and 75, but few and ambiguous in the final nine pages. The terms ΒΑΠΤΙϹΜΑ and ΕΥΧΑΡΙϹΤΕΙΑ are not used at all, while ΧΡΙϹΜΑ is used only once.

ΝΥΜΦⲰΝ is present three times,[31] and its near synonym ΚΟΙΤⲰΝ four times.

The passage from 81.34 to 82.25 circles around the secrecy of marital intercourse, as it belongs not to the "marriage of pollution" but to the "unpolluted marriage" which is "a genuine mystery." The cultural ideal of the seclusion of women, especially of a new bride, is invoked to make a strong statement about the hidden nature of this mystery. "The bride has committed fornication not only if she accepts the sperm of a different man, but even if she leaves her bedroom (ΚΟΙΤⲰΝ) and is seen," at least, by anyone other than her parents and the best man and the "children of the bridegroom" or "bridegroom's attendants"—yet it would seem to be inherently impossible for anyone else to see her, since it is also stated that "no one can see a bridegroom or a bride except by becoming such." The passage spins off of a reflection (from 81.14-34) on the difference between creating and begetting. It is tempting to see the two passages as linked, but the second does not resume the themes of the first in a way that would make it clear that they are an integrated whole rather than a creative juxtaposition.

The images that form the link between the two are the secrecy of begetting, in contrast to the visibility of (artistic or technical) creation. As a sequel to 81.14-34, 81.34-82.25 serves as a parable illustrating the secret or hidden nature of the process of begetting. If the latter passage once had an independent existence, it would have been as a reflection on marriage customs and their resemblance to some corresponding, sacramental reality; presumably joined by a collector to the former passage as a potential illustration of one aspect of it. If, on the other hand, we read the two as a single continuous passage, that passage moves from a distinction between the modes of creation or emanation which are possible to humans (and this distinction was surely meant on a metaphoric level) to a parabolic reflection on marriage customs and a corresponding spiri-

---

[31] Not counting de Catanzaro's emendation of ⲚⲚϢⲎⲢⲈ ⲘⲠⲚΥⲘΦΙΟⳞ to ⲚⲚϢⲎⲢⲈ ⲘⲠⲚΥⲘΦⲰⲚ at 82.16-17.

tual reality, given as a concrete illustration of the secret or hidden nature
of one of these modes of creation or emanation. In both of these scenarios, the latter passage makes a connection between actual worldly marriage and "unpolluted marriage;" this is the context of the terms "children
of the bridegroom" (or "of the bridal chamber" or "bridegroom's attendants": ϢΗΡЄ ΜΠΝΥΜϕΙΟⲤ or ΜΠΝΥΜϕⲰΝ),[32] bedroom (ΚΟΙΤⲰΝ),
bridal chamber (ΝΥΜϕⲰΝ), which are therefore meant to be read on two
registers, that of (idealized) marriage customs and that of another reality,
probably expressed in ritual. But as the passage appears, joined to 81.14-
34, the entire comparison has been made to illustrate another point. We
do not know whether this subordination of ritual imagery was the work
of a collector who joined the two passages, or of an author who wrote the
piece 81.14-82.25 as a whole; nor do we know whether the person who
used this two-leveled discussion of marriage was a participant in a
sacramental system which corresponded to the spiritual register of the illustration, or was someone who knew about it and found it an illuminating metaphor.

The passage from 84.14-85.20 also employs the term ΚΟΙΤⲰΝ, bedroom. Its contrast of the visible and the hidden is not a reflection on the
emptiness of material wealth and beauty, but on the referential and provisional nature of sacramental elements, the (comparatively) weak and
contemptible representations that open the holy of holies to some. The
key to the passage, which we lack, is how its author understood the present to relate to the cataclysmic events surrounding the rending of the
veil. The desolation of the house and the refuge of some people with the
lower divinity under the wings of the cross sounds like a future resolution
of things into their true elements, as does the entrance of those of the
priesthood into the holy of holies with the priest. The immediately following meditation on why the veil was rent from top to bottom—so the
lower and upper realms could both be revealed—seems to reflect on a
present state of reality, however, a "realized eschatology," as does the
nuanced appreciation of "contemptible representations" that uncover the
holy of holies and invite us into that bedroom.

The passage is an appreciation of sacramental usage by others, whom
the author considers to be at a lower level of reality, who (it seems) will
never be able to enter the hidden reality directly. Possibly those at a

---

[32] ϢΗΡЄ, like the Greek παῖς, could mean "son" or "boy" or "servant;" probably the
compounds ΝϢΗΡЄ ΜΠΝΥΜϕΙΟⲤ and ΝϢΗΡЄ ΜΠΝΥΜϕⲰΝ both meant "wedding
attendants" or "bridegroom's attendants."

higher level are not yet able to enter directly either, but will be able to at
the time of eschatological consummation. In any case, the term ΚΟΙΤΩΝ,
bedroom, is equated here with the reality behind the types and images,
the holy of holies, where the lesser deity and certain people will not able
to enter. Thus a presumably sacramental term is employed here in a
catachresis—a somewhat violent overextension of its meaning—to refer
to a hidden reality unmediated by sacraments.

The concluding passage, 85.21-86.18, employs ΚΟΙΤΩΝ again, and
ΝΥΜϕΩΝ (in the compound ϢΗΡΕ ⲘΠΝΥΜϕΩΝ) and, seemingly, the
word ΧΡΙCΜⲀ, though the first half of the word is lost. Its exact relation
to sacramental matters is less clear.

The references to chrism, "ransom," and the "bedroom" here have
been transposed into an eschatological frame of reference, and expressed
in the future: ϨΟΤⲀΝ ⲆΕ ΕϤϢⲀϬΩΛΠ ΕΒΟΛ ΤΟΤΕ ΠΟΥΟΕΙΝ
ΝΤΕΛΕΙΟC ΝⲀϨⲀΤΕ ΕΒΟΛ ΕΧⲚ [Ο]ΥΟ(Ν) ΝΙΜ ⲀΥⲰ ΝΕΤⲚϨΗΤϤ
ΤΗΡΟΥ CΕΝ[ⲀΧΙ ΧΡΙ]CΜⲀ "When it [the seed of the Holy Spirit] is revealed, then perfect light will stream forth upon each person, and all who
belong to it will [be] anointed"[33] This is not a reference to chrism as a ritual, but a portrayal of an eschatological consummation clothed in the imagery of ritual. At that time also, ⲚCΕCⲰΤΕ ⲚⲀΙΧΜⲀΛⲰΤΟC, "captives
will be ransomed."[34] The use of CⲰΤΕ here does not refer to a ritual,
since this is a standard item in lists of eschatological reversals. Similarly,
the reference to "everyone who [enters] the bedroom" seems probably to
belong to this same metaphorical eschatological future, although the
statement stands before a lacuna.

The reference to becoming a ϢΗΡΕ ⲘΠΝΥΜϕΩΝ is more ambiguous:

ΕΡϢⲀ ΟΥⲀ ϢⲰΠΕ ⲚϢΗΡΕ ⲘΠΝΥΜϕΩΝ ϤΝⲀΧΙⲘΠΟΥΟΕΙΝ	If someone becomes a bride- groom's attendant, that person will receive the light.
ΕΤⲘ ΟΥⲀ ΧΙΤϤ ΕϤⲚΝΕΕΙΜⲀ ϤΝⲀΧΙΤϤ ⲀΝ ⲘΠΚΕΜⲀ	If one does not receive it while here, one cannot receive it else- where.[35]

The passage is full of urgency and of the possibility (and necessity) of
claiming eschatological goods in the present. The temporal restriction, it
should be noted, applies to receiving the light, not to becoming a bridegroom's attendant. Nevertheless, we just do not know enough about the

---

[33] *Gos. Phil.* 85.24-28, translation modified.
[34] *Gos. Phil.* 85.29.
[35] *Gos. Phil.* 86.4-7.

business of the bridal chamber, or the sense of ϢHPE ⲘⲠⲚYⲘϕⲰN, or
the meaning of "receive the light," to be able to interpret this well. The
passage concludes with paradoxical assertions which are claimed to apply now as well as in the eschaton. Most—perhaps all—of its uses of
sacramental terminology have been transposed into the future and used as
metaphors to describe the consummation then—and then reapplied to the
present as realized or realizable.

There are few uses of the terminology associated with sacraments in
the final quarter of the *Gospel according to Philip*. When the imagery of
sacraments is present, it is either employed metaphorically (as on pages
78-79), or attached to the imagery of an eschatological cataclysm in
which an overwhelming reality does away with sacraments, but is also
available now, perhaps by means of sacraments, or perhaps by a con-
templative realization partially or wholly independent of sacraments (as
on pages 84-85 and 85-86).

Conclusions and Conjectures

The material from 77.15 to the end of the *Gospel according to Philip*
stems from a milieu which is rhetorically and philosophically sophisticated, permeated by scripture but not seeing it as an essential source of
authority or authenticity, and associated with the *Gospel of Truth*. While
subscribing to some form of a doctrine of natures, the formulations we
find in the final quarter do not locate the center of their teaching in
elaborate systematizations, and are not preoccupied with the harmful
influences of archons. Rather, they seem to revolve around the simple
mystical solution of the Valentinian formulation known from the *Gospel
of Truth* and Irenaeus. Such a form of Valentinianism could be seen as
either early or conservative; both possibilities take seriously Tertullian's
claim that Valentinus' own doctrine underwent a radical expansion later
in his life. Somewhat less likely, the material in the final quarter of the
Gospel according to Philip could represent "exoteric" communications of
a more complex system of the Valentinian type.[36]

---

[36] Less likely, because it seems unlikely that the *Gospel of Truth* is either disingenuous or holding back a more complicated system (at least, not as the heart of its teaching—perhaps as a provocative thing to play with), because its overarching point is that
beneath the nightmarish complications produced by error, everything is absolutely
simple, the Father of the entirety immediately present and accessible. (See Attridge,
"Gospel of Truth as an Exoteric Text," for an opposed view.)

Moreover, it seems likely that the collector of the materials in the *Gospel according to Philip* was also a Valentinian of some sort. Valentinianism was probably born as a synthesis of several strands of earlier traditions, and may have continued to show a lively interest in those traditions for a long time, particularly in geographical areas where it was in continuing contact with them. If the collection that is the *Gospel according to Philip* falls early in the history of Valentinianism, it represents some of the raw materials of the synthesis that went to make up that movement. Most provocatively, could the author of the extended passages in the final quarter have been Valentinus himself? And if so, were these extracts from his writings excerpted and anthologized by another, or could the *Gospel according to Philip* be Valentinus' own notebook, something like Pliny's or Clement's, which contain both materials assembled from other traditions and his own experimental synthesis of these traditions? This possibility, while real, is probably impossible either to prove or to disprove.[37] If, on the other hand, our document was assembled later in the story of that movement, its existence chronicles an ongoing relation between Valentinianism and the traditions represented in the first three quarters of the work.

---

[37] The rhetorical characteristics of this block correspond well to those isolated by Benoit Standaert from the fragments of Valentinus and from the *Gospel of Truth*. They also correspond, in a general way, to most of the trends detected by Jacqueline Williams in the use of scripture in the *Gospel of Truth*, with the exception that there are few traces here of that document's predilection for the term "Father." See Benoit Standaert, "L'Évangile de Vérité: Critique et lecture" *New Testament Studies* 22 (1976) 243-275, and Jacqueline Williams, *Biblical Interpretation in the Gnostic Gospel of Truth from Nag Hammadi*. (Atlanta, GA: Scholars Press, 1988).

CHAPTER NINE

SOME SPECIFIC TRADITIONS IN 51.29-77.14

The material from 51.29-77.14 is much more diverse than that of the final quarter, indicating a greater diversity of sources used. A large number of characteristics mark it off from the final section, indicating that at least some of its sources are significantly different in outlook from the source or sources behind the final quarter. Some of these characteristics also distinguish it from much of the rest of the Nag Hammadi corpus.

It is possible to isolate and describe some specific strands of tradition within the first three quarters of the *Gospel according to Philip*. Some passages show multiple connections with the literature of the "Thomas" traditions, particularly the *Gospel according to Thomas* and the *Acts of Thomas*. These passages do not, however, occur in a large block, as does the material examined in chapter 7, but have been interspersed with other materials, some of which are diametrically opposed to the Thomas material in outlook (hostility toward "apostles" and the "apostolic") or approach (radical rereadings of the creation story in Genesis). Two somewhat longer passages showing marked similarities to the material of the final quarter also appear.

MATERIAL ASSOCIATED WITH THE "THOMAS" TRADITIONS

A number of characteristics link the *Gospel according to Philip* and the braided strands of the "Thomas" traditions.

Use of the Gospel according to Thomas

Quotation of or dependence on other written documents, provided those documents are not widely used, is one instance of a shared, unusual trait. At least ten parallels between the *Gospel according to Philip* and the *Gospel according to Thomas* have been suggested by various scholars,[1] but only two passages show a unmistakable literary

---

[1] Mostly by Hans-Martin Schenke and Bentley Layton. Neither claimed that the parallels noted constituted dependence of one text upon another.

dependence: 64.9-12 and 67.30-37. The two passages should probably
be taken together despite their lack of other shared features, because of
their common appropriation of the *Gospel according to Thomas*' text.
The passage on page 67 of the *Gospel according to Philip* has further
ties to the Thomas tradition, as well.

The passage on page 64 is a direct quotation of the opening statement of the *Gospel according to Thomas* 19, albeit with the quotation
formula shifted from "Jesus said" to "The Lord said." *Gos. Thom.* 19a
reads:

ⲡⲉⲭⲉ ⲓ̄ⲥ̄ ⲭⲉ ⲟⲩⲙⲁⲕⲁⲣⲓⲟⲥ ⲡⲉ	Jesus said, "Blessed is that which
ⲛⲧⲁ2ϣⲱⲡⲉ 2ⲁ ⲧⲉ2ⲏ	existed before coming into being."
ⲉⲙⲡⲁⲧⲉϥϣⲱⲡⲉ	

This statement is part of a larger unit in *Gospel according to Thomas*,
which certainly includes 18, where the disciples ask about their end and
Jesus tells them that "the end will be where the beginning is," and possibly all of the rest of 19, which goes on to say that "these stones will
minister to" those who exist as Jesus' disciples and who listen to his
sayings, and also a statement about the "five trees in paradise," which
ends with the same promise (about not tasting death) as found at the
end of 18. In the *Gospel according to Philip* the core statement appears
in a slightly elaborated form, but is not visibly connected with the
material which surrounds it, nor does that material bear any resemblance
to the surrounding material in *Gospel according to Thomas*.

ⲡⲉⲭⲉ ⲡ̄ⲭⲟⲉⲓⲥ ⲭⲉ	The Lord said, "Blessed is that
ⲟⲩⲙⲁⲕⲁⲣⲓⲟⲥ ⲡⲉ ⲡⲉⲧϣⲟⲟⲡ 2ⲁ	which existed before it came into
ⲧⲉ2ⲏ ⲉⲙⲡⲁⲧⲉϥϣⲱⲡⲉ	existence.
ⲡⲉⲧϣⲟⲟⲡ ⲅⲁⲣ ⲁϥϣⲱⲡⲉ ⲁⲩⲱ	For the existent came into
ϥⲛⲁϣⲱⲡⲉ	existence, and will exist."[2]

Here, the statement has been extended by an explanatory clause reminiscent of Rev 1:8.[3] Beyond pointing to the existence of a "Thomas"
strand among the traditions in the *Gospel according to Philip*, we learn
that this strand of tradition has been refracted through the prism of
scriptural—or perhaps liturgical—phraseology.

---

[2] *Gos. Phil.* 64.9-11.
[3] See Ménard's comments on this expansion, *L'Évangile*, 34.

Sacramental Exemplarism and Exemplar Epicleses

The paraphrase of *Gos. Thom.* 22 on page 67 of the *Gospel according to Philip* is embedded in a page-long catena of (potentially) free-standing units, bearing on the issue of sacraments and the principle of their functioning. The page is found at the beginning of a section of the text with a very high concentration of references to ritual matters, pages 67 to approximately 75. These nine or so pages do not constitute a coherent block of material, for they include much that does not relate to sacraments or to the principles behind them, and the sacramental material they do contain does not seem to represent a single viewpoint. In contrast, the catena of passages on pages 67-68 is uninterrupted by non-sacramental materials and repeatedly expresses a distinctive and unusual understanding of sacramental functioning.

The clearest example of this understanding in the *Gospel according to Philip* is, however, found in a passage outside of the most densely ritual section (pages 67 to 75), on page 57:

ϨΙΤⲚ ΟΥΜΟΟΥ ΜⲚ ΟΥΚⲰϨⲦ	By water and fire the entire place is
ⲈΥΤΟΥΒΟ ⲘⲠΜⲀ ΤΗΡϤ	sanctified—the visible (elements of
ΝⲈΤΟΥΟΝϨ ϨΙΤⲚ ΝⲈΤΟΥΟΝϨ	it) by the visible, the hidden by the
ⲈΒΟⲖ ΝⲈⲐΗⲠⲦ ϨΙΤⲚ ΝⲈⲐΗⲠⲦ	hidden.
ΟΥⲚ ϨΟⲈΙΝⲈ ⲈΥϨΗⲠⲦ ϨΙΤⲚ	Some (elements) are hidden by the
ΝⲈΤΟΥΟΝϨ ⲈΒΟⲖ	visible:
ΟΥⲘΜΟΟΥ ϨⲚ ΟΥΜΟΟΥ ΟΥⲚ	there is water within water, there is
ΚⲰϨⲦ ϨⲚΝΟΥΧΡΙⲤΜⲀ	fire within chrism.[4]

This seems to match, in a rather more theoretical mode, a very exceptional understanding of sacramental functioning found in the *Acts of Thomas*. We will examine the form in which it is found in the *Acts of Thomas* before returning to consider other examples in the *Gospel according to Philip*.

In chapter 52 of the *Acts of Thomas,* there is a prayer which clearly shows the idea of a heavenly counterpart to the earthly water used in a ritual. This prayer does not occur in an initiatory context, but as an invocation over water to be used for the healing of a young man who, after his initiation, committed murder.

Ἔλθετε τὰ ὕδατα ἀπὸ τῶν	Come, waters from the living
ὑδάτων τῶν ζώντων,	waters,

---

[4] *Gos. Phil.* 57.22-28.

τὰ ὄντα ἀπὸ τῶν ὄντων καὶ ἀποσταλέντα ἡμῖν·	realities from what is real and that have been sent to us;
ἡ ἀνάπαυσις ἡ ἀπὸ τῆς ἀναπαύσεως ἀποσταλεῖσα ἡμῖν,	rest that has been sent us from rest;
ἡ δύναμις τῆς σωτηρίας ἡ ἀπὸ τῆς δυνάμεως ἐκείνης ἐρχομένη τῆς τὰ πάντα νικώσης καὶ ὑποτασσούσης τῷ ἰδίῳ θελήματι,	salvific power that comes from power which conquers all and subdues all things to its own will,
ἐλθὲ καὶ σκήνωσον ἐν τοῖς ὕδασι τούτοις,	come and dwell in these waters,
ἵνα τὸ χάρισμα τοῦ ἁγίου πνεύματος τελείως ἐν αὐτοῖς τελειωθῇ.	so that the gift of the Holy Spirit might be brought to perfect completion in them.[5]

While this prayer is an epiclesis in that it calls down heavenly power onto the water, notice that it does not ask the Father to send the Holy Spirit, nor even, on a more "primitive" model common in Syria, ask Jesus to send his spirit or his power. God is not addressed here at all. The prayer addresses "waters:" "Come, waters from the living waters. . . come and dwell in these waters." The ordinary water is made efficacious because heavenly water has come to dwell in it. We may provisionally call this understanding of the operation of sacraments "sacramental exemplarism" (and any epiclesis which depends upon it an "exemplar epiclesis"), because the spiritual reality conveyed by the matter is understood to be the heavenly exemplar or type of that matter, rather than some other good or grace. The *Acts of Thomas* contains several more examples.

The Syriac version of the *Acts of Thomas*, which in very many other particulars has been moved in the direction of a later orthodoxy,[6] contains a similar prayer.

| *Greek* | *Syriac* |
| Come, waters from the living waters, | Water given us from Living Water; |

---

[5] *Acts Thom.* 52. English translation of Greek and Syriac from an unpublished translation by Harold W. Attridge.

[6] The extant Greek text seems to be closer to the original than the extant Syriac, despite the probability that the work was originally written in Syriac. See Harold W. Attridge, "The Original Language of the Acts of Thomas" in *Of Scribes and Scholars*, ed H. Attridge, J. Collins, T. Tobin (Lanham, MD: University Press of America, 1990) 241-250, and further references given there.

realities from what is real and that have been sent to us;

Light sent us from the glorious Light;

rest that has been sent us from rest;

Gift come to us from Love;

salvific power that comes from power which conquers all and subdues all things to its own will,

Life sent us from Life;

Grace sent us from Grace;

come and dwell in these waters,

let your victorious power come;

so that the gift of the Holy Spirit might be brought to perfect completion in them.

may your healing and your mercy alight on and dwell in these waters over which your life-giving name, Jesus, is proclaimed.

The Syriac version of the prayer addresses "Water given us from Living Water" but substitutes Light, Gift, Life and Grace for Realities and Rest; both versions end the list with Power, though the Greek objectifies it in a way the Syriac does not. Nevertheless, the Syriac is structured like the Greek until its end: "let your victorious power come"—note that the only antecedents so far for "your" have been Waters, Light, Gift, Life, and Grace—"may your healing and your mercy alight on and dwell in these waters over which your life-giving name, Jesus, is proclaimed." This awkward shift to an address to Jesus, together with the logically and syntactically consistent structure of the Greek version, are strong indications that the Syriac version of this epiclesis has been modified, clumsily, from one that addressed heavenly waters into one that addresses Jesus.

In chapter 121, Thomas says this prayer while pouring the pre-baptismal oil:

Ἔλαιον ἅγιον εἰς ἁγιασμὸν ἡμῖν δοθέν,

Holy oil given for our sanctification,

μυστήριον κρυφιμαῖον ἐν ᾧ ὁ σταυρὸς ἡμῖν ἐδείχθη,

secret mystery in which the cross was revealed to us,

σὺ εἶ ὁ ἁπλωτὴς τῶν κεκαλυμμένων μελῶν·

you are the one who discloses covered parts.

σὺ εἶ ὁ ταπεινωτὴς τῶν σκληρῶν ἔργων·

You are the one who humiliates stubborn deeds.

σὺ εἶ ὁ δεικνὺς τοὺς κεκρυμμένους θησαυρούς·

You are the one who reveals hidden treasures.

σὺ εἶ τὸ τῆς χρηστότητος βλάστημα·

You are the offshoot of beneficence.

ἐλθέτω ἡ δύναμίς σου·

Let your power come.

ἰδρυνθήτω ἐπὶ τὴν δούλην σου   Let it be established in your servant
Μυγδονίαν· καὶ ἴασαι αὐτὴν διὰ   Mygdonia and heal her through this
τῆς ἐλευθερίας ταύτης.   freedom.[7]

While here the oil, presumably the heavenly oil, is addressed and the petition is "Let your power come," this epiclesis fails to correspond to the pattern just examined in that it is an epiclesis over the initiand rather than over the earthly exemplar of the heavenly oil. In the Syriac, however, the prayer shifts, awkwardly, from address of the oil to address of Jesus about half-way through, but it remains an epiclesis over the oil: "let your [that is, for the Syriac, Jesus'] power come and rest upon this oil and let your holiness abide in it." Most probably this prayer originally followed the same pattern as the prayer over the healing water: Heavenly oil, come and dwell in this oil.

The third example of this sort of epiclesis in *Acts of Thomas* is found in chapter 157. It also addresses the oil, very elaborately and somewhat elliptically, but never comes to any petitionary verb: its structure is all invocation plus relative clause: "you, who. . . ."

Ὁ ὡραῖος καρπὸς τῶν ἄλλων   O fruit more beautiful than the
καρπῶν, ᾧ οὐδεὶς συγκρίνεται   other fruits, to which no other can
ὅλως ἕτερος·   be compared

ὁ πάνυ ἐλεήμων· ὁ τῇ τοῦ λόγου   Altogether merciful one, heated by
ὁρμῇ ζέων·   the force of the word,

δύναμις ἡ τοῦ ξύλου ἧν οἱ   Power of the wood, clothed with
ἄνθρωποι ἐνδυόμενοι τοὺς   which people overcome their ad-
ἑαυτῶν ἀντιπάλους νικῶσιν·   versaries,

ὁ στεφανῶν τοὺς νικῶντας·   You who crown the victors

σύμβολον καὶ χαρὰ τῶν   Symbol and joy of those who are
καμνόντων·   weary,

ὁ εὐαγγελισάμενος τοῖς   You who proclaimed to people
ἀνθρώποις τὴν ἑαυτῶν   their salvation,
σωτηρίαν·

ὁ δεικνὺς φῶς τοῖς ἐν σκότει·   You who showed forth light in
          darkness.

ὁ τὰ μὲν φύλλα πικρός, τὸν δὲ   You whose leaves are bitter, but
γλυκύτατον καρπὸν εὐειδής·   who are well formed with fruit
          most sweet,

ὁ τραχὺς μὲν τὴν θέαν, ἁπαλὸς   You who are rough to the sight,
δὲ τὴν γεῦσιν·   but smooth to the taste,

---

[7] *Acts Thom.* 121.

ὁ ἀσθενὴς μὲν δοκῶν, τῇ δὲ τῆς δυνάμεως ὑπερβολῇ τὴν τὰ πάντα θεωποῦσαν βαστάζων δύναμιν·	You who seem to be weak, but in an abundance of power bear the power that contemplates all things.[8]

After this lengthy address, the narration breaks in with "when he has said these things" and a single unintelligible word,[9] and then resumes, "Jesus, let your victorious power come and let it be established in this oil . . . let your gift come . . . and may it dwell in this oil on which we invoke your holy name." In the Syriac the address of the oil is drastically shortened and the transition "having said these things" omitted, but the prayer to Jesus retained in full.

It may well be that the prayer over the healing waters in chapter 52 of the *Acts of Thomas* escaped revisionistic attention because it did not deal with a rite of as major significance as initiation, while the prayers over the oil in 121 and 157 were remade either into prayers to Jesus or prayers over those being initiated.

In the *Gospel according to Philip*, this same principle is presented in more theoretical terms in a passage contained in the chain of sacramental materials, beginning on page 67:

ΤΑΛΗΘΕΙΑ ΜΠΕⲤΕΙ ΕΠΚΟⲤΜΟⲤ ΕⲤΚΑΚΑ2ΗΥ	Truth did not come into the world nakedly;
ΑΛΛΑ ΝΤΑⲤΕΙ 2Ν ΝΤΥΠΟⲤ ΜΝ Ν2ΙΚⲰΝ	rather, it came in types and images:
ⳠΝΑ⳦ΙΤⲤ̄ ΑΝ Ν̄ΚΕⲢΗΤΕ	the world will not accept it in any other form.
ΟΥΝ̄ ΟΥ⳦Πⲟ Ν̄ΚΕⲤⲟⲡ ⳡΟΟⲡ ΜⲚⲚΟΥ2ΙΚⲰΝ Ν̄⳦Π⳪ Ν̄ΚΕⲤⲟⲡ	Rebirth exists along with an image of rebirth:
ⳡⳡΕ ΑΛΗΘⲰⲤ ΑΤⲢΟΥ⳦⳪ΟΟΥ Ν̄ΚΕⲤⲟⲡ 2ΙΤⲚ Τ2ΙΚⲰΝ	by means of this image one must be truly reborn.[10]

In this understanding, the action of sacraments is a matter of the relation of types and images (Ν̄ΤΥΠΟⲤ ΜΝ Ν2ΙΚⲰΝ): "Truth did not come to the world nakedly; rather, it came in types and images: the world will not accept it in any other form."[11] The relation of image to type is quite direct: "Rebirth exists along with an image of rebirth."[12]

---

[8] *Acts Thom.* 157.
[9] ταῦτα εἶπων περιωχείμας. The phrase is transcribed thus in *Acta Philippi et Acta Thomae* ed. M. Bonnet, 267.
[10] *Gos. Phil.* 67.9-14 (translation altered).
[11] *Gos. Phil.* 67.9-11.
[12] *Gos. Phil.* 67.13-14.

The initial statement of the catena seems to belong to the same tradition, although it is a less full statement of the principle; it opens with a speculative anthropology based on a theory of sacramental (and, specifically initiatory) functioning:

ЄΒΟΛ 2Ñ ΟΥΜΟΟΥ ΜÑ ΟΥΚШ2Τ ÑΤΑ ΤΨΥΧ[H] ΜÑ ΤΤΠΝΑ ШШΠЄ	Soul and spirit are constituted of water and fire;
ЄΒΟΛ 2Ñ ΟΥΜΟΟΥ ΜÑ ΟΥΚШ2Τ ΜÑΝΟΥΟЄΙΝ ÑΤΑ ΠШHPЄ ΜΠΝΥΜΦШΝ	a bridegroom's attendant is constituted of water, fire, and light.
ΠΚШ2Τ ΠЄ ΠΧΡΙCΜΑ ΠΟΥΟЄΙΝ ΠЄ ΠΚШ2Τ	Fire is chrism; light is fire—
ЄЄΙШΑΧЄ ΑΝ ΑΠЄЄΙΚШ2Τ ЄΤЄ ΜÑΤΑϥ ΜΟΡΦH ΑΛΛΑ ΠΚЄΟΥΑ ЄΤЄ<ΤЄ>ϥΜΟΡΦH ΟΥΑΒШ ЄΤΟ ÑΟΥΟЄΙΝ ЄΝЄCШϥ ΑΥШ ЄΤϯ ÑΤΜÑΤCΑ	I do not mean worldly fire, which has no form, but another kind of fire, whose appearance is white, which is beautifully luminous, and which bestows beauty.[13]

Explicit sacramental references continue from the beginning of page 67 through the famous list, "The Lord [did] all things by means of a mystery: baptism, chrism, eucharist, ransom, and bridal chamber," and beyond. Immediately following that list, page 67 ends with a dominical saying, which is the second citation of *Gospel according to Thomas* in the *Gospel according to Philip*. Its exegesis extends onto page 68; the material shared with *Gospel according to Thomas* compares the terminology of upper and lower with that of inner and outer.

[. . .]ЄΙ Π[ЄΧ]Αϥ ΧЄ ΑЄΙ ЄΤΡΑЄΙPЄ [ÑΝΑ ΠCΑ ΜΠΙ]ΤÑ ÑΘЄ ÑΝΑ ΠCΑ Ñ[ΤΠЄ	[. . .] said, "I have come to make [the lower] like the [upper
ΑΥШ ΝΑ ΠCΑ Ν]ΒΟΛ ÑΘЄ ÑΝΑ ΠC[Α Ν2ΟΥΝ	and the] outer like the [inner,
ΑΥШ ЄΤΡΑ2ΟΤ]ΡΟΥ ΜΠΜΑ ЄΤΜ̄[. . . ΝЄ]ЄΙΜΑ 2ΙΤÑ 2ÑΤΥ[ΠΟC . . .]	and to join] them in [. . .] here by means of type(s) [. . .]."[14]

The *Gospel according to Thomas'* longer version reads:

2ΟΤΑΝ ЄΤЄΤÑШΑⳁ ΠCΝΑΥ ΟΥΑ ΑΥШ ЄΤЄΤÑШΑⳁ ΠCΑ Ν2ΟΥΝ ÑΘЄ ΜΠCΑ ΝΒΟΛ	When you make the two one and make the inside like the outside

---

[13] *Gos. Phil.* 67.2-9.
[14] *Gos. Phil.* 67.30-34 (translation altered).

ⲁⲩⲱ ⲡⲥⲁ ⲛⲃⲟⲗ ⲛ̄ⲑⲉ ⲙ̄ⲡⲥⲁ ⲛ̄Ϩⲟⲩⲛ ⲁⲩⲱ ⲡⲥⲁ(ⲛ)ⲧⲡⲉ ⲛ̄ⲑⲉ ⲙ̄ⲡⲥⲁ ⲙ̄ⲡⲓⲧⲛ̄	and the outside like the inside and the above like the below,
ⲁⲩⲱ ϣⲓⲛⲁ ⲉⲧⲉⲧⲛⲁⲉⲓⲣⲉ ⲙ̄ⲫⲟⲟⲩⲧ ⲙⲛ̄ ⲧⲥϨⲓⲙⲉ ⲙ̄ⲡⲓⲟⲩⲁ ⲟⲩⲱⲧ	and that you might make the male and the female be one and the same,
ⲭⲉⲕⲁⲁⲥ ⲛⲉ ⲫⲟⲟⲩⲧ ⲣ̄Ϩⲟⲟⲩⲧ ⲛ̄ⲧⲉ ⲧⲥϨⲓⲙⲉ ⲣ̄ⲥϨⲓⲙⲉ	so that the male might not be male nor the female be female,
Ϩⲟⲧⲁⲛ ⲉⲧⲉⲧⲛ̄ϣⲁⲉⲓⲣⲉ ⲛ̄Ϩⲛ̄ⲃⲁⲗ ⲉⲡⲙⲁ ⲛ̄ⲟⲩⲃⲁⲗ ⲁⲩⲱ ⲟⲩϬⲓⲭ ⲉⲡⲙⲁ ⲛ̄ⲛⲟⲩϬⲓⲭ ⲁⲩⲱ ⲟⲩⲉⲣⲏⲧⲉ ⲉⲡⲙⲁ ⲛ̄ⲟⲩⲉⲣⲏⲧⲉ ⲟⲩϨⲓⲕⲱⲛ ⲉⲡⲙⲁ ⲛ̄ⲟⲩϨⲓⲕⲱ(ⲛ)	when you make eyes in place of an eye and a hand in place of a hand and a foot in place of a foot, an image in place of an image—
ⲧⲟⲧⲉ ⲧⲉⲧⲛⲁⲃⲱⲕ ⲉϨⲟⲩⲛ ⲉ̣[ⲧ̣]ⲙⲛ̣̄[ⲧⲉⲣ̣]ⲟ	then you will enter [the kingdom].[15]

The citation formula which introduces Jesus' saying is damaged in the *Gospel according to Philip*, but unquestionably was there, although without anything like the context in *Gospel according to Thomas* of comment on nursing infants. The paraphrase has retained the poles of inner and outer and upper and lower, and the reference to some kind of joining, but has omitted the longer consideration of sexual polarity and the application of the substitution of image in place of image to the parts of the body.

The passage in the *Gospel according to Philip* continues, after the paraphrase, in an interpretive mode, using two other sayings of Jesus known from canonical traditions, and focusing on a preference of inside-outside contrasts over higher-lower contrasts, on the grounds that the latter mean approximately the same thing, but are potentially misleading. Thus the heavenly types should be understood as the innermost, presumably spiritual, types of material things or images. The outer images are of lesser value, but they are understood to be essential for attainment of the inner realities.

In the *Gospel according to Philip*, the immediate context of this saying shows that it was interpreted to mean that the sacramental element is efficacious by its participation in its heavenly type, alternatively understood as its inner reality. In the *Gospel according to Thomas*, the depiction of salvation as the process of becoming an accurate expression of one's reality—spiritual nature?—is a parallel conception.

---

[15] *Gos. Thom.* 22.

Another passage may be joined to these, on a very much more speculative basis. The passage in question is so extremely lacunose that it is not entirely clear even what its topic is; nevertheless, it seems to contain some of the same terminology. While it is quite speculative to join this passage to the others showing an exemplaristic understanding of sacraments, the text and translation below include only some small and conservative restorations.

[ ] ⲚⲦⲀⲨⲬⲠⲞϤ ⲈⲂⲞⲖ ⳒⲘ̄	[ ] born from [ ]
ⲠⲈⲦⲦⲒ[Ⲉ]ⲂⲞⲖ Ⳓ ⲓⲦⲘ̄ ⲠⲚⲞⲨⲦⲈ	[ ] by god.
ⲀⲠ[ⲈⲂ]ⲞⲖ ⳒⲚ̄ ⲚⲈⲦⲘⲞⲞⲨⲦ	The [ ] from the dead
[Ϣ]ⲞⲞⲠ ⲀⲖⲖⲀ ⲚⲈ	[ ] exist(s), but
[ ] ⲈϤⲞ Ⲛ̄ⲦⲈⲖⲈⲒⲞⲚ	[ ] is perfect
[ ] Ⲛ̄ⲤⲀⲢⳅ ⲀⲖⲖⲀ ⲦⲈⲈⲒ	[ ] flesh, but
[ⲞⲨⲤ]ⲀⲢⳅ ⲦⲈ Ⲛ̄ⲀⲖⲎⲐⲈⲒⲚⲎ	[ ] it is genuine flesh
[ ]Ⲉ ⲞⲨⲀⲖⲎⲐⲈⲒⲚⲎ ⲀⲚ ⲦⲈ ⲀⲖ	[ ] is not genuine; rather
[ⲖⲀ] Ⲛ̄ⳒⲒⲔⲰⲚ Ⲛ̄ⲦⲀⲖⲎⲐⲈⲒⲚⲎ	[ ] image of the genuine one.[16]

The relation of a "genuine flesh" to flesh which is not genuine seems to be an instance of the relation of type to image, and the relation seems to be of importance to the question of rebirth and resurrection. It is tempting to say that this is a sacramental passage, although it is unclear what sacrament is involved; it exhibits enough of the pattern of "sacramental exemplarism" to be tentatively included in the "Thomas" strand.

Acts of Thomas alone contains prayers of epiclesis addressed to the heavenly Water or Oil, asking *that* Water or *that* Oil to come and dwell in *this* water or *this* oil; the *Gospel according to Thomas* contains statements that could be read as reflecting such an understanding. The *Gospel according to Philip* contains a passage in which one such statement from the *Gospel according to Thomas* was read in just that way, along with a number of other statements of the same principle. This, together with the two instances of literary dependence, make a relatively secure connection between one of the strands of the *Gospel according to Philip* and some part of the Thomas tradition. It should be noted, however, that this "Thomas" strand in the *Gospel according to Philip* seems to represent an earlier version of the tradition than is expressed in either the extant Syriac or the extant Greek text of the *Acts of Thomas*.

---

[16] *Gos. Phil.* 68.29-37.

Sacramental Exemplarism and the Mystery of Marriage

There are two passages which assert the principle in relation to the "mystery of marriage" and "the act of joining between males and females" (neither passage uses the term "bridal chamber" or its synonyms). The passage on page 64, while lacunose (as well as pertaining to debatable matters), clearly attaches great importance to a "mystery of marriage" which is spiritual or heavenly or something of that sort. This "mystery" exists in a particular relationship to the marriage which involves sexual intercourse: the latter is the "image" of the former, while the former (if one may supply the expected symmetry) must be the "type" of the latter. It reads:

[ⲡⲙ]ⲩ̣ⲥⲧⲏⲣⲓⲟⲛ ⲙⲡⲅⲁⲙ[ⲟⲥ] ⲟⲩⲛⲟϭ [ⲡⲉ ⲁϫⲛ̄]ⲧ̣ϥ ⲅⲁⲣ ⲛⲉ ⲡⲕⲟⲥ[ⲙⲟ]ⲥ̣ ⲛⲁϣⲱ[ⲡⲉ ⲁⲛ	[The] mystery of marriage [is] a great mystery, for [without] it the world would [not] exist.
ⲧⲥ]ⲩ̣ⲥⲧⲁⲥⲓⲥ ⲅⲁⲣ ⲙ̄[ⲡⲕⲟ]ⲥ̣ⲙⲟ[ⲥ . . .]ⲙⲉ	For [the] structure of [the world. .]
ⲡⲥⲩⲥⲧⲁⲥⲓⲥ ⲇⲉ [. . . ⲡⲅ]ⲁ̣ⲙⲟⲥ	But the structure [. . .] marriage.
ⲉⲣⲓⲛⲟⲉⲓ ⲛ̄ⲧⲕⲟⲓ[ⲛⲱⲛⲓⲁ . . . ϫ]ⲱϩⲙ̄ ϫⲉ ⲟⲩⲛ̄ⲧⲁⲥ ⲙ̄ⲙⲁⲩ[. . .] ⲇ̣ⲩⲛⲁⲙⲓⲥ	Consider the sexual intercourse [. . .] pollute(s), for it possesses [. . .] force(s).
ⲧⲉⲥϩⲓⲕⲱⲛ ⲉⲥϣⲟⲟⲡ ϩⲛ̄ ⲟⲩϫⲱ̣[ϩⲙ̄]	It is in pollution that its image resides.[17]

The passage on page 76 is similar:

ⲉⲡϩⲱⲧⲣ̄ ϣⲟⲟⲡ ϩⲙ̄ ⲡⲉⲉⲓⲕⲟⲥ-ⲙⲟⲥ ϩⲟⲟⲩⲧ ϩⲓ ⲥϩⲓⲙⲉ ⲡⲙⲁ ⲉⲧϭⲟⲙ ⲙⲛ̄ ⲧⲙⲛ̄ⲧ̄ϭⲱⲃ	It is in the world, where power and weakness exist, that the act of joining between males and females occurs;
ϩⲙ̄ ⲡⲁⲓⲱⲛ ⲕⲉⲟⲩⲁ ⲡⲉ ⲡⲉⲓⲛⲉ ⲙ̄ⲡϩⲱⲧⲣ̄	but in the eternal realm there is a different sort of joining.
ⲉⲙⲙⲟⲩⲧⲉ ⲇⲉ ⲉⲣⲟⲟⲩ ⲛ̄ⲛⲉⲉⲓⲣⲁⲛ ⲟⲩⲛ ϩⲛ̄ⲕⲟⲟⲩⲉ ⲇⲉ ϣⲟⲟⲡ ⲥⲉϫⲟⲥⲉ ⲡⲁⲣⲁ ⲣⲁⲛ ⲛⲓⲙ ⲉⲧⲟⲩⲣ̄ⲟⲛⲟⲙⲁⲍⲉ ⲙ̄ⲙⲟⲟⲩ ⲁⲩⲱ ⲥⲉϫⲟⲟⲥⲉ ⲉⲡϫⲱⲱⲣⲉ	Although it is with these names that we refer to things, yet other names also exist, above every current name, indeed, above the most potent.
ⲡⲙⲁ ⲅⲁⲣ ⲉⲧⲉ ⲟⲩⲛ̄ ⲃⲓⲁ ⲙ̄ⲙⲁⲩ ⲉⲩϣⲟⲟⲡ ⲙ̄ⲙⲁⲩ ⲛ̄ϭⲓ ⲛⲉⲧⲥⲟⲧⲡ ⲉⲧϭⲟⲙ	For where brute force exists there are those who are superior to power.

[17] *Gos. Phil.* 64.31-65.1.

ΝΕΤΜ̄ΜΑΥ ΚΕΟΥΑ ΑΝ ΠΕ ΑΥω	These are not two different things,
ΚΕΟΥΑ ΠΕ ΑΛΛΑ Ν̄ΤΟΟΥ	rather one and the same.
Μ̄ΠΕϹΝΑΥ ΠΙΟΥΑ ΟΥωΤ ΠΕ	
ΠΑΕΙ ΠΕ ΕΤϥΝΑϢΙ ΑΝ Ε2ΡΑΪ	It is this which is incomprehensible
ΕΧΝ̄ ϤΗΤ Ν̄ϹΑΡ2	to hearts of flesh.[18]

Quite apart from the understanding of sacraments which may be seen in them, these two passages probably constitute the best data available on which to base an argument that the "mystery of marriage" or "bridal chamber" is not entirely a metaphoric matter in the *Gospel according to Philip* (or parts of the *Gospel according to Philip*), but refers simultaneously to a more spiritual reality and a less spiritual, more material counterpart of that reality. One possible interpretation of these two passages, in keeping with the analysis pursued above, would be that ordinary physical marriage is recommended as the sacramental vehicle by which one receives the spiritual counterpart of marriage, and that the "image" is necessary to the reception of the spiritual gift corresponding to it. This would be a surprising opinion to find within a strand of tradition related to the Thomas literature—but we may know less than we imagine about "Thomas" traditions.

The *Gospel according to Thomas* contains two different resolutions to the problem of sexuality: the attainment of androgyny (as in *Gos. Thom.* 22) and the transformation of the female into the male (as in *Gos. Thom.* 114). The *Acts of Thomas* rejects human marriage because of the bitter results it finds in the intoxication of lustful desire, and in favor of a spiritual marriage to the heavenly bridegroom, Jesus. The *Book of Thomas the Contender* repeats such negative assessments of the nature and effects of sexual desire, along with the punishments which it will meet, but offers only escape from these, together with a few hints at the concept that sexuality is alien to the chosen, and that chastity renders one compatible with the "light," more or less along the lines of the *Gospel according to Thomas*' emphasis on personal transformation.[19] All seem to agree, however, in rejecting marriage. It is important to remember that the criterion of an exemplaristic understanding of sacramental efficacy has guided us to some part of the Thomas tradition—not necessarily to its entirety, or to the exact stage represented by any of its

---

[18] *Gos. Phil.* 76.6-17.

[19] Arguments based on the reattainment of a primordial union of the sexes (as androgyny?) and on the compatibility or connaturality of purity and spiritual things are the only two of these concepts found in the Gospel according to Philip

extant documents, but one which shows itself in some of the material in the *Gospel according to Thomas* and in a primitive tradition which has already been partially obscured by redaction in extant texts of the *Acts of Thomas*. Nevertheless, there seem to be at least four possibilities. (1) These two passages may not belong to the "Thomas" strand in the *Gospel according to Philip*, or may have been edited out of recognition on this point by a proponent of a quite different tradition. (2) This strand of the "Thomas" tradition may, against expectations, have embraced marriage as a sacrament necessary to the attainment of a certain grace. (3) The material, physical "image" to which the spiritual "type" corresponded may have been something other than ordinary marriage: perhaps a celibate "spiritual" marriage, or perhaps a monastic or eremetical isolation, conceived of as parallel to the "enclosure" in the women's quarters which was an ideal for upper-class matrons. (4) The paradigm of sacramental type and image may be used here in a slightly different way, allowing that "the act of joining between males and females" and the "pollution" of sexual intercourse contain an image of something higher, but that the enactment of this particular image, far from being necessary to the attainment of the reality, must be rejected. The last two possibilities are not incompatible, and either or both correspond to concepts and imagery in the *Acts of Thomas*. The issue of the meaning of the "mystery of marriage" and related terms in the *Gospel according to Philip* is a difficult one, and will not be resolved here. I would tentatively suggest either or both of the last two possibilities above as interpretations of these passages, and attach them to the "Thomas" strand in the *Gospel according to Philip*, although with a considerable degree of hesitation.

While neither of the two passages analyzed above uses the term "bridal chamber" or its synonyms, they have usually been interpreted together with the "bridal chamber" passages. The probability that they have different affiliations seriously undermines one of the mainstays in the exegesis of the *Gospel according to Philip*, the idea that all bridal chamber/mystery of marriage passages go together and are necessarily Valentinian.

Anointing as a Sufficient Form of Christian Initiation

The *Gospel according to Philip* contains some statements about Christian initiation which are unusual; one of them, at least, seems to have parallels only in the *Acts of Thomas*.

The Greek text of the *Acts of Thomas* shows four different sequences of ritual actions in its five initiatory episodes.[20] Two of the initiations describe an anointing of the head only, followed by the water bath.[21] Another describes an anointing of the head, followed by an anointing of the whole body, which is then followed by the water bath.[22] Another account of initiation in the *Acts of Thomas*, however, consists of a 'seal' of some kind requiring oil, followed by an anointing of the head and an epiclesis over the initiands.[23] There is no water bath mentioned at all. One other account of initiation in the *Acts of Thomas* consists merely of an epiclesis over the initiand and the laying on of hands, with no mention of either oil or water, but this account is brief and could perhaps be defective.[24] All five episodes describe the transition of someone from a pagan existence into a Christian one; the transition in all five cases is followed by a first partaking of the eucharist.

While the *Acts of Thomas* is clearly meant to entertain as well as to instruct, the work presents its community as one founded and authorized by the apostle Thomas; practices which seemed exotic or archaic to its readers would be in line with this intention, but not practices which seemed unacceptable or heretical. Presumably, then, the anticipated readers of the work would have found all of these initiatiory sequences acceptable and valid, if perhaps also glamorously exotic or archaic. Thus we have in *Acts Thom.* 26-27 and 49 an understanding that the water rite is not an indispensable part of Christian initiation, and that one could be validly initiated by the use of oil alone.

A passage on page 77 probably also belongs with this material because, while the *Acts of Thomas* ignores the Pauline understanding of the water rite as baptism into Jesus' death, the *Gospel according to Philip* is openly critical of it:

---

[20] The Syriac, which has been adapted to a later orthodoxy, shows only three patterns of initiatory action in the same five episodes. There is also a Greek epitome which does not include the whole book; it contains only one initiation episode.

[21] *Acts Thom.* 120-121 and 132-133. This pattern has sometimes been taken as normative of "early Syrian baptism," for example, by Gabriele Winkler, who ignores most of the variety of practice documented in *Acts of Thomas* to construct a model of "earliest practice." See Gabriele Winkler "The Original Meaning of the Prebaptismal Anointing and its Implications," *Worship* 52 (1978) 24-45.

[22] *Acts Thom.* 157-158.

[23] *Acts Thom.* 26-27.

[24] *Acts Thom.* 49.

ⲛ̄ⲑⲉ ⲛ̄ⲧⲁ ⲓ̄ⲥ̄ ϫⲱⲕ ⲉⲃⲟⲗ ⲙ̄ⲡⲙⲟⲟⲩ ⲙ̄ⲡⲃⲁⲡⲧⲓⲥⲙⲁ ⲧⲁⲉⲓ ⲧⲉ ⲑⲉ ⲁϥⲡⲱϩⲧ ⲉⲃⲟⲗ ⲙ̄ⲡⲙⲟⲩ	Just as Jesus perfected the water of baptism, so too he drew off death.
ⲉⲧⲃⲉ ⲡⲁⲉⲓ ⲧⲛ̄ⲃⲏⲕ ⲙⲉⲛ ⲉⲡⲓⲧⲛ̄ ⲉⲡⲙⲟⲟⲩ	For this reason we go down into the water
ⲧⲛ̄ⲃⲏⲕ ⲇⲉ ⲁⲛ ⲉⲡⲓⲧⲛ̄ ⲉⲡⲙⲟⲩ ϣⲓⲛⲁ ϫⲉ ⲛⲟⲩⲡⲁϩⲧⲛ̄ ⲉⲃⲟⲗ ϩⲙ̄ ⲡⲡⲛ̄ⲁ̄ ⲙ̄ⲡⲕⲟⲥⲙⲟⲥ	but not into death, so that we are poured out into the wind of the world.
ϩⲟⲧⲁⲛ ⲉϥϣⲁⲛⲛⲓϥⲉ ϣⲁⲣⲉϥ ⲧⲉ ⲧⲡⲣⲱ ϣⲱⲡⲉ	Whenever the latter blows, winter comes:
ⲡⲡⲛ̄ⲁ̄ ⲉⲧⲟⲩⲁⲁⲃ ϩⲟⲧⲁⲛ ⲉϥϣⲁⲛⲛⲓϥⲉ ϣⲁⲣⲉ ⲧⲉ ⲧϣⲁⲙⲏ ϣⲱⲡⲉ	whenever the holy spirit blows, summer comes.[25]

A passage about chrism on page 74 of the *Gospel according to Philip* also reflects such a tradition.

ⲡⲭⲣⲉⲓⲥⲙⲁ ϥⲟ ⲛ̄ϫⲟⲉⲓⲥ ⲉⲡⲃⲁⲡⲧⲓⲥⲙⲁ	Chrism has more authority than baptism.
ⲉⲃⲟⲗ ⲅⲁⲣ ϩⲙ̄ ⲡⲭⲣⲓⲥⲙⲁ ⲁⲩⲙⲟⲩⲧⲉ ⲉⲣⲟⲛ ϫⲉ ⲭⲣⲓⲥⲧⲓⲁⲛⲟⲥ ⲉⲧⲃⲉ ⲡⲃⲁⲡⲧⲓⲥⲙⲁ ⲁⲛ	For because of chrism we are called Christians, not because of baptism.
ⲁⲩⲱ ⲛ̄ⲧⲁⲩⲙⲟⲩⲧⲉ ⲉⲡⲉⲭ̄ⲥ̄ ⲉⲧⲃⲉ ⲡⲭⲣⲓⲥⲙⲁ	And the anointed (Christ) was named for chrism,
ⲁⲡⲉⲓⲱⲧ ϥⲁⲣ ⲧⲱϩⲥ ⲙ̄ⲡϣⲏⲣⲉ ⲁⲡϣⲏⲣⲉ ⲇⲉ ⲧⲱϩⲥ ⲛ̄ⲁⲡⲟⲥⲧⲟⲗⲟⲥ ⲁⲛⲁⲡⲟⲥⲧⲟⲗⲟⲥ ⲇⲉ ⲧⲁϩⲥⲛ̄	for the father anointed the son, and the son anointed the apostles, and the apostles anointed us.
ⲡⲉⲛⲧⲁⲩⲧⲟϩⲥϥ ⲟⲩⲛ̄ⲧⲉϥ ⲡⲧⲏⲣϥ ⲙ̄ⲙⲁⲩ	Whoever has been anointed has everything:
ⲟⲩⲛ̄ⲧⲁϥ ⲧⲁⲛⲁⲥⲧⲁⲥⲓⲥ ⲡⲟⲟⲩⲟⲉⲓⲛ ⲡⲉⲥ⳨ⲟⲥ ⲡⲡⲛ̄ⲁ̄ ⲉⲧⲟⲩⲁⲁⲃ	resurrection, light, cross, holy spirit;
ⲁⲡⲉⲓⲱⲧ ϯ ⲛⲁϥ ⲙ̄ⲡⲁⲉⲓ ϩⲙ̄ ⲡⲛⲩ[ⲙ]ⲫⲱⲛ̣	the father has given it to that person in the bridal chamber, and the person has received (it).[26]

The statement "The Father anointed the Son, and the Son anointed the apostles, and the apostles anointed us," taken with "because of chrism we are called Christians," makes it unambiguously clear that this passage

[25] *Gos. Phil.* 77.7-15.
[26] *Gos. Phil.* 74.12-22.

originated in a group that called themselves Christians and understood this claim in terms of a succession of anointing going back through the apostles and Christ to the Father. Far from deriding the apostles and the idea of apostolic authority (as some texts within the *Gospel according to Philip* do), they saw their community as based on it—as did the people responsible for the *Acts of Thomas*. The group behind the statements on page 74 seem also to have accepted (and may have practiced) an initiation rite in which anointing was central (as it was for much of Syria), and in which the water bath was not only secondary but also optional. It is this peculiar evaluation of the anointing rite, taken along with the emphasis on it and the interpretation of apostolic authority under this image, that place the passage within the "Thomas" source.

Apostolic Authority and Initiation by Anointing

A group of material possibly related to the Thomas tradition can be discovered by analysis of the pro-apostolic statements in the *Gospel according to Philip*. This "pro-apostolic" strand (or strands) of tradition is not necessarily equivalent to the position of the opponents of the "anti-apostolic" statements, nor need they constitute a unity: many kinds of early Christians claimed some form of apostolic authority. One of these passages, however, shows strong links with the Thomas material in its understanding of a variant form of Christian initiation.

A passage on page 62 gives the names which "the apostles before us" used to refer to Jesus; we learn that they used "Messias," which has been abandoned by the group in question and must be explained as "Christ." Of the four interpretations which follow, three depend on Semitic roots and one, seemingly, on fantasy. Thus we have a group which, at the very least, retrieved apostolic usages and interpreted them on the basis of their original cultural context, which has now grown foreign to the group. This is not distinctive enough to allow us to attach this passage to the Thomas material, although it is certainly compatible with Thomas Christianity.

Much more can be learned from the passage about anointing on page 74. "The apostles" are a constitutive link in the conception of corporate identity here, which is also imaged in terms of a *chain of initiation:* "The Father anointed the Son, and the Son anointed the apostles, and the apostles anointed us." This is coupled with a strong interpretation of the gifts conveyed by anointing: "Whoever has been anointed has everything: resurrection, light, cross, Holy Spirit," and, "Chrism has more authority than baptism. For because of chrism we are called Christians, not because of baptism." This emphasis on anointing is, as the last quoted statement shows, linked to a critique of over-evaluations of baptism, and also to an acceptance of Christian initiation practices which used oil and no water bath. The passage on page 74 thus shows several points of contact with the Thomas tradition(s). Intriguingly, this strand of tradition is one which uses the term "bridal chamber," ΝΥΜΦϢΝ.

The Christianity depicted in *Acts of Thomas* claimed the authority of apostolic foundation and was certainly "pro-apostolic" in some strong sense; nevertheless, it would be rash to attribute all of the *Gospel according to Philip*'s "pro-apostolic" materials to the "Thomas" source on that ground alone. As there are no overlaps between the passages on pages 62 and 74, beyond their high evaluation of apostles, there are no strong reasons for either identifying or differentiating the strands of tradition they embody. Other Christians claimed apostolic ties too: the "proto-orthodox," and Valentinians, for example. Even some of the "classical" or "Sethian" gnostic works have been more or less superficially "apostolized," with or without the use of the word. The *Apocryphon of John* is presented as a revelation given to John the brother of James, one of the sons of Zebedee; although the word "apostle" does not occur in the text, the work claims some connection to the apostolic circle. Some "Christianization" (and "apostolization") is superficial, however. The *Apocryphon of John* does not mention Christ or the events surrounding the incarnation until the final lines, which are probably a scribal colophon. The introductory paragraph of the *Hypostasis of the Archons* quotes Eph 6.12 in support of the reality of the rulers it proposes to discuss, and attributes the quotation to "the great apostle." The rest of the document, like the *Apocryphon of John*, consists of an elaborated retelling of the creation mythology from Genesis; beyond the first paragraph, there is nothing distinctively Christian (or apostolic) about the work. An approving use of the word "apostle" or a link to the circle of apostles can appear in documents which do not make other claims to being Christian, but one would tend to expect such superficial reworking at the beginning and/or end, and would not expect such material to be very fully developed.

The strongest of the "pro-apostolic" passages in the *Gospel according to Philip*, however, shares further characteristics with the *Acts of Thomas*. The passage on page 74 depicts a chain of authority involving the apostles and imaged as ritual anointings; the prominence of anoint-

ing here corresponds to the prominence given it in the initiations depicted in *Acts of Thomas*; both betray an unusual evaluation of its importance in Christian initiation. It is this peculiar evaluation of the
anointing rite, taken along with the emphasis on it and the interpretation
of apostolic authority under this image that place provides a stronger
warrant for attaching this "pro-apostolic" passage to the "Thomas"
strand in the *Gospel according to Philip*.

Images of Eating and Becoming

Yet another group of passages involves the concept of "sacramental exemplarism" along with the image of eating and becoming, both of which
are found in the Thomas tradition also.

One of these passages alludes to and builds on the "bread of heaven"
discourse in John 6. The *Gospel according to Philip* does not portray
Jesus as a second Moses, associated with manna, but as a corrector of an
(implicitly) deficient paradise in which Adam had no proper food!

2Δ TЄ2H ЄMΠΔTЄ ΠЄⲬⲤ ЄI NЄ MN ОЄIK 2M ΠKOCMOC	Before the anointed (Christ) came there was no bread in the world:
NⲐЄ MΠΠΔPΔΔICOC ΠMΔ NЄPЄ ΔΔΔM MMΔY NЄYNTΔϤ 2Δ2 NⲰHN NNTPOϤH NNⲐHPION NЄ MNTΔϤ COYO NTTPOϤH MΠPⲰMЄ NЄPЄ ΠPⲰMЄ COЄIⲰ NⲐЄ NNⲐHPION	just as paradise, where Adam was, had many trees for the food of the animals but did not have wheat for the food of human beings, and human beings were nourished like the animals.
ΔΛΛΔ NTΔPЄ ΠЄⲬⲤ ЄI ΠTЄΛIOC PPⲰMЄ ΔϤЄINЄ NOYOЄIK ЄBOΛ 2N ΤΠЄ	But when the anointed (Christ), the perfect human being, came, he brought bread from heaven
ⲰINΔ ЄPЄ ΠPⲰMЄ NΔPTPЄϤЄCⲐΔI 2N TTPOϤH MΠPⲰMЄ	so that human beings might be fed with the food of the human be-ing.[27]

No use is made here of the link in John 6 between the "bread of heaven"
and Jesus' flesh; rather, it is the proper food for human beings—a statement that implies that the humans are of a heavenly origin or somehow
connatural with heavenly things.

Two more passages in the *Gospel according to Philip* speak of humans eating food that is linked with animals or with death and becoming, as a result, animals or mortal.[28]

---

[27] *Gos. Phil.* 55.6-14.

[28] A number more passages in the Gospel according to Philip deal with eating

ОУⲚ ϢHN CNAY ⲢHT [2]Ⲙ ⲦⲦⲀⲢⲀⲀⲒⲤⲞⲤ ⲦⲞYⲀ ⲬⲦⲈ Θ[HⲢⲒⲞⲚ] ⲦⲞYⲀ ⲬⲦⲈ ⲢⲰⲘⲈ	There are two trees growing in paradise: one produces [animals], the other produces human beings.
ⲀⲀⲀⲘ Ⲟ[YⲰⲘ] ⲈⲂⲞⲀ 2Ⲙ ⲦⲦϢH(N) ⲚⲦⲀ2ⲬⲦⲈ ΘHⲢⲒ[ⲞⲚ]	Adam [ate] from the tree that had produced animals;
ⲀⲩϢ]ⲰⲦⲈ ⲚⲞHⲢⲒⲞⲚ ⲀⲩⲬⲦⲈ ΘH[ⲢⲒⲞⲚ]	he became an animal and begot animals.
ⲈⲦⲂⲈ ⲦⲀⲓ̈ ⲤⲈⲢⲤⲈⲂⲈⲤΘⲈ ⲀⲚΘ[HⲢⲒⲞⲚ] Ⲛ6]Ⲓ ⲚϢHⲢⲈ ⲚⲀⲀⲀⲘ	For this reason the children of Adam worship the [animals].[29]

The passage continues with a parallel development of the tree that produces human beings, but is too lacunose to tell much about. When undamaged text resumes at the top of the next page, the discussion has taken an ironical turn in weighing the relative merits of human beings and the gods whom they create. The first part of the passage, and section lost to lacuna (if it is a parallel development), propose an equation between eating and identity.

The other passage based on the effects of what humans eat is on page 73:

ⲦⲈⲈⲒⲔⲞⲤⲘⲞⲤ ОУⲀⲘⲔⲰϢⲤ ⲦⲈ ⲚⲔⲈ ⲚⲒⲘ ⲈⲦОУⲰⲘ Ⲙ̄ⲘⲞОУ 2ⲢⲀⲓ̈ Ⲛ̄2HⲦⲩ ⲤⲈⲘⲞ[Y] 2ⲰⲞY ⲞⲚ	The world devours corpses: everything eaten within it also dies.
ⲦⲀⲀHΘⲈⲒⲀ ОУⲀⲘⲰⲚ2 ⲦⲈ ⲈⲦⲂⲈ ⲦⲀⲈⲒ ⲘⲚ̄ ⲀⲀⲀY 2Ⲛ̄ ⲚⲈⲦⲤⲞⲚϢ 2Ⲛ̄ Ⲧ[ⲘⲈ] ⲚⲀⲘⲞY	The realm of truth devours life: thus no one of those who live on [truth] is dying.
ⲚⲦⲀ Ⲓ̄Ⲥ̄ ⲈⲒ ⲈⲂⲞⲀ 2Ⲙ̄ ⲦⲘⲀ Ⲉ[ⲦⲘ̄]ⲘⲀY ⲀYⲰ ⲀⲩⲈⲒⲚⲈ Ⲛ̄2Ⲛ̄ⲦⲢⲞⲪH ⲈⲂⲞⲀ Ⲙ̄ⲘⲀY	From that realm did Jesus come, and he brought food from there.
ⲀYⲰ ⲚⲈⲦОУⲰϢ Ⲁⲩⲧ̄ ⲚⲀY [ⲚОY]Ϣ[Ⲛ2] ⲬⲈ[ⲔⲀⲀⲤ] Ⲛ̄ⲚОУⲘⲞY	And he gave [life] to whomever wished it, so that they might not die.[30]

---

from some perspective, but only these develop the idea that one takes on the nature of what one eats from the perspective of human eating and becoming. For a survey of all the passages in the Gospel according to Philip dealing with eating, see Jorunn Jacobsen Buckley, "Conceptual Models and Polemical Issues in the Gospel of Philip," *Aufstieg und Niedergang der römischen Welt* II.25.5 (Berlin: De Gruyter, 1988), 4167-4194, especially 4175-4179.

[29] *Gos. Phil.* 71.22-28.
[30] *Gos. Phil.* 73.19-27.

These passages correspond to material found not only in the *Gospel according to Thomas* but also to the *Book of Thomas the Contender*. In the latter, animal nature and particularly sexual reproduction are linked to eating:

ⲁⲩⲱ ⲛⲉⲩⲕⲁⲣⲡⲟⲥ ⲡⲉⲧⲥⲁⲁⲛⲩ ⲙⲙⲟⲟⲩ	And it is their fruits that nourish them.
ⲛⲉⲉⲓⲥⲱⲙⲁ ⲛ̄ⲧⲟⲟⲩ ⲉⲧⲟⲩⲟⲛ̄ ⲉⲃⲟⲗ ⲉⲩⲱⲙ ⲉⲃⲟⲗ ϩⲛ̄ ⲛ̄ⲥⲱⲛⲧ ⲉϯⲛⲉ ⲙ̄ⲙⲟⲟⲩ	These visible bodies themselves eat of the creatures that resemble them.
ⲉⲧⲃⲉ ⲡⲁⲓ̈ ϭⲉ ⲛ̄ⲥⲱⲙⲁ ⲥⲉⲩⲓⲃⲉ	So for this reason bodies are mutable.
ⲡⲉⲧⲩⲓⲃⲉ ⲇⲉ ϥⲛⲁⲧⲉⲕⲟ ⲛ̄ϥⲱⲭ̄ⲛ̄ ⲁⲩⲱ ⲙⲛ̄ⲧⲉϥ ϩⲉⲗⲡⲓⲥ ⲛ̄ⲱⲛϩ ⲭ̄ⲙ̄ ⲡⲧⲓⲛⲁⲩ	But what is mutable will perish and cease to be, and from that moment on it has no hope of living.
ⲭⲉ ⲡⲓⲥⲱⲙⲁ ⲅⲁⲣ ⲟⲩⲧⲃ̄ⲛⲏ ⲡⲉ	For the body is a domestic animal.
ⲛ̄ⲛ̄ⲑⲉ ϭⲉ ⲛ̄ⲛ̄ⲧⲃⲛⲟⲟⲩⲉ ⲉⲩⲁⲣⲉ ⲡⲟⲩⲥⲱⲙⲁ ⲧⲉⲕⲟ ⲧⲉⲉⲓ ⲧⲉ ⲑⲉ ⲛ̄ⲛⲉⲉⲓⲡⲗⲁⲥⲙⲁ ⲥⲉⲛⲁⲧⲉⲕⲟ	Indeed, just as the bodies of domestic animals perish, so too these modeled forms will perish.
ⲙⲏⲧⲓ ⲟⲩⲉⲃⲟⲗ ⲁⲛ ⲡⲉ ϩⲛ̄ ⲧⲥⲩⲛⲟⲩⲥⲓⲁ ⲛ̄ⲑⲉ ⲙ̄ⲡⲁ ⲛ̄ⲧⲃ̄ⲛⲟⲟⲩⲉ	Does it (the body) not result from sexual intercourse like that of the domestic animals?[31]

They are also strongly reminiscent of two passages in *Gospel according to Thomas*. Logion 7 is a macarism blessing the lion that the human being devours so that the lion becomes human, and cursing the human being that the lion devours, again (and puzzlingly) with the result that the lion becomes human. One might expect the same results in both cases: either eater should become like the one eaten, or vice versa; but instead, in both cases, the result is the lion becoming human. Possibly the point is a psychological one, about a better and a worse path to achieving the spirit's mastery over the passions. In any case, unless the text is corrupt, its point has to do with the unexpected asymmetry of the situation. It is not a sacramental passage (at least, not obviously), but it depends upon the equation of eating and identity, and so testifies to this metaphor's use in the Thomas tradition. Another example of the metaphor in *Gospel according to Thomas* is in logion 60, in which Jesus comments to his disciples, on seeing a Samaritan carrying a lamb, that he must slaughter it before eating it, and so he will eat its carcass. This is

---

[31] *Th. Cont.* 139.1-12.

reminiscent of the *Gospel according to Philip*'s talk of the world eating corpses,[32] as is the warning to the disciples which concludes this logion, "You, too, seek for yourselves a place for repose, lest you become a carcass and be devoured."

"CLASSICAL" OR "SETHIAN" PASSAGES

Both of the passages in the *Gospel according to Philip* which show a hostility toward "apostles" and those who claim to be their heirs also involve traditions about the fallen Sophia. One of these two quotes the *Hypostasis of the Archons* (or is quoted by it, or both depend on a common source). In addition, the first three quarters of the document also contains four other passages which involve harsh criticism of the creator.

The passage on page 55 fuses a Christian legend with a strand of gnosticism which is not overtly Christian, by taking a category from the latter and using it to interpret the former. Mary the mother of Jesus is described here as "the virgin whom the forces did not defile" a phrase identical to that applied to Norea in *Hypostasis of the Archons*.[33] It is this interpretation of Mary which the passage reports as having been declared anathema by "the Hebrews, meaning the apostles and apostolic persons." If the entire passage about the conception of the Lord (55.23-36) comes from the same source as the interpretation of Mary, a few more things can be learned about them and their apostolic opponents. This larger passage denies the virginal conception of Jesus and seems to flirt with portraying the Holy Spirit as kin to "the forces," possibly as the lower Sophia. The apostolic opponents assert that Mary conceived by the Holy Spirit.

The other passage exhibiting conflict with apostles is the account on page 59 of the apostles' remark to the disciples: "May all our offering get salt!" The apostolic group, according to this text, interprets the ritual requirements of Leviticus allegorically, equating "salt" with "wisdom." The text criticizes their remark together with their understanding of it by applying a category widespread in gnostic circles of various types: a

---

[32] *Gos. Phil.* 73.19-27.

[33] *Gos. Phil.* 55.23-32: ⲘⲀⲢⲒⲀ ⲦⲈ ⲦⲠⲀⲢⲐⲈⲚⲞⲤ ⲈⲦⲈ ⲘⲠⲈⲆⲨⲚⲀⲘⲒⲤ ⲬⲀϨⲘⲈⲤ; Hyp. Arch. 91.34-93.1, especially 92.2-3: ⲦⲀⲈⲒ ⲦⲈ ⲦⲠⲀⲢⲐⲈⲚⲞⲤ ⲈⲦⲈ ⲘⲠⲈ(Ⲛ)ⲆⲨⲚⲀⲘⲒⲤ ⲬⲀϨⲘⲈⲤ.

personified "Wisdom" who is somehow problematic, possibly again the lower Sophia. The well-known and disastrous consequences of salt on land are paralleled with traditions of the barrenness of Sophia. From the perspective of this passage, the apostles have unwittingly specified their folly in their remark. No positive position can be gleaned from the passage, at least in its lacunose state, beyond the fact that a saying of the apostles is deemed worthy of report and evaluation.

These passages show multiple points of contact. They are both hostile toward the apostles and those who claim to be their heirs; they are both concerned with Christian traditions (Mary, Jesus, discussions between Jesus and his disciples); they are both concerned with teachings about a lower power or powers;[34] they both construe some other Christians' teaching as based on a mistaken attachment to that lower power or powers; both associate what they find wrong in other Christians' teaching with the Law or with being Hebrew. The large number of shared characteristics makes it probable that these two passages come from the same source or derive from the same group.

Three extremely revisionistic retellings of Genesis also belong outside the Thomas material.

One of the most revisionistic interpretations of Genesis in the *Gospel according to Philip* is found on page 60. It seems to combine in itself two logically incompatible traditions, perhaps because they are capable of being read as having the same point.

[ⲡⲉⲛⲧ]ⲁ̄ⲩⲡⲗⲁⲥⲥⲉ ⲙ̄ⲙⲟϥ ⲛⲉ[ⲥ]ⲱ̣ϥ ⲁⲗⲗⲁ ⲛ̣ⲉ̣ⲕ̣ⲛⲁ2ⲉ <ⲁⲛ> ⲁⲛⲉϥϣⲏⲣⲉ ⲉⲩⲟ ⲙ̄ⲡⲗⲁⲥⲙⲁ ⲛ̄ⲉⲩⲅⲉⲛⲏⲥ	[The one who] was modeled was beautiful, [but] his offspring were <not> like noble modeled forms.
ⲉϣϫⲉ ⲙ̄ⲡⲟⲩⲣ̄ⲡⲗⲁⲥⲥⲉ ⲙ̄ⲙⲟϥ ⲁⲗⲗⲁ ⲁⲩϫⲡⲟϥ ⲛⲉⲕⲛⲁ2ⲉ ⲁⲡⲉϥⲥⲡⲉⲣⲙⲁ ⲉϥⲟ ⲛ̄ⲉⲩⲅⲉⲛⲏⲥ	If he had not been modeled but rather born, his posterity would be like what is noble.
ⲧⲉⲛⲟⲩ ⲇⲉ ⲁⲩⲡⲗⲁⲥⲥⲉ ⲙ̄ⲙⲟϥ ⲁϥϫⲡⲟ	But as a matter of fact he was modeled, and then produced offspring.
ⲁϣ ⲛ̄ⲉⲩⲅⲉⲛⲉⲓⲁ ⲡⲉ ⲡⲧⲁⲉⲓ ϣⲟⲣⲡ̄ ⲁⲧⲙ̄ⲛⲧⲛⲟⲉⲓⲕ ϣⲱⲡⲉ ⲙ̄ⲙⲛ̄ⲛ̄ⲥⲱⲥ ϥⲱⲧⲃⲉ	What sort of nobility is this? First adultery occurred, then murder!

---

[34] See *Hyp. Arch.* 94.2-18.

ⲁⲩⲱ ⲁⲩϫⲡⲟϥ ⲉⲃⲟⲗ 2Ⲛ	And he was born of adultery; for
ⲦⲘⲚⲦⲚⲞⲈⲒⲔ ⲚⲈ ⲠϢⲎⲢⲈ ⲄⲀⲢ	he was the son of the snake.
Ⲙ̄ϤⲞϥ ⲠⲈ	
ⲆⲒⲀ ⲦⲞⲨⲦⲞ ⲁϥϣⲱⲡⲈ	Therefore he became a murderer
Ⲛ̄2ⲀⲦⲂ̄ⲢⲰⲘⲈ Ⲛ̄ⲐⲈ Ⲙ̄ⲠⲈϥⲔⲈⲈⲒⲰⲦ	like his father, and slew his
ⲁⲩⲱ ⲁϥⲘⲞⲨⲞⲨⲦ Ⲙ̄ⲠⲈϥⲤⲞⲚ	brother.[35]

The premise of the passage is that Cain's defect is linked to his father's defect. The passage begins with a discussion of the inadequacy of Adam's creation in Genesis 2.7. Modeling a being from clay results in a statue, a doll, not a creature capable of reproduction according to its kind. Adam is unable to pass on his nobility because he did not really possess it: his offspring are morally monsters. The fault lies in the way Adam was made and implies the same failure of the creator to bestow a nature which could be passed on.

The second half of the passage shifts to another tradition about human origins. Rather than failing to inherit what his father only appeared to have, Cain did inherit his father's nature: but his father was not Adam, but the snake![36] In this passage, the creator does not appear except in the implication in the first part that Adam was inherently mis-made; the second part extends the biblical themes of the snake's disastrous temptations and Cain's sin by asserting that the snake seduced Eve and so became the father of Cain. There are resonances here with the story in Genesis 6 about the Nephilim seducing human women, but stronger resonances with stories in the *Apocryphon of John, Apocalypse of Adam,* and (with a somewhat different twist) *Hypostasis of the Archons,* in which the craftsman or rulers of some kind father some of Eve's children.

Another of the three revisionistic retellings occurs on page 70. The passage is lacunose toward the end, but the first eight lines deal with the giving of Adam's soul and, separately, his spirit—the latter is said to be his mother. The undamaged text seems a little garbled here, but some

[35] *Gos. Phil.* 60.35-61.12.
[36] In line 9 there is an element which does not appear in Layton's translation above: -ⲔⲈ-, which can mean "other" or, just as often, can merely emphasize—translatable (if at all) as "too" or "as well". If we understand it here in its emphasizing function, we might say "just like his father." If, on the other hand, we take -ⲔⲈ- in its sense of "other" or "another," the phrase reads "his other father." If the latter could be shown to be the case, we would have caught a redactor in an attempt to harmonize two explanations of Cain's flaw which were felt to be incompatible! In either case, the explanations are distinct and rest on conflicting accounts of Cain's parentage.

thing very much like the stories in which Sophia sneaks the spirit into Adam while his creator is unaware must underlie the passage.

The third revisionistic treatment of Genesis deals with the tree of gnosis and appears on pages 73 and 74. The text is full of lacunas at the bottom of page 73, and may also be a confused or corrupt translation. In it, Adam was placed in a defective paradise with a malfunctioning tree of knowledge, identified with the law, which killed him. Its author understands a present and future tree of knowledge to function in the opposite way, bestowing life. The positive valuation of gnosis could fit with any number of traditions, but the negative valuation of paradise—and, implicitly, its creator—and the Law put this passage clearly outside of the Thomas tradition. The double bind created by the Law is presented in terms reminiscent of, and probably dependent on, Romans 7: "The law was the tree. It is able to impart acquaintance of good and evil; and it neither made him (that is, Adam) cease from evil nor allowed him to be in the good."

The most explicit reference to an ignorant creator in the *Gospel according to Philip* occurs on page 75:

ⲀⲠⲔⲟⲤⲘⲟⲤ ϢⲰⲠⲈ ⲘⲚ ⲞⲨⲠⲀⲢⲀⲠⲦⲰⲘⲀ	The world came into being through a transgression.
ⲠⲈⲚⲦⲀϨⲦⲀⲘⲒⲟϤ ⲄⲀⲢ ⲚⲈϤⲞⲨⲰϢ ⲀⲦⲀⲘⲒⲟϤ ⲈϤⲟ ⲚⲀⲦⲦⲀⲔⲞ ⲀⲨⲰ ⲚⲀⲐⲀⲚⲀⲦⲞⲤ	For the agent that made it wanted to make it incorruptible and immortal.
ⲀϤϨⲈ ⲈⲂⲞⲗ ⲀⲨⲰ ⲘⲠⲈϤⲘⲈⲦⲈ ⲀⲐⲈⲗⲠⲒⲤ	That agent fell, and did not attain what was expected.
ⲚⲈⲤϢⲞⲞⲠ ⲄⲀⲢ ⲀⲚ ⲚϬⲒ ⲦⲘⲚⲦⲀⲦⲦⲈⲔⲞ ⲘⲠⲔⲟⲤⲘⲟⲤ	For the world's incorruptibility was not;
ⲀⲨⲰ ⲚⲈϤϢⲞⲞⲠ ⲀⲚ ⲚϬⲒ ⲦⲘⲚⲦⲀⲦⲦⲀⲔⲞ ⲘⲠⲈⲚⲦⲀϨⲦⲀⲘⲒⲈ ⲠⲔⲟⲤⲘⲟⲤ	furthermore, the incorruptibility of the agent that made the world was not.
ⲤϢⲞⲞⲠ ⲄⲀⲢ ⲀⲚ ⲚϬⲒ ⲦⲘⲚⲦⲀⲦⲦⲀⲔⲞ ⲚⲚ2ⲂⲎⲨⲈ ⲀⲗⲗⲀ ⲚⲚϢⲎⲢⲈ	For there is no such thing as the incorruptibilty of things—only of offspring.
ⲀⲨⲰ ⲘⲚ ⲞⲨϨⲰⲂ ⲚⲀϢϪⲒ ⲚⲞⲨⲘⲚⲦⲀⲦⲦⲀⲔⲞ ⲈϤⲦⲘϢⲰⲠⲈ ⲚϢⲎⲢⲈ	And no thing can receive incorruptibility unless it is an offspring:
ⲠⲈⲦⲈ ⲘⲚ ϬⲞⲘ ⲆⲈ ⲘⲘⲞϤ ⲈϪⲒ ⲠⲞⲤϢ ⲘⲀⲗⲗⲞⲚ ϤⲚⲀϢϯ ⲀⲚ	that which cannot receive (it) certainly cannot bestow (it).[37]

---

[37] *Gos. Phil.* 75.2-14.

The first half of this passage alludes to a common gnostic mythology of origins. Its high level of abstraction makes it impossible to attach to any particular version of the myth. The reader is presumed to be acquainted with the creation stories involving Sophia and her Craftsman son, and the disappointing outcomes of their antics, but the details are not at the focus of attention here.

The principle of defective creation serves to preface the last two statements contrasting "things" and "offspring." The making of perishable things belongs to the realm of transgression, corruptibility and mortality. Offspring, metaphorically understood, belong outside the realm of "creation" and its shortcomings. Offspring are of another order of being, and show it not only by their incorruptibility but also by their ability to bestow what they have received. The passage is one of a number in the *Gospel according to Philip* which muse on the idea of procreation, as distinct from creation, transposed into a spiritual sphere.

These passages share the use of "classical" or "Sethian" concepts and imagery: the ignorant creator, a Sophia with some qualities of the trickster. They come from a tradition which was in conflict with traditions tracing their authority to apostles, so they belong neither with the "Thomas" materials discussed above, nor with the Valentinian movement.

TWO PASSAGES RELATED TO THE VALENTINIAN BLOCK

Two passages, one on pages 53 and 54, and the other on pages 56 and 57, stand out among the materials in the first three quarters of the *Gospel according to Philip* for their length, their rhetorical approach, their high degree of sophistication, and their opinions. Both combine vivid, concrete imagery with abstraction; in both, mythological motifs and philosophical reflections alike clothe an underlying mysticism of radical simplicity. These features correspond to those of the material which makes up all (or nearly all) of the final quarter of the document. The two passages seem to be isolated excerpts derived from the same source as that underlying the final quarter.

A reflection on language begins at 53.14 and continues through 54.31, fully one and a half manuscript pages. It opens with a statement that duality is only apparent, not real. Polar opposites—those involved in ethical and mystical imagery, at that—are declared to be brothers or siblings, an image implying derivation from the same source. This implication is underlined by the following statement that such opposites will be dissolved into their original source. This is then contrasted with the indissoluble, eternal nature of things which are above the world. The passage then turns explicitly to language, the source of these false oppositions, and particularly to the deceptive nature of theological and ecclesiological terminology. Although such words are meant to refer to realities, they create unreal images in the minds of those who use them. Another sort of language could be imagined: a language of the eternal realm, which could not be used in the world, which not only does not deceive, but which creates.[38] This paradoxical anti-language consists of only one word, but it is enough: the name of the Father. Bestowed by the Father on the Son, it allows the Son in turn to become father; some humans possess this name as well, but do not speak it. The imagery of the name of the Father as the single name which is not only real but creative is closely akin to the extended meditation on the name of the Father running from *Gospel of Truth* 38.6 to 41.2. The *Gospel according to Philip* nevertheless goes on to assert that even the deceptive and multiple words encountered in the world tend toward truth—for language, with its faults, is the loving accommodation of truth to our nature, allowing us to express at least an approximation of truth by means of multiplicity. A playfully mythological development follows, paralleling this: the rulers tampered with language, misassigning the names of the good and the non-good, mixing up the polar oppositions of the opening of this passage. Their scheme backfires, however: this ruse simply creates a critical awareness of the limitations of language, and a corresponding caution which allows humans to evade their grasp.

The passage is the work of a flamboyant thinker. Its author has dared to relativize the imagery of ethics, mysticism, theology, and ecclesiology, but has done so in order to present a mystical and intellectual piety. In the final, mythological section, the rulers are depicted as malevolent, but their defeat is contained in their actions themselves, and requires no adversarial activity, no precautionary measures, no ruse or trickery, no powerful figure's protection. Their plan melts away on its own, in a way paralleling images in the *Gospel of Truth* of light replacing darkness, waking consciousness replacing nightmare and panic: here, the deceptions of language melt away before the consciousness of their relativity,

---

[38] Plato's *Cratylus* 439 C traces some of the capacity of language to confuse rather than illumine to the fact that the referents of words are themselves unstable, and to the mistaken opinion held by their makers that all is in flux.

a consciousness which they themselves help to create. Salvation is found by mystical awareness of the utter simplicity at the heart of reality; the obstacles to that awareness are clothed only loosely in mythical, demonic imagery, which cannot help but dissolve into nothingness. Only a thoroughly self-assured writer, with a flair for combining the abstract with vivid mythological and experiential imagery, such as Valentinus seems to have been, would be likely to write such a mythological denouement to an abstract discussion of the nature of language. While the underlying mysticism of this passage is based on simplicity, its application here to the nature of language seems to be addressed to an audience of some intellectual sophistication.

The passage from 56.26 to 57.19 begins with a vivid image involving a seemingly naive fear about the resurrection: some people are afraid they may arise naked. This is immediately softened into a more realistic conceptuality: they are afraid they may somehow arise without a body, they look toward a resurrection of the body. More teasing involving the chasm between these two images follows: those wearing the flesh are naked (in a sense which will be developed later: lacking in something essential), but of course only those wearing the flesh could be literally naked (in the sense of having an unclothed, exposed body). Such playful mockery is better calculated to instruct those who basically agree than to convert an opponent.

The passage continues, giving another image, then withdrawing it. The body we are wearing will not inherit the kingdom of God, but Jesus' flesh, along with his blood, will. An image of the eucharist is offered— by eating and drinking Jesus' flesh and blood one can come to have a different sort of body, one which could be resurrected. But the image, offered both in the words of this passage's author and those of Jesus from John 6.53, is then revalued:

Ⲇⲓⲁ ⲦⲞⲨⲦⲞ ⲠⲈⲬⲀϤ ⲬⲈ ⲠⲈⲦⲀⲞⲨⲰⲘ ⲀⲚ ⲚⲦⲀⲤⲀⲢⲌ ⲀⲨⲰ ⲚϤⲤⲰ ⲘⲠⲀⲤⲚⲞϤ ⲘⲚⲦⲀϤ ⲰⲚⲆ ⲆⲢⲀⲓ ⲚⲆⲎⲦⲀϤ	Therefore he said, "He who does not eat my flesh and drink my blood does not have life within him."
ⲀϢ ⲦⲈ ⲦⲈϤⲤⲀⲢⲌ ⲠⲈ ⲠⲖⲞⲄⲞⲤ ⲀⲨⲰ ⲦⲈϤⲤⲚⲞϤ ⲠⲈ ⲠⲠⲚⲀ ⲈⲦⲞⲨⲀⲀⲂ ⲠⲈⲚⲦⲀⲆⲬⲒ ⲚⲀⲈⲒ ⲞⲨ(Ⲛ)ⲦⲈϤ ⲦⲢⲞⲫⲎ ⲀⲨⲰ ⲞⲨⲚⲦⲀϤ ⲤⲰ ⲆⲒ ⲂⲤⲰ	What is meant by that? His "flesh" means the Word, and his "blood" means the Holy Spirit: whoever has received these has food, and has drink and clothing.[39]

---

[39] *Gos. Phil.* 57.3-8.

Translators and commentators have sometimes taken this as a eucharistic passage,[40] but the quotation from John 6 is interpreted in explicitly non-sacramental terms. From here, the passage's author goes on to make explicit his or her disagreement with both the position that the flesh will arise and with the position that it will not, or that only the spirit will arise. What will arise is Jesus' flesh (and hence those clothed in it), but a eucharistic understanding of this is denied, and an understanding of Jesus' flesh and blood as Word and Holy Spirit is asserted in its place. This position differs from the position that only the spirit arises, in that here, the power to arise is derived from intimate contact with Jesus, and a concomitant reception and incorporation of Word and Holy Spirit. This playful advocacy of an "impossible" excluded middle is a sophisticated rhetorical maneuver.

The inclusion of "clothing" along with food and drink is interesting: the clothing in a white robe after baptism is a minor element in some relatively early Syrian initiation rites, while the image of the oil or the water as a garment clothing the person is prominently featured in the understanding of the change wrought by initiation in several. By including "clothing" along with food and drink, our author extends his spiritualized interpretation of John 6:53 and the eucharist to an important metaphor associated with Christian initiation: whoever has received the "Word" and the "Holy Spirit" has the effect sought from baptism as well as that of the eucharist.

This complex and ambivalent use of sacramental imagery is similar to that found in the final quarter of the text, where (as here) such images are introduced and developed to convey an idea, but ultimately transcended. The multiple distinctions made here, and the complex deployment of imagery, again suggest a sophisticated audience.

This perspective of 56.26-57.19 is in sharp contrast to the sacramental perspective of 57.22-27, interpreted above as a passage from the "Thomas" tradition. In that passage, (1) visible things (such as human bodies) are sanctified; (2) sacraments work on two levels at once: their visible element sanctifies the visible, while their invisible element sanctifies the invisible; (3) the invisible elements in question are the heavenly exemplars of visible ones, rather than unrelated graces.

---

[40] See, for example, Wilson, *The Gospel of Philip*, 87-89; Ménard, *L'Évangile*, 147-148; Layton, *The Gnostic Scriptures*, 333.

A single statement intervenes between 56.26-57.19 and 57.22-27. It reads: "In this world those who wear garments are superior to the garments; in the kingdom of heavens the garments are superior to those who put them on." This has some connections with the imagery of argument preceding it: the metaphor of garments is related to the discussion of "wearing" the flesh; the inclusion of "clothing" along with food and drink prevents this statement from seeming jarring. The passage is, however, reminiscent of early Syrian initiatory imagery, and is very strongly reminiscent of the Hymn of the Pearl contained in the *Acts of Thomas*; moreover, it seems to propose an image-type relationship between the baptismal garments and heavenly garments. It seems probably that 57.19-22 was juxtaposed redactionally with the argument which precedes it.

SUMMARY

While not all assignments are equally secure, we have identified three strands of tradition within the *Gospel according to Philip,* which represent material drawn from three sources or groups of sources.

One such strand can be linked to the Thomas tradition of early Christianity, principally by means of quotations and allusions, a shared and highly distinctive understanding of sacramental functioning, and a tendency to view anointing as essential to Christian initiation and the water bath as less important or optional. Some of the pro-apostolic passages belong here, and possibly some of the material based on Semitic etymologies as well.

Two extended passages near the beginning of the work seem to correspond to the material of the final nine pages. It is recognized principally by its longer coherent units, high level of sophistication, distinctive use of imagery and rhetoric, and an ambivalent interest in the sacraments. These passages, like the final quarter, seem to derive from an early or a conservative variety of Valentinianism.

Six more passages may not derive from a single source, but have been provisionally grouped together because they show characteristics which are at odds with what we know about the Thomas tradition: open hostility toward "apostles" and their followers, teachings about the fallen Sophia, and revisionistic retellings of the creation story from Genesis which are harshly critical of the creator. One of these shows verbal similarities with the *Hypostasis of the Archons*; all belong, if not to a single source or tradition, a considerable distance across the gnostic spectrum from Thomas Christianity and from the elegantly simple mysticism of the "primitive" Valentinian material.

We have already encountered a number of organizing principles in the course of examining this material; these will be the focus of the next chapter.

PART THREE

THE *GOSPEL ACCORDING TO PHILIP* AS A COLLECTION

INTRODUCTION TO PART THREE

This final section will survey the characteristics which the *Gospel according to Philip* shares with other collections of late antiquity, and will attempt to clarify the ways in which such a document can be studied.

Chapter 10 returns to the organizing practices examined in chapter 4 and uses them to illuminate the structures of the *Gospel according to Philip*—including some aspects of it which have been claimed as evidence that the document cannot be a collection but must have had a single author.

Chapter 11 speculates, briefly, on the particular kind of recombinant mythography the collector of the *Gospel according to Philip* practiced, and the questions and criteria he or she seems to have used in selecting material for inclusion.

CHAPTER TEN

A COLLECTION AMONG COLLECTIONS

The range of phenomena from unedited personal notebooks, through minimally edited miscellanies, to carefully edited collections encompasses documents shaped almost wholly by chance and by practical considerations, and also documents belonging to self-consciously literary genres and subgenres. Many of the latter imitated the characteristics of private notebooks as well as earlier literary models. Because all such works were embedded in a matrix of closely related possibilities, "generic experimentation" did not require great originality or daring. Genres and subgenres mutated easily and rapidly within such a generic field, and as a consequence, this field was crisscrossed by the trajectories of their evolution. Many of the characteristics and organizing principles employed within this generic field can also be traced in the *Gospel according to Philip.*

This document lacks a narrative frame. It does not show much grouping of its materials according to either their formal characteristics or their content. It therefore belongs to the less deliberately "literary" end of the spectrum, along with genuine notebooks such as Pliny's private notes or Clement's *Excerpta ex Theodoto*, as well as collections like the works about which Gellius and Pliny complained, which preserve (or imitate) the circumstantial order of collecting of notebooks.

On the other hand, some passages in the *Gospel according to Philip* show signs of deliberate editorial activity, including, in places, editorial activity of a very considerable sophistication. This activity may sometimes have been the work of the compiler of our document and, at other times, have been contained in his or her sources. Further, as we have seen, collectors sometimes found organizing principles present in their sources and extended them beyond their original scope and materials, as was the case with the successive editors of the *Greek Anthology,* and with the traditions related to the *Sentences of Sextus.*

This makes for a messy evidentiary situation, which must be treated cautiously. Ideally, we would like to find specific organizational principles applied to groups of passages clearly derived from disparate sources, showing the activity of the compiler/editor of the present document, and (perhaps) other specific organizational principles restricted to materials from a single source only, representing authorial or redactorial markings already present in that source. Such clarity may be attained at some future stage in the investigation of the *Gospel according to Philip*, but I am not able to offer it here. Nevertheless, a number of examples of organizing principles documented in other composite works are easily found. They identify many large and small structures in the work as structures formed by widely used compilatory practices.

The relative simplicity of these practices does not imply that the excerpts themselves were, or were regarded as, trite; nor does it imply that the processes of their combination, because they can be described by formulae, were therefore thoughtless and "mechanical." As argued in chapter 5, some of the redactional principles of reorganization and juxtaposition common to multiple kinds of collections became heuristic as well as editorial tools in the hands of gnostic thinkers. Materials already regarded as conveying important truths were juxtaposed, perhaps systematically, in a search for further insight. Nonetheless, the mechanisms of rearrangement and juxtaposition were shared with other collectors and compilers in the late ancient world.

ORGANIZING PRINCIPLES IN THE *GOSPEL ACCORDING TO PHILIP*

Repeated Word Linkages, Simple and Complex

The term "catch word association" is a label which has lead to many misunderstandings, because (1) it covers a number of different phenomena, and (2) it carries with it, at least for some readers, a prejudgment about the nature of these phenomena, namely, that items so joined have no other connection with each other. The same kinds of linkages that tend to be called "catch word associations" when they occur in a multi-source wisdom collection (the *Sentences of Sextus*, for example) are more likely to be identified as rhetorical devices when they appear in an original work. Curiously, the more specific names for such phenomena are applied in both cases: anaphora, chiasmus, climax, sorites, and the like. The deployment of these devices can range from the crudely mechanical to the subtly sophisticated. We need a term for the group of rhetorical devices that involve the repetition of one or more words, and "catch word association" can serve, if we remember to see in it neither a judgment about the origins of the material in which it appears nor an observation that no other link is present, nor yet that only a crude kind of verbal association is being made.

The *Gospel according to Philip* begins with a series of potentially independent units, each grammatically complete in itself, each couched in a deliberately enigmatic style, and each involving one or more pairs of antithetical terms. In their present state, these units have been arranged in such a way as to suggest a chain of loosely analogous relationships between each antithesis and the next. The analogies are far from perfect, and their imperfection invites the reader to ponder their similarities and differences, to play with equating each pair of terms with the next pair, to test their potential interchangeability, or to limit his or her construal of each pair by the senses it has (or might have) in common with the previous or next pair. A hermeneutical situation is set up which is involving in the extreme, as most commentators on the document have noted.

The passage is a breathtakingly elegant and complex example of multiple, paired catch word connections. Nevertheless, a catena of statements involving paired opposites provocatively related to each other does not necessarily cloak a preexisting esoteric doctrine. Such a catena can be created, with a some effort, by taking an assortment of loosely related excerpts, each drawing a contrast, removing them from any clarifying context, and arranging them so that those which bear suggestive analogies to each other are juxtaposed. Below, the antithetical pairs are set in the far right column.

51.29-52.2

ΟΥ2ЄΒΡΑΙΟϹ Ṗ̄ΡШΜЄ	A Hebrew makes a	Hebrew/
[Ш]ΑЧΤΑΜΙЄ 2ЄΒΡΑΙΟϹ ΑΥШ	Hebrew, and such a	proselyte
ШΑΥΜΟΥΤЄ [ЄΝΑ]ЄΙ	person is called a	
Ñ̄ΤЄЄΙΜΙΝЄ ΧЄ ΠΡΟϹΗΛΥΤΟϹ	convert. But a convert	make or
ΟΥΠ[ΡΟϹΗ]ΛΥΤΟϹ ΔЄ	does not make a	create/
ΜΑЧΤΑΜΙЄ ΠΡΟϹΗΛΥΤΟϹ	convert. [. . .] are as	exist
[. . .] Є ΜЄ(Ν) ϹЄШΟΟΠ Ñ̄ΘЄ	they [. . .] and they	
ЄΤΟΥШ[. . .] ΑΥШ ϹЄΤΑΜЄΙΟ	make others [. . .] is	
Ñ̄2Ñ̄ΚΟΟ[ΥЄ. . . ΔЄ] ΜΟΝΟ[Ν	enough that they exist.	
ЄϹ]ΡШШЄ ЄΡΟΟΥ ШΙΝΑ		
ЄΥΝΑШШΠЄ		

52.2-5

Π[2Μ]Ϩ̅Α̅Λ ΜΟΝΟΝ ΕϤϢΙΝΕ
ΑϤ̅ΕΛΕΥΘΕΡΟ[C] ΜΑϤϢΙΝΕ
ΔΕ Ν̅CΑ ΤΟΥCΙΑ
Μ̅ΠΕϤΧΟ[ΕΙ]C ΠϢΗΡΕ ΔΕ ΟΥ
ΜΟΝΟΝ ΧΕ ϤΟ Ν̅ϢΗΡΕ ΑΛΛΑ
ΤΚΛΗΡΟΝΟΜΕΙΑ Μ̅ΠΕΙШΤ
ϢΑϤCΑϨϤ̅ Ν̅CШϤ

All that a slave wants is to be free; the slave does not hope for the riches of its master. But a child is not merely a child; rather, the child lays claim to the father's legacy.

slave/ (free) son

hope for/ lay claim to

freedom/ inheritance (or οὐσία)

52.6-15

ΝΕΤϤ̅ΚΛΗΡΟΝΟΜΕΙ
Ν̅ΝΕΤΜΟΟΥΤ Ν̅ΤΟΟΥ ϨШΟΥ
CΕΜΟΟΥΤ ΑΥШ
ΕΥΚΛΗΡΟΝΟΜΕΙ
Ν̅ΝΕΤΜΟΟΥΤ
ΝΕΤϤ̅ΚΛΗΡΟΝΟΜΕΙ
Μ̅ΠΕΤΟΝϨ Ν̅ΤΟΟΥ CΕΟΝϨ
ΑΥШ CΕϤ̅ΚΛΗΡΟΝΟΜΕΙ
Μ̅ΠΕΤΟΝϨ ΜΝ̅ ΝΕΤΜΟΟΥΤ
ΝΕΤΜΟΟΥΤ
ΜΑΥϤ̅ΚΛΗΡΟΝΟΜΕ Λ̅ΛΑΑΥ
ΠШC ΓΑΡ ΠΕΤΜΟΟΥΤ
ϤΝΑΚΛΗΡΟΝΟΜΕΙ
ΠΕΤΜΟΟΥΤ
ΕϤϢΑΚΛΗΡΟΝΟΜΕΙ
Μ̅ΠΕΤΟΝϨ ϤΝΑΜΟΥ ΑΝ
ΑΛΛΑ ΠΕΤΜΟΟΥΤ ΕϤΝΑШΝϨ
Ν̅ϨΟΥΟ

Those who inherit dead things are also dead, and what they inherit are dead things. Those who inherit the living are alive, and they inherit both the living and the things that are dead. Dead things inherit nothing, for how could a dead thing inherit anything? If a dead person inherits the living, that person will not die, but rather will greatly live.

dead/ living

inheriting dead things/ inheriting that which lives

52.15-19

ΟΥϨΕΘΝΙΚΟC Ρ̅ΡШΜΕ
ΜΑϤΜΟΥ Μ̅ΠΕϤШΝϨ ΓΑΡ
ΕΝΕϨ ϨΙΝΑ ΕϤΝΑΜΟΥ
ΠΕΝΤΑϨΠΙCΤΕΥΕ ΕΤΜΕ
ΑϤШΝϨ ΑΥШ ΠΑΪ
ϤϬΝ̅ΔΥΝΕΥΕ ΕΜΟΥ ϤΟΝϨ ΓΑΡ

A gentile does not die, for the gentile has never become alive so as to die. One who has believed in the truth has become alive; and this person runs the risk of dying, because of being alive.

gentile/ believer

has not lived/ lives and so risks death

52.19-21

ΧΙΝ̅ ΠϨΟΟΥ Ν̅ΤΑ ΠΧ̅C̅ ΕΙ
CΕCШΝΤ Μ̅ΠΚΟCΜΟC
CΕϤ̅ΚΟCΜΕΙ Ν̅Μ̅ΠΟΛΕΙC CΕϤΙ
Μ̅ΠΕΤΜΟΟΥΤ ΕΒΟΛ

Since Christ came, the world has been created, cities have been organized, and the dead have been buried.

(implicit before and after)

activities of life/ burial of dead

52.21-24

ⲚϨⲞⲞⲨ ⲚⲈⲚϢⲞⲞⲠ
ⲚϨⲈⲂⲢⲀⲒⲞⲤ ⲚⲈⲚⲞ ⲚⲞⲢⲪⲀⲚⲞⲤ
ⲚⲈⲨⲚⲦⲀⲚ ⲚⲦⲘⲘⲀⲀⲨ
ⲚⲦⲀⲢⲚϢⲰⲠⲈ ⲆⲈ
ⲚⲬⲢⲎⲤⲦⲒⲀⲚⲞⲤ ⲀⲈⲒⲰⲦ ϨⲒ
ⲘⲀⲀⲨ ϢⲰⲠⲈ ⲚⲀ(Ⲛ)

When we were Hebrews we were orphans with (only) our mother, but when we became Christians we got father and mother.

Hebrews/ Christians

orphans/ children with father

52.25-35

ⲚⲈⲦⲤⲒⲦⲈ ϨⲚ ⲦⲠⲢⲰ ϢⲀⲨⲰⲤϨ
ϨⲘ ⲠϢⲰⲘ ⲦⲠⲢⲰ ⲠⲈ
ⲠⲔⲞⲤⲘⲞⲤ ⲠϢⲰⲘ ⲠⲈ
ⲠⲔⲈⲀⲒⲰⲚ ⲘⲀⲢⲚⲤⲒⲦⲈ ϨⲘ
ⲠⲔⲞⲤⲘⲞⲤ ⲬⲈⲔⲀⲀⲤ
ⲈⲚⲚⲀⲰϨϨ ϨⲘ ⲠϢⲰⲘ ⲆⲒⲀ
ⲦⲞⲨⲦⲞ ϢϢⲈ ⲈⲢⲞⲚ
ⲈⲦⲘⲦⲢⲚϢⲖⲎⲖ ϨⲚ ⲦⲠⲢⲰ
ⲠⲒⲈⲂⲞⲖ ϨⲚ ⲦⲠⲢⲰ ⲠⲈ ⲠϢⲰⲘ
ⲈⲢϢⲀ ⲞⲨⲀ ⲆⲈ ⲰⲤϨ ϨⲚ
ⲦⲈⲠⲢⲰ ⲈϥⲚⲀⲰⲤϨ ⲀⲚ ⲀⲖⲖⲀ
ⲈϥⲚⲀϨⲰⲖⲈ ϨⲰⲤ ⲠⲀⲈ[Ⲓ
Ⲛ]ⲦⲈⲈⲒⲘⲈⲒⲚⲈ ⲈϥⲚⲀⲦⲈⲨⲈ
ⲔⲀⲢⲠⲞⲤ [ⲚⲀϤ] ⲀⲚ ⲞⲨ
ⲘⲞⲚⲞⲚ ⲈϥⲚⲚⲎⲨ ⲈⲂⲞ[Ⲗ. . .]
ⲀⲖⲖⲀ ϨⲘ ⲠⲔⲈⲤⲀⲂⲂⲀⲦⲞⲚ
[. . . Ⲟ]ⲨⲀⲦⲔⲀⲢⲠⲞⲤ ⲦⲈ

Whoever sows in the winter reaps in the summer. "Winter" means the world; "summer" means the other realm. Let us sow in the world so that we might reap in the summer. For this reason we ought not to pray in the winter. What emerges from winter is the summer. But if one reaps in the winter, one will not acutally reap but only pluck out young plants, for such will not bear a crop. Not only does it come [. . .] but even on the sabbath   [. . .] is barren.[1]

sow/reap

winter/ summer

this world/ the other realm

reaping/ plucking up

fruitful/ barren

While pairs of opposites are not infrequent in the material contained in the *Gospel according to Philip*, this section is by a very wide margin the densest concatenation of paired oppositions anywhere in the document. Its prominent placement at the beginning of the document has lured a number of commentators to greatly overestimate the dominance of this, as principle of composition or as mode of thought, in their understanding of the *Gospel according to Philip*.[2]

Beyond the aggregation of teachings containing provocatively similar antitheses, the passage is given a further sense of coherence by the use of multiple associating words. As a rhetorical figure used in arrangements of collected materials, it is very similar to one of the ordering principles

---

[1] *Gos. Phil.* 51.29-52.35.
[2] See chapter 2, especially the discussion there of Gaffron.

Miriam Lichtheim isolated in the *Instruction of Ankhsheshonqy*.[3] Here, of course, the individual units of text are longer, but a similar network of linking words spreads through it. Note that some, but not all, of the paired oppositions form part of this network. Only a few oppositions are repeated immediately, forcing the reader to look beyond their particular referents to the analogy of the successive series of pairs. When a pair is, at some length, repeated, it is sometimes transformed as well.

The opening section introduces the contrasts Hebrew/proselyte and make/exist, both of which will become involved in the associative web. In section 52.2-5, the word used for the master's "estate," οὐσία, also means "being," forming an associative connection back to "exist" in 51.29-52.2, although there is no logical connection, since that mere existence seems negative, while this evokes all the richness of the God's being. The sense of "estate" or "riches" is logically connected to the new key word, "inherit/inheritance." The section 52.6-15 rings multiple changes on the themes of "inheritance" and "death." "Gentile/believer" in 52.15-19 recalls the "Hebrew/proselyte" opposition (in 51.29-52.2), and "die/live" is continued in the form of "die/become alive," which is vaguely evocative of the dichotomy "make/exist" (in 51.29-52.2). The new topic of "belief" is introduced, as is a "before-and-after" temporal scheme. In 52.19-21, the topic of "death" recurs, and the unit has a "before-and-after" scheme which is unrelated to that of the last. The new key word "world" (κόσμος) is given verbal but not logical stress by the use of the related verb κοσμέω (Ⲣ̄ⲔⲞⲤⲘⲈⲒ, "organize" or "adorn" [cities]) in the same section. The appearance of "Christ" in 52.19-21 is echoed in "Christians" in 52.21-24, and is linked by conceptual rather than verbal association to the idea of "believing the truth" (in 52.15-19). The unit again involves a "before and after" schema. The key terms "Hebrews" and "father" reappear, the latter linked to "orphans" and its opposite, children with fathers (recalling the "father" and "son" of 52.2-5). 52.25-35 returns to the key term "world" (from 52.19-21), while the ideas of "plucking out" and "barrenness" recall the themes of "death" and "never having been alive." "Sabbath" evokes again the set of terms derived from Judaism: "Hebrews" and "proselytes" (in 51.29-52.2), "Gentiles" (in 52.15-19), and "Hebrews" again (in 52.21-24).

This densely interwoven catena of excerpts occurs at the beginning of our work. The placement of a more tightly constructed sequence of indi-

---

[3] See Lichtheim, *Late Egyptian Wisdom Literature*, 64.-65, and chapter 4 above.

vidual units at the beginning of a work was also found in the *Sentences of Sextus*, where Christian and Pythagorean monostichs were arranged into a sorites. Both seem to be compiled introductions, and both function to announce the interests and approaches of the compilers.

Motif Clusters and Analogous Associations

Pairs and trios of excerpts appear in the *Gospel according to Philip* which seem to be associated by the analogous structures of their argument or presentation. They seldom involve an explicit verbal link. On the other hand, these groupings do not usually seem make any particular point beyond the individual points of their units—or at least, not one that observers agree about.

Other small clusters do not show an analogy in thought or structure, but a similar idea or motif. It is impossible, working (as we must) from the Coptic translation, to be sure whether these were always linked by idea, motif, or image, or whether in the original they might also have been linked by repeated words. Some of them may even have placed a repeated word(s) at the beginning of each unit (resulting in anaphora), or at the end (antistrophe), or even both (anastrophe), or in chiastic or other patterns. Sadly, however, translation inevitably blurs the distinctions between association by the various sorts of verbal figures and association by image or idea.[4]

The mythological ending to the Valentinian meditation on language (*Gos. Phil.* 53.14-54.31) seems to have provided a place for another development on the plans of malevolent powers. The link here is partly a matter of similar ideas and images, partly one of analogous points being made:

ⲁⲛⲁⲣⲭⲱⲛ ⲟⲩⲱϣ ⲁⲡⲁⲧⲁⲧⲁ	The rulers wanted to deceive
ⲙ̄ⲡⲣⲱⲙⲉ ⲉⲧⲉⲓⲁⲏ ⲁⲩⲛⲁⲩ ⲉⲣⲟϥ	humanity, inasmuch as they saw
ⲉⲩⲛ̄ⲧⲁϥ ⲙ̄ⲙⲁⲩ	that it had kinship with truly good
ⲛ̄ⲛⲟⲩⲥⲩⲅⲅⲉⲛⲉⲓⲁ ϣⲁ	things; they took the names of the
ⲛⲉⲧⲛⲁⲛⲟⲩⲟⲩ ⲛⲁⲙⲉ ⲁⲩϥⲓ	good (plur.) and gave them to the
ⲧⲡⲣⲁⲛ ⲛ̄ⲛⲉⲧⲛⲁⲛⲟⲩⲟⲩ ⲁⲩⲧⲁⲁϥ	nongood (plur.),
ⲁⲛⲉⲧⲛⲁⲛⲟⲩⲟⲩ ⲁⲛ	

---

[4] Similarly, translation would have obliterated any alphabetical arrangements, other patterns formed by initial letters or words of units, along with most word-plays.

ⲬⲈⲔⲀⲀⲤ ϨⲒⲦⲚ Ⲣ̄ⲢⲀⲚ
ⲈⲨⲀⲢⲀⲡⲀⲦⲀ ⲘⲘⲞϤ ⲀⲨⲰ
ⲚⲤⲈⲘⲞⲢⲞⲨ ⲈϨⲞⲨⲚ
ⲀⲚⲈⲦⲚⲀⲚⲞⲨⲞⲨ ⲀⲚ ⲀⲨⲰ
ⲘⲘⲚ̄Ⲛ̄ⲤⲰⲤ ⲈϢϪⲈ ⲈⲨⲈⲒⲢⲈ ⲚⲀⲨ
ⲚⲞⲨϨⲘⲞⲦ Ⲛ̄ⲤⲈⲦⲢⲞⲨⲤⲈϨⲰⲞⲨ
ⲈⲂⲞⲖ Ⲛ̄ⲚⲈⲦⲚⲀⲚⲞⲨⲞⲨ ⲀⲚ ⲀⲨⲰ
Ⲛ̄ⲤⲈⲔⲀⲀⲨ Ϩ̄Ⲛ ⲚⲈⲦⲚⲀⲚⲞⲨⲞⲨ
ⲚⲀⲈⲒ ⲚⲈⲨⲤⲞⲞⲨⲚ ⲘⲘⲞⲞⲨ
ⲚⲈⲨⲞⲨⲰϢ ⲄⲀⲢ ⲈⲦⲢⲞⲨϤⲒ
ⲦⲈⲖⲈⲨⲐⲈⲢ[Ⲟ]Ⲥ Ⲛ̄ⲤⲈⲔⲀⲀϤ ⲚⲀⲨ
Ⲛ̄ϨⲘ̄ϨⲀⲖ̄ ϢⲀ ⲈⲚⲈϨ

to deceive humanity by the names
and bind them to the nongood
and—then what a favor they do
for them!—to remove them (the
names) from the nongood and
assign them to the good! These
they were acquainted with: for
they wanted the free to be taken
and enslaved to them in
perpetuity.[5]

ⲞⲨⲚ ϨⲚ̄ⲆⲨⲚⲀⲘⲒⲤ ϢⲞⲞⲡ ⲈⲨⲦϨ̄
[. . .] ⲡⲢⲰⲘⲈ ⲈⲤⲈⲞⲨⲰϢ ⲀⲚ
ⲀⲦⲢⲈϤⲞⲨ[ϪⲀⲈⲒ] ⲬⲈⲔⲀⲀⲤ
ⲈⲨⲚⲀ ϢⲰⲡⲈ ⲈⲨⲘ[. . .]Ⲁ̄ ⲈⲢϢⲀ
ⲡⲢⲰⲘⲈ ⲄⲀⲢ ⲞⲨϪ[ⲀⲈⲒ
Ⲛ̄ⲚⲞⲨ]ⲬϢⲰⲡⲈ Ⲛ̄ϬⲒ ϨⲚ̄ⲐⲨⲤⲒⲀ [. . .]
ⲀⲨⲰ ⲚⲈⲨⲦⲀⲖⲈ ⲐⲎⲢⲒⲞⲚ ⲈϨⲢⲀⲒ
Ⲛ̄Ⲛ̄ⲆⲨⲚⲀⲘⲒⲤ ⲚⲈ [Ϩ]Ⲛ̄[Ⲑ]ⲎⲢⲒⲞⲚ
ⲄⲀⲢ ⲚⲈ ⲚⲈⲦⲞⲨⲦⲈⲖⲞ ⲈϨⲢⲀ̇Ⲓ̇
ⲚⲀ[Ⲩ] ⲚⲈⲨⲦⲈⲖⲞ ⲘⲈⲚ Ⲙ̄ⲘⲞⲞⲨ
ⲈϨⲢⲀ̇Ⲓ̇ ⲈⲨⲞⲚϨ Ⲛ̄ⲦⲀⲢⲞⲨⲦⲈⲖⲞⲞⲨ
ⲆⲈ ⲈϨⲢⲀⲒ̇ ⲀⲨⲘⲞⲨ ⲡⲢⲰⲘⲈ
ⲀⲨⲦⲈⲖⲞϤ ⲈϨⲢⲀⲒ̇ Ⲙ̄ⲡⲚⲞⲨⲦⲈ
ⲈϤⲘⲞⲞⲨⲦ ⲀⲨⲰ ⲀϤⲰⲚϨ

There exist forces that [. . .]
human beings, not wanting them
to [attain salvation], so that they
might become [. . .]. For if human
beings attain salvation, sacrifices
[will not] be made [. . .], and
animals will not be offered up
unto the forces. Indeed, the ones to
whom offerings used to be made
were animals. Now, they were
offered up alive; but when they
had been offered up, they died. A
human being was offered up dead
unto God; and became alive.[6]

The first of these passages serves as a summarizing conclusion, in mythological imagery, to a quite sophisticated discussion of language. Its point is that the rulers tamper with language in order to ensnare humans, but their plan backfires: they only succeed in pointing out the relativity of language, thus freeing their intended victims from taking it too literally. The second passage is quite different in its thrust: it identifies the "forces" with the gods of paganism, abusively notes their animal nature, and states that their power was such that sacrifices of live animals made to them died, whereas sacrifices of dead human beings made to God become alive. The second passage uses different vocabulary to refer to the hostile powers, and seems to make a completely fresh start with its assertion that these powers exist. In fact, this re-introduction of a topic apparently already under discussion is one of the few clear markers of a redac-

---

[5] Gos. Phil. 54.18-31 (translation altered).
[6] *Gos. Phil.* 54. 31-55.5 (translation altered).

tional seam in the *Gospel according to Philip*. The two passages are thus clearly distinct, juxtaposed because of shared concepts. The two share the idea that the rulers or forces are actively hostile to humans, and they both open by presenting this situation in parallel statements:

54.18ff	*54.31ff*
The rulers wanted to deceive humanity,	There exist forces that [. . .] human beings,
inasmuch as they saw that it had kinship with truly good things; . . .	not wanting them to [attain salvation], ...

Different points are made, using different terms, and reflecting different underlying approaches, but both are related to the general category of hostile beings, and both explore the overcoming of such beings.

The next two pairs of examples depend more on the principle of analogy alone.

NE OYⲚ ϢOMTE MOOϢE ⲘN ⲠXOEIC OYOEIϢ NIM MⲀPIⲀ TEϤMⲀⲀY ⲀYⲰ TEϤCⲰNE ⲀYⲰ MⲀⲄⲆⲀⲀHNH TⲀEI ETOYMOYTE EPOC XE TEϤKOINⲰNOC MⲀPIⲀ ⲄⲀP TE TEϤCⲰNE ⲀYⲰ TEϤMⲀⲀY TE ⲀYⲰ TEϤ2ⲰTPE TE	Three women always used to walk with the Lord—Mary his mother, his sister, and the Magdalene, who is called his companion. For "Mary" is the name of his sister and his mother, and it is the name of his partner.[7]
ⲠEIⲰT MⲚ ⲠϢHPE Ⲛ2ⲀⲠⲖOYN NE ⲢⲢⲀN ⲠⲦⲦⲚⲀ ETOYⲀⲀB OYPⲀN TE ⲚⲆIⲠⲖOYN CEϢOOⲠ ⲄⲀP ⲘMⲀ NIM CEⲘⲦⲠCⲀ NTⲦE CEⲘⲦⲠCⲀ MⲠITⲚ CE2Ⲛ ⲠEⲐHⲠ CE2Ⲛ NETOYON2 EBOⲀ ⲠⲦⲦⲚⲀ ETOYⲀⲀB Ϥ2Ⲙ ⲠOYⲰN2 EBOⲀ Ϥ2Ⲙ ⲠCⲀ MⲠITⲚ Ϥ2Ⲙ ⲠEⲐHⲠ Ϥ2Ⲙ ⲠCⲀ NTⲦE	"Father" and "Son" are simple names: "Holy Spirit" is a two-part name. For they exist everywhere— —above, below; in the hidden, in the visible. The Holy Spirit is in the visible, and in the below; and in the hidden, and in the above.[8]

These statements are linked because both deal with a trio of characters, and both discuss the names of those characters in teasing, riddling ways. In each case, the presence of manifest difference in things which can be described in synonymous predicates is at issue.

Another pair depends on the presence of an originating relationship considered over a period of time, and the effects thereof:

---

[7] *Gos. Phil* 59.6-11.
[8] *Gos. Phil* 59.11-18.

ΠΕΤΕΥⲚΤΑϤϤ Ⲛ̄ϬΙ ΠΕΙⲰΤ ΝΑ
ΠϢΗΡΕ ΝΕ ΑΥⲰ Ⲛ̄ΤΟϤ ϨⲰⲰϤ
ΠϢΗΡΕ ΕΝϨΟϹΟΝ ϤΟ Ⲛ̄ΚΟΥΕΙ
ΜΑΥΠΙϹΤΕΥΕ ΝΑϤ ΑΝΕΤΕ ΝΟΥϤ
ϨΟΤΑΝ ΕϤϢΑϢⲰΠΕ Ⲣ̄ΡⲰΜΕ
ϢΑΡΕ ΠΕϤΕΙⲰΤ † ΝΑϤ
ΝΕΤΕΥⲚ̄ΤΑΒϹΕ ΤΗΡΟΥ

What a father owns belongs to his
child. And so long as the child,
too, is little, it will not be entrusted
with its own. When the child
grows up, its father will give it all
that it owns.[9]

ΝΕΤϹΟΡΜ ΝΕΤΕ ΠΠⲚ̄Ⲁ Ⲭ̄ΠΟ
Μ̄ΜΟΟΥ ϢΑΥϹⲰΡΜ ΟΝ ΕΒΟⲖ
ϨΙΤΟΟΤϤ ΔΙΑ ΤΟΥΤΟ ΕΒΟⲖ
ϨΙΤΜ̄ ΠΠⲚ̄Ⲁ ΟΥⲰΤ ϤⳜΕΡΟ Ⲛ̄ϬΙ
ΠΚⲰϨΤ ΑΥⲰ ϤⲰϢⲘ̄

It is the ones who have gone astray
that the spirit gave birth to.
Moreover, they go astray because
of the spirit. Thus from one and
the same spirit the fire is kindled
and quenched.[10]

The first of these units is strongly reminiscent of Gal 4.7 (as well as of
Gos. Phil. 52.2-5); the second is quite distinct, seemingly either blaming
the Spirit for those who "go astray," or defending "going astray" as the
work of the Spirit. The juxtaposition makes one notice more clearly the
implication of the first, that the child is unworthy of trust while young—
perhaps the "going astray" is a temporary thing? But here we have, again,
taken up the invitation to attempt to superimpose the values of the one
onto the other, and make sense of the result. Each of these units could be
used as an extended analogy to generate an unusual interpretation of the
other. Nevertheless, they show no links beyond this provocative paralleling of concepts: there is no syntactic or rhetorical connection between
them, nor any logical development linking them. There is no reason to
believe that they are anything but independent excerpts which have been
creatively juxtaposed.

The clusters of units containing the same motif, especially as seen in
the demotic *Instructions*, the *Garland of Meleager* (and probably that of
Philip, although the evidentiary problems are greater there), and the
Sentences of Sextus show considerable similarity to these pairs. The de-
ployment of the same principles in the *Gospel according to Philip* is,
however, far removed from the cluster of epigrams about grasshoppers in
Meleager, and closer to the thoughtful groupings in the demotic
Instructions and in Sextus. Many of the pairs found in the *Gospel ac-
cording to Philip* are sophisticated, involving second order abstractions.
We are dealing here with a collector for whom this kind of similarity of

---

[9] *Gos. Phil.* 60.1-6.
[10] *Gos. Phil.* 60.6-9.

concept was sometimes more important than either doctrinal content or
literary shape.

Thematic Sequences

Some thematic sequences appear in the *Gospel according to Philip*.
Pages 67 and 68 present a catena of excerpts, all from the Thomas tradition of Christianity and all dealing with sacraments.[11] These units of material are not connected syntactically or rhetorically or logically or in any
other way, except their circling around a general theme. They undoubtedly were once independent texts, or at least independent of each other.

A series of short units on pages 55 and 56 are connected only by all
referring to "the Lord" or "Jesus" or "the Christ." The series begins with a
dominical saying which interprets Jesus' phrase "My father who is in the
heavens" as proof that he must have had an earthly father as well—if not,
there would be no need to specify which father.[12] Another dominical saying follows immediately,[13] and then an etymological exegesis of the
names "Jesus," "Christ," and "the Nazarene" (although it is not one of the
passages which gives good evidence as to the linguistic milieu of its origin).[14] Then follow two doctrinal teachings. Again, these units of text
seem unrelated except by their interest in Jesus.[15]

The *Gospel according to Philip* also contains sequences which are
apparently random, in which each unit seems to be a complete non se-
quitur. These sequences may follow the circumstantial order of collecting, or may artificially imitate it. Pages 61 through 64 are the best example of this "inconsequential" organization, even in the opinions of some
of the most forceful defenders of the document's overall coherence.[16]

The densely sacramental section which begins with the chain of passages on page 67 seems to lose momentum after a few pages. A markedly
increased interest in sacraments continues until the division at the middle
of page 77, with excerpts relating to sacraments in some way making up
over half of the material, but (1) texts unrelated or doubtfully related to

---

[11] *Gos. Phil.* 67.2-68.16. For an analysis of this passage, see chapter 8.

[12] *Gos. Phil.* 55.33-36. The passage is loosely associated with the material on
Mary's conception (with its verbal similarity with *Hypostasis of the Archons*); perhaps
it prompted the small collection which follows it.

[13] *Gos. Phil.* 55.37-56.3.

[14] See chapter 3.

[15] *Gos. Phil.* 56.13-15 and 15-19.

[16] See particularly Giversen and Borchert.

sacraments are included as well; (2) the approaches to the subject broaden; and (3) some clearly non-Thomas material is included, which levels harsh criticism against the creator.[17]

The Division and Dispersal of Source Materials

The interspersing of excerpts from a tradition distinct from the Thomas tradition in the first three-quarters of the *Gospel according to Philip* suggests editorial activity, as do the presence of two Valentinian units (on pages 53-54 and 56-57). Such editorial activity seems to have been motivated by the aesthetic of variety and (roughly) uniform texture. Long blocks of homogenous material were clearly avoided by both Aulus Gellius and Meleager; the sprinkling in of passages involving the fallen Sophia, or sharply critical of the Creator, seems to point to a similar editorial policy in the *Gospel according to Philip*. As we saw in chapter 4, the evidence of documents related to the *Sentences of Sextus* points to a dismantling of compound sentences into briefer, monostichic units. The dissolving of compound and complex sentences also occured in the demotic instructions tradition. A dismantling of materials at the sentence or paragraph level is quite possible in the *Gospel according to Philip* as well: though, if the traditions related to *Sextus* are comparable, such dismantling would not have left any visible traces. Isenberg's basic insight that longer and more cohesive blocks of text have been dismembered and distributed throughout the document is almost certainly accurate, even though the examples he put forward fail to convince. In known examples, a stylistic preference for gnomic brevity controlled such activity.

The *Gospel according to Philip* contains one pair of (loosely) monostichic units:

ⲘⲠⲢ̄ⲔⲀⲦⲀⲪⲢⲞⲚⲈⲒ ⲘⲠⲦ2ⲒⲈⲒⲂ ⲀⲬⲚ̄ⲦⳐ ⲄⲀⲢ ⲘⲚ̄ ⳝ6ⲞⲘ ⲈⲚⲀⲨ ⲈⲠ<Ⲣ̄>ⲢⲞ	Do not despise the lamb, for without it one cannot see the door [or, the king].
ⲘⲚ̄ ⲖⲀⲀⲨ ⲚⲀⳝⳁ ⲠⲈⳑⲞⲨⲞⲈⲒ Ⲉ2ⲞⲨⲚ ⲈⲠⲢ̄ⲢⲞ ⲈⳑⲔⲎⲔⲀ2ⲎⲨ	No one can encounter the king while naked.[18]

If there are others, they have been woven into larger discussions and have disappeared as such. Many of the units in the *Gospel according to*

---

[17] *Gos. Phil.* 70.22-33, 73.28-74.11, 75.2-14.
[18]*Gos. Phil.* 58.14-17.

Philip are quite short; while sense-divisions and paragraph-divisions are both quite disputed, seventeen excerpts take up almost exactly four pages in the long randomly ordered sequence on pages 61-64: an average length of a little under a fourth of a manuscript page. On the other hand, several passages run to over a page (400% of the average length of unit on pages 61-64), and the final section contains several longer passages which are tightly organized. This very substantial variation in the size of the units excerpted is the only characteristic which pertains both to the notebook and the pseudo-notebook examined in chapters 3 and 4 (the *Excerpta ex Theodoto* and the *Attic Nights*), but to none of the other collections examined. It may be a distinguishing mark of the unedited and the lightly edited collection of private notes.

THE *GOSPEL ACCORDING TO PHILIP* AMONG COLLECTIONS

The characteristics isolated (in chapters 3 and 4) from genuine and pretended notebooks and from collections of several kinds may be arranged into the following schema.

1. Inclusion of material extrinsic to excerpts:
    1.1 Introductions:
        1.1.1 Introduction authored for this purpose
        1.1.2 Introduction composed from excerpted material
    1.2 Comments and passages authored by the compiler
        1.2.1 Occasional brief comments on excerpts
        1.2.2 Longer development or rebuttal of ideas in excerpts
        1.2.3 Contextualizing of excerpted material

2 Attribution of excerpted material:
    2.1 Consistent (or nearly so)
    2.2 Sporadic
    2.3 Removed, or source of material obscured

3 The division and rearrangement of excerpted material

4 Length of excerpted units:
    4.1 Unit size:
        4.1.1 Monostichs (or largely monostichs)
        4.1.2 Relatively short units
        4.1.3 Inclusion of some longer units
    4.2 Variation in unit size:

4.2.1 Relatively uniform size
4.2.2 Substantial variation in unit size

5 Order of excerpted units:
    5.1 Apparently random sequences
    5.2 Ordering of excerpts by extrinsic characteristics:
        5.2.1 Order by author/speaker
        5.2.2 Chronological ordering
        5.2.3 Geographical ordering
    5.3 Ordering of excerpts by rhetorical means:
        5.3.1 Clustering of units sharing a motif
        5.3.2 Anaphoric sequences of excerpted units
        5.3.3 Alphabetic sequences of excerpted units
        5.3.4 Formulaic sequences[19]
        5.3.5 Parallel or antithetical pairs of units
        5.3.6 Multiple catchword associations
    5.4 Ordering by logical means
        5.4.1 Thematic sequences or chapters
        5.4.2 Creation of logically coherent sequence from individual units
        5.4.3 Creation of chain syllogisms or sorites from individual units

The distribution of these characteristics in the *Gospel according to Philip* and in the other collections surveyed in chapters 3 and 4 is shown in the table on the next page.

---

[19] Such as lists of a given number of items, or patterned sequence of paradoxes.

The Characteristics and Organizing Principles
of Notebooks and Collections

	Gospel according to Philip	Aulus Gellius Attic Nights	Excerpta ex Theodoto	Instruction of Ankhsheshonqy	Instruction of P. Insinger	Garland of Meleager	Garland of Philip	Plutarch's collections	Pirqe 'Abot	Sentences of Sextus
1.1.1 authored intro		X		X	X	X	X	X	X	
1.1.2 compiled intro	X									X
1.2.1 occ. comments	?	X	X					X	X	
1.2.2 longer dev. ideas	?	X	X					X		
1.2.3 contextualizing		X		1	1			X	X	
2.1 consistant attrib.		X				X	X	X	X	
2.2 sporadic attrib.			X							
2.3 attrib. removed	X			X	X					X
3 division and re-arrangement of units	X	X			X	X	X			X
4.1.1 monostichs				X	X					X
4.1.2 rel. short units	X	X	X			X	X	X	X	
4.1.3 longer units incl.	X	X	X							
4.2.1 rel uniform size				X	X	X	X	X	X	X
4.2.2 substantial variation in size	X	X	X							
5.1 app. random order	X	X		X	X	X	X			X
5.2.1 order by speaker			X					X	X	
5.2.2 chronol. order								X	X	
5.2.3 geog. order								X		
5.3.1 motif clusters	X	X		X	X	X	?		X	X
5.3.2 anaphoric seq.				X	X	X				
5.3.3 alphabetic seq.								X	X	2
5.3.4 rigidly patterned					X				X	
5.2.5 parallel/antithetical pairs	X			X	X	X	?			X
5.3.6 multiple catch-word associations	X			X						
5.4.1 thematic seq.	X	X	X	X	X	X	?	X		X
5.4.2 logically coh. seq.				X	X					X
5.4.3 sorites				X						X

Key: :   X characteristic present   ? characteristic possibly present
      (1) in introductions only   (2) in derived traditions only

The congruence of the *Gospel according to Philip* with the characteristics of this continuum suggests that the work is a notebook which has been rearranged a little, to conform to the aesthetic of an even texture without excessively large blocks of any one author, source or subject—a simple aesthetic which also controlled the organization of the epigram collections of Meleager and Philip, and the organization of the maxims in the *Sentences of Sextus*. The thematic sequences probably reflect both the collector's interests and the thematic coherence of his or her sources. Juxtapositions of conceptually analogous material were determined by the collector's approach to religious speculation, which will be considered in the next chapter. An introduction for the whole has been carefully crafted, however. This, together with the dispersal throughout the first three quarters of the document of small amounts of material at odds with the Thomas tradition, constitute good evidence that some efforts were made to prepare the book for publication. Such a scenario would not be at all unusual in the second or third century, when miscellanies and "pseudo-notebooks" were popular, and the abrupt style of anthologies influenced the way even writers of original material expressed themselves.

SOME IMPLICATIONS OF THIS STUDY

The findings of this study have implications for both the interpretation of the *Gospel according to Philip* and for the understanding of the traditions it represents, particularly in their mutual interactions.

The importance of these findings for the interpretation of the *Gospel according to Philip* is obvious. If there was no one author, and if the materials derive from multiple communities of faith, we cannot talk meaningfully of the document's position, its author's beliefs, or its community's practices (although, of course, these are all possible approaches to material from any one source within it). Unless redactional contributions can be clearly identified and isolated, we cannot talk of the "redactor's meaning," either. Passages from specific sources should be interpreted (1) in relation to other passages from the same source, and (2) in relation to each source's wider tradition. Whenever these cannot be discerned, passages must be treated as isolated materials of unknown provenance, and interpreted accordingly.

Secondly, deciding that the *Gospel according to Philip* is a collection does not place it outside the realm of all coherence, either conceptually or organizationally. The organizing principles characteristic of collections can involve some very substantial artistry, and have the power to explain and illumine some of the most characteristic passages in this document. Moreover, some careful conjecture about the interests and criteria which guided the choice and assembly of these excerpts is also possible.

Thirdly, the discovery of this particular combination of traditions in the *Gospel according to Philip* is important for the history of the relations between some groups of early Christians. Within what seems to be a lightly edited notebook, we have substantial materials from the Thomas tradition, several small excerpts in which material related the *Apocryphon of John* or the *Hypostasis of the Archons* is taken over and given a Christian twist, and some more extended passages in a style and theology similar to Valentinus' fragments or the *Gospel of Truth*. Further insight into the date of this document relative to the development of the traditions on which it drew will be necessary before these data can be fully utilized, but documentary evidence of the confluence of these three traditions should be of considerable interest to investigators of all three.

CHAPTER ELEVEN

ON STUDYING A SOURCEBOOK FOR SPECULATION

There is a tension inherent in the position presented in this volume. A sourcebook for speculation such as the *Gospel according to Philip* offers a strong invitation to speculate, to attempt to trace the possible connections between the diverse materials contained in it. Its materials were chosen both for the individual merits of each excerpt and for their mutual relevance (or possible relevance). Its redaction, though light, strove to create provocative juxtapositions of these excerpts. The "pre-constrained" nature of the borrowed imagery creates a web of apparent inter-relationship and cross-reference between and among its components. Moreover, the excerpts included in the *Gospel according to Philip* were chosen for their potential to shed light on some specific questions, or at least to help focus those questions. To refuse to speculate is to distance one's self from the collector's interests, and to decline the invitation of the redactor.[1]

One may, of course, accept the invitation: but then, for the time being, one has become a gnostic speculator, albeit belated. Since sympathy tends to foster insight, this might be worthwhile to the scholar. But if the document is a sourcebook of provocative materials from which to speculate, rather than the shattered remains of a system born of accomplished speculation, we should take pains to be clear when we are studying the document and when we are, as it were, its dinner guests.

The connections to which these combinations of material seem to point are not made explicit in the work. It is inherently unlikely that anyone now living, turned loose on the same set of provocative but disparate texts as a second or third century gnostic Christian, would make from them the same synthesis, however great their sympathy. It is unlikely that any two gnostic Christians from those times would do so! The variety of scholarly interpretations of this text testifies that there are multiple configurations of its elements possible (as does the difficulty in making any more incisive critique of many of them than "plausible, but

---

[1] I do not mean to imply that they were, or were not, the same person: I am concerned here only with distinguishable functions.

not compelling"). In any case, there is no evidence that the collector/redactor of this material ever made any synthesis from it.

Historical understanding is perhaps doomed always to be anachronistic, a hybrid between one time's sensibilities and another's. But to pursue it at all means to attempt to minimize and transcend this doom, at least when we can see a way to do so. If the *Gospel according to Philip* is a collection, a speculator's sourcebook, it would be desirable to find a way to glean from the text the collector's questions and interests, without extrapolating the answers to which he or she might have come.

The evidence surveyed in this volume suggests that, like the *Excerpta ex Theodoto* in several respects, the *Gospel according to Philip* is an assemblage of materials from multiple sources. One major difference is that the *Gospel according to Philip* has been edited in accordance with some of the principles which were common to published collections of excerpts in late antiquity. A more important difference between the two documents, however, lies in their attitudes toward the material included. Clement mostly excerpted material with which he disagreed, and which he intended to refute, as his interspersed comments make clear. A smaller amount of Clement's material, on the other hand, seems to have been collected with the intention of borrowing or adapting it to his own thought, perhaps the better to persuade those familiar with gnostic ideas. The collector of the *Gospel according to Philip*, in contrast, seems to have had little or no interest in refuting the material collected: while he or she could hardly have agreed with every opinion expressed, each excerpt seems to have been selected for its positive value. (A few excerpts are, themselves, controversial in nature: see, for example, 55.23-36, or 56.15-57.22.)

The apparent lack of interest in controversial issues is a clue that the center of our collector's interest lay elsewhere. Controversies such as those behind the use or non-use of sectarian labels like "Christian," "Hebrew," "apostolic," "perfect," and the like seem to have been of very little interest. Our collector was eclectic in the materials chosen for inclusion.

Themes and concerns which appear repeatedly, especially in materials derived from disparate contexts, form the evidence for the collector's interests. The *Gospel according to Philip* may, of course, also contain other redactorial contributions such as comments and revisions, but we would need to find a way to distinguish them in order to talk meaningfully about the redactor's point of view.

The collector's interests, so far as I can discern them, seem to lie with large patterns of thought, meta-patterns by which possibilities and constellations of possibilities can be organized. Most previous analyses of "Philip's" ideas can be re-read, *mutatis mutandis,* as pointing to the collector's interests. Rather than survey these opinions, I will try to add what I can to them.

What follows is surely conjectural—even speculative—but I have tried to speculate about the document as we have it and its possible functions, rather than about systems which might be made from it. I have tried to speculate as an historian, within the understanding of the *Gospel according to Philip* developed here.

The document is a tinker's collection of odds and ends, an assortment of texts that might come in handy in gnostic *bricolage*. That is, it is composed of passages provocative of new insights and approaches, raw materials for possible syntheses. Nevertheless, it is not an undiscriminating collection of junk: its materials are ones which might come in handy for a very specific task.

The collector of the *Gospel according to Philip* assembled a great deal of material which dealt with, or could be read as dealing with, a particular set of themes, often by means of dichotomies. These dichotomies are not especially unusual in themselves. The connecting themes were not always even present in the passages, as they occurred in their original contexts. They seem to have been chosen for their capacity to allow a certain set of concerns to be read into them; a few already expressed these concerns, but most did not.

The gathering together of these passages formed a new context, however, in which passages could reverberate off each other. Interests and questions from material derived from one source could easily be read into material from another. Some redactional juxtapositions actively encourage new readings. That is, the assembly of such a collection makes—almost forces—a somewhat violent re-reading of its component excerpts.

Placed together like this, very many passages in the *Gospel according to Philip* can be read as circling around the theme of modes of existence. In good gnostic fashion, these are reflections of each other on different levels; by assembling them, our collector was toying with the possibility that they could interpret each other.

Two pairs of antitheses lie close to the heart of the cluster: true God/inferior Demiurge, and procreating/creating. Begetting or emanating (or something like them) is the proper action of the true God; a technical, approximate, and lifeless making is the proper action of the inferior Demiurge. From there, chains of analogy run out to many other dichotomies (some of them originally innocent of such concerns).

The collector who produced the *Gospel according to Philip* seems to have been absorbed with the idea of emanation. This is no surprise: the intricate systems of archons emanating from each other was the feature most apparent to the ancient Christian opponents of gnosticisms, and is extremely conspicuous in a number of the Nag Hammadi texts. It is, moreover, present in middle Platonist thought, and central to Plotinus' schema. It was "in the air" in the second and third centuries.

Gnostics have been stereotyped as an anti-cosmic lot, denying goodness to the visible world and to its creator. While this stereotype contains a great deal of truth, it is not entirely and universally just, of course. The conceptual grounding of this anti-cosmic mind set was one which was susceptible of more benign interpretations as well. Rather than being founded on a radical dualism of opposed powers, several gnostic systems proposed a series of emanations from the high God to successively lower entities, until at some number of removes, something went wrong with the process of emanation itself. Attenuation somehow ended in distortion, perversion—and a world of trouble followed. The key questions on which systems of this type meditate are: what, exactly, went wrong? how actively malevolent is the result? and, how can such a breech be healed?

More originally and perhaps more daringly, our collector has also assembled materials which reflect on the processes of pure and flawed emanation as human possibilities. Again, this is not unusual. The image of sexual reproduction pervades the mythology of many gnostic systems. Aeons appear as syzygies on each level of being, up to (and sometimes including) the high God. Other modes of production are not encountered until the catastrophic events leading to the world outside the pleroma. It is a truism that, in gnostic mythologies, activities depicted in the pleroma point, at least in part, to possibilities open to human nature and human choice. It was never very clear what all this pleromatic reproductive activity meant for human life, however. Ancient rumors of extremes of both ascetic and libertine attitudes toward sexuality in gnostic groups reflect this unclarity as one shared by ancient observers of gnostic phenomena, and probably by gnostic thinkers and communities themselves.

The distinction between creation and procreation, between Artisan-artifact and Parent-offspring, is central to many passages in the *Gospel according to Philip*. It differentiates the Demiurge from God, and also differentiates between the earthly and heavenly modes of human existence. Not only are the origins of different sorts of humans traced to these different modes of "making," but these modes of activity are operative in present human life.

These questions can be read through much of the *Gospel according to Philip*—again, with violence to the original contexts of at least some of these excerpts, but such is the price of speculative collecting and recombinant mythography. Their relevance to the *Gospel according to Philip* is not that they are generally gnostic questions, much less my own, but that they seem to be the level of abstraction at which the document's disparate contents intersect with greatest density.

The collector of the *Gospel according to Philip* sought to address two interrelated problems—the origin and nature of evil in the world, and the nature of the highest possibilities open to human beings—by means of the single paradigm of emanation. There is no answer put forward: just excerpts which help focus the question or offer splinters of insight. Nevertheless, most of the "odds and ends" assembled in this curious text can be seen as texts which show some promise of coming in handy for the illumination of these problems by means of some aspect or analog of the chosen paradigm. Not infrequently, this criterion seems to have relaxed, allowing in some other striking passages of marginal relevance to these issues: but who can predict what might come in handy to a tinker?

Somewhat like Aulus Gellius, or the elder Pliny, it seems that our collector jotted down and kept these notes as an aid to memory, creating a storehouse of material from which he or she could conveniently draw—except, a hedgehog to Pliny's or Gellius' fox, our collector sought not to know many things, but one big thing.

BIBLIOGRAPHY

SCHOLARSHIP ON THE *GOSPEL ACCORDING TO PHILIP*

Agourides, Sabbas. "To Euaggelio tou Philippou." *Deltion Biblikon Meleton* 17 (1988) 44-67.

Arai, Sasagu. "Philiponi yoru Fukuinshoni okeru Kiristo [Jesus Christ in the Gospel according to Philip]." *Fukuinshono Kenkyû Takayanagi Isaburô Kyôju Kentei Ronbunshû Takayanagi [Studies on the Gospels: Essays in Honor of Prof. Isaburo Takayanagi]*, ed. N. Tajima, A. Satake, K. Kida. Tokyo: Sôbunsha, 1967, 159-87. Reprinted in Arai Sasagu. *Genshikirisutokyô to Gunôshisushugi [Early Christianity and Gnosticism]*. Tokyo: Iwanami Shoten, 1971. [English summary 377-97.]

Barc, Bernard. "Les noms de la triade dans l'Evangile selon Philippe." In *Gnosticisme et monde hellénistique: Actes du Colloque de Louvain-la-Nueve (11-14 mars 1980)*, ed. J. Ries, Y. Janssens and J.-M. Sevrin. Louvain-la-Nueve: Institute Orientaliste, 1982, 361-76.

Bauer, Johannes Baptist. "Zum Philippus-Evangelium Spr. 109 und 110" *Theologische Literaturzeitung* 86 (1961) 551-54.

——. "Das Evangelium nach Philippos." *Theologische Revue* (?)61 (1965) 236-238.

—— "Das Philippusevangelium." *Bibel und Liturgie* 39 (1966) 136-39.

——. "De Evangelio secundum Phillippum coptico." *Verbum domini* 41 (1963) 290-98. Reprinted in *Scolia Biblica et Patristica*. Graz: Akademische Druck- u. Verlagsanstalt, 1972, 131-40.

Betz, Otto. "Der Name als Offenbarung des Heils (Jüdische Traditionen im koptisch-gnostischen Philippusevangelium)." In *Das Institutum Judaicum der Universität Tübingen in den Jahren 1971-1972*, Tübingen, 1971 121-29. Reprinted in *Jesus, der Herr der Kirche. Aufsätze zur biblischen Theologie 2*, Tübingen: J. C. B. Mohr (Paul Siebeck) 1990.

Borchert, Gerald Leo. *An Analysis of the Literary Arrangement and Theological Views in the Gnostic Gospel of Philip*. Dissertation, Princeton Theological Seminary, 1967. Ann Arbor: University Microfilms, 1983.

——. "Insights into the Gnostic Threat to Christianity as Gained through the Gospel of Philip." In *New Dimensions in New Testament Study*, ed. R. N. Longenecker & M. C. Tenney. Grand Rapids, MI: Zondervan, 1974, 79-93.

Buckley, Jorun Jacobsen. "A Cult Mystery in the Gospel of Philip." *Journal of Biblical Literature* 99 (1980) 569-81.

——. "Conceptual Models and Polemical Issues in the Gospel of Philip." In *Aufstieg und Niedergang der römischen Welt (ANRW)/ Rise and Decline of the Roman World* Part 2, vol 25.5, Berlin: Walter de Gruyter, 1988, 4167-94.

—— 'The Holy Spirit' is a Double Name." Chapter 6 in *Female Fault and Fulfilment in Gnosticism*. Chapel Hill: Univeristy of North Carolina Press, 1986. Reprinted, in a reworked and condensed version, in *Images of the Feminine in Gnosticism* ed. Karen L. King. Philadelphia: Fortress, 1988, 211-227.

de Catanzaro, Carmino Joseph. "The Gospel According to Philip." *Journal of Theological Studies* n.s. 13 (1962) 35-71.

Craveri, M. "Vangelo di Filippo" In *I Vangeli apocrifi*, ed I. Millenni. Torino: Giulio Einaudi, 1969.

Dembska, Albertyna, and Wincenty Myszor. "Evangelie gnostyckie z Nag Hammadi." In *Apokryfy Nowego Testamentu I: Evangelie apokryficzne*, ed. M. Starowieyskiego. Lublin: Towarzypstwo Naukowe Katolickiego Uniwersytetu Lubelskiego, 1980, 119-37.

Eijk, A. H. C. van, "The Gospel of Philip and Clement of Alexandria: Gnostic and Ecclesiastical Theology on the Resurrection and the Eucharist" *Vigiliae christianae* 25 (1971) 94-120.

Emmel, S. "Indexes of Words and Catalogues of Grammatical Forms." In *Nag Hammadi Codex II, 2-7*, ed B. Layton. Leiden: E. J. Brill, 1989, 261-336.

Erbetta, M. "Il Vangelo di Filippo" *Euntes docete* 23 (1970) 317-70.

Foerster, W. *Gnosis: A Selection of Gnostic Texts. II Coptic and Mandean Sources.* English transl. by Robert McL. Wilson. Oxford: Clarendon, 1974.

Frid, Bo. *Filippusevangeliet: Inledning och översättning från koptiskan.* Symbolae Biblicae Upsalienses, Supplementhäften til SEÅ, 17. Lund: Berlingska Boktryckeriet/C. W. K. Gleerup, 1966.

Gaffron, Hans-Georg, "Studien zum koptischen Philippusevangelium unter besonderer Berücksichtigung der Sakramente" (Dissertation, Bonn: Rheinische-Friedrich-Wilhelms-Universität, 1969).

Gero, Stephen. "The Lamb and the King: 'Saying' 27 of the Gospel of Philip Reconsidered" *Oriens christianus* 63 (1979) 177-82.

Giversen, Søren. *Filipsevangeliet: Indledning, studier, oversaettelse og noter.* Copenhagen: G. E. C. Gads Forlag, 1966.

Grant, Robert M. "Two Gnostic Gospels." *Journal of Biblical Literature* 79 (1960) 1-11. = Chapter 16 in *Christian Beginnings: Apocalypse to history*. London: Variorum Reprints, 1983. [unpaginated]

——. "The Mystery of Marriage in the Gospel of Philip." *Vigiliae christianae* 15 (1961) 129-140. Reprinted in *After the New Testament*. Philadelphia: Fortress, 1967, 183-94.

Haardt, R. "Gnosis und Freiheit--'Die Gnosis ist Freiheit' (Evangelium nach Philippus 132,10): Einige Bemerkungen zur Exposition des Problems" *Ex orbe religionum: Studia Geo Widengren*, vol. 1. Leiden: E. J. Brill, 1972, 440-48.

Helmbold, Andrew K. "Translation Problems in the Gospel of Philip." *New Testament Studies* 11 (1964/5) 90-93.

Hoeller, S. A. "Means of Transformation: The Gospel of Philip." Chapter 12 in *Jung and the Lost Gospels: Insights into the Dead Sea Scrolls and the Nag Hammadi Library*, ed. S. A. Hoeller. Wheaton/Madras/London: Theosophical Publishing House, 1989.

Isenberg, Wesley William. "The Coptic Gospel according to Philip." Dissertation, University of Chicago, 1968.

——. Introduction and English translation in *Nag Hammadi Library in English*, ed. J. M. Robinson. New York: Harper & Row, 1977 & 1988, 131-51.

——. Introduction and English translation in *The Other Bible* (ed. W. Barnstone; San Francisco: Harper & Row, 1984) 87-100.

──. "Tractate 3: The Gospel according to Philip." In *Nag Hammadi Codex II, 2-7*, ed. B. Layton. Leiden: E. J. Brill, 1989, 131-217. [Introduction and English translation.]

Janssens, Yvonne. "L'Évangile selon Philippe." *Muséon* 81 (1968) 79-133.

──. *Évangiles gnostiques dans le corpus de Berlin et dans la bibliothèque copte de Nag Hammadi* (Homo religiosus 15). Louvain-la-Neuve: Centre d'histoire des religions, 1991.

Kasser, Rodolphe. "L'Évangile selon Philippe: Propositions pour quelques reconstitutions nouvelles." *Muséon* 81 (1968) 407-14.

──. "Bibliothèque gnosticque VIII: L'Évangile selon Philippe." *Revue de théologie et de philosophie* ser. 3.20 (1970) 12-35, 82.106.

Koschorke, Klaus. "Die 'Namen' im Philippusevangelium" *Zeitschrift für die neutestamentliche Wissenschaft* 64 (1973) 307-22.

Labib, Pahor. *Coptic Gnostic Papyri in the Coptic Museum at Old Cairo. volume 1.* Cairo: Government Press (Antiquities Department), 1956, plates 99-134

Layton, Bentley. *The Gnostic Scriptures. A New Translation with Annotations and Introductions.* Garden City, NY: Doubleday, 1987, 325-53.

──. "Tractate 3: the Gospel according to Philip." In *Nag Hammadi Codex II, 2-7*, ed B. Layton. Leiden: E. J. Brill, 1989, 142-216. [edition of Coptic text.]

Luttikhuizen, Gerard P. *Gnostische Geschriften I: Het Evangelie naar Maria, het Evangelie naar Filippus, de Brief van Petrus aan Filippus.* Kampen: J. H. Kok, 1986.

McNeil, Brian. "New Light on Gospel of Philip 17." *Journal of Theological Studies* 29 (1978) 143-6.

Ménard, Jacques-É. "La sentence 53 de l'Évangile selon Philippe." *Studia Montis Regii* 6 (1963) 149-52.

──. "L'Évangile selon Philippe." *Studia Montis Regii* 6 (1963) 67-73.

──. *L'Évangile selon Philippe.* Montréal: Université de Montréal/Paris: P. Lethielleux, 1964.

──. "L'Évangile selon Philippe: Présentation et texte." *Studia Montis Regii* 7 (1964) 193-282.

──. "L'Évangile selon Philippe et la gnose." *Revue des sciences religieuses* 41 (1967) 305-17.

──. *L'Évangile selon Philippe: Introduction, texte, traduction, commentaire.* Strasbourg, 1967/ Paris: Letouzey & Ané, 1967.

──. "Le milieu syriaque de l'Évangile selon Thomas et de l'Évangile selon Philippe." *Revue des sciences religieuses* 42 (1968), 261-66.

── "Syrische Einflüsse auf die Evangelien nach Thomas und Philippus." In *XVII. Deutscher Orientalistentag vom 21 bis 27 Juli 1968 in Würzburg, Vorträge, Teil 2.*, ed. W. Voigt, Wiesbaden: Franz Steiner, 1969, 385-91

──. "Das Evangelium nach Philippus und der Gnostizismus." In *Christentum und Gnosis*, ed. W. Eltester, Beihefte zur ZNW 37, Berlin: Alfred Töpelmann, 1969, 46-58.

──. "L' 'Évangile selon Philippe' et l' 'Exégèse de l'âme.'" In *Les textes de Nag Hammadi: Colloque du Centre d'histoire des religions (Strasbourg, 23-25 octobre 1974)*, Nag Hammadi Studies 7. Leiden: E. J. Brill, 1975, 56-67.

——. "Beziehungen des Philippus- und Thomas-Evangeliums zur syrischen Welt." In *Altes Testament-Frühjudentum-Gnosis. Neue Studien zu "Gnosis und Bibel,"* ed. K.-W. Tröger. Berlin: Evangelische Verlagsanstalt, 1980, 317-25.

Meyer, Marvin W. "The Gospel of Philip." In *The Ancient Mysteries: A Source book: Sacred Texts of the Mystery Religions of the Ancient Mediterranean World.* San Francisco: Harper & Row, 1987, 235-42.

Montserrat-Torrents, J. "Evangelis gnòstics: Introducció, traducció i notes." In *Apòcrifs del Nou Testament*, ed. A. Puig. Clàssics del cristianisme 17. Barcelona: Edicions Proa, 1990, 67-178.

Moraldi, Luigi. *I vangeli gnostici: Vangeli di Tomaso, Maria, Verità, Filippo.* Milan: Adelphi Edizioni, 1984.

Müller, C. D. G. "Evangelium nach Philippus (kopt.)." In *Kindlers Literatur Lexicon* 2, ed. V. Bompiani. Zürich: Kindler, 1966, 2548-9.

Myszor, Wincenty, and Albertyna Dembska. *Teksty z Nag-Hammadi: Z jezyka koptyjskiego przetlumaczyli.* (Pisma Starochrzescijanskich Pisarzy 20). Warsaw: Akademia Teologii Katolickiej, 1979.

Niederwimmer, K. "Die Freiheit des Gnostikers nach dem Philippusevangelium--Ein Untersuchung zum Thema: Kirche und Gnosis." In *Verborum Veritas. Festschrift für Gustav Stählin zum 70 Geburtstaf,* ed. O. Böcher and K. Haacker. Wuppertal: R. Brockhaus, 1970, 361-74.

Pagels, Elaine. "Pursuing the Spiritual Eve: Imagery and Hermeneutics in the *Hypostasis of the Archons* and the *Gospel of Philip*." In *Images of the Feminine in Gnosticism*, ed. Karen L. King. Philadelphia: Fortress, 1988, 187-210.

——. "The 'Mystery of Marriage' in the *Gospel of Philip* Revisited." In *The Future of Early Christianity*, ed. Birger A. Pearson. Minneapolis: Fortress Press, 1991, 442-454.

Rewolinski, Edward Thomas. "The Use of Sacramental Language in the Gospel of Philip (*Cairensis Gnosticus* II,3)." Dissertation, Harvard University, 1978.

Rudolph, Kurt. "Response to "'The Holy Spirit is a Double Name': Holy Spirit, Mary, and Sophia in the *Gospel of Philip*" by Jorunn Jacobsen Buckley." In *Images of the Feminine in Gnosticism*, ed. K. King. Philadelphia: Fortress, 1988.

Schenke, Hans-Martin. "Das Evangelium nach Philippus: Ein Evangelium der Valentinianer aus dem Funde von Nag-Hamadi." *Theologische Literaturzeitung* 84 (1959) 1-26.

——. "Das Evangelium nach Philippus" in *Koptisch-gnostische Schriften aus den Papyrus-Codices von Nag Hamadi.* Johannes Leipoldt and Hans-Martin Schenke. Hamburg: Herbert Reich, 1960.

——. "Die Arbeit am Philippus Evangelium." *Theologische Literaturezeitung* 90 (1965) 321-32.

——. "Das Evangelium nach Philippus." §5 in *Neutestamentliche Apokryphen in deutscher Übersetzung I. Evangelien*, ed. W. Schneemelcher and E. Hennecke. Tübingen: J. C. B. Mohr [Paul Siebeck], 1987, 148-73. = ET: R. McL. Wilson. *New Testament Apocrypha I. Gospels.* Louisville, KY: Westminster/John Knox Press, 1991, 179-208.

Segelberg, Eric. "The Coptic-Gnostic Gospel according to Philip and its Sacramental System" *Numen* 7 (1960) 189-200.

——. "The Antiochene Background of the Gospel of Philip." *Bulletin de la Société d'Archéologie Copte* 18 (1965/66), 205-23.

——. "The Antiochene Origin of the 'Gospel of Philip' II." *Bulletin de la Société d'Archéologie Copte* 19 (1967/68 publ. 1970) 207-10.

——. "The Gospel of Philip and the New Testament." In *The New Testament and Gnosis. Essays in honour of Robert McL. Wilson*, ed. A. H. B. Logan and A. J. M. Wedderburn. Edinburgh: T. & T. Clark, 1983, 204-12.

Sevrin, Jean-Marie. "Pratique et doctrine des sacrements dans l'Évangile selon Philippe." Dissertation, Université Catholique de Louvain, 1972.

——. "Les noces spirituelles dans l'Évangile selon Philippe." *Muséon* 87 (1974) 143-93.

Sfameni Gasparro, Giulia. "Il personaggio di Sophia nel 'Vangelo secondo Filippo.'" *VC* 31 (1977) 244-81. Reprinted in *Gnostica et hermetica: Saggi sullo gnosticismo e sull'eremetismo*, Rome: Edizioni dell'Ateneo, 1982, 75-119.

——. "Aspects encratites dans l'Évangile de Philippe." In *Gnosticisme et monde hellénistique*, ed. Ries & Sevrin. Louvain-la-Neuve: Institute Orientaliste, 1980, 115-18. = "Aspetti encratiti nel 'Vangelo secondo Filippo'" in *Gnostica et hermetica. Saggi sullo gnosticismo e sull' eremetismo*. Rome: Edizioni dell'Ateneo, 1982, 123-160.

——. "Il 'Vangelo secondo Filippo:' rassegna degli studi e proposte di interpretazione." In *Gnostica et hermetica . Saggi sullo gnosticismo e sull' eremetismo*. Rome: Edizioni dell'Ateneo, 1982, 17-71. Reprinted with additions in *Aufstieg und Niedergang der römischen Welt*. Berlin: Walter de Gruyter, 1988, 4107-4166.

Siker, Jeffrey S. "Gnostic Views on Jews and Christians in the Gospel of Philip." *Novum Testamentum* 31 (1989) 276-88.

Stroud, W. J. "Ritual in the Chenoboskion Gospel of Philip." *Iliff Review* 28 (1971) 29-35.

——. "The Problem of Dating the Chenoboskion Gospel of Philip." Dissertation, Iliff School of Theology, 1971.

Till, W. C. *Das Evangelium nach Philippos*. Patristische Texte und Studien 2. Berlin: Walter de Gruyter, 1963.

Trautmann, Catherine. "La Parenté dans l'Évangile selon Philippe." In *Colloque international sur les textes de Nag Hammadi (Québec, 22-25 aout 1978)*, ed. B. Barc. Bibliothèque copte de Nag Hammadi, Section "Études" 1. Québec: Université Laval/Louvain: Éditions Peeters, 1981, 267-78.

——. "Le schéme de la croix dans l'Évangile selon Philippe." In *Deuxiéme journée d'etudes coptes. Strasbourg 25 mai 1984*, ed. J.-M. Rosenstiehl. Cahiers de la bibliothèque copte 3. Louvain/Paris: Peeters, 1986, 123-9.

Tripp, David H. "The 'Sacramental System' of the Gospel of Philip." In *Studia Patristica* 17.1, ed. Elizabeth A Livingstone. Oxford/New York: Pergamon, 1982, 251-60.

Unnik, Willem Cornelis van. "Three Notes on the Gospel of Philip" *New Testament Studies* 10 (1963/64) 465-9. Reprinted in *Sparsa collecta: The Collected Essays of W. C. van Unnik. Part 3: Patristica, Gnostica, Liturgica*. Leiden: E. J. Brill, 1973, 238-43.

Williams, Michael A. "Realized Eschatology in the Gospel of Philip." *Restoration Quarterly* 14 (1971) 1-17.

Wilson, Robert McLachlan. *The Gospel of Philip: Translated from the Coptic Text with an Introduction and Commentary*. New York and Evanston: Harper & Row/London: Mowbray, 1962.

———. "The New Testament in the Nag Hammadi Gospel of Philip." *New Testament Studies* 9 (1962/3) 291-4.

———. "The Gospel of Philip." In *Church History* vol. 1, ed. C. W. Dugmore and C. Duggan. London: Nelson, 1964, 98-103.

ANCIENT LITERATURE: EDITIONS AND TRANSLATIONS CITED

Acts of Thomas
English translations quoted are from an unpublished translation by Harold W. Attridge.
Acta Apostolorum Apocrypha. ed. R. A. Lipsius & M. Bonnet. Hildesheim: Georg Olms, 1959.

Ankhsheshonqy
"The *Instruction of Ankhsheshonq"* in *Ancient Egyptian Literature. A Book of Readings. Volume III: The Late Period.* Berkeley: University of California Press, 1980.

Book of Thomas the Contender
"The Book of Thomas the Contender Writing to the Perfect" Coptic text edited by Bentley Layton (with English translation by John D. Turner) in *Nag Hammadi Codex II, 2-7*, Vol 2. Leiden: E. J. Brill, 1989, 180-205.
"The Book of Thomas the Contender Writing to the Perfect." English translation by Bentley Layton in *The Gnostic Scriptures.* Garden City, NY: Doubleday & Co., 403-409.

Clement of Alexandria
The Excerpta Ex Theodoto of Clement of Alexandria. Ed. and transl. by Robert Pierce Casey, London: Christophers, 1934.
Clément d'Alexandrie. Extraits de Théodote. Ed. F. Sagnard. Paris: Éditions du Cerf, 1948.
Clemente Alessandrino. Estratti Profetici. Ed. Carlo Nardi. Firenze: Nardini, 1985.

Epiphanius
The Panarion of Epiphanius of Salamis. Transl. Frank Williams. Leiden: Brill, 1987.

Galen
Galen. On Anatomical Procedures. Περι Ανατομικων Εγχειρησεων. De Anatomicis Administrationibus. Transl. and ed. Charles Singer. London: Oxford University Press, 1956.
Galen On Bloodletting. Transl. Peter Brain. Cambridge: Cambridge University Press, 1986.

Aulus Gellius
The Attic Nights of Aulus Gellius. Transl. John C. Rolfe. Cambridge: Cambridge University Press, 1984.

Gospel according to Thomas
"The Gospel According to Thomas." Coptic text edited by Bentley Layton (with English translation by Thomas O. Lambdin) in *Nag Hammadi Codex II, 2-7*, Vol 1. Leiden: E. J. Brill, 1989, 52-93.
"The Gospel According to Thomas." English translation by Bentley Layton in *The Gnostic Scriptures.* Garden City, NY: Doubleday & Co., 380-399.

Gospel according to Philip
"The Gospel According to Philip." Coptic text edited by Bentley Layton (with English translation by Wesley W. Isenberg) in *Nag Hammadi Codex II, 2-7*. Leiden: E. J. Brill, 1989, 142-216.
"The Gospel According to Philip." English translation by Bentley Layton in *The Gnostic Scriptures*. Garden City, NY: Doubleday & Co., 329-53.

Gospel of Truth
"The Gospel of Truth." Coptic text edited and translated by Harold W. Attridge and George W. MacRae in *Nag Hammadi Codex I (The Jung Codex)*. Leiden: E. J. Brill, 1985.

Greek Anthology
The Greek Anthology. Ed. and transl. W. R. Paton. Cambridge, MA: Harvard University Press, 1960. 5 volumes.

Irenaeus of Lyon
St. Irenaeus of Lyons. Against the Heresies. English translation by Dominic J. Unger. Vol. 1, book 1. With further revisions by John J. Dillon. Ancient Christian Writers 55. New York: Paulist Press, 1992.
Irénée de Lyon: Contre les hérésies. Livre 1. Latin text and Greek fragments edited (with French translation) by A. Rousseau and L. Doutreleau, *Irénée de Lyon: Contre les hérésies. Livre 1*. Vol 1: Introduction and notes; Vol. 2: Text and translation. Sources chrétiennes 263 and 264. Paris: Éditions du Cerf, 1979.

Nag Hammadi Codex II
The Facsimile Edition of the Nag Hammadi Codices. Codex II. Leiden: Brill, 1974.

Papyrus Insinger
"The *Instruction of Papyrus Insinger*." In Miriam Lichtheim, *Late Egyptian Wisdom Literature in the International Context. A Study of Demotic Instructions*. (Orbis Biblicus et Orientalis 52). Göttingen: Vandenhoeck & Ruprecht, 1983.

Papyrus Oxyrhynchus 3724
The Oxyrhynchus Papyri. Volume 54. Ed. Peter Parsons. London: Oxford University Press, 1987.

Photius
Photius. Bibliothèque. Ed. René Henry. Paris: Société d'Édition "Les Belles Lettres," 1960.

Pistis Sophia
Pistis Sophia. Ed. Carl Schmidt, transl. Violet MacDermot. Leiden: Brill, 1978.

Pliny the Elder
Pliny. Natural Histories, Preface and Books 1-2. Transl. H. Rackham. Cambridge, MA: Harvard University Press, 1949.

Pliny the Younger
Pliny. Letters and Panegyricus. Vol. 1, Letters, Books 1-7. Ed. with an English translation by Betty Radice. Cambridge, MA: Harvard University Press, 1969.

Quintillian
The Institution Oratoria. Ed. with an English translation by H. E. Butler. Cambridge, MA: Harvard University Press, 1979.

Sentences of Sextus
The Sentences of Sextus. Ed. Richard A. Edwards & Robert A. Wild. Chico, CA: Scholars Press, 1981.
Les Sentences de Sextus (NH XII,1). Ed. Paul-Hubert Poirier. Quebec: Presses de l'Université Laval, 1983.

SECONDARY LITERATURE CITED

Attridge, Harold W. "The Gospel of Truth as an Exoteric Text." In *Nag Hammadi, Gnosticism, and Early Christianity.* Ed. C. W. Hedrick and R. Hodgson. Peabody, MA: Hendrickson, 1986.

———. "The Original Language of the Acts of Thomas." *Of Scribes and Scholars.* Ed. H. Attridge, J. Collins, T. Tobin. Lanham, MD: University Press of America, 1990, 241-250.

Aune, David Edward "The Phenomenon of Early Christian 'Anti-Sacramentalism.'" In *Studies in New Testament and Early Christian Literature,* ed. D. Aune. Leiden: Brill, 1972, 194-214.

Barnes, J. W. B., G. M. Browne and J. C. Shelton, eds. *Nag Hammadi Codices. Greek and Coptic Papyri from the Cartonnage of the Covers.* Leiden: E. J. Brill, 1981.

Bascom, William. "The Forms of Folklore: Prose Narratives." In *Sacred Narrative. Readings in the Theory of Myth,* ed. Alan Dundes. Berkeley: University of California Press, 1984, 5-29.

Bauer, Walter. *Orthodoxy and Heresy in Earliest Christianity.* Philadelphia: Fortress, 1971.

Brock, Sebastian. "The Syrian Baptismal Ordines (with special reference to the anointings)." *Studia Liturgica* 12 (1977) 177-183.

———. "Introduction." *Horizons in Semitic Studies.* Ed. J. H. Eaton. n.p.: 1980.

Brooke, George J. *Exegesis at Qumran. 4QFlorilegium in its Jewish Context.* JSOT Supplement Series 29. Sheffield, England: JSOT Press, 1985.

Cameron, Alan. *The Greek Anthology from Meleager to Planudes.* Oxford: Clarendon, 1993.

Cauderlier, Patrice. "Quatre cahiers scolaires (Musée de Louvre): Présentation et problèmes annexes." In *Les débuts du codex,* ed. Alain Blanchard (Bibliologia 9). Turnhout: Brepols, 1989, 43-59.

Chadwick, Henry. *The Sentences of Sextus.* Cambridge: Cambridge University Press, 1959.

———. "Florilegium." In *Reallexikon für Antike und Christentum.* Stuttgart: Anton Hiersemann, 1969, 7.1131-1160.

Conybeare, F. C. *The Ring of Pope Xystus.* London: Williams and Norgate, 1910.

Daly, Lloyd W. *Contributions to a History of Alphabetization in Antiquity and the Middle Ages.* Brussels: Latomus, 1967.

Dawson, David. *Allegorical Readers and Cultural Revision in Ancient Alexandria.* Berkeley: University of California Press, 1992.

Edwards, Richard A. and Robert A. Wild. *The Sentences of Sextus.* Chico, CA: Scholars Press, 1981.

Egan, Rory B. "Two Complementary Epigrams of Meleager (A. P. vii 195 and 196)" *Journal of Hellenic Studies* 108 (1988) 24-32.

Farmer, William R. and Denis M. Farkasfalvy. *The Formation of the New Testament Canon. An Ecumenical Approach.* Ed. Harold W. Attridge. New York: Paulist Press, 1983.

Firth, Raymond. "The Plasticity of Myth: Cases from Tikopia." In *Sacred Narrative. Readings in the Theory of Myth,* ed. Alan Dundes. Berkeley: University of California Press, 1984, 207-216.

Funk, Wolf-Peter. "How Closely Related are the Subakhmimic Dialects?" *Zeitschrift für ägyptische Sprache* 112 (1985) 124-139.

Gow, A. S. F. and D. L. Page. *The Garland of Philip and Some Contemporary Epigrams. Volume 1. Introduction, Text and Translation. Indexes of Sources and Epigrammatists.* Cambridge: Cambridge University Press, 1968.

———. *The Garland of Philip and Some Contemporary Epigrams. Volume 2. Commentary and Indexes.* Cambridge: Cambridge University Press, 1968.

Heinrichs, Wolfhart. *Studies in Neo-Aramaic.* Atlanta, GA: Scholars Press, 1990.

Henry, René. "Remarques a propos des 'codices' 161 et 239 de Photius." *L'Antiquité Classique* 7 (1938) 291-93.

Holford-Strevens, Leofranc. *Aulus Gellius.* Chapel Hill: University of North Carolina Press, 1988.

Jonas, Hans. "Evangelium Veritatis and the Valentinian Speculation." *Studia Patristica* 6. Berlin: Akademie-Verlag, 1962.

———. *The Gnostic Religion. The Message of the Alien God and the Beginnings of Christianity.* Boston: Beacon Press, 1963.

Kasser, Rodolphe. *Compléments au Dictionnaire copte de Crum* . Cairo: Institut Français d'Archéologie Orientale, 1964, vii-xviii.

Kirk, G. S. *Myth. Its Meaning and Functions in Ancient and Other Cultures.* Cambridge: Cambridge University Press, 1970.

Klijn, A. J. F. "Baptism in the Acts of Thomas." *In Studies on Syrian Baptismal Rites,* ed. J. Vellian. Kottayam: C. M. S. Press, 1975, 57-62.

Kloppenborg, John S. *The Formation of Q.* Philadelphia: Fortress, 1987.

Koester, Helmut. "GNOMAI DIAPHOROI: The Origin and Nature of Diversification in the History of Early Christianity." In *Harvard Theological Review* 58 (1965) 279-318; reprinted in James M. Robinson and Helmut Koester, *Trajectories through Early Christianity.* Philadelphia: Fortress, 1971, 114-157.

———. *Ancient Christian Gospels, Their History and Growth.* Philadelphia: Trinity, 1990.

Küchler, Max. *Frühjüdische Weisheitstraditionen.* Göttingen: Vandenhoeck & Ruprecht, 1979.

Layton, Bentley. *The Gnostic Scriptures.* Garden City, NY: Doubleday, 1987.

———. *Nag Hammadi Codex II,2-7, Vols 1 & 2.* Leiden: Brill, 1989.

Lévi-Strauss, Claude. *The Raw and the Cooked, Introduction to a Science of Mythology.* New York: Harper, 1969.

———. *The Savage Mind.* Chicago: University of Chicago Press, 1966.

Lewis, Naphtali. *Papyrus in Classical Antiquity.* Oxford: Clarendon, 1974.

Lichtheim, Miriam. *Ancient Egyptian Literature. A Book of Readings. Volume III: The Late Period.* Berkeley, CA: University of California Press, 1980.

——. *Late Egyptian Wisdom Literature in the International Context. A Study of Demotic Instructions.* (Orbis Biblicus et Orientalis 52). Göttingen: Vandenhoeck & Ruprecht, 1983.

Marache, René. *Aulu-Gelle. Les Nuits Attiques.* Paris: Société d'édition "Les belles lettres," 1967.

Markschies, Christoph. *Valentinus Gnosticus?* Tübingen: Mohr/Siebeck, 1992.

Morris, Brian. *Anthropological Studies of Religion. An Introductory Text.* Cambridge: Cambridge University Press, 1987.

Myers, Ruth A. "The Structure of the Syrian Baptismal Rite." In *Essays on Early Eastern Initiation,* ed. P. Bradshaw. Bramcote: Grove, 1988, 31-43.

Nardi, Carlo. *Clemente Alessandrino: Estratti profetici.* Firenze: Nardini Editore, 1985.

Nautin, Pierre. "La fin des Stromates et les Hypotyposes de Clément d'Alexandrine." *Vigiliae Christianae* 30 (1976) 268-302.

Neusner, Jacob. *Form-Analytical Comparison in Rabbinic Judaism. Structure and Form in The Fathers and The Fathers According to Rabbi Nathan.* Atlanta: Scholar's Press, 1992.

Ogden, L. K. "The Binding of Codex II." In *Nag Hammadi Codex II, 2-7,* ed B. Layton. Leiden: E. J. Brill, 1989, 19-25.

——. "Anti-Heretical Warnings in Codex IX from Nag Hammadi." In *Gnosticism, Judaism, and Egyptian Christianity.* Minneapolis: Fortress, 1990, 183-93.

Pagels, Elaine Hiesey. *The Gnostic Paul. Gnostic Exegesis of the Pauline Letters.* Philadelphia: Fortress, 1975.

Pettazzoni, Raffaele. "The Truth of Myth." In *Sacred Narrative. Readings in the Theory of Mythology.* ed. Alan Dundes. University of California Press, Berkeley, 1984, 98-109.

Pintaudi, Rosario. "Tavolette lignee e cerate della biblioteca vaticana." In *Les débuts du codex,* ed. Alain Blanchard (Bibliologia 9). Turnhout: Brepols, 1989, 61-67.

Pouillon, Jean. "Remarks on the Verb 'To Believe.'" In *Between Belief and Transgression. Structuralist Essays in Religion, History, and Myth* ed. Michel Izard and Pierre Smith. Chicago: University of Chicago Press, 1982, 1-8.

Puhvel, Jaan. *Comparative Mythology.* Baltimore: Johns Hopkins University Press, 1987.

Richard, Marcel "Florilèges spirituels grecs." In *Dictionnaire de la spritualité.* Paris: Beauchesne, 1964, 5.475-512.

Roberts, Colin H., and T. C. Skeat. *The Birth of the Codex.* London: Oxford University Press, 1987.

Roberts, Louis. "The Literary Form of the *Stromateis*" *The Second Century* 1 (1981) 211-222.

Robinson, James M. "From the Cliff to Cairo: The Story of the Discoverers and Middlemen of the Nag Hammadi Codices." In *Colloque international sur les textes de Nad Hammadi (Québec, 22-25 août 1978),* ed B. Barc. Québec and Louvain: Presses de l'Universtié Laval and Éditions Peeters, 1981, 21-58.

——, ed. *The Facsimile Edition of the Nag Hammadi Codices, Introduction.* Leiden: Brill, 1984.

Rochais, Henri-Marie. "Florilèges spirituels latins." In *Dictionnaire de la spritualité.* Paris: Beauchesne, 1964, 5.435-460.

Sagnard, F. *Extraits de Théodote.* Sources chrétiennes 23. Paris: Éditions du Cerf, 1948.

Sider, David. "Looking for Philodemus in P. Oxy. 54.3724." *Zeitschrift für Papyrologie und Epigraphik* 76 (1989) 229-236.

Siegert, Folker. *Nag-Hammadi-Register.* Tübingen: J. C. B. Mohr (Paul Siebeck),

Stadter, Philip. *Plutarch's Historical Methods. An Analysis of the Mulierum Virtutes.* Cambridge, MA: Harvard University Press, 1965.

Standaert, Benoit. "L'Évangile de Vérité: Critique et lecture." *New Testament Studies* 22 (1976) 243-275.

Strutwolf, Holger. *Gnosis als System.* Göttingen: Vandenhoeck & Ruprecht, 1993.

Treadgold, Warren T. *The Nature of the Bibliotheca of Photius.* Washington, DC: Dumbarton Oaks/Harvard University Press, 1980.

Tripp, David H. "The Original Sequence of Irenaeus 'Adversus haereses' I: A Suggestion." *The Second Century* 8 (1991) 157-162.

van Baaren, Th. P. "The Flexibility of Myth." In *Sacred Narrative. Readings in the Theory of Myth* ed. Alan Dundes. Berkeley: University of California Press, 1984, 217-224.

van Haelst, Joseph. "Les origines du codex." In *Les débuts du codex,* ed. Alain Blanchard (Bibliologia 9). Turnhout: Brepols, 1989, 13-35.

Volten, Aksel. *Kopenhagener Texte zum demotischen Weisheitsbuch. (Pap. Carlsberg II, III verso, IV verso und V).* Copenhagen: Munksgaard, 1940.

Wilken, Robert L. "Wisdom and Philosophy in Early Christianity." In *Aspects of Wisdom in Judaism and Early Christianity.* Notre Dame, IN: University of Notre Dame Press, 1975, 143-168.

Williams, Jacqueline A. *Biblical Interpretation in the Gnostic Gospel of Truth from Nag Hammadi.* Atlanta, GA: Scholars Press, 1988.

Willis, G. G. "What Was the Earliest Syrian Baptismal Liturgy?" *Studia Evangelica 6* (1973), 651-654.

Wilson, Robert McL. "Twenty Years After." In *Colloque international sur les textes de Nag Hammadi (Québec, 22-25 août 1978),* ed B. Barc. Québec and Louvain: Presses de l'Universtié Laval and Éditions Peeters, 1981, 59-67.

Winkler, Gabriele. "The Original Meaning of the Prebaptismal Anointing and its Implications." *Worship* 52 (1978), 24-45.

INDEX

NAG HAMMADI AND MANICHAEAN STUDIES

FORMERLY

NAG HAMMADI STUDIES

19. FRICKEL, J. *Hellenistische Erlösung in christlicher Deutung*. Die gnostische Naassenerschrift. Quellen, kritische Studien, Strukturanalyse, Schichtenscheidung, Rekonstruktion der Anthropos-Lehrschrift. 1984. ISBN 90 04 07227 6

20-21. LAYTON, B. (ed.). *Nag Hammadi Codex II, 2-7, together with XIII, 2* Brit. Lib. Or. 4926(1) and P. Oxy. 1, 654, 655*. I. Gospel according to Thomas, Gospel according to Philip, Hypostasis of the Archons, Indexes. II. On the origin of the world, Expository treatise on the Soul, Book of Thomas the Contender. 1989. 2 volumes. ISBN 90 04 09019 3

22. ATTRIDGE, H.W. (ed.). *Nag Hammadi Codex I* (The Jung Codex). I. Introductions, texts, translations, indices. 1985. ISBN 90 04 07677 8

23. ATTRIDGE, H.W. (ed.). *Nag Hammadi Codex I* (The Jung Codex). II. Notes. 1985. ISBN 90 04 07678 6

24. STROUMSA, G.A.G. *Another seed. Studies in Gnostic mythology*. 1984. ISBN 90 04 07419 8

25. SCOPELLO, M. *L'exégèse de l'âme*. Nag Hammadi Codex II, 6. Introduction, traduction et commentaire. 1985. ISBN 90 04 07469 4

26. EMMEL, S. (ed.). *Nag Hammadi Codex III, 5*. The Dialogue of the Savior. 1984. ISBN 90 04 07558 5

27. PARROTT, D.M. (ed.) *Nag Hammadi Codices III, 3-4 and V, 1 with Papyrus Berolinensis 8502,3 and Oxyrhynchus Papyrus 1081*. Eugnostos and the Sophia of Jesus Christ. 1991. ISBN 90 04 08366 9

28. HEDRICK, C.W. (ed.). *Nag Hammadi Codices XI, XII, XIII*. 1990. ISBN 90 04 07825 8

29. WILLIAMS, M.A. *The immovable race*. A gnostic designation and the theme of stability in Late Antiquity. 1985. ISBN 90 04 07597 6

30. PEARSON, B.A. (ed.). *Nag Hammadi Codex VII*. 1996. ISBN 90 04 10451 8

31. SIEBER, J.H. (ed.). *Nag Hammadi Codex VIII*. 1991. ISBN 90 04 09477 6

32. SCHOLER, D.M. *Nag Hammadi Bibliography*. (in preparation)

33. WISSE, F. & M. WALDSTEIN, (eds.). *The Apocryphon of John*. Synopsis of Nag Hammadi Codices II,1; III,1; and IV,1 with BG 8502,2. 1995. ISBN 90 04 10395 3

34. LELYVELD, M. *Les logia de la vie dans l'Evangile selon Thomas*. A la recherche d'une tradition et d'une rédaction. 1988. ISBN 90 04 07610 7

35. WILLIAMS, F. (Tr.). *The Panarion of Epiphanius of Salamis*. Book I (Sects 1-46). 1987. ISBN 90 04 07926 2

36. WILLIAMS, F. (Tr.). *The Panarion of Epiphanius of Salamis*. Books II and III (Sects 47-80, De Fide). 1994. ISBN 90 04 09898 4

37. GARDNER, I. *The Kephalaia of the Teacher*. The Edited Coptic Manichaean Texts in Translation with Commentary. 1995. ISBN 90 04 10248 5

38. TURNER, M.L. *The Gospel according to Philip*. The Sources and Coherence of an Early Christian Collection. 1996. ISBN 90 04 10443 7